DEATH RITES

DEATH RITES

Law and ethics at the end of life

Edited by

Robert Lee and Derek Morgan

London and New York

First published 1994
by Routledge
11 New Fetter Lane, London EC4P 4EE

Simultaneously published in the USA and Canada
by Routledge
29 West 35th Street, New York, NY 10001

First published in paperback 1996

Typeset in Garamond by
Florencetype Ltd, Stoodleigh, Devon
Printed and bound in Great Britain by
TJ Press (Padstow) Ltd, Padstow, Cornwall

British Library Cataloguing in Publication Data
A catalogue record for this book is available from the British Library

Library of Congress Cataloguing in Publication Data
A catalogue record for this book is available from the Library of Congress

ISBN 0-415-14026-9

Contents

CONTENTS

List of contributors

Peter Alldridge is a Lecturer at Cardiff Law School. He specialises in criminal law and evidence.

Ruth F. Chadwick is Professor of Moral Philosophy in the Centre for Professional Ethics, University of Central Lancashire, Preston. With Win Tadd, she is author of *Ethics and Nursing Practice: A Case Study Approach* (London: Macmillan, 1992) and is herself editor of *Ethics, Reproduction and Genetic Control*, rev. edn (London: Routledge, 1992).

Martyn Evans is University College Fellow in the Centre for Philosophy and Health Care at University College Swansea. He is the author of a number of journal papers and book contributions on the definition of human death and the associated ethical problems in organ transplantation. In the field of philosophical aesthetics he is the author of *Listening to Music* (London: Macmillan, 1990).

Marie Fox is a Lecturer in law at the University of Manchester. With Simon Lee she is co-author of *Learning Legal Skills* (London: Blackstone Press, 1991) and she has written on abortion law in Ireland with Therese Murphy.

Nicky James is Senior Lecturer in the Department of Nursing and Midwifery Studies in the Faculty of Medicine, University of Nottingham. She has a long-standing research interest in hospices and palliative care, more recently extending these to a comparison with neonatal care. Publications include 'Care = organisation + physical labour + emotional labour' (Sociology of Health and Illness) and 'Divisions of emotional labour: disclosure and cancer', in Fineman (ed.), *Emotion and Organisations* (London: Sage 1993).

Robert Lee is Director of Research and Education at Wilde Sapte,

Solicitors, London. He is a visiting research fellow at the Centre for Science Policy, University of Lancaster and is co-author of *Blackstone's Statutes on Public Law* (London: Blackstone Press, 1990), *Blackstone's Guide to the Human Fertilisation and Embryology Act 1990* (London: Blackstone Press, 1991), co-editor of *Birthrights: Law and Ethics at the Beginnings of Life* (London: Routledge, 1989), co-author of *Housing Act 1988: A Practical Guide to Private Residential Lettings* (Oxford: BSP Professional Books, 1989) and author of numerous articles and essays in a wide variety of legal disciplines.

Jonathan Montgomery lectures in law at the University of Southampton. He is co-author of *Nursing and the Law* (London: Macmillan, 1989), co-editor of the *Encyclopedia of Health Services and Medical Law* (London: Sweet & Maxwell, 1991) and has written numerous articles on health care law. His textbook *Health Care Law* is to be published by Oxford University Press. He is the Chief Law Examiner for the Institute of Health Services Management, a member of the Ethics Advisory Committee of the British Paediatric Association, the Southampton and South West Hampshire Research Ethics Committee and a non-executive director of the Southampton Community Health Services NHS Trust.

Derek Morgan is Senior Fellow in Health Care Law at University College Swansea. With Bob Lee he is the co-editor of *Birthrights: Law and Ethics at the Beginnings of Life* (London: Routledge, 1989) and co-author of *Blackstone's Guide to the Human Fertilisation and Embryology Act: Abortion and Embryo Research the New Law* (London: Blackstone Press, 1991).

Frances Price is a Senior Research Associate at the University of Cambridge. She is the co-author of *Three, Four and More: A Study of Triplet and Higher Order Births* (London: HMSO, 1990) and of *Technologies of Procreation: Kinship in the Age of Assisted Conception* (Manchester: Manchester University Press, 1993).

John Saunders is a Consultant Physician, Nevill Hall Hospital, Abergavenny, Gwent and an Honorary Fellow of the Centre for Philosophy and Health Care, University College Swansea.

Keith Smith is Professor of English Law at Brunel University, London. His most recent book in criminal jurisprudence is *A Modern Treatise on Criminal Complicity* (Oxford: Oxford University Press, 1991).

Stuart F. Spicker is Emeritus Professor, School of Medicine, University of Connecticut Health Center, Farmington, Connecticut, and Visiting Professor, Center for Ethics, Medicine and Public Issues (and Department of Community Medicine), Baylor College of Medicine, Houston, Texas. With H.T. Engelhardt, Jr, he is co-editor of the *Philosophy and Medicine* book series (Dordrecht, Netherlands, and Boston, USA: Kluwer Academic Publishers), and co-editor with J.W. Ross of *HEC (Healthcare Ethics Committee) Forum* (Kluwer Academic Publishers). He serves as Project Director for 'Educating Healthcare Ethics Committees: A National Dissemination Project', a three-year programme supported by FIPSE, US Department of Education.

Celia Wells lectures at Cardiff Law School, University of Wales. She is co-author of *Reconstructing Criminal Law* (London: Weidenfeld & Nicolson, 1990) and author of *Corporations and Criminal Responsibility* (Oxford: Clarendon Press, 1993). Her essay in this collection is based on an article published in (1991) 11 *Legal Studies* 71.

Preface
Law, ethics and death: silence and symbolism

With all of the essays completed and the intricacies of editing almost over, Bob's father died, and our work stopped for a while to allow a journey north and the business of the funeral. The family gathered together on the chosen day with his mother remarkably collected and concerned that everything should go just right. So it was that she admonished the younger brother – looking unusually smart in his suit – for forgetting to put a flower in his buttonhole. And having arranged lifts for the various mourners without cars, she answered promptly when queried by Bob about the precise address of one of them, 'Ask your Dad.' With the funeral over the guests drank long and hard, and Uncle Tom (Dad's brother) was kind enough to say that he hadn't enjoyed himself so much in a long time.

This was true for many of the guests not so ready to articulate it. For in that very northern catholic way, there is a strong sense of family; and yet, in spite of largely living in the same town, there is rarely an excuse to get together. Fine though the occasion was, it served only to impress upon the immediate family afterwards that they had been abandoned, a feeling which receded a little when within the month Bob became a father.

THE SYMBOLISM

No man, as Donne wrote, is an island.[1] To write about death is to write about life; 'death is an important and permanent aspect of the human condition, affecting the meaning and value of life'.[2] And yet we do not live life in order to experience our own death; 'death is not an event in life. Death is not lived through'.[3] It would former-ly have been the case that death was not negotiable in the

way of other facts of life,[4] although we may begin to wonder the sense in which we use these very words. As we drafted this introduction, newspapers in the United Kingdom reported the suggestion that a deceased woman should be allowed to give evidence in a criminal trial recorded on videotape before her death.[5] A man has recorded on videotape his wish that his frozen sperm should be used after his death to impregnate his former wife in order that she might bear a child genetically related to both of them. And, as Jonathan Montgomery records in this collection, the desire to ensure that medical treatment which the patient deems desirable while competent should be respected when they are no longer able to do that, has given rise to the notion of the 'living will'. These are indeed times of change and renegotiation in one area of life that seemed to be fixed and certain, that of death.

But as John Saunders points out in his essay, fear of dying, of the possible manner of death and indeed of death itself are important parts of the human condition. So it is that the story of the practices and rituals of death tells us as much about the living as the dead or dying. 'Ask your Dad' expresses the solitude of someone who within the common structures of our society had quietly lived a life of mutual dependence, and would have to learn to live an identifiable individual life over again. The mistaking of the funeral for wedding, or wake for wedding feast is not so surprising. Each sealing in its own way a relationship, each marked by ceremony and by the formal requirements of legality; each is part of what Gabriel Garcia Marquez has called the 'ritual of eradication'.[6]

Indeed one feature of the funeral arrangements was how most of the knowledge on what was required – who to inform, how to get the death certificate, how to dispose of the body – belonged to the older members of the family who had lived through other deaths. So too the shaping of this book, to follow an earlier collection of essays on birth, served only to illustrate the ignorance (of the editors at least) of what constitutes the practices and rituals of death in our own, clever, advanced, changing society. We are indeed sometimes apt to forget how contemporary and relative our attitudes to death really are. From 1541 to as late as 1871, the English expectation of life at birth fluctuated only between 27 and 42 years. Not until the end of the nineteenth and the beginning of the twentieth centuries did the pattern begin to show any marked change in distribution and shape. Against this cultural backdrop Alldridge's titular question 'who wants to live for ever?' takes on its particular significance.

We have extraordinarily little knowledge as citizens of our laws in respect of death. Yet, as Celia Wells's essay in this volume reminds us the formal processes and procedures by which we signify the fact of death become a crucial part of responding to death itself. Several of the essays in this collection are distinguished by taking a look at some currently fashionable ideas and arguments in respect of death and dying and, subjecting them to searching and critical analysis, presenting some decidedly challenging and unfashionable conclusions. Of this kind particularly are the essays by Evans, Saunders, Spicker, Wells and Smith. Each of these (and we hope the other) essays helps to remind us that not all death is the same. The symbolic reaction differs for each death. Much of what is written concerns perceptions of and responses to death: to the death of the human, the animal, the foetus, to the death by disaster and that by disease; to death as a danger and a threat; or to death as a release. In dealing in death we are trading values. We confront tricky ethical issues as we rub against deeply ingrained cultural practices. Medical science may provide the arena for such confrontations and promote ever more complex contests.

As with birth, which we treated in an earlier volume called *Birthrights*, the notion of hospitalisation assumes a critical importance in death and discussions of some of the ethical issues with respect to dying. Here, that is reflected particularly in the essays of Spicker, Saunders, James, Alldridge, Montgomery and Chadwick. John Saunders in his essay on the ethics of cardiopulmonary resuscitation illuminates issues not yet widely discussed in literature on medical ethics. However, the use of CPR as a life-prolonging intervention following acute insult has been developing from the 1960s as an alternative to open chest massage. But as medical practices change, so too might our responses and reactions to death. This may be true even to the point that our views of what constitutes death may shift, even as the necessity to establish death remains as important as ever for the formality of law. What are the reponsibilities of the medical profession, of relatives, of society generally to a patient in 'persistent vegetative state?' May artificial feeding be discontinued to allow them to 'die with dignity' or are these cases never to be regarded as 'hope-less'?

To ask the question of what constitutes death is to ask also what separates life from death and at what point life may hold no greater worth than death. These are issues variously explored by Alldridge, Montgomery and Evans. It may be because of the symbols and forms with which we surround death that it is very difficult for the law to allow that for some life and death may be indistinguishable, or that death may appear preferable to life. The classic recent example of this is provided in the Canadian case of *Malette* v. *Shulman*[7] in which a young woman was brought unconscious into a casualty department. She was carrying with her a card which stated clearly that she was a Jehovah's Witness and that consequently there were no circumstances in which a blood transfusion was to be given, even if this were the only way of saving her life. The court rejected the doctor's submission that refusal of treatment must be informed, and in her suit against the hospital for wrongfully transfusing her, the court accepted that an assault had been committed and awarded her substantial damages. For her, the jewel of life, a 'pearl beyond price' as it is sometimes referred to,[8] had come to be seen as an insult or injury, a paste diamond of little value or worth.

This is not to say that the law treats all deaths the same, any more than the law treats all lives the same way. At the most obvious level law is concerned with death as the antithesis of life, so that it is concerned with death as the wrongful taking of life. But what is wrong? Can killing be a kindness? Should we kill animals? Is the termination of pregnancy killing – and if not does the law nonetheless have legitimate concerns over the how and why of termination? From this simple concept of wrongful death many public interests emerge, but from there these interests spread further. Thus many of the essays here concern questions of rationing (Chadwick, Saunders, James and Morgan) and the resources that we can and should expend to postpone death. Lee and Smith identify and address the wider interest in seeking to protect the public from death. Wells and Morgan lead us back to the symbolic role of the law as the arbiter of the harms that death cause to the living. Many of the questions raised above concern what type of death the law considers important. We might also raise the question of whose death is considered important. For although most living adults have been touched by the death of family or friends and have had their own perceptions of death and dying shaped accordingly, there are certain deaths which touch a society. Hence the symbolism of the state funeral to mark exactly that. Thus our ability to bring to mind pictures of a limousine on the highways of Dallas and the shocking images which followed. In this volume, Alldridge opens his essay with the poignantly ironic words sung by Freddie Mercury, and it is beyond doubt that our ideas of the deadly disease of AIDS have been shaped far more by his death, or that of Rock Hudson, than by thousands of deaths in Africa.

THE SILENCE

Yet although much of the concern of the law in dealing with death seems to surround the symbols and signifiers of the end of life, at the same time the law preserves a strange silence on the many issues concerning death. Many of the essays here struggle to identify what it is that the law is saying about death, for often it speaks in euphemism.

For example, Frances Price returning to amplify a theme which she has scored elsewhere, attends to the under-researched and almost silent face of death before birth. Rather than the usual scenario of abortion, however, she focuses on selective reduction of multiple pregnancy; what she here calls multiparity. Within this essay she brings to bear on a new issue in reproductive technology old ethical dilemmas in medicine and public life – on what basis should selection decisions be made when death has to be chosen for some to allow others to live? Is this a proper understanding of ancient notions of sacrifice thrown into new relief, or is it the misapplication of science to produce deaths which are avoidable, unnecessary and unethical? As she catalogues, the term selective reduction is part of a vocabulary of life and death in which the directness of the action that brings about death is occluded. Her essay discloses an important aspect of response to death, that those who bring about death have sometimes to live with the consequences of that in a stark and clamorous form.

Elsewhere it does not speak at all. Fox points to issues which the law will not address; Wells suggests a seduction of the law to address only marginal issues; many of the essays identify a reluctance or failure of the law to give even an ethical signpost, let alone a moral lead. Saunders and James highlight issues not widely debated, particularly in legal literature. What appears to be an instinctive fear of death seems to be reflected in an eerie silence on the part of the law. This dread of death shapes much of what is done. Thus Saunders's essay speaks of our perceptions of death and reminds us that in our dread we are capable of doing much harm. In Saunders's instance of CPR this includes harm to patients, their families, the medical team and society at large. This raging against the dying of the light is reflected in the many decisions made and choices exercised in the shadow of death. The work by Alldridge and by Montgomery exposes our inabilities to make what we see as agonising choices. That of Lee and Smith shows that desire to avoid the danger of death leads us into treacherous moral territory. This denial of death is most relevant in James's essay on the development and dynamic of the hospice movement. Care of the terminally ill in the context of a soulless medicalisation may reflect not only a denial of the fact of the person's death but a denial to the patient to even talk about dying. In this, as in many of the contributions in this collection (Spicker, Saunders, Price, Lee, Alldridge), doctors become intermediaries – often between life and death. Implicit in the work of Evans and of others is the notion of the doctor as arbiter of death, rather than as agent of the patient. Here, the issue is not only one of the cultural role ascribed to the doctor but also one of legal status. The devolution of responsibility to doctors is often a process of concealing tragic choices from the glare of wider public debate.

Yet through the silence it is undeniable that there is a terrible morbidity to the law. Homicide is the most terrible crime, still justifying, as we see in the United States, execution and the taking of life in the name of the law. In the UK, as Montgomery explains, suicide itself was, until 1961, an offence and assisting suicide remains so. Although this only leads us into sterile arguments about whether, for example, starvation is suicide so that a doctor withdrawing hydration commits a crime or whether someone apparently starving herself to death can be treated against her wishes.[9] It seems however that despite the importance which the law ascribes to the moment of death and to its causes, it is incapable of answering even some of the most obvious questions about death – not least, what is death?[10] As such, the law has hardly served doctors well, as the trials in 1981 of Leonard Arthur and in 1992 of Nigel Cox demonstrate. And, as Peter Alldridge suggests in his preliminary consideration of the case of Tony Bland[11] – which was concluded in the House of Lords as proof pages came to hand – when some assistance is sought, the echoes which breach the silence are often more shrill than the muted notes which they succeed.

But doctors are not alone in this. In its incapacity the law disables many. We see that, at common law, consent from a family member in relation to potentially deadly medical interventions may achieve little. The patient's own advance choice is questionably efficacious at common law. As Derek Morgan and Celia Wells both illustrate, the law may deny effective redress to those harmed by disaster and death. It may fail to reconcile the interests of those who do not wish to be touched by that shadow. And in its very failure to address issues law helps us hide from moral dilemmas which we would rather not face – as the essay by Marie Fox makes clear.

CONCLUSION

We present these essays in the hope that they address some of the issues: that they speak in the silence and strip bare the symbolism. In exploring how we deal with death perhaps they can inform us of the sorts of life we had and the sort of world we live them in.

Derek Morgan
Robert Lee
1992

NOTES

1 Devotions, XII (1624).
2 Oswald Hanfling, *Life and Meaning: A Reader* (Oxford: Basil Blackwell, 1987): 2.
3 Ludwig Wittgenstein, *Tractatus Logico-Philosophicus*, trans. C. K. Ogden (London and New York: Routledge, 1922 (reprinted 1992)): 6.4311.
4 P. Ramsey, 'Death's pedagogy', *Commonwealth* 20 (1974): 497–502.
5 See, for example, *Guardian* (15 June 1992).
6 Gabriel Garcia Marquez, *Love in the Time of Cholera*, trans. Edith Grossman (Harmondsworth: Penguin, 1988): 279.
7 (1988) 63 OR (2d) 243, and see in England and Wales, *ReT* (Adult: Refusal of Treatment) [1992] 3 WLR 782.
8 See, for example, Guido Calabresi, *Ideals, Beliefs, Attitudes and the Law* (New York: Syracuse University Press, 1985): 16.
9 *Re J (A Minor) (Wardship Medical Treatment)* [CA] [1992] 4 All ER 614.
10 Only recently have the Courts determined the (legally accepted) definition of death; see *Re A (A Minor)* [1993] 3 Med LR 303.
11 *Airedale National Health Service Trust* v. *Bland* [1993] 1 All ER 821.

1

Against the definition of brainstem death

Martyn Evans

The quest for a definition of death, adequate to those patients whose condition is 'masked' by the technology of intensive-therapy units, has become the quest for the ultimate seat of human life: for the physiological and anatomical core of human life, whose loss constitutes the death of the human being as a whole. There is a general acceptance that this core is identified with the brain: British medical practice employs the further identification of a physiological 'kernel' within the brain itself, namely the brainstem whose functioning underpins the functioning of the brain as a whole, and thence of the human being.

On this view, most formidably articulated and championed by Dr Pallis,[1] the death of the brainstem can be understood as providing the necessary and sufficient conditions for the death of the human being as a whole. Although the formal clinical diagnosis of 'brainstem death' is appropriate only under certain circumstances,[2] the death of every human being can be understood in terms of the death of their brainstem. In the vast majority of deaths, however, the formal diagnosis of brainstem death is unnecessary, since the classical cardiac diagnosis is perfectly adequate. It is in the desperate and extraordinary circumstances of the intensive-therapy unit, where a patient's underlying condition may be disguised by the artificial maintenance of his breathing and perhaps other vital functions, that greater acuity and discrimination appears to be needed – to penetrate the mask of maintained functions and to diagnose the true underlying state of the unfortunate patient. If we construe human death in terms of the final loss of brainstem function, it is held, we shall wield diagnostic criteria with the appropriate discriminatory power.

The arguments in support of this conception of human death rest

1

on the notion of distinguishing that which is essential to meaningful human life; thus they are explicitly conceptual arguments, acknowledged as such by Pallis.[3] From the establishment of a conception of human death, diagnostic criteria may follow; it is of the anatomical nature of the brainstem that such diagnostic criteria can follow straightforwardly.[4]

I believe the arguments in favour of this conception of human death (and hence of their associated diagnostic criteria) to be flawed. My purpose here is to show why this is so, and further to support the case for retaining classical cardiac criteria, as a necessary part of the diagnosis of human death, against the objections which Pallis puts forward. The serious implications of my view are acknowledged and discussed.

I shall present Dr Pallis's arguments in what I hold to be their logical form; then I shall summarise my challenge to them. Following this, a more detailed discussion will pay attention to important questions arising in the presentation and summarised challenge. This discussion will explore the significance of the cardiac criteria, and will reject Dr Pallis's attempt to exclude cardiac criteria by analogy with decapitation. Lastly I will review the implications of what I have said for intensive therapy and for organ transplantation.

In my view Pallis employs essentially two arguments for the brainstem conception of death, though they are entangled in each other and require separation.

I *characterise* the two arguments, once separated, like this:

1 The central, critical and irreplaceable characteristics of human life are functions of the brain – the brain is the 'critical system' of the human being.[5] Thus the death of the brain as a whole implies the death of the human being.[6] Furthermore, the brainstem is the 'critical system' within the brain. Thus the death of the brainstem implies the death of the brain as a whole.[7] Ergo, the death of the brainstem implies the death of the human being as a whole.[8]

2 The central, critical and irreplaceable characteristics of human life are functions of the brainstem, namely the capacities for respiration and for consciousness. The death of a human being just is the irreversible loss of these capacities.[9] Ergo, the death of the brainstem implies the death of the human being as a whole.[10]

I *challenge* the arguments like this:

1   If we accept that the death of the brain implies the death of the human being as a whole, then we need a clear notion of what counts as the death of the brain. Instead we are offered a further implication: that the death of the brainstem implies the death of the brain as a whole. I argue that this process of implication must come to an end somewhere: there must be some point at which a set of functions that are identified as crucial or 'critical' are tested exhaustively and found comprehensively to be finally lost. The point at which this 'criticality' comes to an end must, of course, be identified and defended. For Pallis, of course, this point is the brainstem.

Of his *defence* of the brainstem as the appropriately critical level, two things should be said. First, the criticality of the brainstem can provide no independent support for the conception of human death which Pallis offers, unless it is defended otherwise than by appeal to the functions which embody that conception of death: such an appeal would be circular. However, it is clear that this is effectively the appeal which Pallis makes.[11] Second, and from this, the defence must face any objections that could be put concerning the conception of human death which is being advocated. Of course, at this point argument (1) gives way to argument (2) and we shall consider it below.

His *identification* of the brainstem as the critical point occasions the methodological confusion in his argument. The burden of showing the death of the brain as a whole now rests on demonstrating the exhaustive loss of function of the entire brainstem; yet this is neither shown nor particularly envisaged by the 'brainstem argument'.[12] Although Pallis quite clearly thinks that the proffered criteria, when met, do imply the death of the entire brainstem,[13] he does not tell us why this should be so. I argue that further, undefended, assumptions of deeper levels of criticality are at work here; and that in the absence of any defence they offer no support to the claim that the brainstem is dead. Thus with neither such support nor an exhaustive demonstration of the total loss of brainstem function, a brainstem cannot be held to be dead.

Critics from within medicine are complaining that some brainstem functions, above all vasomotor functions, persist even in individuals declared 'brainstem dead' within British practice. Such persistent functions would refute, on Pallis's own terms, the notion of a dead brainstem in those individuals.[14] By extension they would,

3

if substantiated, refute the claim that those individuals are dead according to the brainstem criteria.

2   I argue that the brainstem criteria for human death must in any case be perceived as in competition with other rival criteria for death, since scientific criteria arise out of a given conception, and do not adjudicate among different conceptions (a point ably made by Pallis himself). Thus the argument over the appropriate diagnostic criteria is in essence an argument over the appropriate way to see and understand human death. The centrality of the brain does not exclude the vital significance of the beating heart. Though the heart may be replaceable, this cannot disqualify it from 'counting for life'[15] where it has not been replaced and continues to beat spontaneously. Though we concede the centrality of the brain, we have no reason to ignore the persistent heartbeat in the so-called 'beating-heart cadaver'.

In this context, I argue that our *reactions* to an individual who is warm, pink and perfused may be categorically different from our reactions to an individual who is cold and grey; and that our reactions are morally significant, indeed, they can be morally decisive. The brainstem conception of death is unacceptable precisely because in such cases it is counter-intuitive. Our responsibilities, to those whose lives are stretched out in the ITU, of course remain.

DISCUSSION

The logic of 'criticality'

The death of the brainstem is taken, on the argument we are challenging, to imply the death of the human being as a whole. The question now arises, in what does the death of the brainstem consist? The justification for concentrating on the brainstem has been that it facilitates the essential characteristics of human life – that it is, in Lamb's phrase, the critical system within the human being as a whole.

It is a matter of logic that successive identifications of 'criticality' must sooner or later come to a stop: otherwise we are never able to say anything about any given critical system, nor, hence, about the human being as a whole. Although there may be no objection in logic to settling on any given level of criticality, we can certainly insist that the chosen level be exhaustively described.

Were we, therefore, to concede the criticality of the death of the

4

brainstem with respect to the death of the human being as a whole, this criticality would entail the absolute necessity of demonstrating the total, comprehensive and final loss of all the brainstem's functions. To claim otherwise is clearly to appeal to some set of necessary and sufficient conditions within the brainstem, that is, to appeal to the further criticality of some set from among the brainstem's functions. Such a set requires to be identified and defended as critical. Since Pallis does not envisage a comprehensive testing of the functions of the brainstem, he is clearly either making such an appeal covertly, or he is failing to grasp the logical requirements of the central status which he ascribes to the brainstem.

The more narrowly we pursue the identification of a critical system, the more explicit is our logical requirement to describe that system definitively. When the testing of such a system underpins our diagnosis of the death of a human being, our *moral* obligation is hardly less demanding.

The prognostic certainty of death

In reply, a proponent of the brainstem criteria might appeal to the prognostic certainty of the current diagnoses of brainstem death: that one who is certified brainstem dead according to the British criteria is doomed to develop asystole within days, perhaps hours. I do not dispute this; what I dispute is whether the entailed eventual loss of life within hours is the same as being dead now.[16] A condition which entails death is not identical with death, because entailment and identity are not the same thing. I shall say more about this in my concluding remarks concerning the implications of the view that I am proposing.

The possibility of exhaustive tests

It may further be objected that we could, in principle, produce an exhaustive series of tests for the death of the brainstem that would meet the logical requirement I have set down. In this case, would we not have a perfectly respectable criterion for the death of the human being as a whole, located in the demonstrable death of the brainstem? There are two things to be said in reply: first, that according to critics, such tests would exclude from a diagnosis of death many patients who are currently declared dead on the existing British criteria;[17] second, that the burden of argument once again falls on establishing that the death of the brainstem does indeed entail the loss of the essential characteristics of human life. This is of course the conceptual argument concerning the identity of those characteristics; specifically, whether persistent spontaneous heartbeat counts among them.

The significance of the spontaneously beating heart

There are two very general authorities for the significance of the persistent and spontaneous heartbeat: public intuition and traditional medical wisdom. Unlike Pallis I continue to be satisfied by these; in this I am joined by, among others, the authors of the 1981 President's Commission Report[18] and their eminent critics[19] alike. Furthermore, I take it that the burden of proof lies upon any attempted revision of the conception of human death to show why, for instance, cardiac criteria should not signify among them.

Together with the rise and fall of the chest, it is the perfusion of the body with blood which offers the clearest visible sign of life in an otherwise motionless and unconscious individual. Our attitude to someone we see as alive is fundamentally different from our attitude to someone we see as dead. The relevant difference is plausibly charted by the change from a pink, warm and perfused individual to a cold, grey, non-perfused body; in contrast it is not plausibly charted by the information, from a doctor, that certain tests have indicated the absence of certain reflexes and capacities – and that, *spontaneously persistent* heartbeat to the contrary, this really means that so-and-so is dead.

This is not to say that human life *essentially* consists in the heartbeat, nor to make any other metaphysical statement of that sort. It is to insist that the spontaneously persistent heartbeat is a sign that the individual is not dead: that the heartbeat, as Jonas put it, 'counts for life'.

Those who would exclude the spontaneously persistent heartbeat from counting for life must convince us of their case. If we can resist their case, the moral and conceptual significance of the beating heart will remain. To Pallis's case I now return.

Pallis devotes much energy to discounting the significance of the persistent heartbeat in the 'brainstem dead' patient, in accordance with his conception of human death.[20] In particular, he appeals to an analogy with the decapitated individual whose heart continues to beat after the head has been severed: the absurdity of thinking such a victim alive whilst his heart continues to beat is supposed to entail the irrelevance of a persistently beating heart in the 'brainstem dead' patient. This is intended as a *reductio* against the cardiac conceptions of death. But the analogy soon breaks down. After decapitation the heartbeat is not seriously persistent, for a variety of gross physiological reasons. In decapitation, the heart dies – among other reasons – because its normally integrated environment is disrupted; but the brainstem dies because, among other things, it is no longer perfused. Of course, it would indeed seem strange to deny that the decapitated individual was dead on the grounds that the heartbeat persisted briefly; but a comparable denial, on the grounds that the brainstem would not for some minutes cease functioning, appears equally bizarre. Yet the brainstem criteria require precisely such a denial. Therefore we see that the *reductio* cuts both ways.

Of course it is patients, and not decapitation victims, who interest us. Even in a patient who meets the criteria for a declaration of brainstem death, the heartbeat may persist spontaneously; it does so in a milieu which is still largely, albeit temporarily, integrated. It is no objection to point out that mechanical ventilation is necessary to prevent asystole: patients with end-stage renal disease need mechanical dialysis to prevent eventual asystole. The result may be delayed, but it is no less certain. Furthermore, the non-spontaneity of contributory functions is no threat to the spontaneity of the first-order function in question, as Jonas has powerfully argued.[21]

Nor is the potential replaceability of the human heart a convincing argument against its 'counting for life' in those patients where it has not in fact been replaced. Transplanted hearts, it is true, enjoy no neural connection with the brainstems of their new owners. Original hearts, however, do, and it is with the spontaneous and persistent beating of such hearts that we are typically concerned.

Conceding the centrality of the brain in the maintenance of human life does not entail relinquishing the vital significance of the persistent heartbeat, where it is spontaneously maintained. I would concede that the brain is central; I would insist that the persistent heartbeat also counts for life. Therefore although I have complained of a methodological confusion in Pallis's argument, my principal objection to the brainstem conception of death is itself a conceptual one; as Pallis would himself insist, science cannot adjudicate between rival conceptions. However, I claim that my conception of human death – the final loss of all of those bodily characteristics which *count for life*, persistent heartbeat prominent among them – is in accordance with classical medical wisdom and public conviction. Here the heartbeat takes its place alongside respiration, the brainstem reflexes and evidence of the capacity for consciousness.

Those who doubt the need to include the persistent heartbeat as spontaneous must ask themselves the following simple question: would their confidence, that a 'beating-heart cadaver' was actually dead, extend to cremating the 'cadaver' whilst the heartbeat spontaneously persisted? Taking 'brain death' or 'brainstem death' seriously logically entails a willingness to do precisely this. Some proponents of brain-centred formulations of death might draw back from this repugnant conclusion, by acknowledging their emotional development to be some way in arrears with regard to their logic. Unfortunately, such proponents owe us an account of why eviscerating such patients of their vital organs is acceptable when cremation is not.

Implications

Although I have specifically argued against the brain*stem* conception of death, my insistence on the inclusion of cardiac criteria would clearly commit me against current whole-brain formulations of death as well. This has essentially two sets of implications, concerning the fate of the maintained patient in the intensive-therapy unit and the prospects for transplant organ procurement.

I argue that the fate of the ITU patient is largely untouched. In Britain there is no legal requirement that the patient be dead before the ventilator is switched off, so the inclusion of cardiac criteria do not, in Britain, commit us to the horrors of 'ventilating to asystole'. When the patient's condition is recognised as completely hopeless, the ventilator can be withdrawn, and the patient allowed to die with dignity, in a manner and according to criteria which all would recognise and accept.

By contrast, the implications for organ procurement are profound, and must be faced. Of the major organs, only kidney procurement could survive the re-inclusion of cardiac criteria in the diagnosis of death.[22] Let it first be noted that those who, like Dr Pallis, have resolutely denied any connection between the need for organs and the redefinition of death are in no position to argue the need for organs as an objection to the reassertion of traditional cardiac criteria. Others may feel less inhibited. However, since, in general, the proponents of brainstem and whole-brain conceptions

8

of death scrupulously insist that prudential consideration should not influence conceptual clarification, let us take them at their word: ends do not justify means. As uncontroversial evidence of this, no amount of practical benefit would (I take it) justify either the explantation of organs from those in a persistent vegetative state, or any further revision of the notion of death to accommodate *them*.

If we wish to benefit from the terminal prognosis of those brain-damaged, comatose patients whose hearts nonetheless beat spontaneously, let us do so openly, by general consent and agreement. I doubt whether such consent would be forthcoming, but let the question still be put. As things stand, the condition of the terminally comatose patient is masked by more than technology: it is masked by a diagnosis which regards the dying as already dead.

NOTES

1 C. Pallis, *ABC of Brainstem Death* (London: British Medical Association, 1983); C. Pallis, 'Death', in *Encyclopedia Britannica*, 1986 edn.
2 See Pallis, *ABC*: 10–21.
3 ibid.: 1, 2, 7, 32.
4 ibid.: 7–8.
5 This phrase is not used by Pallis himself; it is offered by David Lamb, *Death, Brain Death and Ethics* (London: Croom Helm, 1985), and it serves as a useful shorthand for the notion which Pallis does employ: the role of an organ whose loss implies the death of some larger organ as a whole or, in the ultimate case, of the human being as a whole.
6 Pallis, *ABC*: 1, 5.
7 ibid.: 1, 6, 7, 8.
8 ibid.: 1, 7.
9 ibid.: 2, 7, 8.
10 ibid.: 2, 7, 32.
11 ibid.: 2, 6, 7.
12 The tests essentially concern persistent apnoea and areflexia – ibid.: 14 *et seq*. Although Pallis acknowledges the brainstem's role in vasomotor function (ibid.: 7), for instance, no test for this is envisaged. Instead the emphasis is on a 'battery' of sufficient tests (ibid.: 7). Pallis is noncommittal on the adequacy of 'partial data' (ibid.: 20).
13 The claim is unambiguous: see ibid.: 29.
14 See D. W. Evans and D. J. Hill, 'The brainstems of organ donors are not dead', *Catholic Medical Quarterly* XL 3 (243) (August 1989) for a detailed and authoritatively referenced discussion of persistent brainstem functions.
15 The phrase is Jonas's; see H. Jonas, 'Against the stream: comments on the definition and redefinition of death', reprinted in D. Beauchamp and

L. Walters (eds), *Contemporary issues in bioethics*, 2nd edn (Belmont, Calif.: Wadsworth Pub. Co., 1982): 288–93.

16 Pallis's attempt to resist this is no more than a restatement of his premisses; since we deny the premisses, our charge on this point is sustained. Pallis, *ABC*: 23.

17 Evans and Hill, op. cit.

18 President's Commission for the Study of Ethical Problems in Medicine and Biomedical and Behavioral Research, *Defining Death – medical, legal and ethical issues in the determining of death* (Washington DC: US Government Printing Office, July 1981). Persistent cardiac function is taken to be a 'reliable sign' of 'systemic integration' (ibid.: 37).

19 J. L. Bernat, C. M. Culver and B. Gert, 'Defining death in theory and practice', *Hastings Center Report* 12 (1) (February 1982): 5–9. Here I take it that cardiopulmonary function may be conceived of as two distinct functions, and that the persistence of the cardiac component would satisfy these authors' understanding of the non-fulfilment of necessary conditions for death (ibid.: 8).

20 Pallis, *ABC*: 3, 9, 17, 22–3.

21 Jonas, op. cit.: 290.

22 Since writing, this statement has been overtaken by events. See the special issue of the *Kennedy Institute of Ethics Journal*, 3:2 (June 1993), for discussions of a new proposal for the procurement of organs from 'single non-heart-beating cadavers'.

2

'Who wants to live forever?'[1]

Peter Alldridge

A fear which has for years affected many people, and which is the basis of many legends, is the fear of becoming 'undead'. A person who is 'undead' lacks qualities both of the live and the dead. The combination of advancing medical technology, cruel courts and the fanaticism of the protoplasm obsessed, *soi-disant* 'pro-life' school have made the prospect of being numbered among the undead very much more of a reality than any vampire or werewolf ever has.

In *Cruzan* v. *Director, Missouri Department of Health*[2] the Supreme Court of Missouri and then the Supreme Court of the United States had to consider the law relating to the giving of hydration and nutrition to a patient in a persistent vegetative state (PVS). Commencing with the decision in *Re Quinlan*[3] there had, until 1988, been an emerging consensus in the various jurisdictions of the US that courts should order the withdrawal of nutrition and hydration from patients who entered the PVS. A counter trend has now emerged, in the decisions of

1   the Supreme Court of Washington in *In re Grant*;[4]
2   the New York Court of Appeals in *In re Westchester County Medical Centre*;[5] and especially
3   the Supreme Court of Missouri in *Cruzan*.

In each of these cases the state supreme courts have refused to authorise the withdrawal of food and fluids from incompetent patients who were not terminally ill, in the absence of an informed refusal of care by the patient while competent. Since it went on appeal to the Supreme Court of the United States, *Cruzan* will acquire the greatest significance.[6]

11

PETER ALLDRIDGE

THE FACTS

Nancy Beth Davis, née Cruzan, had been in a PVS since an accident on 11 January 1983. She was oblivious to her surroundings and the prognosis was that she would remain so. Her body twitched only reflexively, without consciousness. The areas of her brain that once thought, felt and experienced sensations had degenerated badly and were continuing to do so. The cavities remaining were filling with cerebrospinal fluid. The cerebral cortical atrophy was irreversible, permanent, progressive and ongoing. Nancy would never have interacted meaningfully with her environment again. She would have remained in a persistent vegetative state until her death. Because she could not swallow, her nutrition and hydration were delivered through a tube surgically implanted in her stomach.[7]

WHAT EXACTLY IS THE PERSISTENT VEGETATIVE STATE?

Cranford and Smith[8] offer the following definition of the PVS: 'In this state the neocortex is largely and irreversibly destroyed, although some brain stem functions persist.'[9] It is very doubtful whether patients in the PVS experience pain. Karen Quinlan's family believed that she did, inferring this from her groans, grimaces and increased muscular tension in response to stimuli.[10] But the medical evidence was that these were simply reflex responses.[11] In approving the withdrawal of life-support equipment the President's Commission[12] concluded from irreversibly vegetative patients:

[T]reatment ordinarily aims to benefit a patient through preserving life, relieving pain and suffering, protecting against disability, and returning maximally effective functioning. If a prognosis of permanent unconsciousness is correct, however, continued treatment cannot confer such benefits. Pain and suffering are absent, as are joy, satisfaction, and pleasure. Disability is total and no return to an even minimal level of social or human functioning is possible.

Whilst it is not possible to provide accurate figures on the numbers of people maintained in the PVS in the United Kingdom, it is clear that the significance of the problem can only increase with advances in medical technology. And the possibility of maintaining people in the PVS will inevitably generate calls for intervention by the courts or for legislation. A decision on treatment of patients in the PVS, indicative as it is of the mood of the courts, is not the last word on many other questions. The PVS is not a terminal condition. It is not covered as one of the conditions to which many 'living will' statutes (including that of Missouri) apply.[13] In the Supreme Court of Missouri Blackmar J said, at the outset of his strong dissent: 'Distinguishable cases include mechanical respirators, radical surgery, blood transfusions, dialysis, chemotherapy, treatment of infection or . . . surgical implantation of feeding tubes after all hope of amelioration has vanished.'[14] Nonetheless if it is accepted that it can be lawful to withdraw nutrition and hydration to PVS patients, those other cases must follow *a fortiori*.

NANCY'S VIEWS

One of the approaches to litigants in 'right to die' cases has been to reconstruct the ideology of the patient, in order to locate his/her views upon what s/he would have liked to happen in the events which have happened. This is easiest, in the absence of a living will, in the case of an obedient member of a religious community.[15] The evidence of Nancy's views was less clear, but might have been held to be compelling by another court:

> Ms. Comer [a friend of Nancy] testified that: 'Nancy said she would never want to live [in a vegetative state] because if she couldn't be normal or even, you know, like half way, and do things for yourself, because Nancy always did, that she didn't want to live . . . and we talked about it a lot.' She said 'several times' that 'she wouldn't want to live that way because if she was going to live, she wanted to be able to live, not to just lay in a bed and not be able to move because you can't do anything for yourself. . . . [S]he said that she hoped that [all the] people in her family knew that she wouldn't want to live [as a vegetable] because she knew it was usually up to the family whether you lived that way or not.' The conversation took place approximately a year before Nancy's accident and was described by Ms. Comer as a 'very serious' conversation that continued for approximately half an hour without interruption.[16]

So the only expression of view by the patient of which there was evidence before the court was to the effect that she would wish not to be treated.

THE MISSOURI DECISION

An application was made by Nancy Cruzan's parents, before the courts of Missouri, asking for an order permitting[17] the withdrawal of hydration and nutrition.

By a 'tenuous majority'[18] of 4–3 the Supreme Court of Missouri held that no such order should be made. The reasoning is sometimes difficult to follow, because three layers of constitutional law need to be considered and reconciled. There was argument as to the common law of Missouri, the constitutional rights guaranteed by the state constitution, and also as to the rights enshrined in the Constitution of the United States.

What was held by the majority of the court was that:

1   Under the common law of Missouri, in order for there to be a withdrawal of medical treatment, there had to be 'clear and convincing evidence' to the effect that the patient would not wish, under the circumstances which obtain, to be treated. Without such clear and convincing evidence hydration and nutrition had to continue.[19]

2   Under the state constitution of Missouri, the rights to liberty and equal protection of the laws (protected both under Article I sections 2 and 10 of the state constitution and the Fourteenth Amendment to the US constitution) do not operate in such a way as to grant a right to have nutrition and hydration terminated. The courts of Missouri do not regard the Missouri constitution as conferring a right of privacy.[20]

3   Under the Constitution of the United States, the right of privacy which had been developed by the Supreme Court to protect the right to contraception within marriage,[21] and then used to provide a constitutionally-protected right to abortion,[22] had no application. The right of privacy in US constitutional law is under attack. The Supreme Court refused in 1986 to extend the right 'beyond a common theme of procreation and relationships within the bonds of marriage'.[23] The Supreme Court of Missouri expressed grave doubts as to whether the privacy decisions could be applied in cases such as this.[24] Although the Supreme Court of New Jersey had based its decision in *Quinlan* partly upon decisions such as *Roe and Griswold* upon privacy rights, the

14

Supreme Court of Missouri held that those arguments did not apply in this case.[25]

THE APPEAL TO THE US SUPREME COURT

The constitutional position as between the state's and the federal jurisdiction explains some of the differences in emphasis in the two decisions. The US Supreme Court had to decide only whether the law of Missouri, as determined by the Supreme Court of the state, was consistent with the US constitution. Save in so far as it was inconsistent with the US constitution, the US Supreme Court had neither the right nor the duty to determine the law of Missouri.

So the question for the US Supreme Court was whether the state could, consistently with the US constitution, require clear and convincing evidence of the wishes of the patient to be produced before it would act upon them; and whether it could, consistently with the equal protection clause in the Fourteenth Amendment permit rights (to refuse treatment) to competent patients which were not permitted to incompetent patients.

The Supreme Court held by 5–4 that the State of Missouri was within its powers to adopt the law laid down in *Cruzan* (Mo.). Chief Justice Rehnquist and Justices White, O'Connor, Scalia and Kennedy joined in the majority opinion. Justices O'Connor and Scalia filed concurring opinions, of which O'Connor J's was more liberal, Scalia J's more conservative than the judgment of the court.

Justice Scalia takes reverence for the founding fathers to extremes. He considers the law of suicide which obtained in 1789 in the states which signed the US constitution, and argues that since the preponderance of them criminalised suicide, that could not be a constitutionally-protected right, and consequently the right to refuse treatment could not be constitutionally protected either.

> It seems to me, in other words, that [the minority's] position ultimately rests upon the proposition that it is none of the State's business if a person wants to commit suicide. . . . This is a view that some societies have held, and that our States are free to adopt if they wish. But it is not a view imposed by our constitutional traditions, in which the power of the State to prohibit suicide is unquestionable.[26]

As on many questions in the court as constituted in the years before the retirement of Brennan and Marshall JJ, O'Connor J's

15

vote was pivotal, and, in the words of the dissent, 'less parsimo-nious'. She recognised that:

Today's decision, holding only that the Constitution permits a State to require clear and convincing evidence of Nancy Cruzan's desire to have artificial hydration and nutrition withdrawn, does not preclude a future determination that the Constitution requires the States to implement the decisions of a patient's duly appointed surrogate. Nor does it prevent States from developing other approaches for protecting an incompetent individual's liberty interest in refusing medical treatment. As is evident from the Court's survey of state court decisions, no national consensus has yet emerged on the best solution for this difficult and sensitive problem. Today we decide only that one State's practice does not violate the Constitution; the more challenging task of craft-ing appropriate procedures for safeguarding incompetents' liberty interests is entrusted to the 'laboratory' of the States,[27] in the first instance.[28]

The dissenting judgment was by Brennan J,[29] with Blackmun, Marshall, Stevens JJ (who committed himself to paper separately, but to the same effect) concurring. It is a very powerful and eloquent rebuttal of the arguments for the State of Missouri, and ranks highly in the common law tradition of dissenting judgments.

Now there is a reaction which can be made to many US Supreme Court decisions which goes something like this: that what has to be decided is often not a substantive issue about what the law should be in this or that state, but whether the laws adopted by a particular state comply with the federal constitution – that is, a question of *vires*, not of substance. If this position is taken then the utterances of the Supreme Court judges on the substantive question are neither here nor there. Given that there is a federal constitution, there must be areas of legislative autonomy for the states (otherwise there is no federation at all), and there must be areas where the states are subject to the federal consti-tution (because otherwise they would be independent).

If the decision in *Cruzan* (US) is read as saying simply that the federal courts are adopting a 'hands-off' posture, then the reader's response will vary according to his/her constitutional philosophy. It must always be remembered, in this case as well as *Roe* v. *Wade*,[30] that the argument is a constitutional one, and the mere fact, for example, that there is no constitutionally-protected right to refuse treatment does not mean that any of the states are going to legislate to take it away. All it means is that the citizens of the US are in the position held by citizens of the UK before the European Convention on Human Rights came to be taken at all seriously. That is, they are at the mercy of an unconstrained legislature.

But such an approach is not really consistent with the manner in which the US Supreme Court, during some passages at least of its history, has perceived its function. Unavoidably, arguments about constitutionality and appropriateness become mingled. This essay will take the following questions in turn:

1 Can the distinction between ordinary and extraordinary means of securing survival be defended?
2 What is the interest of a patient in the PVS?
3 Does the competent patient have a constitutionally-protected right to refuse treatment?
4 What is the significance of the finality argument?
5 What is the position of the doctor and the family?
6 What is the standard of proof of the patient's prior expression?

THE DISTINCTION: ORDINARY/EXTRAORDINARY MEANS

The question arose whether any satisfactory distinction could be made between 'ordinary' and 'extraordinary' means of preserving the life of the patient. The argument has sometimes been made by those trying to tread the tightrope between 'killing' and 'not striving officiously to keep alive' that 'extraordinary' means do not need to be taken to preserve life:[31] in the case of the PVS patient the argument is then that all that is needed to preserve the patient in the PVS is nutrition and hydration – and what could be more ordinary than that?

In spite of some equivocal support for the distinction in *Cruzan* (Mo.)[32] only Scalia J regarded the delivery of nutrition and hydration to a patient in the PVS as not falling within the category of 'medical treatment'. Brennan J said:[33]

No material distinction can be drawn between the treatment to which Nancy Cruzan continues to be subject – artificial nutrition and hydration – and any other medical treatment. The artificial delivery of nutrition and hydration is

17

undoubtedly medical treatment. The technique to which Nancy Cruzan is subject – artificial feeding through a gastrostomy tube – involves a tube implanted surgically into her stomach through incisions in her abdominal wall. It may obstruct the intestinal tract, erode and pierce the stomach wall or cause leakage of the stomach's contents into the abdominal cavity. . . . Artificial delivery of food and water is regarded as medical treatment by the medical profession and the Federal Government.

In neither Supreme Court was a satisfactory foundation laid for a distinction between nutrition and hydration and other treatments. There is anecdotal evidence that doctors in the United Kingdom continue to supply nutrition and hydration to patients in the PVS but do not treat pneumonia when it arises, as commonly it will. This would accord with the attitude of the criminal law to the distinction between acts and omissions. But in the context of the relationship between a doctor and an entirely helpless patient the distinction between acts and omissions is difficult to defend. A law adopting such a policy seems to be directed more towards the psychological well-being of the doctor than to any particular physical benefit to the patients. Whatever else, the refusal of the Supreme Court to perpetuate the distinction between ordinary and extraordinary means is to be applauded.

THE PATIENT'S INTEREST

A traditional legal approach to the problem of how a particular person or class of persons should be treated, when the objects are not in a position, or supposed not to be in a position, to express their views, is to have someone, an official or a court or some other nominee, decide what is in the best interest of the person concerned. In this way the decision of the nominee can be regarded as endorsed by the object – which is as close as the law can get to treating him/her as an autonomous subject.

So, if a patient in the PVS has interests,[34] the question arises whether feeding by tube is in his/her interests? Harris and Bostrom,[35] after a long exposition of feeding by tube to establish the normality of the treatment, regard the treatment as being in her interest. If it means anything to say that a patient has interests independent of his/her capacities to be satisfied, can it be in the

18

patient's interest to have nutrition and hydration withdrawn? Buchanan faces the problem squarely: 'Withholding life-support seems to be no more in [the comatose patient's] best interest than refraining from watering a plant could be said to be good for it.'[36]

Conversely, of course, the argument that with nutrition and hydration withdrawn the patient would die a particularly unpleasant death is specious. The PVS patient is non-sentient. What appeared to some members of the court in *Cruzan* (Mo.)[37] to be horrifying – the idea of the woman dying of thirst – is not horrifying because of her reaction, but theirs. It is difficult to see how any significant difference is made to the non-sentient patient by the means of his/her death. Rhoden's view is highly persuasive:

> Looking to the present physical or psychological interests of the permanently comatose yields no reason either to treat them or to stop. If one adds the exceedingly remote possibility that the diagnosis is wrong and the patient will regain consciousness, then the scale tips slightly toward treatment and the lives of the comatose must be sustained.[38]

One solution by definition would be, of course, to define the PVS patient as being already dead.[39] This would require wholesale reconsideration of the legal definition of death, which is not within the cope of this essay.[40]

The inevitable conclusion is that to ask what is in the interest of the patient is a procedure better suited towards alleviating the feelings of responsibility in the decision-taker, than actually for deciding what to do. It is perfectly understandable as a matter of psychology[41] that this course is adopted – but it is also unfortunate and unhelpful. It is in the consideration of the interests of the patient, and the analytical cul-de-sac which it presents, that the basis can be seen for the idea of treating the PVS patient as the object of the rights of others.

IS THERE A RIGHT IN A COMPETENT PATIENT TO REFUSE TREATMENT?

It was necessary for the Supreme Court to consider the possibility that there may be a constitutionally-protected right for a competent patient to refuse treatment. The reason for this was that one of the arguments for the family was that Nancy was being deprived of equal protection of the laws (guaranteed by the Fourteenth

Amendment to the US constitution). The argument was that the competent patient has this right, and that it denies the incompetent patient equal protection not to have some mechanism by which the right can be exercised for him/her. The argument did not succeed, and in rejecting it (or at least, in allowing the imposition by the state of stringent requirements for its exercise) the Supreme Court cast doubt upon the assumption that had previously been made that the competent patient has such a right and that the right is constitutionally-protected.

The clearest US decision in which a right to refuse treatment had been granted was *Bouvia* v. *Superior Court*.[42] Elizabeth Bouvia was a woman with a disability who decided to refuse treatment to the point at which she died. The Californian courts permitted her so to do. Greeted by some writers as a glorious vindication of personal autonomy, the decision has been shown by Longmore to be less unequivocally welcomed.[43] He argues that Elizabeth Bouvia was the victim of a social construction of a person with her disability as being worthless.[44]

The majority of the US Supreme Court judgment in *Cruzan* equivocated as to whether the right to refuse treatment was constitutionally-protected. The judgment expressly states that it assumes – without deciding – for the purpose of the instant appeal that there is a constitutionally-protected right – either because of the right to privacy developed by the court without being mentioned in the constitution[45] or because of the provisions of the Fourteenth Amendment. But it is worth quoting the judgment in full on this question:

> But determining that a person has a 'liberty interest' under the Due Process Clause does not end the enquiry; whether the respondent's constitutional rights have been violated must be determined by balancing his liberty interests against the relevant state interests. Petitioners insist that under the general holdings of our cases, the forced administration of life sustaining medical treatment, and even of artificially delivered food and water essential to life, would implicate [*sic*] a competent person's liberty interest. Although we think the logic of the cases discussed above [i.e., *Bouvia* etc.] would embrace such a liberty interest, the dramatic consequences involved in refusal of such treatment would inform the enquiry as to whether the deprivation of that interest is constitutionally permissible. But

for purposes of this case,[46] we assume that the United States Constitution would grant a competent person a constitutionally protected right to refuse lifesaving hydration and nutrition.[47]

Brennan J thundered in response:

Although the right to be free of unwanted medical intervention, like other constitutionally protected interests, may not be absolute, no State interest could outweigh the rights of an individual in Nancy Cruzan's position. Whatever a State's possible interests in mandating life-support treatment under other circumstances, there is no good to be obtained here by Missouri's insistence that Nancy Cruzan remain on life-support systems if it is indeed her wish not to do so. Missouri does not complain, nor could it, that society as a whole will be benefited by Nancy's receiving medical treatment. No third party's situation will be improved and no harm to others will be averted. If Missouri were correct that its interests outweigh Nancy's interest in avoiding medical procedures as long as she is free of pain and physical discomfort, . . . it is not apparent why a State could not choose to remove one of her kidneys without consent on the ground that society would be better off if the recipient of that kidney were saved from renal poisoning. Nancy cannot feel surgical pain. Nor would removal of one kidney be expected to shorten her life expectancy. . . . Patches of her skin could also be removed to provide grafts for burn victims, and scrapings of bone marrow to provide grafts for someone with leukemia. Perhaps the State could lawfully remove more vital organs for transplanting into others who would then be cured of their ailments, provided the State placed Nancy on some other life-support equipment to replace the lost function. Indeed, why could the State not perform medical experiments on her body, experiments that might save countless lives, and would cause her no greater burden than she already bears by being fed through the gastrostomy tube? This would be too brave a new world for me and, I submit, for our Constitution.[48]

21

FINALITY AND MEDICAL MIRACLES

There is an argument which appears from time to time in debates as to the termination of life. It goes like this: there is something particular about a decision to terminate life, which distinguishes it from all other decisions: there is no means of correcting a mistake. The argument is a difficult one to understand because it is, of course, in the nature of the process of deciding anything finally that the decision is irrevocable. There is a connected argument for preserving the status quo in PVS cases, and that is the possibility of a medical miracle. But the problem of finality and the possibility of diagnostic mistake or subsequent 'medical miracle' was something which concerned the majority in the Supreme Court. Brennan J dealt with the issue elegantly:

> The majority claims that the allocation of the risk of error is justified because it is more important not to terminate life-support for someone who would wish it continued than to honor the wishes of someone who would not. An erroneous decision to terminate life-support is irrevocable, says the majority, while an erroneous decision not to terminate 'results in a maintenance of the status quo.' But, from the point of view of the patient, an erroneous decision in either direction is irrevocable. An erroneous decision to terminate artificial nutrition and hydration, to be sure, will lead to failure of that last remnant of physiological life, the brain stem, and result in complete brain death. An erroneous decision not to terminate life-support, however, robs a patient of the very qualities protected by the right to avoid unwanted medical treatment. His own degraded existence is perpetuated; his family's suffering is protracted; the memory he leaves behind becomes more and more distorted.[49]
>
> The majority also misconceives the relevance of the possibility of 'advancements in medical science,' by treating it as a reason to force someone to continue medical treatment against his will. The possibility of a medical miracle is indeed part of the calculus, but it is a part of the patient's calculus. If current research suggests that some hope for cure or even moderate improvement is possible within the life-span projected, this is a factor that should be and would be accorded significant weight in assessing what the patient himself would choose.[50]

THE FAMILY

The way in which the *Cruzan* litigation arose was such that the only interested parties were Nancy Cruzan and the State of Missouri. The possibility did not arise that her family or relative may have had rights.[51] That had to follow directly from the fact that there were claims being made on her behalf which had she been a competent patient would have been assertions of patient autonomy. If anyone was to have the right to terminate her hydration and nutrition, it was she.

But there is another, radically different approach which the law could adopt to the problem, and that would be to regard the PVS patient not as being the subject of rights, but as their object. Such an approach would take account of the sorts of problems which are faced by family and friends of PVS patients, and various other consequentialist arguments which were excluded by the form of the litigation. First, there is the cost. Care for Nancy Cruzan cost $9,000 per month.[52] Long before the litigation began her own resources of health care insurance had been exhausted. The case proceeded on the basis of the state's undertaking to meet whatever costs were incurred. But no such undertaking need have been given. It is by no means clear what the position would be where the state was not paying: or perhaps the right which *Cruzan* (US) confers on the states is subject to their paying.

Following at least in part from the question of cost, there is the effect upon the treatment of people coming into a hospital. Pressure will be placed upon doctors not to commence treatment. Any rational approach would make it easier to withdraw treatment which has been commenced and proved hopeless rather than not to treat someone coming into a hospital. *Cruzan* is likely to produce the opposite approach:

> if there is any call to draw a moral distinction between withholding and withdrawing [treatment], it generally cuts the other way from the usual formulation: greater justification ought to be required to withhold than to withdraw treatment. Whether a particular therapy will have positive effects is often highly uncertain before the therapy has been tried. If a trial of therapy makes clear that it is not helpful to the patient, this is actual evidence (rather than mere surmise) to support stopping because the therapeutic benefit that earlier was a possibility has been found to be clearly unobtainable.[53]

23

We need a medical culture which recognises that withdrawing treatment is psychologically more difficult, but also ethically easier to justify and which thus avoids the dangerous 'cycle of commitment' – where treatment continues because it continues.

Last, there is the effect upon families of having a member in a PVS. There is strong evidence that to have one of its number in a PVS for any length of time has a serious effect upon the mental and physical health of the rest of the family.[54] Now, of course, the consequence of regarding a PVS patient as an object, not a subject of rights would be that the law would have to consider the uncomfortable question of when there is to be a right vested in a parent (or other relative or appointee) to authorise the killing of the patient. But it is by no means an alien notion to the English lawyer that the family should be consulted. In a series of decisions the English courts have made it clear that the family does have a role to discharge in the taking of decisions in this area. They have all dealt with the treatment of neonates, in respect of whom there is a presumption that the parents' consent is a relevant matter,[55] but nevertheless the same principles may well apply. In the case of Re J[56] the question was whether a child should be treated in the event that it suffered a further seizure of a type which, if not treated, could prove fatal.

Lord Donaldson MR said:[57]

No one can dictate the treatment to be given to the child, neither court, parents nor doctors. There are checks and balances. The doctors can recommend treatment A in preference to treatment B. They can refuse to adopt treatment C on the grounds that it is medically contra-indicated or for some other reason is a treatment which they could not conscientiously administer. The court or parents for their part can refuse to consent to treatment A or B or both, but cannot insist on treatment C. The inevitable and desirable result is that choice of treatment is in some measure a joint decision of the doctors and the court or parents.

What this case[58] contemplates is that there are circumstances under which the wishes of the parents can make the difference whether non-treatment is authorised by the court or not. In the case of a PVS patient the relative simplicity of the medical decision (whether or not to supply nutrition and hydration) makes the choice more stark: there is not the range of treatments which is contemplated by Lord

Donaldson. Nor, of course, does anyone have the rights conferred by the law upon the parents, but *Re J* does at least suggest a way forward – the possibility of someone else making the decision, rather than some attempt to second-guess what the patient might have thought.

STANDARD OF PROOF

The decision against which the appeal was taken was that the law of Missouri requires 'clear and convincing' evidence that the wishes of the person in a PVS were that s/he would want treatment withdrawn. The 'clear and convincing' standard is one between the usual civil and criminal standards of proof. What it does is to create a strong presumption in favour of treatment. This is of the utmost importance because in the majority of such cases there will be no absolutely clear evidence, and the question what is to happen will be determined by the onus and standard of proof. It was the evidential issue upon which the appeal centred. As with any system of jurisprudence for the protection of rights, the issue which arises is whether there can be a right in circumstances where procedural and evidential restrictions are imposed which are so tight as to restrict the exercise of the right substantially.[59] It would in practice be quite difficult to produce 'clear and convincing' evidence of an expression of the wishes of the patient, in the absence of a living will. The argument for the 'clear and convincing' standard was made by Rehnquist CJ and those who agreed with him:

It is also worth noting that most, if not all, States simply forbid oral testimony entirely in determining the wishes of parties in transactions which, while important, simply do not have the consequences that a decision to terminate a person's life does. At common law and by statute in most States, the parole evidence rule prevents the variations of the terms of a written contract by oral testimony. The statute of frauds makes unenforceable oral contracts to leave property by will, and statutes regulating the making of wills universally require that those instruments be in writing.[60]

The differences between the choice made by a competent person to refuse medical treatment, and the choice made for an incompetent person by someone else to refuse medical treatment, are so obviously different that the State is warranted in

25

establishing rigorous procedures for the latter class of cases which do not apply to the former.[61]

To the contrary effect came Brennan J's dissent:

Missouri may constitutionally impose only those procedural requirements that serve to enhance the accuracy of a determination of Nancy Cruzan's wishes or are at least consistent with an accurate determination. The Missouri 'safeguard' that the Court upholds today does not meet that standard. The determination needed in this context is whether the incompetent person would choose to live in a persistent vegetative state on life-support or to avoid this medical treatment. Missouri's rule of decision imposes a markedly asymmetrical evidentiary burden. Only evidence of specific statements of treatment choice made by the patient when competent is admissible to support a finding that the patient, now in a persistent vegetative state, would wish to avoid further medical treatment. Moreover, this evidence must be clear and convincing. No proof is required to support a finding that the incompetent person would wish to continue treatment. . . . Just as a state may not override Nancy's choice directly, it may not do so indirectly through the imposition of a procedural rule.[62]

Rhoden[63] wrote of the arguments for the 'clear and convincing' standard of evidence of a patient's desire to have treatment discontinued, that:

unsatisfactory and subtly dishonest opinions predominate in this area . . . the medical presumption for treatment incorporates not only the overt and noble commitment to saving life, but also covert and highly questionable psychological, technological and professional drives . . . doctors should be required to justify medical interventions that are unwanted by the patient's nearest relatives, and to justify them as beneficial in human, not merely biological terms.

WHAT'S LEFT FOR THE UNITED STATES?

[W]e think a State may properly [i.e., constitutionally] decline to make judgments about the 'quality' of life that a particular individual may enjoy, and simply assert an unqualified interest in the preservation of human life to be weighed against the constitutionally protected interests of the individual.[64]

The question is still an open one under US constitutional law whether or not there is a constitutionally-protected right to refuse life-sustaining treatment, or whether the question is one for the states to determine. Advances in medical technology will force each state to adopt one of two positions. On the one hand, the state may go down the road taken by the state of Missouri in this case, incurring a self-imposed obligation to invest in building coma wards in which to keep increasing numbers of comatose patients, in training staff to maintain the equilibrium of these patients and in training psychiatrists to take care of the depressive illnesses occasioned in the families of the patients it maintains. The alternative is to make statutory provision, or to interpret the common law as having made provision, for the termination of care to patients in the PVS.

Of course, it is possible that the development of differing rules in differing states will lead to the prospect of families or relatives toting around a PVS patient to find the state with the least restrictive requirements in order to terminate his/her 'life'.[65] This is regarded by some as gruesome or offensive, but it is difficult to see how the objection differs in principle from an objection to differential divorce statutes which lead to trips to Reno.

ENGLAND AND WALES

If *Cruzan* leaves almost everything to be decided in the individual states, what then of the position in England and Wales? First, is there a right in England and Wales to refuse treatment, even if it involves the death of the patient? Writing of the law as at December 1988, Kennedy and Grubb[66] cite *Re Conroy*[67] in support of that proposition, and go on to say: 'Although *Conroy* is an American case, we are confident that it reflects the English common law (see *R v. Blaue* [1975] 3 All ER 446, [1975] 1 WLR 1411).' The question which must now be addressed is whether this judgment must be changed in the light of the disapproval expressed for *Conroy* in *Cruzan*. In fact *Blaue*[68] cannot be relied upon as giving very strong support for any proposition in this area. It is a case on causation. The question was whether the defendant had caused the death of the victim notwithstanding that she, a Jehovah's Witness, had refused a

blood transfusion. The case is silent upon the question of the rights
of the victim to refuse consent. Even if she did something which she
had no legal right to do (for example, aggravated an injury by
committing a trespass), that does not necessarily imply that it would
have broken the chain. Nor is *Blaue* inconsistent with the proposition that the doctor had a duty or a liberty to give a blood
transfusion. It does not decide that the doctor had a duty not to give
the transfusion. What would have been required to decide that was
either a successful prosecution or tortious action for assault against
a doctor who had treated under such circumstances,[69] or altern-
atively an unsuccessful murder prosecution. Nonetheless, even with
this absence of English authority, it can be predicted with a fair
degree of confidence that the sorts of arguments which commended
themselves to Brennan J would also meet the approval of an English
court. The right to refuse treatment would be protected by the
courts.[70]

More generally, how are PVS patients to be treated? The US
attitude to questions of law and medical ethics does appear to be
'when in doubt, litigate', and this is why there has been a great deal
of case law developed in many US jurisdictions. But there may be
good reasons why it would be better for litigation not to take place.
In the case where treatment has been withdrawn, it is highly unlikely that a doctor would ever be convicted of murder, even if the
judge decided that, as a matter of law, there was a duty to continue
treatment. And litigation whilst the patient remains comatose
would clearly be an appalling strain for family and friends.

There had until very recently been no case in which a court has
been asked to adjudicate *ex ante* upon the lawfulness of ceasing life-
support measures.[71] Such case law as has developed has either been
(very rare) murder charges brought against doctors[72] or in causation
questions.[73] But in the case of *Airedale NHS Trust* v. *Bland*[74] the
House of Lords made a declaration approving [75] the cessation of the
supply of nutrition, hydration and antibiotics to a PVS patient. Sir
Stephen Brown P had heard evidence from doctors to the effect that
it was their opinion as experts that nutrition and hydration should
be withdrawn, and from Bland's father that this was also his wish.
No argument for the cessation was made on the basis of the
preferences of the patient. The judge held that the medical opinion
was relevant, and determinative. In the Court of Appeal, Hoffman
LJ[76] in particular was clear in regarding questions about the
patient's interests as being philosophical in nature.[77] In the House

of Lords Lord Goff, with whom two others purported[78] to agree, did treat the evidence as relevant, and the withdrawal of consent justifiable, in effect, on *Bolam*[79] grounds. The speech of Lord Browne-Wilkinson[80] also treated the doctor's view as being of importance. He argued that the prior justification for invasive treatment had ceased by the time PVS was diagnosed and that the answer to the question whether it was in the patient's interest to continue[81] was in the negative.[82]

All the judges in *Bland* regarded the case as revolving solely around the legal position of the patient as subject, and were not prepared to countenance explicitly the intervention of any other kind of consideration. The way in which the case was presented to the courts was very favourable to those advocating cessation of hydration and nutrition. The only further variable which could have been more favourable to termination would have been a living will. Consequently *Bland* leaves open a further series of questions.

If the views of relatives are to be taken into account, what is to be the position where they are not in agreement? The answer seems to be that the views of the relatives are evidence as to the best interests of the patient, and that differences between them are to be resolved in the same way as any other conflicts of testimony.

What is to be the position either where the relatives are in favour of continuation of hydration and nutrition, or, more difficult yet, where there is very clear (most probably written) evidence of the wishes of the patient that s/he wished to be maintained in the PVS for as long as possible? These are really the critical questions, because they lay bare the reality, veiled in *Cruzan* and *Bland*, that what is in dispute is not so much what is meant by life and how we value it, but a rather less exalted decision about resource allocation. Perhaps *Bland* works at a rhetorical level because it purports to enshrine a right (not to have treatment cease in the face of the patient's wishes) which, it is contemplated, will never be used. If even one patient is actually to be maintained in the PVS on the grounds of his/her previously expressed wishes, but at the cost of other NHS resources, then a strong justification is required.

Notwithstanding *Bland*, there is still little evidence, other than anecdotal,[83] as to English practice, but there is a belief abroad that whereas practice might differ as between doctors in supplying nutrition and hydration to PVS patients, when pneumonia develops there is a great hesitance to treat. There is no doubt that this practice would gain the approval of the courts, but also that failure to heed the calls by the judges for legislative intervention in this difficult area will generate further difficulties.

THE EUROPEAN DIMENSION

A comatose patient in a PVS does not have a constitutionally-protected right in the United States to have nutrition and hydration withdrawn. English law is at best equivocal on the subject. What of the European Convention on Human Rights? It may be that it is within the jurisprudence of the European Convention that this issue will be resolved. There are two major provisions of the European Convention which might be germane. The possibility either of euthanasia or of the termination of nutrition and hydration to patients in a PVS might be affected by article 2. This provides:

> 1 Everyone's right to life shall be protected by law. No one shall be deprived of his life intentionally save in the execution of a sentence of a court following his conviction of a crime for which this penalty is provided by law.

Jacobs[84] states that:

> The legalisation of Euthanasia, which would seem prima facie contrary to the express terms of article 2 . . . might raise the difficult question how far the consent of the victim may negate what would otherwise be a violation of the Convention.[85]

Euthanasia has been justified by Van Dijk and Van Hoof[86] under article 3 of the convention, which provides that: 'No one shall be subjected to torture or to inhuman or degrading treatment or punishment.' The argument here would be that if preserving somebody's life involves subjecting them to inhuman or degrading treatment, then the right not to be subjected to inhuman or degrading treatment prevails. It is difficult to imagine it succeeding.

A MODEST PROPOSAL

What is the best way forward? The merits of living wills are addressed elsewhere in this volume.[87] For some conditions it may be that living wills will provide an answer in the case of those people well enough informed and prescient enough to make them so as to cover every eventuality. But irrespective of the merits of permitting living wills, the law should permit the appointment of health care proxies.[88] This could be done by the patient when competent (in the way that executors are appointed) or, in the case of incompetence, by the court.

The advantages of having proxies are clear: if one person is fixed as the proxy, there can be no dispute as to whom the doctor should address. The convenience of the neonate cases is that the parents are located by the law as the decision-takers, and that there are mechanisms for the resolution of disputes between them. When the patient is an adult in the PVS, there may be any number of people who may reasonably claim to be the best person to tell the doctor. It may well be that the patient does not want a member of his/her family to make the decision. Even the court may recognise that. It is, of course, a very difficult decision to ask anyone to make, but a person could always be empowered to refuse appointment or cease operating as proxy. An objection which is sometimes raised to allowing the appointment of proxies is that the proxy may not be there when an important decision is required. But this objection carries no weight in the case of the PVS patient. If it is a decision to cease hydration and nutrition to a terminally ill patient then the timing does not matter. There is ample time for consideration.

THE AFTERMATH

There was a good deal of scepticism as to the way in which the courts of Missouri treated the evidence:

> The Missouri court's disdain for Nancy's statements in serious conversations not long before her accident, for the opinions of Nancy's family and friends as to her values, beliefs and certain choice, and even for the opinion of an outside objective factfinder appointed by the State evinces a disdain for Nancy Cruzan's own right to choose. The rules by which an incompetent person's wishes are determined must represent every effort to determine those wishes. The rule that the Missouri court adopted and that this Court upholds, however, skews the result away from a determination that as accurately as possible reflects the individual's own preferences and beliefs.

It is a rule that transforms human beings into passive subjects of medical technology. . . . [I]t is still possible for others to make a decision that reflects [the patient's] interests more closely than would a purely technological decision to do whatever is possible. Lacking the ability to decide, [a patient] has a right to a decision that takes his interests into account.[89]

Further evidence came to light from friends of expressions by Nancy Cruzan of her wishes in the events which occurred. No opposition was made to a further application for disconnection of nutrition and hydration. Nutrition and hydration were disconnected and Nancy died on 26 December 1990 after a fortnight short of eight years in the PVS.

ACKNOWLEDGEMENTS

For assistance with this essay I am grateful to the participants in a seminar in the Centre for the Philosophy of Health Care, University College, Swansea and, most particularly, to Derek Morgan.

NOTES

1 Brian May, 'Who wants to live forever', Queen Productions 1986.
2 On appeal from *Cruzan* v. *Harmon* 760 SW 2d 408, (Mo. 1989) (citation) 111 L Ed 2d 224 (1990) (where it is necessary to distinguish the issues decided in the Supreme Court of Missouri and the Supreme Court of the US the cases will be called *Cruzan* (Mo.) and *Cruzan* (US)).
3 (1976) 70 NJ 10, 355 A. 2d 647 (1976).
4 109 Wash 2d 545, 747 P. 2d 445 (1987) modified 575 P. 2d 534 (1988).
5 72 NY 2d 517, 534 NYS 2d 886, 531 NE 2d 607 (1989).
6 The literature is already enormous. See, for example, Symposium, 'Cruzan and the "right to die" ', *Georgia Law Review* 25(5) (1991); A. M. Capron (ed.). 'Medical decision-making and the right to die after Cruzan', *Law, Medicine and Health Care* 19(1–2) (1991).
7 *Per* Brennan J, dissenting, *Cruzan* (US) at p. 256.
8 Ronald Cranford and Harmon Smith, 'Some critical distinctions between brain death and the Persistent Vegetative State', *Ethics in Science and Medicine* 6 (1979): 199.
9 Wanzer *et al.*, 'The physician's responsibility toward hopelessly ill patients', *New England Journal of Medicine* 310 (1984): 955, 958.
10 R. Burt, *Taking Care of Strangers: The Rule of Law in Doctor–Patient Relations* (New York: The Free Press, 1979): 147.
11 Ronald Cranford, 'Termination of treatment in the Persistent Vegetative State', *Seminars in Neurology* 4 (1984): 36; cited by Nancy

K. Rhoden, 'Litigating life and death', *Harvard Law Review* 102 (1988): 375, 405. Data utilising positron emission tomography indicates that the metabolic rate for glucose in the cerebral cortex is greatly reduced in persistent vegetative state patients, to a degree incompatible with consciousness. 'Position of the American Academy of Neurology on certain aspects of the care and management of the Persistent Vegetative State patient', *Neurology* 39 (January 1989): 125.

12 President's Commission for the Study of Ethical Problems in Medicine and Biomedical and Behavioral Research, *Deciding to Forgo Life-Sustaining Treatment* (Washington DC: US Government Printing Office, 1983): 181–2.

13 On living wills see Montgomery, Chapter 3.

14 *Cruzan* (Mo.) at p. 427.

15 See the case of Brother Joseph Fox in *Eichner* 52 NY 2d 353, 420 NE 2d 64 (1981) – who had specifically stated in formal circumstances and in accordance with his religious beliefs that he did not wish to be maintained in the PVS.

16 Brennan J, at p. 269, references being to the transcript of the trial. And for the further decision see *infra*, p. 15 *et seq*.

17 Note the use of permission rather than mandate: in cases where there is permission to disconnect it will be rare that the doctor will not regard him/herself as mandated.

18 *Per* Welliver J, at p. 442 in his stinging dissent. The regular judges of the Supreme Court of Missouri were divided 3–3: the majority arose as a result of the appointment of a 'special judge' to the court.

19 Presumably, though this is not made clear, at the risk of a murder prosecution.

20 *State* v. *Walsh* 713 SW 2d 508 (1986).

21 *Griswold* v. *Connecticut* 381 US 479 (1965).

22 *Roe* v. *Wade* 410 US 113 (1973).

23 *Bowers* v. *Hardwick* 478 US 186 (1986).

24 *Cruzan* (Mo.) at p. 417 *et seq*.

25 For liberal arguments based upon privacy see David A. Richards, 'Constitutional privacy, the right to die and the meaning of life: a moral analysis', *William and Mary Law Review* 22 (1981): 327; and Linda Fentiman, 'Privacy and personhood revisited: a new framework for substitute decisionmaking for the incompetent, incurable adult', *George Washington Law Review* 57 (1989): 801.

26 At p. 252.

27 She cites the famous judgment of Brandeis J, dissenting in *New State Ice Co.* v. *Liebmann*, 285 US 262, 311 (1932).

28 At p. 251.

29 William Brennan retired in July 1990, at the age of 84, as the longest-serving Justice of the United States Supreme Court. He was described, in the chair's introduction to his HLA Hart lecture ('Why have a Bill of Rights?', *Oxford Journal of Legal Studies* 9 (1989): 425), as 'the greatest judge in the greatest court in the world'. One of his last judgments is therefore the dissent he delivered on 26 June 1990 in *Cruzan*. It does him justice.

30 *Roe* v. *Wade* 410 US 113 (1973).
31 Grant 747 P. 2d at p. 461; Westchester 534 NYS 2d at p. 894.
32 760 SW. 2d at pp. 419 and 423.
33 At p. 260.
34 This is a controversial question. See, for example, Joel Feinberg, *Harm to Others* (New York: Oxford University Press, 1984): 79 *et seq*. But in view of the argument in the text, it is unnecessary to look into it.
35 Curtis E. Harris and Barry A. Bostrom, 'Is the continued provision of food and fluids in Nancy Cruzan's best interests?', *Issues in Law and Medicine* 5 (1990): 415.
36 Allen B. Buchanan, 'The limits of proxy decision-making for incompetents', *University of California Los Angeles Law Review* 29 (1981): 386 at p. 402.
37 At p. 423.
38 Rhoden, op. cit.: 375, 400–1 and accompanying footnote drawing attention to religious questions.
39 Buchanan, op. cit.
40 Though see Evans, Chapter 1 *supra*.
41 In much the same way that, after someone dies, things are done in the name of 'what s/he would have wanted', as a means of making the living feel better, and absolved from the behaviour to which their grief drives them.
42 225 Cal. Rptr. 297 (1986).
43 B. Longmore, 'Elizabeth Bouvia, assisted suicide and social prejudice', *Issues in Law and Medicine* 3 (1987): 141.
44 And see, to the same effect, Jenny Morris, *Pride Against Prejudice* (London: Women's Press, 1990).
45 The decisions in *Griswold and Roe* (*supra*) take their lead from Samuel D. Warren and Louis D. Brandeis, 'The right to privacy', *Harvard Law Review* 4 (1890): 193.
46 Emphasis added.
47 At p. 242.
48 At p. 269.
49 Brennan J, at p. 268.
50 Brennan J, at p. 269.
51 See generally H. Krasik, 'The role of the family in medical decision making for incompetent adult patients: a historical perspective', *University of Pittsburg Law Review* 48 (1987): 539.
52 Harris and Bostrom, op. cit.
53 President's Commission for the Study of Ethical Problems in Medicine and Biomedical and Behavioral Research: at p. 240.
54 See Martin Livingstone, 'Head injury: the relatives' response', *Brain Injury* 1 (1987): 8. Also T. C. M. Carnwath and D. A. W. Johnson, 'Psychiatric morbidity among spouses of patients with stroke', *British Medical Journal* 294 (1987): 409; M. Livingstone, 'Families who care', *British Medical Journal* 291 (1985): 919. Nancy Cruzan's husband had to go through the harrowing business of getting a divorce. Such property as she had could not be distributed.
55 *Re B* [1990] 3 All ER 927 CA.

56 [1990] 3 All ER 930 CA.
57 At p. 934h.
58 And the antecedent case of *Re B* (1981) [1990] 3 All ER 927.
59 This was the issue dealt with in a classic liberal manner – that is, by striking down the restrictions – by the Supreme Court of Canada in *Morgantaler* v. *R* (1988) 44 DLR 3d 385.
60 Per Rehnquist CJ, at p. 245.
61 Per Rehnquist CJ, at p. 244. We should beware of differences which are so obvious that they need no explanation.
62 Brennan J, at p. 265.
63 *Harvard Law Review* 102 (1988): 375, 420.
64 At p. 244.
65 This could not be done in circumstances (as in the *Cruzan* case) where the patient is made a ward of court – in which case transporting the patient outside the jurisdiction would constitute a contempt of court – but could well occur in other cases where the relatives act first and ask courts afterwards. See *Re Busalacchi* (Mo. Court of Appeals, 1991) LEXIS 315 for just such a case.
66 Ian Kennedy and Andrew Grubb, *Medical Law: Text and Materials* (London: Butterworth, 1989): 1071.
67 98 NJ 321, 486 A. 2d 1209 (1985).
68 And see H. L. A. Hart and Tony Honore, *Causation in the Law*, 2nd edn (Oxford: Oxford University Press, 1985): 360–1.
69 *Malete* v. *Shulman* (1988) 63 OR (2d) 243.
70 Treatment without consent would also constitute a breach of the European Convention, as to which see *infra*, p. 13.
71 That did not mean that the position was necessarily unsatisfactory. In *Bland* Lord Mustill, at p. 885, expressed serious doubts as to the justiciability of the issue.
72 *R* v. *Arthur* (1991) 3 Med. LR 1.
73 *R* v. *Malcherek and Steel* [1981] 1 WLR 690; *R* v. *Blaue*, *supra*.
74 [1993] 1 All ER 821 (FD, CA, HL).
75 In so far as a declaration is able to do so, Lord Goff (at p. 868) invited the use of a *nolle prosequi* in the event of a prosecution being brought.
76 [1993] 1 All ER 821 at p. 849.
77 He cited, *inter alia*, Isaiah Berlin, *Four Essays on Liberty* (Oxford: Oxford University Press, 1969); and Ronald Dworkin, *Life's Dominion* (forthcoming) and concluded, with Brennan J in *Cruzan*, that 'The best interests of the patient in my judgment embrace not only recovery or the avoidance of pain . . . but also a dignified death' (at p. 857f). It is not immediately clear why it is the patient and not those who care about him/her who has an interest in the dignity of his/her death.
78 Lords Keith and Lowry. *Sed quaere*. Lord Keith stated (at pp. 860j–861a) that:

> In the case of the permanently insensate being, who if continuing to live would never experience the slightest actual discomfort, it is difficult, if not impossible, to make any relevant comparison between continued existence and the absence of it. It is, perhaps,

permissible to say that to an individual with no cognitive capacity whatever, and no prospect of recovering any such capacity, it must be a matter of complete indifference whether he lives or dies.

Lord Lowry (at p. 877c), together with Lords Browne-Wilkinson and Mustill, was unable to explain why it should be permissible to withdraw nutrition and hydration but not administer a lethal injection.

79 [1957] 1 WLR 582.
80 At p. 883.
81 It is unclear whether this implies a *duty*, rather than a *liberty* to withdraw treatment.
82 There is insufficient space in which to deal with the memorable and agonised speech of Lord Mustill.
83 I am grateful to Dr Alan Sinclair, Senior Lecturer in the University of Wales School of Medicine, for conversations on this point.
84 Francis G. Jacobs, *The European Convention on Human Rights*, 2nd edn (Oxford: Clarendon Press, 1980): 472. And see J. E. S. Fawcett, *The Application of the ECHR*, 2nd edn (Oxford: Clarendon Press, 1987): 36.
85 Giving fatal drugs to a patient whose death was certain was found not to be contrary to article 2 in *Verwaltungsgericht Bremen* NJW [1960] 400.
86 P. Van Dijk and G. J. H. Van Hoof, *Theory and Practice of the ECHR*, 2nd edn (Deventer, Netherlands: Kluwer Law and Taxation Publishers, 1990): 188.
87 See Montgomery, Chapter 3.
88 See Kennedy and Grubb, op. cit.: 300 *et seq*.
89 Per Brennan J, at p. 271.

3

Power over death: the final sting

Jonathan Montgomery

The idea that patients have rights sits ill with the general shape of English health care law.[1] Issues of informed consent are governed by ordinary malpractice principles, not by the right of self-determination.[2] Confidentiality is justified by reference to the public good, not individual privacy rights.[3] For practical purposes, rights to health care under the National Health Service Act 1977 are unenforceable.[4] Some progress towards a rights-based model can be seen in legislation giving access to health reports and records.[5] Even here, however, the rights created are subject to being overridden by a professional judgment that patients would be better off not being able to exercise them.[6]

In this infertile ground it is, however, possible to assert that English law now recognises a limited right to die. It is a right carved out of a mixture of general principle and the relaxation of the suicide laws. This right to die is neither strong nor extensive. It is read out of the gaps in the law not expressly stated. It is in nature negative rather than positive. It is protected by obligations on others not to interfere with the patient's choice but it does nothing to secure assistance in putting that choice into effect. Nevertheless, it is there.

This essay is concerned with the right to die in English law. It will begin by substantiating the argument just sketched for the existence of such a right. The power over death thus established will quickly be seen to be a precarious one. It depends on the capacity of the patient to make a rational choice; without this capacity a patient will be given the treatment thought best by the responsible professionals. Yet the line between capacity and incapacity is both obscure and fluid. Professionals caring for the patient may effectively remove the right to die by declaring them no longer capable of making the choice. In this sense patients may be subjected to a

37

con-trick. The law represents that they may choose to be left to die, but allows this power over their dying to be withheld from them at the very point at which its exercise is sought.

If the right to die is to mean anything it must be secured against being undermined in this way. This essay will consider two means of achieving this objective. The first is the development of what have been called 'advance declarations' or 'living wills'. These provide for the legal effect of a choice to die to endure beyond the point when a patient loses the capacity to give or withhold consent to treatment. This would ensure that a choice to die could not be overridden by professionals. The second way in which the right to die might be given more substance is by giving patients the power to appoint proxies to make life and death decisions on their behalf. This would provide a mechanism by which they could ensure that their values prevailed over those of the health professionals. Although such powers of attorney have been recognised in respect of property belonging to those no longer able to manage it for themselves,[7] their use in the health care context has not been fully explored.

Two reports published in 1988 reached different conclusions on both the merits and the legal effect in England of these two approaches. The British Medical Association's (BMA) *Working Party on Euthanasia* argued that neither the selection of a surrogate to take decisions on the patient's behalf nor an advance declaration of intent should be treated as legally or ethically binding. They should be treated with respect, but:

> When a medical crisis arises the medical team cannot solely rely upon projected and hypothetical expressions of intent which may or may not show a full appreciation of the problem. The team are cast upon subtle and intersubjective judgments, made in the light of the advance declaration and appropriate consultation, but also crucially dependent on medical intuitions and guidance in the light of past clinical experience and a considered regard for the patient's best interests.[8]

They were persuaded that the current state of English law reflected this stance.[9]

A report produced by a joint working party of Age Concern and the Centre of Medical Law and Ethics based at King's College, London, expressed a contrary view.[10] They saw advantages in the

38

use of living wills, but found that the demand for their use in the UK was uncertain, and recommended a cautious move towards their use in order to assess their role on a more informed basis. On the current legal position, the report agreed with the BMA so far as the appointment of proxies was concerned. If these were to be made available, this would involve statutory intervention. However, the report argued that advance declarations would have legal effect in England under the common law, provided that the patient foresaw the circumstances which actually arose.[11]

The disagreement between these two reports and the growing acceptance of the need to establish patients' rights indicates the need for further consideration of the issues. The focus of this essay will therefore be on securing for those at the end of their life the power over death which the law already promises but fails to deliver. This represents only part of the proper discussion of the right to die. Questions about the merits of permitting active steps to be taken to end someone's life will receive no more than a cursory glance. Nevertheless, protecting patients from the final sting, the broken promise which leaves them powerless to control their last days, is in itself a significant step.

THE RIGHT TO DIE IN ENGLISH LAW

It is a basic principle of health care law that no patient may be treated without their consent.[12] This principle is not absolute. Some actions may not require consent because they are acceptable in the course of everyday life.[13] Consent may not be available because the patient is incapable of giving it, either temporarily or permanently. If this is so, then the consent requirement is suspended and professionals must act in what they perceive to be the patient's best interests.[14] Exceptionally, it may be permissible to override a refusal of consent, or necessary to reinforce a consent which has been given by a mentally disordered person for the purposes of treatment for such disorder.[15] As a general principle, however, the need for consent is fundamental.

It follows from this principle that patients may not be treated against their will. This creates a right to refuse treatment that will permit patients to choose to die by opting out of their care. At one stage it appeared that this right could be trumped by an obligation on health professionals to keep their patients alive.[16] Such an obligation could be based on three arguments. First, on the general argument that steps taken to save life are justified by the principle of necessity. The House of Lords has held that this applies in relation to those who are incapable of consenting, but that it does not permit treatment against the known wishes of a patient.[17] Thus, it appears that the root of the doctrine is the assumption that the patient would agree, and it follows that if it is known that this is a false assumption treatment cannot be justified. It has been suggested that the basis of the necessity principle is not such an imputed consent, but a 'public interest'.[18] Even if this is correct, suggestions that the public interest requires health professionals to keep their patients alive at all costs are precluded by the series of decisions permitting severely handicapped newborn children to die.[19] In the Court of Appeal in the *Berkshire* case, without deciding the point, Neill LJ suggested that the right to refuse treatment 'exists even where there are overwhelming medical reasons in favour of the treatment and even where if the treatment is not carried out the patient's life will be at risk'.[20]

A second argument which has been used to justify overriding a refusal of life-saving treatment has been the duty to prevent crimes. The Criminal Law Act 1977 allows people to take reasonable steps to prevent the commission of a crime.[21] However, since attempting suicide is no longer a criminal offence this justification is no longer available.[22] The third argument rests on a case in which it was held that the force-feeding of a hunger-striking prisoner was justified.[23] It is probable that the decision rests in part on the fact that attempting suicide was then still a crime and in part on the special obligations on prison authorities. Neither of these justifications are now thought to be adequate to justify force-feeding.[24]

So far, the argument has established that patients who are capable of exercising choice have the right to decide to die by refusing to allow others to keep them alive. It goes no further than this, as taking active steps to cause death will constitute the crime of assisting suicide.[25] It is therefore perhaps better to say that there is a right to be left to die, rather than a right to die. This right is not deliberately created for the benefit of the terminally ill, but depends entirely upon the application of the general consent principle.

As has already been noted, this principle does not apply when a patient does not have the capacity to consent. Whether a patient has this capacity depends on their ability to understand the choice with which they are presented.[26] Exactly what this entails is unclear. The better view is that it is the physical nature of the treatment which must be understood, but it is possible to argue that understanding of the moral and social implications of the choice must also be appreciated.[27] If the latter view is taken then a health professional may argue that any decision to die illustrates a failure to appreciate the negative moral status of suicide.[28] Even on the former view a similar argument might succeed. Given that the health professional's judgment of capacity is likely to be the main evidence on which a court would judge the patient's state of mind should a dispute arise, it is unlikely that a bona fide opinion could be challenged in the courts. Ultimately, therefore, even this limited power over death depends largely on the goodwill of the health professionals.

This has led Kennedy to point out that

> the supposed right to self-determination may not be the creature it is thought to be. . . . Its theoretical weaknesses are implicit in the fact that it rests on the vague and easily manipulated notion of consent. Once such theoretical weaknesses are identified, it is but a simple step to weaken the right as it operates in practice. The persuasive power of paternalism supplies the motive for this step to be taken.[29]

If the right to die is to be more than an empty promise it is necessary to explore the possibility of strengthening the position of the values of the patient against their being superseded by those of the professionals caring for them.

ADVANCE DECLARATIONS

A range of terms has been used to describe this approach to ensuring respect for the past decisions of incompetent patients, including advanced directives and living wills. At its core lies a statement of the patient's wishes, made while they were competent, in contemplation of future circumstances about which they have views which they fear may be ignored. The principal benefits of advance declarations are the protection of patient autonomy and greater certainty for the health professionals, which would in turn reduce unnecessary interventions carried out in order to play safe.[30]

The first statutory recognition of the need for some kind of advance directive governing treatment at the end of life was the Californian Natural Death Act of 1976.[31] A large number of US jurisdictions have since followed the Californian example. A brief

41

consideration of the Act can serve to identify some of the major issues which need to be tackled in a satisfactory scheme to allow patients to provide their carers with directions as to their terminal care in advance. It will then be possible to consider the state of English law in the light of these concerns.

Problems of regulation

Scope

The first problem which any statutory scheme would have to face is the nature of the declarations which should be recognised. The Californian Act provides a standard form on which a person may record their wish not to be kept alive in the face of imminent death if they have 'an incurable injury, disease or illness certified to be a terminal condition'. The use of a standard form reduces the flexibility of advance directives, and enshrines a degree of legislative paternalism in that it limits the circumstances for which directives may be made. An interesting example of this is inclusion of a clause suspending the operation of the directive during pregnancy, inscribing the assumption that foetal interests will be held to outweigh the dying person's wishes to die whatever the stage of pregnancy.[32]

Subsequent developments in the USA have departed from the Californian model in two important respects. First, the Uniform Rights of the Terminally Ill Act produced by the National Conference of Commissioners on Uniform State Laws in 1985 does not restrict declarations to the standard form, although it does provide one.[33] Second, the President's Commission on Bioethics considered that advance directives should be available for treatment other than that designed to sustain life.[34] This acknowledges the fact that the root of the directive is the patient's right of self-determination and that advance directives are merely a way of allowing this right to be exercised when a view cannot be formed and or communicated.

There are good reasons for not taking declarations into account in relation to temporary incapacities when the issue is a matter of life and death. In such circumstances, patients will be able to take the decision to die when they become able to do so. In this situation a refusal to act on the directive would not be a denial of the right to die. It is possible that they will be unable, due to paralysis for example, to execute that decision. This raises an important issue as to whether patients should be entitled to request others to take their life, a form of mercy killing, but this is beyond the scope of this paper.[35] In general it would be better to consider this problem in that context rather than to confuse matters by tinkering with it within advance declaration legislation. There are, however, no good reasons for restricting directives to life and death issues; indeed the arguments for recognising them at all seem less difficult in this wider context. The dangers of abuse are reduced by the fact that abuses can be rectified. In the former case it will be too late.

A more fundamental point must be made, however. By limiting the scope of its provisions in this way, the Californian Act does not cover all the circumstances in which a competent patient could lawfully refuse treatment. A patient who had suffered serious, but not life-endangering, disablement would not come within the terms of the statute. The Natural Death Act deals only with hastening already inevitable death, not ending sustainable life.[36] Yet a competent patient could lawfully refuse sustenance and thus end their life in such circumstances. On this basis to respect fully the common law right to die, living wills legislation would need to extend to non-life-threatening cases.

Abuse

Whilst there is no reason of principle to disregard oral declarations, it is common to assume that advance declarations should be required to be made in writing. This has significant practical advantages. It provides concrete evidence of the patient's wishes which would reduce the likelihood of disputes. It will also overcome the weaknesses of memory of those in whom the patient confided. This leaves less scope for the existence of directions to be forgotten or for mistakes as to their terms. Oral instructions to the physicians caring for a terminally ill patient can be taken into account in the usual way, but it would be unwise to make them binding without clear evidence as to their content. Requiring written evidence of the patient's views also guards against the risks of abuse.

The Californian Act seeks to guard against abuse in the forms of forgery and undue influence. The declaration has to be witnessed by two persons who are neither the responsible health carers nor beneficiaries under any existing will of the declarant. These rules are modelled on the formalities required for the making of wills. They seek to ensure that the document was made genuinely and freely by the patient. In recognition of the difficulties of making a free choice in an institution, an added requirement applies to Californians who wish to make a declaration when they are already patients in a nursing institution.[37] In these circumstances, one of the witnesses must be an official patient advocate or specially appointed ombudsman.

The Californian provisions do not go further and seek to guarantee the quality of the decision. Thus there is no requirement that the witnesses play an active role. Given the irreversibility of a decision to die, a case might be made for using the witness requirement as a means to ensure the involvement of persons skilled in counselling. A more paternalistic system might make it mandatory to consult such a person. The proposal to introduce qualifications for witnesses would fall short of requiring counselling before any declaration would be recognised, but would guarantee that the person making the declaration had the opportunity to consult counsellors if they wished. In the same way, the requirement that a patient advocate be involved ensures that help is at hand to overcome professional pressure if the patient wishes to take advantage of it.

Effects

A third area in which there is scope for a considerable range of variation in the nature of living will schemes concerns the legal effect. A refusal made by a competent patient would be binding upon the health professionals. It would make any further treatment illegal, backed up by (in theory at least) both criminal and civil sanctions. It would be possible to give advance declarations a similar status. This would entail establishing their exact wording in order to be certain that a professional had ignored them. This in turn would increase the need for formality. If so much turns on the details of the direction, then clarity must be guaranteed.

There is a danger here that the usefulness of directives will be undermined. The more significant the legal effect of advance directives, the more detailed they will need to be in order to win recognition. Unless the circumstances in which it is to take effect have been precisely defined, a court would be unlikely to allow a professional to be penalised heavily for ignoring the provisions of a living will. However, the more precisely that the events are described, the more likely it is that the actual scenario would be different and that the declaration would be held to be inapplicable.

Thus the practical effect of increasing the force given to directives might be to reduce the number which would be effective.

Under the Californian code the effects of a declaration are less forceful than an explicit refusal by a competent patient. The code declares first that no civil, criminal or professional liability will be incurred by a health care professional who withholds or withdraws treatment in accordance with an advance directive.[38] It goes on to provide that no civil or criminal liability will attach to a professional who disregards a directive, but that it would constitute professional misconduct unless the patient is referred to someone who will give it effect.[39] This approach recognises the rights of conscience of the health professionals, but, unlike the conscience clause in the English Abortion Act 1967, protects the rights of the patient by ensuring that there will be referral.[40]

It also provides for some remedy through proceedings for professional misconduct. In the English context the adequacy of this type of remedy must be considered carefully. The regimes of professional discipline differ according to the profession in question. Under the Medical Act 1983 no disciplinary offence is committed unless there is 'serious professional misconduct'.[41] In relation to pharmacists it has been held that a single act or error can constitute 'misconduct',[42] but it must be doubtful whether a single action would in itself be considered 'serious'.[43] This presents less of a problem in relation to nurses or pharmacists where 'misconduct' is sufficient to give rise to the possibility of disciplinary action by the relevant professional body.[44] Thus to use professional disciplinary proceedings to back up living wills would probably be of little effect in relation to doctors who are, in practice, the most significant professional group in this context. Reform of the Medical Act would be needed to make the professional sanction effective.[45]

Duration

Finally, a statutory scheme recognising advance directives would need to specify the period for which a directive would be valid and by what means it would be revocable. The Californian law automatically revokes a declaration after five years, but allows for revocation through the destruction or cancellation of the document, a written statement or an oral expression of the intention to revoke.[46] In contrast to the formal requirements for creation, no witnesses are required to make the revocation effective. It will only take effect, however, once the attending physician has been notified.

The comparative ease of revocation is justified by the presumption in favour of life. If mistakes are to be made, it is better that they are made in favour of continuing life. It is then possible to put things right later. It may also be necessary to consider whether recognition should be given to implied revocations. The Age Concern report discusses the situation where 'the patient, although confused, is at present requesting' treatment.[47] How should such a request, made by an incompetent patient, be approached? The first possibility is that it should be ignored as being inconsistent with the advance direction and not genuinely representing the patient's views. The second is that it should be taken as an indication of competence and suspend the operation of the advance directive. The third is that it should take effect as a revocation of the declaration itself. The Age Concern report describes the first approach as 'invidious' and it can be argued that the presumption in favour of life should operate to oust it. Instead it opts for the third solution.

The difficulty with this position is that it gives effect to a confused expression of the patient's wishes not only for the time at which it was made, but also for the future. Consider the case of a patient who declared that they did not wish to be kept alive in a senile state. Early in the drift towards senility they demand treatment, but later are unable to express any coherent view. If the request for treatment is regarded as a revocation no advance directive would apply to their final situation. If, however, it is regarded as suspending the operation of the 'living will' the request would have the effect of indicating that the patient had not yet reached the degree of senility which they regarded as an unacceptable quality of life. Although in particular circumstances it may be difficult to be certain, suspending the operation of the directive rather than revoking it completely would seem to be closer to the wishes expressed while the patient was fully competent.

It is perhaps even more difficult to decide whether advance declarations should have limited life. It can be argued that matters of life and death should not be governed by documents created years before and possibly no longer representing the views of the person making them. This was one of the reasons which led the British Medical Association to reject the idea of binding advance directives outright.[48] On the other hand, the likelihood of people forgetting to renew their advance directives seems high. This persuaded the working party set up by Age Concern to reach the view that no

46

automatic revocation should be introduced.[49] There is strength in both views, and clearly the presumption in favour of life would point towards the former. It may be possible, however, to steer a middle road. Directives might be given an indefinite life, but the patient's general practitioner could be required to draw the document to their attention at any consultation which occurs over five years from its execution. The patient could then choose whether to revoke it. The document would in any event need to be recorded in the patient's notes if there is any likelihood of it coming to the attention of the relevant health professionals.

English law

There have been no reported cases dealing directly with the validity of a living will, so any assessment of English law must proceed from first principles. It may be helpful to consider the ordinary case of consent to operations under the National Health Service. Consent will be given expressly on the basis that no particular doctor will perform the operation. It will probably be given to and recorded by a doctor other than the one who performs it. Consent will be given before, although usually only shortly before, the procedure and any accompanying anaesthetic is administered. It is good practice to allow for a period of delay between discussing the treatment, obtaining consent and carrying it out. It permits the patient to think the matter over and if necessary withdraw their agreement without the pressure and anxiety created by the presence of the medical professionals.

The recognition of an advance directive differs from this situation only in degree. No one could suggest that consent to an operation is revoked when a patient becomes unconscious under a general anaesthetic. Nor is it acceptable to override a refusal of consent once this happens.[50] Consequently, it is clear that the force of a consent to or refusal of treatment can endure longer than the period of the patient's capacity to express a choice. On this basis, there would appear to be no reason of principle why living wills should not be recognised at common law and two recent decisions have indicated that they would be.[51] Their legal force would seem to be necessarily the same as if the patient was competent and was refusing to consent. It is probable that they would have to be precisely worded and clearly cover the circumstances which arise because this means that their recognition would entail rendering any treatment in

47

disregard of the refusal they contain completely unlawful.

In principle, therefore, it can be said that an advance directive would bind a health professional under English common law. However, it would not be difficult for a court to argue that the circumstances in respect of which a living will was made were materially different from those actually arising. This was done in *Re T* so as to disregard an earlier refusal of a blood transfusion on the basis that it did not apply to the new situation.[52] It is possible that the English courts would use this possibility to avoid giving recognition to most documents. In the light of this, it would be best to introduce specific legislation.

PROXY CONSENT

The second approach to giving effect to the right of a patient to die is the appointment of proxies or surrogates to make decisions on their behalf. American states have tended to adopt this possibility alongside that of advance declarations. The proxy may be given a free hand, or may be entrusted with the responsibility of interpreting the wishes of the patient as expressed in an advance declaration. The latter approach will help overcome the ambiguities of living will documents. Patients can select proxies whom they are confident will understand what they meant by the words they used rather than relying on a court or health care professional to do so.

There is no reason in English law why a patient cannot appoint someone to act as his agent in relation to medical decisions.[53] The problem is that at common law such appointments are automatically revoked when the commissioning person ceases to be competent to make them.[54] For this reason it was necessary to enact the Enduring Powers of Attorney Act 1985 in order to facilitate the appointment of persons to administer the property of those who become mentally incompetent. This Act applies only to property and thus is of no relevance to treatment decisions.[55] It seems, therefore, that there is no scope for the use of proxy decision-makers in English law once patients lose their capacity to choose for themselves without statutory intervention.

There are, however, a number of advantages in recognising surrogate decision-makers. The difficulty of tailoring the terms of a living will to the circumstances which arise can be avoided. The patient protects their values by selecting a proxy whom they can tell, or can trust already to know, what they regard as important. The proxy can then apply those values to whatever situation has arisen. There is also the advantage that lack of knowledge of the medical possibilities can be overcome by discussion between the proxy and the health care professionals. Any refusal of treatment can then be based on an informed assessment of the patient's position. The poor quality of the information on which advance declarations will usually be made was a major reason behind their rejection by the British Medical Association.

There is also scope for negative features of proxy consent. The criticism of the existing legal position from which this essay has developed was that it offered the promise of a right without providing the means to guarantee it. The patient could be conned where the doctors decided to declare them incompetent. In the context of proxy consent the possible sting is slightly different. It is that the person appointed will not in fact apply the criteria which the patient would have desired. The proxy might operate on the basis of what they believe is best for the patient; a form of paternalism where the patient has chosen the person whose paternalism is most attractive. They might act as they believe the patient would have done, the substituted judgment approach.[56] They could act in accordance with the express wishes of the patient, possibly set out in an advance declaration.

All of these approaches are legitimate, in that it is the patient's welfare which governs the decision. But there is scope also for abuse. Unless proxies are monitored they may take their own interests into account. A system of regulation might be in order, such as that under the Enduring Powers of Attorney Act 1985 requiring registration, the notification of relatives (with a chance to object) and the supervision of the Court of Protection. These dangers are perhaps less serious in the health care context because any decisions will necessarily be known to the health care professionals. They can then challenge inappropriate actions. The dangers nevertheless remain.

As with advance declarations, it is necessary to consider the legal effect of treatment decisions emanating from the proxy. They might be given the same weight as would have been accorded to the patient's own decisions. This would give them an absolute veto. Anything less could perhaps be said to perpetuate the ability of health professionals to override the right to die. On the other hand, without the possibility of review there would be no defence against the abuse of power by the proxy. Extending the *parens patriae* jurisdiction might provide a solution.[57] As with children whose parents are thought to be acting against their interests the decision could be placed in the hands of the court.[58] The proposal is thus for a system which gives neither proxy nor health professional absolute power, sacrificing some of the right to die in the interests of protection from abuse.

CONCLUSION

This essay has been concerned with reflecting on the weakness of the right to die in English law. It has not argued that the right to die is ethically sound, it has instead sought to show that it can be of practical value only if the existing law is reinforced by the introduction of some type of living will. As has become clear, it is not easy to determine exactly what shape legislation in this area should take, but it has been possible to discuss some of the options. The debate must continue and must range more widely. It is impossible to select a path from among the many available without considering why we believe the granting of power over death to be important. It is by no means obvious that the atomistic, individualist model of the patient on which a strong right to die would be based best reflects the position in which most people find themselves. The claims of other members of the family may be thought to be stronger in the face of likely bereavement than they would be in the case of ordinary treatment. The ethical debate which this essay has eschewed cannot be avoided for long. For this reason the discussion has been tentative. The nettle must, however, be grasped, no matter how bitter the sting. For death comes to us all and the fear of dying is widespread:

> And therefore never send to know for whom the bell tolls; it tolls for thee.
>
> (John Donne, Devotions XVII)

NOTES

1 J. Montgomery, 'Victims or threats? The framing of HIV', *Liverpool Law Review* xii (1990): 25, 35–9.
2 Compare *Schloendorf* v. *Society of New York Hospital* 105 NE 92 (1914) and Lord Scarman's judgment in *Sidaway* v. *Bethlem RHG* [1985] 1 All ER 643 with the majority speeches in the latter case. See also J. Montgomery, 'Power/knowledge/consent: medical decision-making', *Modern Law Review* 51 (1988): 245.

3 *W* v. *Egdell* [1990] 1 All ER 835 (CA), leave to appeal to the House of Lords refused [1990] 1 WLR 1502.
4 *R* v. *Secretary of State for Social Services, ex p. Hincks* [1980] 1 BMLR 93; *R* v. *Central Birmingham HA, ex p. Walker* [1987] 3 BMLR 32; *R* v. *St Mary's Hospital, ex p. Harriott* [1988] 1 FLR 512.
5 Data Protection Act 1984 (computerised information only); Access to Medical Reports Act 1987 (reports for employment and insurance purposes only); Access to Health Records Act 1990 (with effect from 1 November 1991).
6 For the 1984 Act, see the Data Protection (Subject Access Modification) (Health) Order 1987 (SI 1987/1903). For the 1987 Act see s. 7. For the 1990 Act see s. 5.
7 Enduring Powers of Attorney Act 1985.
8 British Medical Association, *Euthanasia* (London: BMA, 1988), ch. 12: 'Advance Declarations', para. 236.
9 ibid.: para. 271, the grounds given for this view are frustratingly brief. For support for this view see D. A. Lush, 'Living wills', *Law Society's Gazette* 86(12) (1989): 21.
10 Age Concern Institute of Gerontology and Centre of Medical Law and Ethics King's College, London, *The Living Will: Consent to Treatment at the End of Life* (London: Edward Arnold, 1988).
11 ibid.: 35 approving the position taken by P. Skegg, *Law, Ethics and Medicine* (Oxford: Oxford University Press, 1984): 116. See also M. Hurwitt, 'The right to die', *Law Society's Gazette* 88(26) (1991): 20.
12 *Chatterton* v. *Gerson* [1981] 1 All ER 257.
13 *Collins* v. *Wilcock* [1984] 3 All ER 374.
14 *F* v. *West Berkshire HA* [1989] 2 All ER 545.
15 See Mental Health Act 1983, part IV.
16 In *F* v. *West Berkshire HA* [1989] 2 All ER 545 the House of Lords indicated that as a matter of policy it would not allow the law of trespass to override the general duty of care on professionals. With respect, this reasoning is suspect in that it was based on the assumption that an action would lie for failure to treat even when the treatment would be unlawful by reason of lack of consent. The better view must be that the unlawfulness of the treatment would provide a complete answer to a claim that the failure to provide it was negligent.
17 *F* v. *West Berkshire HA* [1989] 2 All ER 545, 566 *per* Lord Goff.
18 See Neill LJ in the Court of Appeal in *Re F* [1989] 2 FLR 376, at 401–2. For discussion of the possible foundations for such a public interest, see R. Dworkin, 'The right of death', *New York Review of Books* (31 January 1991).
19 *Re C* [1989] 2 All ER 782; *Re J* [1990] 3 All ER 930. See also *Airedale NHS Trust* v. *Bland* [1993] 2 WLR 316.
20 *Re F* [1989] 2 FLR 376, 401C.
21 Section 3.
22 Suicide Act 1961, s. 1.
23 *Leigh* v. *Gladstone* (1909) 26 TLR 139.
24 G. Zellick, 'The force feeding of prisoners' [1976] *Public Law* 153; I. Kennedy, 'The legal effect of requests by the terminally ill and aged not

JONATHAN MONTGOMERY

to receive treatment from doctors' [1976] *Crim. Law Rev.* 217; see now
I. Kennedy, *Treat Me Right: Essays in Medical Law and Ethics* (Oxford:
Oxford University Press, 1988); Skegg, op. cit.: 110–16.
25 Suicide Act 1961, s. 2. There is a limited defence under *R* v. *Adams*
[1957] *Crim. Law Rev.* 365 for those who administer medicines to those
who are already terminally ill when it is the 'right and proper treatment'
to control pain even if the effect is to shorten life. See also *Re J* [1990] 3
All ER 930.
26 The leading case on capacity is *Gillick* v. *West Norfolk and Wisbech
AHA* [1985] 3 All ER 402; see also *Re K, Re F* [1988] 1 All ER 358; and
Re R (a minor) (wardship: medical treatment) [1991] 4 All ER 177. For
general discussions see S. Lee, 'Towards a jurisprudence of consent', in
J. Eekelaar and J. Bell (eds), *Oxford Essays in Jurisprudence*, 3rd series
(Oxford: Oxford University Press, 1987); I. Kennedy and A. Grubb,
Medical Law: Text and Materials (London: Butterworth, 1989): 180–
215.
27 For discussion of the problem, see J. Montgomery, 'Children as property?', *Modern Law Review* 51 (1988): 323, 336–9.
28 The fact that suicide has been decriminalised does not necessarily
indicate that it is approved, see *R* v. *Inner London Coroner, ex p. De
Luca* [1988] 3 All ER 414.
29 I. Kennedy, 'The legal effect . . .', in Kennedy, *Treat Me Right:* at 341.
30 For a longer list see Age Concern and Centre of Medical Law and
Ethics, op. cit.: 46–7.
31 California Health and Safety Code, paras 7186ff. Extracts from the
provisions can be found in Kennedy and Grubb, op. cit.: 1123–6.
32 This is also included in the proposals adopted by the Age Concern
report, op. cit., without comment or justification, see p. 60.
33 See Age Concern and Centre of Medical Law and Ethics: 53–6 for
discussion of using prescribed forms and an example of such of a form
which would still allow for further specific requests to be included.
34 President's Commission for the Study of Ethical Problems in Medicine
and Biomedical and Behaviorial Research, *Deciding to Forgo Life-
Sustaining Treatment* (Washington DC: US Government Printing
Office, 1983). See Kennedy and Grubb, op. cit.: 1117–18 for the
relevant passage.
35 See, for example, R. Leng, 'Mercy killing and the Criminal Law
Revision Committee', *New Law Journal* 132 (1982): 76; J. Horder,
'Mercy killings – some reflections on Beecham's case', *Journal of
Criminal Law* 52 (1988): 309; J. Laing, 'Assisting suicide', *Journal of
Criminal Law* 54 (1990): 106.
36 *R* v. *Adams* [1975] *Crim. Law Rev.* 365 is similarly limited, but *Re J*
[1990] 3 All ER 930 is not.
37 Para. 7188.5.
38 Para. 7190.
39 Para. 7191.
40 Abortion Act 1967, s. 4. In *R* v. *Salford AHA* [1988] 2 FLR 370 the
Court of Appeal suggested that a doctor could rely on the conscience
clause to justify refusing to refer a patient. On appeal, the House of

52

Lords declined to decide the point, *Janaway* v. *Salford AHA* [1988] 3 All ER 1079.

41 Medical Act 1983, s. 36.

42 *R* v. *Pharmaceutical Society, ex p. Sokoh*, *The Times* (4 December 1986), under the Pharmacy Act 1954, s. 8.

43 It is not impossible, however. See General Medical Council, *Annual Report 1980* (London: GMC, 1981): 23–4 for an example where a single failure of duty was held to constitute serious professional misconduct.

44 Nurses, Midwives and Health Visitors Act 1979, s. 12. See also the Nurses, Midwives and Health Visitors (Professional Conduct) Rules 1987, r. 1(2)(i). Pharmacy Act 1954, s. 8.

45 This may well be desirable on other grounds, see, for example, J. Robinson, *A Patient Voice at the GMC* (London: Health Rights, 1988). Note that this was written before the amendments made to the General Medical Council Preliminary Proceedings Committee and Professional Conduct Committee (Procedure) Rules 1988 (SI 1988 no. 2255) by the General Medical Council Preliminary Proceedings Committee and Professional Conduct Committee (Procedure) (Amendment) Rules Order 1990 (SI 1990 no. 1587).

46 Para. 7189, 7189.5.

47 At p. 59.

48 British Medical Association, op. cit. para. 234.

49 At p. 59.

50 *F* v. *West Berkshire HA* [1989] 2 All ER 545, 566 *per* Lord Goff; *Re T* [1992] 4 All ER 649, 653 (Donaldson MR); *Airedale NHS Trust* v. *Bland* [1993] 2 WLR 316, 360–1 (Keith), 367 (Goff).

51 *Re T* [1992] 4 All ER 649; *Airedale NHS Trust* v. *Bland* [1993] 2 WLR 316. See A. Grubb (1993) 1 Med L. Rev 84.

52 *Re T* [1992] 4 All ER 649.

53 Skegg, op. cit.: 57.

54 *Drew* v. *Nunn* [1879] 4 QBD 661.

55 The Enduring Powers of Attorney Act 1985 covers the donor's 'property and affairs' (s. 3(1)). In *F* v. *West Berkshire HA* [1989] 2 All ER 545 it was held that the same phrase in the Mental Health Act 1983 did not cover medical decisions.

56 See Kennedy and Grubb, op. cit.: 323–45.

57 For discussion see B. Hoggett, 'The Royal prerogative in relation to the mentally disordered: resurrection, resuscitation or rejection', in M. Freeman (ed.), *Medicine, Ethics and the Law* (London: Stevens, 1988).

58 For example, *Re P* (1981) 80 LGR 305; *Re D* [1976] Fam. 185. This is by no means a perfect solution, see J. Montgomery, 'Rhetoric and "Welfare" ', *Oxford Journal of Legal Studies* 9 (1989): 395; R. Lee and D. Morgan, 'A lesser sacrifice? sterilization and mentally handicapped women', in R. Lee and D. Morgan (eds), *Birthrights: Law and Ethics at the Beginnings of Life* (London: Routledge, 1989).

4

Corpses, recycling and therapeutic purposes

Ruth F. Chadwick

The aim of this article is to examine some of the tensions in current thinking concerning the human body: these may throw light on why, for example, despite the generally perceived usefulness of transplant technology, we remain reluctant to endorse policies which would increase organ supply. Further, given that some parts of the body appear to carry considerably more importance than others, it is my intention to look at what is held to be more shocking than what, and whether there is any rational basis for this. Are there any good reasons for privileging some organs? Should the bodies of foetuses be regarded differently from those of adults? In looking at these questions, the use of language is central – for example, the language of 'donation' requires closer inspection, as does the notion of recycling.

Recycling is a modern concept. It has come to the fore along with a gradual heightening of awareness of the limits to world resources, at a time when people's consciousness of environmental problems is being raised and when the imperative to recycle what is recyclable is being increasingly recognised. The automatic recycling of the human body, however, remains problematic. The science fiction film *Soylent Green*, with its demonstration of the ultimate in human recycling – the production of nondescript tablets of foodstuff made out of human beings – does not present a favourable view of the idea. H. E. Emson is one of the few who has emphasised that the human body should simply be regarded as part of a total pool: 'our bodies are part of a total pool of elements and molecules which is the biomass of our planet, and which interacts with its organic mass'.[1] This view, although it accords with the 'ashes to ashes, dust to dust' tradition, has not been so generally embraced that automatic recycling has unqualified support. There are arguments which suggest that there are definite limits to the ways in which it is permissible to treat corpses, which restrict their availability for therapeutic use. In thinking about the dead body, however, the traditional modes of ethical thought themselves have limits because of the difficulty in regarding the human body in an impartial rational way. Symbolism will be found to be particularly important in this area.

With the rapid advances in transplant technology in the second half of the twentieth century, the question of the proper treatment of corpses has come increasingly to the fore. In earlier times, debate centred on the use of corpses for dissection and teaching purposes in medical schools: this problem was dealt with in the 1832 Anatomy Act, which largely solved the problem of shortage of cadavers until the explosion in organ transplant expertise. Before assessing the argument concerning the use of corpses for therapeutic purposes, however, it is essential to be clear about what counts as a corpse, and what counts as a therapeutic use.

DEFINITIONS

What counts as a corpse?

As the *Oxford English Dictionary* points out, the addition of 'lifeless' to the word 'corpse' is now regarded as pleonastic in ordinary speech, because 'corpse' simply means 'dead body'. So recent debates have turned on *when* death occurs: when what we are dealing with is indeed a dead body. On some proposed definitions of death, those that involve higher brain formulations, an organism could be declared a corpse while still breathing. Of the higher brain formulations Lamb says: 'The notion of a still-breathing corpse is morally repugnant. How, for example, does one dispose of such a being? Should burial or cremation take place while respiration continues? Or should someone take responsibility for suffocating the "corpse" first?'[2] There are several points made in this quotation. The point about indeterminacy carries more weight than that concerning moral repugnance. Intuitions about what is repugnant are notoriously varied. Lamb is right, however, to say that there would be difficulties about the notion of a breathing corpse.

Having suggested that the addition of the epithet 'lifeless' is pleonastic, it would seem odd (though not, of course, beyond revision) to call a corpse an object which still manifested one of the traditional signs of life.[3]

It is beyond the scope of this discussion to examine in detail the rival merits of different definitions of death. For present purposes I shall accept brainstem death as the criterion of the death of the organism as a whole.

What counts as therapeutic?

The Human Tissue Act 1961 makes provision for the use of parts of bodies for 'therapeutic purposes and purposes of medical education and research'. The language on the current donor card offers a choice between a request that 'my kidneys, eyes, heart, liver, pancreas be used for transplantation' and that 'any part of my body be used for the treatment of others'. Corpses, or at least parts of them, are now required for a wide variety of organ transplants. These uses may be said to be therapeutic because they provide medical benefit to the sufferer of renal failure, heart disease and so on.

In the early days of any of these technologies, however, debate rages over the extent to which they are to be classed as experimental rather than therapeutic. There is a sense, of course, in which all medical treatment is experimental. However tried and trusted a form of treatment is, there is always a possibility that it will produce some quite unexpected result when administered to a particular patient. Perhaps what we can say is that in order to count as therapeutic, a procedure must be carried out with at least the *aim* of providing some benefit to the patient, rather than simply for the advancement of knowledge. This condition, while necessary, is not sufficient, however, because it hardly seems possible to describe a procedure as therapeutic, whatever the aim of the health care professional, if there is no evidence whatever to suggest that the procedure might be beneficial.[4] We need a further necessary condition to the effect that there is good reason (normally provided by animal studies, the ethics of which will not be discussed here) to believe that this is the case. Together these conditions are sufficient for a procedure to count as therapeutic, even if in fact it does not benefit a particular recipient.

An example of a fairly recent development is the transplantation of foetal brain cells into victims of Parkinson's disease. This is not covered by the Human Tissue Act but has been the subject of the Polkinghorne Report. The extent to which it constitutes a successful form of therapy is still uncertain, but it counts as a therapeutic procedure because its aim is to relieve the suffering of such patients, and there are grounds for believing that it could be of therapeutic value.

In order to count as therapeutic, however, does a procedure have to be administered to someone who is ill? For example, a report in *The Independent* noted the possibility of infertility 'treatments' for infertile women through retrieval of ovaries from dead women.[5] Whether infertile people can properly be described as ill, or as suffering from a disease, is controversial, but what we can say is that in so far as infertility is thought to be a problem which admits of medical solutions there seems no difficulty in counting such an intervention as therapeutic, and this form of treatment will be discussed below (p. 69).

Using a cadaver to practise and to teach, while covered by the Human Tissue Act's provision regarding the use of corpses for education, could also perhaps be said to be indirectly therapeutic. As Kenneth Iserson points out, an opportunity (and in his view a responsibility) exists 'to prepare the clinician and future clinicians to care for the next critically ill patient'.[6] Therefore, although the corpse is not used to benefit any particular patient, it is done with the aim of benefiting future patients and there is good evidence, this time in the form of the belief that practice makes perfect, for the view that it will.

We must now turn to the question of the sources of the views that we have duties regarding our treatment of corpses.

DUTIES TOWARDS THE DEAD

If we look to traditional theories of ethics we find, as we might expect, conflicting views as to the appropriate treatment of the human corpse.

Consequentialism

From a consequentialist point of view it might seem to be clear that it is desirable, if not a moral requirement, to use recyclable corpses to prolong the lives of those who are desperately ill and in need of organs. The dead have neither interests nor preferences, so any claims that may be made on their behalf are surely unreal.

The matter is not as simple as that, however. Even though the dead indeed have no preferences or interests, we could intelligibly speak in terms of duties *regarding* the dead, rather than duties *towards* the dead, and there are perfectly good reasons of a consequentialist sort for the view that such duties exist. Duties regarding the dead could be seen as indirectly duties towards living persons, who certainly do have preferences about how the dead should be treated. The preferences of living persons include both those of the loved ones of a dead person who cannot bear to think of their friend or relative being disfigured in an organ transplant operation, and the preferences of persons currently alive who do not like the thought of such procedures being carried out on their own bodies after death.

On a consequentialist viewpoint, however, it might be argued that these are preferences that we should all be better off without: that it would be advantageous to society as a whole if people could be brought to see that the benefits of routine recycling of corpses outweigh these somewhat irrational responses. For it is arguable that they *are* irrational. Who, exactly, is harmed, and how, by the salvaging of organs from a corpse? If the harm lies in the (possibly short-term) distress of loved ones, surely these must give way to the benefit of the needy person?

John Harris has suggested that if we think that the interest in establishing truth through the carrying out of an autopsy must outweigh the wishes of relatives, as we do in our society, then it is irrational to allow the preferences of relatives to take priority where organ transplants are the issue.[7]

A possible reply to this would be that society as a whole has an interest in the facilitating of the processes of law to establish the truth about unexpected death. Where salvaging organs is concerned, however, only one or two persons stand to benefit. Against this it could be argued that society has an interest in the availability of technology to extend lives, and surely the rationale behind even the argument for autopsies is that the processes of law are, or should be, instrumental in protecting the lives of individuals. Some have argued, however, that it is not clear that society has an interest sufficient to justify routine recycling if the price is a view which suggests the collective ownership of bodies. Thus Hans Jonas quotes Henry K. Beecher as saying:

> Can society afford to discard the tissues and organs of the hopelessly unconscious patient when they could be used to

restore the otherwise hopelessly ill, but still salvageable individual?[8]

and objects to this that the use of the word 'discard' implies proprietary rights, asking 'Does society then own my body?'

The implications for the living of a view endorsing collective ownership of individuals' bodies have been explored by Rom Harré, who speaks of enforced surrogacy, for example.[9] But it is not clear that such a view, when applied to the dead, need mark the first step on a slippery slope towards collective ownership of the living, *provided that* we have clear criteria of death.

One strand of the anti-collectivist argument is the idea that not only does *society* not have the right to the organs of any particular individual, but nor does the person who desperately needs organs to stay alive. On some views of morality, however, if there are organs available which could be used to save a person X's life, and they are denied by a person Y who could make them available without the sacrifice of anything of comparable significance, then Y has as good as killed X.[10]

One way of objecting to this would be to refuse to accept this particular view of morality. Another is to suggest that there *is* something else of comparable moral significance, and that is the individual's interest in, or right to, control over her own body, even after death. This must now be examined.

Autonomy

Since at least the mid-twentieth century the autonomy model of health care has been dominant, suggesting that patients' autonomous choices about their treatment should be respected. Thus Lamb points to loss of autonomy as one of the major ethical objections to routine salvaging.[11] But Iserson remarks starkly: 'Once the patient has been pronounced dead the physician–patient relationship is over.'[12] The implication here is that the deceased no longer has any capacity for autonomy which provides a grounding for the view that there is a requirement to respect an autonomous person.

The Human Tissue Act 1961, section 1, however, does recognise the relevance of the autonomous wishes of a person expressed while alive. Thus section 1(1) states:

If any person, either in writing at any time or orally in the presence of two or more witnesses during his last illness, has expressed a request that his body or any specified part of his body be used after his death for therapeutic purposes or for purposes of medical education or research, the person lawfully in possession of his body after his death may, unless he has reason to believe that the request was subsequently withdrawn, authorise the removal from the body of any part.

Section 1(2) further provides that the person lawfully in possession of the body may authorise removal if he has no reason to believe 'that the deceased had expressed an objection to his body being so dealt with after his death, and had not withdrawn it'.

As has frequently been noted, 1(1) is an 'opting in' provision, while 1(2) is an 'opting out' provision. The moral argument for respecting the autonomy of individuals with regard to what should happen to their bodies after death is presumably that what is involved in the principle of autonomy is that we respect all the autonomous choices of individuals that are compatible with respecting the autonomy of other individuals, and that these include choices made about the future of one's body.

If the Human Tissue Act stopped there, it would at least be explicable in terms of a readily identifiable and defendable moral position, but it does not. A role is also given to the relatives of the deceased. Thus section 1(2) adds the condition that the person lawfully in possession of the body must have no reason to believe 'that the surviving spouse or any surviving relative of the deceased objects to the body being so dealt with'.

The reference to 'any surviving relative' might seem to indicate an impossibly wide search, but in fact it is limited to 'such reasonable enquiry as may be practicable', and P. D. G. Skegg has argued that since it has long been accepted that a reasonable enquiry normally requires no more than asking the spouse or close relative, it is unlikely that a court would take a different view.[13]

Current practice goes beyond the provisions of the Human Tissue Act, so that even if a dead person is found to be carrying a donor card, enquiries are still made of the spouse. What is the moral argument for this? As Lamb points out, there is a clear inconsistency here: 'if we uphold the right not to donate, as a right which cannot be vetoed, then the right to donate without veto should also exist'.[14] There may be an argument for respecting the autonomous choice of the person while alive, but what is the argument for respecting the choices of their relatives? If the person herself is not to be allowed to decide, why give greater preference to relatives than to ill people who could be helped? If it is simply to spare their feelings, why should they take priority over the feelings of the relatives of people waiting for organs? Perhaps the suggestion is that the relatives have certain *rights* in the matter.

Rights

Who, if anyone, has rights with regard to a corpse? The notion that the *deceased* has a right of self-determination runs into similar problems as those which confront the autonomy argument.

A right commonly appealed to in discussing the living body, at least, is the right to property. This has been at issue in the abortion debate, for example. In the case of the corpse, it might be argued that since a person owns her body when alive, she has the right to dispose of it as she wishes after death.

It is sometimes said that English law does not recognise a right to property in a corpse (it cannot be bequeathed, for example). Paul Matthews has described this as 'one of those charming legal maxims that as general propositions are untrue'.[15] Matthews's point is that to have property in a thing is to have certain rights, powers, duties and liabilities in relation to it, and there are people who have those in relation to a corpse. These are people, however, other than the person whose body it is, and to them it will be necessary to return (p. 62).

What are we to say of the person whose corpse is under consideration? I have argued in another context that although there is a sense in which persons do own their bodies, this is not the same as the sense in which they own tables and chairs.[16] There is so great a difference between our bodies and other material objects that it is just a mistake to apply the institution of property, with what that is normally taken to imply for rights of transfer and sale, to the body. For my body is not simply 'mine': it is in some sense 'me'.

To this it might be objected that the arguments against viewing the body as property during the life of the person, for example, that my body is not 'mine' but 'me', do not apply when the person is dead. The body of the deceased is much more similar to other material objects such as personal effects. Other arguments, however, might be appealed to. The circumstances which make it similar to other material objects are just those which make understandable the claim that it no longer (in so far as it is true to say it ever did) has an owner, for the 'owner' is dead.

Once the person is dead, the Human Tissue Act recognises that there are people who are 'lawfully in possession of it'. Skegg has argued that the person lawfully in possession is not necessarily identical with one who has a right to possession.[17] For example, one who has a right to possession (who may well be a relative) for the purposes of disposal may claim it from one who is in lawful possession of it.

It is clearly necessary for society to assign rights and liabilities with regard to the body because of its status not simply as the remains of a person, nor as a material object of sorts, but because of the fact that it is a potential source of contagion, and may be a public nuisance. In so far as relatives are the likely target for the liabilities, it is understandable (apart from their feelings in the matter) that they also have rights with regard to it.

But should these rights include the right to overrule their loved one's expressed preference on a donor card? Legally, of course they do not. Morally, it is difficult to find an argument for it. In any case, it is arguable that any rights they do have to express a view must surely be prima facie only and give way before the case of the living to a right to a means of extending their lives.

Despite the apparent force of these arguments, however, there remains strong resistance to routine recycling, even to a system with the protection offered by the opportunity to opt out. Is this simply irrational? Part of the resistance can be explained by a fear of being declared dead before one is 'really' dead, but that is not the whole story, and as David Lamb has pointed out there has not been a single occurrence of someone recovering from the state of brainstem death.[18]

There is something more, and that more is the importance the corpse has as a symbol. In part the newly-dead corpse remains a symbol of the person. Leon Kass has drawn attention to the ambiguity of our reactions towards a corpse – it is both more than it seems, in that it is not just a piece of matter, having been associated with a human personality, and also less than it seems, for on viewing a newly-dead corpse we would not be able to tell that the personality was no longer available to us.[19]

Our treatment of the corpse symbolises not only the respect for the individual whose corpse it is but also for human life in general.

The importance of the body and its integrity in different world-views needs to be considered.

Religion

In the context of different ways of life the corpse takes on particular significance. Much turns on whether, for example, the human being is regarded as a body into which God has breathed life, or as an imprisoned soul. The point is frequently made that orthodox Jews resist autopsy, because for them it is important to keep the body whole. Some versions of Christianity have held that the body had to be kept intact for the Resurrection. Hub Zwart says, of Japan:

> The dualism of body and soul, so characteristic for western views on man, does not fit in with Japanese beliefs. Therefore, the willingness to donate organs like the heart is rather limited. The Japanese do not want to go to Buddha without their heart.[20]

So while the corpse has universal importance as a symbol, its precise significance for the individual or society will differ according to the particular world-view adopted.

What are most striking, however, are perhaps the similarities between cultures rather than the differences. Emson points out that respectful funeral rites are as old as humanity itself.[21] One of the most startling things Christ said is 'Leave the dead to bury their own dead',[22] apparently making the point that concern for the dead is futile.

This strand of thought has had little impact. Even those world-views which do not regard the corpse as the shell of a now departed person, still treat the body with respect. Nevertheless, most religions today accept the appropriateness of organ transplantation for the purpose of the relief of suffering, which is regarded as a good, while it is the product of our secular age, cryonics, which cannot approve of recycling of bodies, precisely because its adherents believe in the possibility of being unfrozen at some future point and introduced to a new life.

Organ transplants: culturally relative?

The point about the relativity to world-view of the value of the integrity of the corpse is one that has frequently been made. Less

63

frequent is the point that the value of organ transplants is also culturally specific. Of course it is known that the perceived value of organ transplants is a feature of our own time; that historically, since the technology was not there, *a fortiori* they were not valued.

However, in much of the contemporary discussion, and despite the controversy in the early days of heart transplantation, it is taken for granted that of course organ transplants are a desirable form of therapy, and that the only problems to be addressed are the practical ones of overcoming donor shortage and rejection problems, and the ethical issues of allocating the resources.

Technological advances, however, along with the increase in the demand for cryonics, make us confront the question of what it means to live a human life, and the extent to which we should go in trying to prolong it. The questioning of our lack of acceptance of death, and the realisation that the demand for organ transplants is culturally relative, are of crucial importance when looking at the imperatives which drive us towards ever more demands for bodily parts.

Language

As mentioned above, in looking at social values with reference to corpses the use of language is central. The word 'donor', contrasted as it is with 'source' used for non-humans,[23] is significant. Its importance is linked with the fear of collective ownership mentioned above. Some of the arguments against routine salvaging concentrate on the value of altruism, and the desirability of encouraging the ethics of giving in society.

As we have seen, however, the Human Tissue Act 1961, section 1(2) is already in fact an 'opting out' rather than an 'opting in' provision, and to call the corpse a 'donor' in such a situation masks the reality of what is going on.

It has been argued so far that the arguments in favour of duties regarding the dead and the rights of relatives with regard to the dead are not strong enough to outweigh the claims of seriously ill people who need organs. It has been suggested, however, that these arguments fail to win the day because they fail to take into account the importance of the corpse as a symbol. It might be argued that a sophisticated consequentialism could incorporate such considerations in its calculations. There would still be problems about how to deal with differences in world-view, however, which point to the necessity of questioning the assumptions we make in our society about the use of technology to prolong life. This shows us that the answer is not necessarily simply to switch to a different policy without more ado. We need to re-examine our assumptions regarding attitudes *both* towards the dead body *and* towards transplant technology.

DISTINCTIONS OF KIND AND DEGREE

We can now turn to look at distinctions that are drawn between different kinds of corpse, or between different parts or uses of them.

Concentration camp victims

Matthew Gwyther and Sean McConville have discussed the practice in Germany of using the remains of Nazi victims for study in medical schools such as Heidelberg.[24] They mention that the practice has now been discontinued so that burials can take place. Objections to this are also applied to the use of data gained from Nazi experiments. Arguments include the fact that these data and specimens were gained through the horrific treatment of human beings who had absolutely no say in the matter. To use them now is to condone the violence to which they were subjected.

On the other hand, it is argued, since it has happened and there is nothing that can be done about it, why not try to retrieve something good from the situation and make use of the results?

Several interesting questions arise in this connection. First, why has this become an issue at this point? What does it say about prevailing cultural mores that the demand for a proper burial of these remains has come to the fore? It is not clear what the answer to this is, but what does seem apparent is the depth of the belief that the corpse is not just an object available for exploitation, even for purposes of acquiring information.

There is a suggestion in these cases that the history of the corpse is relevant in determining its proper treatment. Of course, this is always relevant up to a point: the provisions of the Human Tissue Act look into the history of the person whose corpse is in question in order to discover whether she had any objections to the use of her organs for transplant, for example. But in the case of the Nazi victims, although it is obviously significant that they had no

65

opportunity to consent or object to anything that was done to them, there is more to it than that. The treatment of their corpses is seen as symbolic of an attitude to their treatment during life. Thus once more we see the importance of the corpse as a symbol.

D. Gareth Jones has discussed what he calls the 'moral complicity' argument, which suggests that the use of the data now in some way condones what happened then.[25] He effectively, however, submits this to a *reductio ad absurdum*: as the whole of modern medicine is built on anatomy, does that mean every health care professional is condoning the activities of Burke and Hare?

Further, why is it perfectly acceptable to display in a public museum the remains of Lindow Man, who, according to the accounts of the archaeologists, suffered a rather unpleasant end? Is it because such a person is felt to be beyond the confines of our moral community, whereas the Nazi victims are not? It is not clear how the boundaries are to be drawn.

Foetuses

The treatment of the human foetus, and its relationship to the moral community, continues to be an emotive issue, as is shown by recurrent debates on abortion legislation. Whereas abortion concerns the killing of the foetus, however, two recent developments have provoked strong reactions to the treatment of dead foetal remains.

The first was the 'Foetal Earrings' case. An artist, Richard Gibson, and the gallery owner, Peter Sylveire, were found guilty at the Old Bailey of outraging public decency by displaying a model of a human head wearing, as earrings, two human foetuses. In this case the foetuses had been dead for ten years, and had been kept in a medical laboratory during that period, so there was no suggestion that the artist had been involved in the improper procurement of their death.[26]

It is difficult to see exactly what the objection was to this, especially as the artist was asking a perfectly valid question: if we accept the wearing of animal remains, why not the remains of our own species? In this case there was not, as in the Nazi victims case, a demand for 'decent burial' because there is no legal demand or public expectation that dead foetuses should receive this, though there is controversy about the stillborn. The inescapable conclusion seems to be that the outrage caused by this gallery exhibit was due to the fact that it uncomfortably challenged our categories and the vision of the human species as superior.

If the human body in general is a powerful symbol, it is arguable that the foetus is even more so. Part of this is attributable to the vulnerability and so-called 'innocence' of the foetus. Anti-abortionists have sometimes argued that our treatment of the foetus has implications for respect for human life in general.

It is not surprising, therefore, that the suggestion of the salvaging of human foetal remains for brain cells to treat Parkinson's disease has aroused controversy. But if we accept the use of the corpses of adults for therapeutic purposes, why not the use of foetal remains? Consistency is surely desirable. Is there a relevant difference between the two? Apart from the above-mentioned claims of vulnerability and innocence, another important difference is the inability of the foetus to have expressed any wish on the matter. Does this fact make routine salvaging more or less acceptable?

Few advocates of recycling of the bodies of adults go so far as to exclude the possibility of 'opting out'. Hence it is suggested that the mother, as the closest person, should be asked at least whether she has any objection.

The problem with this is that the mother is the one who in most if not all cases will have willed the death of the foetus. We would not, however, allow a murderer to decide whether or not the organs of his/her victim should be available for therapeutic use. This may not be a fair analogy, however. Surely the point is that the mother is thought, in cases of lawful abortion, to have the right to consent to the death of the foetus. The murderer is never thought to have such a right. The positions of the mother and the murderer are therefore fundamentally dissimilar.

The Polkinghorne Committee recommended that the consent of the mother to the use of foetal remains should be sought, but upheld a separation principle.[27] Consent to use the foetus in research or therapy should be separate from consent to abortion. They should not simply be separated in time, but consent should be sought by different people. The point of this is to diminish the likelihood of people being pressurised into having abortions in order to provide foetal material, but it is impossible to eliminate entirely the possibility of individual mothers choosing to have abortions in order to provide a relative with treatment.

Interestingly, some people who are worried about such possibilities are nevertheless willing to accept the use of material produced by spontaneous abortions. Such a view implies that there is no objection to the use of foetal remains for therapeutic purposes *per se*, but only to willing their death in order to provide material. (The principle of double effect might be appealed to here.)

Let us suppose, however, there is no duty regarding the use of foetal remains as such which prevents their being used for therapeutic purposes. Why then should it not be permissible to use them for other purposes such as incorporating them in a work of art? It is arguable that while this defence was not accepted in the Old Bailey case, it should have been.

An important aspect of the Polkinghorne debate is that it concerns the use of foetal brain cells. The Polkinghorne Report has ruled out the transfer of a whole brain. This leads us to the discussion of the extent to which some parts of the body are more controversial than others, and raises the notion of personal identity.

Brains and personal identity

In thinking about the recycling of corpses the notion of personal identity, and the role played in this by the body, is obviously crucial. The dualist view of the person, and the idea of an immaterial soul substance as the guarantor of continuing personal identity, has severe philosophical difficulties concerning not only the evidence, or lack of it, for such a view, but also the question of the mechanism of the relation between the immaterial and the material.

Contemporary philosophical debate centres principally on two rival theories: the view that personal identity consists in psychological continuity; and the view that 'I am my brain' – in other words, that there is a physical criterion of personal identity, but that this does not involve the whole body but only part of it, namely the brain.

These two views have something in common in that, according to the best available evidence, psychological continuity does depend on the continuity of a particular brain. Clearly, these views of personal identity are closely bound up with the definition of death discussed above (p. 55), *viz.* in terms of death of the brain. But as we have seen, the question of how much of the brain is necessary for us to say that a person still exists is controversial.

What is important for us in the context of the present discussion is to note the centrality of the brain in these discussions. In thinking about appropriate treatment of the human body, we need to be aware that it is not the case that all parts of the human body are regarded in the same light. The brain has largely replaced the heart in our culture as the major organ. But this is a cultural matter. In ancient Egypt the 'seat of the soul' was thought to be in the tongue.[28]

The centrality of the brain in our culture, however, explains the worry about the transfer of an entire foetal brain into an adult sufferer of Parkinson's disease. Would this involve a change in the recipient's identity? The question less frequently asked is whether this would be a worse outcome than the continuance of the present person with the disease. This is perhaps because it is not clear for *whom* it would be worse.

Ovaries

The recovery of eggs from the ovaries of dead women has been thought particularly controversial. Andrew Walker is quoted in *The Independent* as saying: 'this is not the same as donation of a major organ such as a kidney. The idea that a new generation might be walking around as a result raises new questions'.[29] What exactly *are* the new questions?

If we already accept the use of frozen sperm, the donor of which may be dead, what is the difference? One point is of course that the sperm are collected while alive, and therefore the procedure is consented to. But presumably the collection of eggs from ovaries could be covered by the same regulations as govern the retrieval of any other organ as far as consent is concerned. If this is so, it is difficult to see why the fact that the genetic mother is no longer alive should be any more significant than the fact that the genetic father is no longer alive. And as far as the treatment of the corpse is concerned, the retrieval of an egg surely raises no more issues than does the removal of a kidney.

In fact it seems that if we accept the use of donated gametes at all, the fact that the donor is dead is irrelevant, except where the donor is known, as when, for example, a woman positively wants to have a child by her dead partner. But in a situation of donor anonymity it is unclear what difference it makes. The worry about the retrieval and use of gametes from corpses may be one of the intuitions regarding the dead that have no rational foundation.

RUTH F. CHADWICK

CONCLUSIONS

It has been argued that rational ethical arguments have failed to hold sway in thinking about the dead because of possible strong intuitions about the respect due to the corpse. It has been accepted, however, that the corpse has importance as a symbol, and that foetal remains and particular parts of the body have especially strong symbolism which cannot be ignored.

What is important, however, is to reveal some of the contradictions in our thinking. How can the language of 'donation' be squared with actual practice? How can the recent controversy over the concentration camp remains be consistent with what is on display in museums? How can different attitudes to the foetus earring case, the widespread abortion and disposal of foetuses and their salvaging for brain cell transplants be reconciled? How can society's acceptance of gamete donation coexist with worries about posthumous retrieval of eggs from ovaries? Even if we accept that the dead body has a symbolism over and above its status as a material object, some of these contradictions need to be exposed.

NOTES

1 H. E. Emson, 'The ethics of human cadaver organ transplantation: a biologist's viewpoint', *Journal of Medical Ethics* 13 (1987): 125.
2 David Lamb, *Organ Transplants and Ethics* (London: Routledge, 1990): 65.
3 A problem with Lamb's view has recently been highlighted by Martyn Evans, who has argued that if respiration counts for life, why not the beating heart? Cf. Martyn Evans, 'A plea for the heart', *Bioethics* (1990): 227–31.
4 Arthur L. Caplan, 'Arguing with success: is in vitro fertilization research or therapy?', in Dianne M. Bartels, Reinhard Priester, Dorothy E. Vawter and Arthur L. Caplan (eds), *Beyond Baby M: Ethical Issues in New Reproductive Techniques* (Clifton, NJ: Humana Press, 1989): 149–70, identifies two criteria to distinguish therapy from research: the state of knowledge about underlying mechanisms, and the efficacy of a procedure.
5 Celia Hall, 'Fertility treatment could use ovaries from dead women', *The Independent* (16 July 1990).
6 Kenneth V. Iserson, 'Using a cadaver to practice and teach', *Hastings Center Report* 16 (1968): 28.
7 John Harris, *The Value of Life* (London: Routledge & Kegan Paul, 1985): 119.
8 Hans Jonas, 'Philosophical reflection on human experimentation', *Daedus* 98 (1969): 227.

9 Rom Harré, 'Body obligations', *Cogito* (1987): 15–19.
10 See, for example, John Harris, *Violence and Responsibility* (London: Routledge & Kegan Paul, 1980).
11 Lamb, op. cit.: 141.
12 Iserson, op. cit.: 28.
13 P. D. G. Skegg, *Law, Ethics and Medicine: Studies in Medical Law*, rev. edn. (Oxford: Clarendon Press, 1988): 249.
14 Lamb, op. cit.: 145.
15 Paul Matthews, 'Property rights in John Merrick's skeleton', *The Independent* (24 June 1987).
16 Ruth F. Chadwick, 'The market for bodily parts; Kant and duties to oneself', *Journal of Applied Philosophy* 6 (1989): 129–39.
17 Skegg, op. cit.: 232ff.
18 Lamb, op. cit.: 36.
19 Leon R. Kass, 'Thinking about the body', *Hastings Center Report* 15 (1985): 21.
20 Dr Hub Zwart, 'Consensus formation or acceptance strategy?', *European Society for the Philosophy of Medicine and Health Care Newsletter* 9 (1990): 28–9.
21 Emson, op. cit.: 125.
22 *St Matthew* VIII.22.
23 Cf. Lamb, op. cit.: 104ff.
24 Matthew Gwyther and Sean McConville, 'Can good come of evil?', *Observer* (19 November 1989): 18–25.
25 D. Gareth Jones, 'Fetal neural transplantation: placing the ethical debate within the context of society's use of human material', *Bioethics* 5 (1991): 23–43.
26 Cf. Heta Häyry and Matti Häyry, 'The bizarre case of the human earrings', *Philosophy Today* 7 (1991): 1–3.
27 John Polkinghorne (Chairman), *Review of the Guidance on the Research Use of Fetuses and Fetal Material* (London: HMSO, 1989): 22–3.
28 Bruce Chatwin, *The Songlines* (London: Picador, 1988): 302.
29 Hall, op. cit.

5

Medical futility: CPR

John Saunders

HISTORICAL PERSPECTIVE

In 1960 Kouwenhaven and his colleagues first reported the technique of external cardiac massage as a means of maintaining the circulation.[1] Twenty patients were successfully resuscitated from cardiac arrest, defined as the sudden cessation of the circulation resulting in loss of consciousness and death if untreated. The technique was used alone or in combination with artificial ventilation. This demonstration that opening the chest to massage the heart directly was not required led to the widespread dissemination of the new technique. It was seen as an increasingly effective treatment for 'victims of acute insult-drowning, electric shock, untoward effect of drugs, anaesthetic accident, heart block, acute myocardial infarction or surgery',[2] i.e., to prevent sudden unexpected death.

The first ten years witnessed reports of increasing successes. In Montreal, for example, an initial success rate of 33.3 per cent in a series of 126 patients was reported in 1963 with 13.5 per cent surviving to discharge from hospital.[3] By 1965 a survival to discharge of 15.8 per cent of 254 patients was reported.[4] At the end of the decade, 1,204 patients had been subjected to cardiopulmonary resuscitation (CPR) and 19.1 per cent had survived to discharge.[5] These experiences were reported from general and special wards: ischaemic heart disease accounted for over 50 per cent of patients. It is significant that in discussing the requirements for success, the selection of patients was not mentioned. Nevertheless, in 1966 the Ad Hoc Committee on CPR of the Division of Medical Sciences, National Academy of Sciences – National Research Committee, representing a conference of thirty organisations, recommended that 'all physicians, dentists, osteopaths, nurses, inhalation therapists

72

and rescue personnel should be trained' in CPR techniques.[6]

A more gloomy view was published in 1976 from the Veterans Administration Hospital, Madison, Wisconsin.[7] Reporting on CPR attempts in all areas of the hospital an initial success rate of 26 per cent of 183 patients with only 14 per cent surviving to discharge was found. Some calls for CPR may result from 'pseudo-arrests' – emergencies such as fits or faints where spontaneous recovery is the norm. When these calls were excluded the discharge rate fell to 7.6 per cent (fourteen patients); five were in a persistent vegetative state (2.7 per cent of all resuscitations). If medical emergencies such as pneumothorax were excluded the success rate from 'true cardiac arrest' was a mere 4.9 per cent (nine patients). Resuscitation in the Coronary Care Unit and in the daytime were associated with higher success rates. More widespread use of CPR was leading to lower success rates and perhaps inappropriate use. It became clear not only that the long-term survival rate of patients undergoing CPR on general wards was poor, but also that the reason for this was the poor prognosis of such patients at the outset.[8] The initial response in such cases may have been the return of vital signs, but in most this was followed by death in an intensive-therapy unit with the patient on a ventilator and receiving intensive circulatory support.

Even for well-trained resuscitation teams, CPR is often a messy affair. Anyone who has practical experience of participating in even a handful of arrest calls will know that outside the intensive-care unit or the emergency department there are often problems. Patients collapse in toilets, other confined spaces or X-ray departments; vomitus, faeces, urine and blood may surround the victim; clothes may need to be cut away; initial discovery and action may be panicky from junior or ill-trained staff – and in the UK standards still leave much to be desired.[9] Fitting may result from cerebral anoxia; difficulties in intravenous access or intubation are common; administration of drugs and fluids is haphazard; while a 300 joule electric shock to the chest produces a convulsive contraction of the limbs. Curtains are pulled round, visitors ushered out of the area and other patients terrified rather that reassured by the frenetic activity as doctors and nurses rush to and fro. This may be followed by artificial ventilation, tracheostomy, central venous monitoring, arterial lines, inotropic support, complex drug regimes, all the paraphernalia of the intensive-therapy unit with, finally, repeated test procedures for diagnosis of (brainstem) death. If the end result is death, a procedure more destructive of a dignified and peaceful end could hardly be devised: an opinion clearly expressed by nurses[10] and echoed by others.[11]

Institutional policies developed in the United States to identify patients for whom CPR was thought appropriate. In 1974 both Massuchusetts General Hospital[12] and the Beth Israel Hospital[13] issued explicit policies for 'do-not-resuscitate' (DNR) orders. In 1981 in New York, a death under mysterious circumstances in a Queens Hospital intensive-care unit led to a grand jury investigation. This exposed a covert system of applying purple dots to the charts of patients indicating DNR status.[14] This led directly to the 1982 guidelines issued by the Medical Society of the State of New York, to the 1985 New York State Task Force on Life and the Law, convened by the governor and to New York's laws specifying the procedure for DNR orders enacted in July 1987 and effective from April 1988. The earlier pronouncement in the Massachusetts Appeal Court in 1978 *In the Matter* of Shirley Dinnerstein had stated that a DNR order presented a question 'peculiarly within the competence of the medical profession of what measures are appropriate to ease the imminent passing of an irreversibly, terminally ill patient in the light of the patient's history and condition and the wishes of her family'.[15] This decision was the first to uphold the legality of a DNR order; ten years later New York State had placed such orders under legal regulation.

In the UK, the tradition of legal regulation in medicine has been less strong. Public interest was aroused by newspaper reports of the NTBR (not to be resuscitated) labels placed at the end of the bed, but the overall trend has been against explicit policies. Bayliss summed up this approach in 1982: 'In Britain, sound unhurried clinical judgment, sympathy, understanding and mutual trust, rather than abstract principles and printed policy statements, have in general stood patients in good stead.'[16] Bayliss also believed that it should be the consultant who decided whether to resuscitate or not in discussion with house staff and ward sister:

> Better than anyone else the consultant and his team know the nature of the patient's disease or diseases and the likelihood of their responding to treatment. Quality of life is relative and should be assessed in relation to the age, state of health, and the personal aptitudes and interests of each individual patient. The age of the patient should not be a prime factor . . . the

younger the consultant the more he should consciously guard against this bias.[17]

A formal DNR policy existed in few British hospitals, even major teaching centres.[18] It is unlikely that this position will be sustained. In his annual report in 1991, the Parliamentary Commissioner for Health ('ombudsman') drew attention to the case of a woman of 88 admitted to hospital with pneumonia.[19] The patient was designated 'not for 222', which the patient's son learned about and realised meant a DNR order. Commenting on the son's complaint, the ombudsman was reported as stating that he 'found surprising the novelty of establishing a written resuscitation policy'. His investigation revealed that neither the admitting doctor nor other junior doctor colleagues thought that relatives would normally be involved in such decisions. The government's Chief Medical Officer has since written to all consultants and in 1993 the British Medical Association published guidelines.

UNIVERSAL CPR?

So why not give CPR to everyone? After all, it might be argued, if death is the outcome the subject will not suffer from a failed attempt. If one accepts a vitalist doctrine that human life is good in a biological sense, then CPR must be universally given – death must be postponed for as long as possible. Few would accept such a position; life with no consciousness is necessarily deprived of meaning, while nobody would choose to prolong his life by an hour if it was characterised by unremitting and excruciating pain, noise and terror. If one compares permanent unconsciousness with death, there is little difference to the subject himself. In either case the individual's life is over, even though his body goes on living. From the (unconscious) subject's position, it can only be a matter of indifference if CPR is instituted at the point of cardiac arrest. We are chiefly concerned with lives and only secondarily with life.[20] The vitalist argument may be dismissed.

Two utilitarian arguments might be advanced for universal CPR. First, universal CPR will maximise the number of lives saved. Of course, as argued above, some of these lives may not be worth saving because biological life alone is not worth preserving. But if life, real living, is a thing of priceless worth, or even of very great worth, saving a few specimens of biological life is a relatively small price to pay. Second, effective CPR requires a well-trained team for its maximum success. Although frequent revision of protocols and practice on mannequins is helpful, there is no substitute for active participation in CPR to maintain skills. The more frequent the CPR, the more finely honed are the practical techniques. In even a moderate sized hospital sufficient experience may not be possible at the optimal level, especially as junior doctors' hours of work and nights on call are reduced, unless every subject of cardiac arrest is resuscitated. Maximising success for those patients for whom it really matters means CPR for all. If the terminally ill are subjected to this procedure, it does them no harm. They die anyway. But they will have served in a valuable way in maximising lives saved. Anyway, cannot a morally good end justify a relatively bad means by a principle of proportionate good?

Almost nobody accepts such arguments. Even groups such as the Roman Catholic Church claiming the highest 'respect for human dignity and reverence for the sacredness of life' would still suggest that there is 'no obligation to prolong life by extraordinary means'.[21] As the Pope expressed it, 'since resuscitation goes beyond ordinary means, the doctor is not obliged to use it'.[22] Indeed Roman Catholics, in particular, may be more likely to forgo CPR. In a comparison of incompetent patients with and without family consent to their DNR status, all of whom were given DNR status by their doctors, it was found that there was no significant difference in race, occupation, insurer or type of service. Only one socio-economic factor distinguished the two groups. There were proportionately fewer Roman Catholics in the group where the family and the physician disagreed.[23] The teaching of the Roman Catholic Church, with its strong emphasis on the sanctity of life, may also lead its adherents to accept death more readily.

HARMS AND CPR

Underlying the suggestion of universal CPR, a sort of ghastly technological last rites, is the assumption that since the alternative is death, CPR is a procedure that at least can do no harm. It is based on the principle of nonmaleficence: *'primum non nocere'*. The assumption is quite simply wrong. CPR may be harmful, first, to the subject, second, to relatives, third, to health care staff and, fourth, to society. Each of these parties, in varying degrees, has an interest.

For a large number of patients initial success in restoring a beating heart may be rapidly followed by a further cardiac arrest. The experience of the fear of death is therefore visited upon the patient not once, but twice. Fear of dying, fear of the possible mode of dying, fear of death itself are part of the human condition. Death's awfulness is easily forgotten by the young and healthy. Awareness of dying, wrote Ramsey in a classic essay, constitutes an experience of ultimate indignity in and to the self who is dying.[24] Death is nothing but dreadful to any human being; it is not a fact of life negotiable like other facts.[25] Such harms are not limited to anxiety in the psychologically orientated. Many such patients awake from CPR confused, totally disorientated, hallucinating in a new and strange environment. To this is added the apparent assault of multiple venepunctures, arterial samples, catheters, drains and monitors. These represent not only an offence against the dignity of the patient but also may involve discomfort, pain and heighten confusion and apprehension. It would not be an overstatement to use the word torture on occasions; certainly cruelty may be inflicted: the aimless infliction or perpetuation of pain, injury, grief or suffering or interruption of a timely death or kindness of nature.[26] By aimless is meant without rational intent of potential benefit.

Families may also suffer harm. As the social unit in which the patient lived, the family will have an interest in the patient's well-being and standard of care, even if they have no legal rights. A patient who belongs to a loving family does not suffer alone. More than this the family has to live with the thwarted hopes of an initially successful CPR, the hours of expectant waiting over an unconscious body in an intensive-care unit and its associated rituals. To these may be added the guilt of decisions that further discussions may involve: the guilt that arises from the history that all families have, confused feelings about the future, the desire to press that everything is done against the desire to accept the predicted outcome, perhaps confusion over considerations of probate.

Relatively early in the history of CPR, it was commented that 'an unfortunate lowering of morale and enthusiasm of all hospital staff may follow a series of unsuccessful attempts to resuscitate hopeless cases'.[27] If health care professional staff are expected to undertake something they do not believe in, it will not be long before cynicism develops. If there is not a 'no code', there will be a 'slow code'. The team will arrive late, it will go through the motions for the sake of appearances and before long the efficiency of the team for everyone may fall. It is also harmful to call overworked, overtired young doctors out of bed at 5 a.m., just after they have got there, for no rational purpose.

Society may suffer harm in two ways. First CPR uses up valuable resources. Intensive care is the most expensive ward of any hospital, while the costs of maintaining a patient in the persistent vegetative state are enormous. Inappropriate use of resources deprives other patients of benefits that could result from their better use. Second, society in the form of other unrelated patients may suffer considerable anxieties and alarms if CPR teams rush into wards to resuscitate an elderly inappropriate patient. Society has a right to expect that the resources it provides will be used wisely and properly, without causing avoidable alarm and distress to others.

AN INCONSISTENT PRACTICE?

In practice many doctors are highly inconsistent in the way decisions about CPR are made. A survey of 108 cardiologists and diabetologists asked how they would have managed three elderly patients with diabetic emergencies, seen recently by one of the authors.[28] In the first case – a moderately demented alcoholic woman of 66 with a recent stroke – 102 (94.4 per cent) were prepared to treat diabetic ketoacidosis if it developed again in hospital, but only eighty-seven (80.7 per cent) were prepared to offer CPR during that treatment, and if cardiac arrest occurred after full recovery from diabetic ketoacidosis, this fell to sixty-eight (62.9 per cent). In the same study, in the third case, who was described as extremely alert, half indicated they would not ask the patient about her attitude to CPR. This compared with 10 per cent who would do so in the severely demented second case.

Lo and Jonsen[29] suggest that there are four grounds for limiting treatment: cost of treatment, the patient's wishes, quality of life and futility of treatment. One suspects that the cardiologists and diabetologists had failed to separate these four strands and certainly weighted them differently. There is the additional consideration of the patient's age, which Lo and Jonsen do not consider.

WITHHOLDING CPR

Cost

In western society, cost of treatment can rarely affect the decision to offer CPR directly. Indirectly, of course, it may be a highly significant factor. For the cost will affect the provision of facilities that may determine the success of the CPR attempt and also of facilities that may affect the quality of life after the successful attempt. Hence cost may determine futility of treatment, quality of life and the patient's wishes.

The patient's wishes

The importance of the patient's wishes stems from the principle of autonomy. It is widely acknowledged that patients have the right to consent or refuse medical treatment, even when such treatments are life-sustaining. Such judgments have been explicitly made by North American Courts.[30] We are offended in cases where fully competent patients' wishes are overridden.[31] Refusal of medical treatment may of course lead to serious injury or death, but provided the patient has been informed and has understood, the decision must be respected. Such refusal may serve as the basis for a DNR order.[32]

In practice, doctors frequently do not discuss CPR with their patients: indeed in the UK such discussion is the exception rather than the rule. Even when physicians profess a belief in the desirability of discussing CPR they do not in practice do so. Bedell and Delbanco found that in the Beth Israel Hospital only 19 per cent of patients had discussed resuscitation before the arrest with either their private physician or a house officer. The physician's perception may not correspond with the patient's stated preference, nor was there consistent agreement between two physicians about the patient's preference. They found these attitudes to be independent of the physician's estimate of the probability of arrest, the location of the patient in hospital or the patient's underlying disease.[33]

At least part of this problem lies either in the circumstances under which the question of CPR arises or in the doctor's view of the wisdom of the decision. Certainly it is difficult to discuss if unexpected and a discussion too far in advance will be seen as irrelevant to the patient's immediate status. It also lies in the complexity of factors in the decision. A slightly deaf, wheezy, bronchitic, elderly

79

patient presents with central severe chest pain in an emergency department. Does he at 85 years of age really want CPR? How do we inform him of the possible need for CPR, the technique and its outcome, the experiences of intensive care, of ventilators and mental impairment and institutionalisation and all the rest, and then assure ourselves that his understanding is not impaired by senile dementia and his consent is informed, that he is truly competent?[34] And how much harder is such a decision likely to be out of hospital?[35] It is often simply impossible to ask for informed consent.

No information is ever value-neutral. Consider this simple example. Propranolol reduces mortality following a myocardial infarction from 10 per cent to 7.5 per cent.[36] This can be presented factually to the patient as a 25 per cent reduction in mortality by the enthusiast or as being of no value in thirty-nine out of forty patients by the therapeutic nihilist. The decision is likely to be made accordingly. Certainly there is good evidence that a full understanding of CPR, either by virtue of experiencing it or a detailed explanation, leaves many patients refusing it. In one study[37] when thirty-eight patients were asked if they wanted a repeat attempt, only 55 per cent said 'yes'. In a study of elderly patients, others speculated that the response to a simple question (such as 'In the event of your heart stopping, would you like us to do everything to get it started?') was inadequate. They state that when a proper explanation is given few elderly subjects were prepared to consent to CPR: 50 per cent said 'no'. Forty-two per cent wanted a doctor to decide and only 7 per cent said 'yes'.[38] Policies in the USA typically require that CPR is always initiated unless a DNR order is written and, furthermore, that patient or family permission must be obtained before the order is written.[39] Current British practice may be indefensibly paternalistic, but a greater degree of paternalism seems justifiable than in American hospitals. This is not an excuse for avoiding a demanding, emotional task, but an acknowledgement that decisions need to be made about CPR in situations where 'informed consent' easily degenerates into a charade of signing a valueless 'consent form'.

So far I have defended a limited paternalism in situations where it is difficult to obtain informed consent, because the implications are so complex and perhaps the likely benefits so remote. Paternalism may also function as a form of social insurance, as a protection against a course of action that in a more reflective moment we would not countenance. Consider a bride and groom involved in a major accident on their wedding night. One is killed, the other seriously injured. Although the survivor passes all the conventional tests of mental competence, would a request for a DNR order be implemented by a good doctor? Surely it would be overruled, and justifiably so, on the grounds that it represents an impulsive opinion, that would never be taken apart from short-lived special circumstances. And if it is thought that this example errs on the side of life, consider the hackneyed example of the driver imprisoned in a furiously burning vehicle. I cannot rescue him, but I do have a gun. Should I relieve his death agonies by its use, and do so, moreover, even if he should impotently cry 'help, rescue me!'? The claim to know what another person would really want is a peculiarly arrogant one, the more so if a contrary opinion is expressed. Yet there may be extreme circumstances that justify such a claim. The covenant relationship between doctor and patient is governed by faith and the doctrine of trust; no prudent patient would wish to entrust his health to a physician who is both powerless and unwilling to resist unreasonable and irrational demands. As Tomlinson and Brody observe,[40] removing power from the physician by complex DNR procedures does not necessarily enhance the autonomy of the patient. Autonomy must be respected, but it must also be sensitively and sometimes rapidly assessed, where the protection against the abuse of professional power lies only in the integrity of the doctor. It should be accepted that autonomy is not enhanced by offering choices where one choice offers no reasonable prospect of a particular outcome. Insisting on the implementation of a policy that forces surrogates to sign forms to authorise DNR orders was expressed by the wife of one dying patient as 'being my husband's murderer or having him tortured'.[41] No one has expressed this better than Ingelfinger[42] in his memorable essay on arrogance:

> I do not want to be in the position of a shopper at the Casbah who negotiates and haggles with the physician about what is best. I want to believe that my physician is acting under a higher moral principle than a used car dealer. I'll go further than that. A physician who merely spreads an array of vendibles in front of his patient and then says 'Go ahead, you choose, it's your life' is guilty of shirking his duty, if not of malpractice.

Quality of life

Quality of life considerations are of two sorts. First, where the patient can make decisions about these for himself; second, where he is demented or permanently psychotic or otherwise mentally disabled. Any fully competent patient who decides rationally against CPR is likely to be making that decision on the grounds of a judgment on the quality of life. 'I believe that no man ever threw away his life, while it was worth keeping', wrote David Hume.[43] This quality of life will refer either to the present quality of living or to the likely quality of life in the near future in the light of the predicted behaviour of already existing disease. For an elderly patient life expectancy may be sufficiently short and of too mediocre a quality to be judged worthy of the risky outcome of CPR. CPR itself, if promptly carried out and rapidly successful, should have no influence on that quality of life. Tomlinson and Brody[44] have divided rationales for DNR orders into poor quality before and poor quality after CPR, but it is difficult to predict that CPR itself will necessarily lower quality of life.

There can be no question that DNR orders on competent patients on quality of life grounds should only be made with the patient's express consent. Only an individual is capable of evaluating his own priorities. Disabled people, in particular, may value life far more highly than their able counterparts would think, especially when free from cerebral damage. For example, the case histories of thirty-seven patients with spinal injuries requiring artificial ventilation between 1968 and 1984 were reviewed in 1985. Of twenty-one patients who were still alive, no less than eighteen said that they would wish to be ventilated again if the need arose. Two were undecided and only one said that she would wish to be allowed to die.[45] It has also been demonstrated that doctors are poor judges of patients' quality of life[46] in so far as it affects resuscitation choice. In a study of 105 physicians and 258 elderly out-patients, the physicians were found generally to consider their older patients' quality of life worse than the patients themselves.

In the case of incompetent patients, judgments are best made by family members acting in a proxy capacity. The family knows the patient best and, all things being equal, is most concerned for the patient's welfare. Emanuel has reviewed two sets of criteria according to which families or in their absence another surrogate should act.[47] The doctrine of substituted judgment suggests that the surrogate decision-maker should ascertain the incompetent person's actual interests and preferences, making a decision as if that person were competent. Inevitably such a standard is highly subjective. The emphasis that it is important to make in practice, however, is that the doctor asking for this opinion is not interested in the relative's opinion, but in the relative's interpretation of what the patient's opinion would have been. The starting-point therefore should be an enquiry into whether the incompetent patient, when competent, had ever expressed any views as to what should happen under the circumstances now prevailing. A similar starting-point is also desirable if applying the second set of criteria, those of the 'best interests' test. Here the surrogate must evaluate the alternative treatments or lack of them and select that in which the benefits outweigh the burdens and thereby best promote the patient's welfare. This standard will be familiar to most British doctors from its advocacy as the duty of care for any incompetent patient for any procedure.[48] In the USA it has been supported both by the President's Commission[49] and the courts, most explicitly in New Jersey.[50] According to the latter, a treatment could be terminated if:

> the net burdens of the patient's life with the treatment clearly and markedly outweigh the benefits that the patient derives from life so that the recurring, unavoidable and severe pain of the patient's life with the treatment would render the life-sustaining treatment inhumane.[51]

Unfortunately the New Jersey adjudication focuses exclusively on pain. There can be no consensus on objective criteria as to what constitutes 'best interests', and pain alone is inadequate. Using either the substituted judgment or best interest tests will lead to disagreements and on occasions these may be strong enough for relatives' views to be overruled by doctors[52] who after all must implement any policy. In this respect advance directives may be of particular value, though lacking legal status in English law. The varying status of families in giving consent to withdrawing or withholding treatment in general has been reviewed elsewhere.[53]

Futility

Futility of treatment is the fourth reason for considering a DNR order. Futility refers to treatment outcome, and to describe a treatment as futile implies it should not be given. If a patient demands a treatment, must that request always be agreed? Is the patient merely a customer? Patients have certainly become more demanding, and many articulate not merely a right to health care in general but a right to choose a specific treatment modality. Partly this results from increased awareness of what treatments are possible, partly from increased expectations of what treatment may achieve. But if I owe a drunkard a sum of money I am under an obligation to pay it even if I know he will spend it on more drink. He has a right to his money and that will trump any concern on my part for his welfare. We cannot refuse a medical treatment merely because it is harmful or does no particular good. Rather it must be asserted that the patient has no right to specific treatments. In licensing doctors to go about their business, society implicitly entrusts the profession to promote health and relieve suffering. A useless or harmful treatment does not achieve this end. If the aim of medicine is health and health is a form of beneficence, then no individual patient can have a right to a useless or harmful (i.e., maleficent) treatment. As Brett and McCullough put it, if there is no potential medical benefit then the whole *raison d'être* of the physician–patient interaction disappears.[54]

But can we actually say that CPR is never potentially beneficial? Historically, we have noted an improving success rate. What is the current position? Bedell *et al.* studied all patients subjected to CPR for eighteen months at the Beth Israel Hospital, Boston.[55] Of 294 patients, 128 (44 per cent) survived initially, thirty-one died within 24 hours and fifty-six in hospital, forty-one (14 per cent) were discharged, of whom twenty-two required one or more emergency hospitalisations and eight died within six months. At discharge the mean score for depression was in the severely depressed range, while at six months 50 per cent were incapacitated by fear (for example, had to live close to medical help). Certain groups did badly. None of the fifty-eight patients with pneumonia and only 3 per cent with renal failure, for example, survived. Hypotension with a systolic blood pressure less than 100 mm Hg was associated with 2 per cent survival. This series is fairly representative, though more detailed in its psychological assessments. As a simple summary we may say that one-third will survive initially, one-third of these will leave hospital, of whom 80 per cent will be alive at six months and 2 per cent in the persistent vegetative state.[56]

The prognosis of the elderly is deserving of special comment. While it has been suggested that age *per se* is only a factor in predicting outcome because of its association with multiple pathologies, the consensus view suggests otherwise. In patients aged over 70 years one study found that an initial survival rate of 31 per cent fell to zero at discharge;[57] in another series of 503 patients an initial survival rate of 22 per cent fell to 3.8 per cent at discharge of whom only 1.6 per cent returned to their own homes.[58] In the latter series an out of hospital unwitnessed arrest had zero survival, asystole or electromechanical dissociation one of 237, CPR lasting over 15 minutes one of 360 and all out of hospital arrests two of 244. In hospital 6.5 per cent survived to discharge only. Results in nursing homes are worse.[59] Hence one might conclude that the elderly only benefit if ventricular fibrillation or ventricular tachycardia are witnessed and sinus rhythm restored in about 5 minutes. The rest are futile.

Or are they? Futility has an air of finality, a ring of clarity, an echo of facts fighting back against values. Or is it one of professionals' expert knowledge fighting back against patients' or relatives' demands or questions? Certainly it has evoked much recent comment.[60] The notion of futility is certainly not the simple one it is intended to imply. Physiological futility is absolute: a failure to restart the heart always under a particular set of circumstances. Cognitive futility is the failure to achieve recovery of cognitive function. Temporal futility is the failure to achieve a significant increase in life expectancy. Qualitative futility is failure to achieve a quality of life that is acceptable. None of these judgments are entirely factual. A statement of physiological futility may simply imply the need for a larger series of patients. Thus in Bedell's series quoted above, none of fifty-eight patients with pneumonia survived. But assuredly none will if this is taken to mean that none can. Nobody can know what will happen to the fifty-ninth. A rational treatment may be used before its value has been proven, especially if the alternative is death. The suggestion that CPR might be given to someone in a persistent vegetative state is surely repugnant. Yet the decision not to offer it is not value-free. It is possible that such a life may be greatly valued, that such an individual may still be a focus of someone's love and concern and that such an individual may have wanted continuing biological life as long as they could continue such a role. To decline CPR is to deny such possibilities. Similarly, the judgment that an increased life expectancy of a few hours or even a few days is not significant is to make a judgment of value. Such a time may enable a will to be written, affairs to be ordered and goodbyes to be made. Qualitative futility involves an explicit value judgment as with any quality of life consideration. The claim that a treatment is futile is therefore not capable of shifting the issue from one of values to one of facts.

That is not to deny utility to the concept. A surgeon cannot be obliged to operate on an elderly patient with renal failure, dementia and a ruptured thoracic aortic aneurysm just because to do so would imply a judgment of value. Not only does the patient not have an unqualified right to demand specific treatments, but the physician also must have the discretion to interpret and apply medicine's own values – defined broadly as a duty to do more good than harm to patients. As Tomlinson and Brody assert,[61] if physicians have any rightful control over the interventions they offer to patients, it is only because they have the authority to act on judgments of value. If decisions about pursuing the merest possibility of survival always belonged to the patient or proxy, then doctors would have no authority to stop CPR. Although paternalism is open to abuse, an appeal to professional integrity carries the weight of medicine's authority as a moral enterprise, part of whose social acceptability stems from its beneficent purposes. In practice doctors do not easily accept that it is better to do less rather than more for a patient.[62] Certainly, they must examine the reasons for a DNR order, but the fear of casual dismissal of the possibility of resuscitation in the incompetent patient with minimal prospects of success is misplaced. No doubt each doctor must define for himself 'minimal prospects' for each individual. He has a duty to do so. For a few elderly patients, resuscitation may be a blessing, for most it is a curse,[63] and for the health care system a misappropriation of precious resources.

SUMMARY

CPR is an effective and successful treatment for small and selected groups of patients. For most it is a desperate measure with slender prospects of success. It may generate harm for patients, their families, health care professionals and society. Universal CPR is indefensible. Fully competent patients should normally determine their own CPR status; but if the expression of autonomy is limited by the contingencies of the situation doctors should act paternalistically and not always resuscitate. Competence to understand the outcome of CPR is necessary for that consent to be informed. There may still be occasions where doctors may institute or refrain from CPR where there are anxieties about serious wrongs resulting from discussion itself or doubts about the wisdom of the decision by the patient due to temporary contingencies. Decisions about quality of life are best determined by the patient, or, if incompetent, by relatives. The views of the latter should be in good faith, and bizarre or suspect decisions may again lead to professional contra-actions on the basis of a best interests' judgment. The concept of futility contains an implicit value judgment. This does not negate its value. Offering false choices reduces rather than enhances autonomy. Doctors cannot refrain from the sensitive value judgments implicit in the moral purpose of medicine.

NOTES

1 W. B. Kouwenhaven, J. R. Jude and G. G. Knickerbocker, 'Closed-chest massage', *Journal of the American Medical Association* 173 (1960): 94–7.
2 J. H. Talbott, 'Introduction', in J. R. Jude and J. O. Elam (eds) *Fundamentals of cardiopulmonary resuscitation*, (Philadelphia, Pa.: F. A. Davis, 1965).
3 G. A. Klassen, C. Broadhurst, D. I. Peretz and A. L. Johnson, 'Cardio-pulmonary resuscitation in 126 medical patients', *Lancet* 1 (1963): 1290–2.
4 H. J. Smith and W. R. Anthonsen, 'Results of cardiac massage in 254 patients', *Lancet* 1 (1965): 1027–9.
5 J. G. Lemire and A. L. Johnson, 'Is cardiac resuscitation worthwhile? A decade of experience', *New England Journal of Medicine* 286 (1972): 970–2.
6 Ad Hoc Committee on CPR of the Division of Medical Sciences, National Academy of Sciences – National Research Council, 'Cardio-pulmonary resuscitation', *Journal of the American Medical Association* 198 (1966): 372–9.
7 B. Messert and C. E. Quaglieri, 'Cardiopulmonary resuscitation. Perspectives and problems', *Lancet* 2 (1976): 410–11.
8 C. O. Hershey and L. Fisher, 'Why outcome of cardiopulmonary resuscitation in general wards is poor', *Lancet* 1 (1982): 31–4.
9 A Report of the Royal College of Physicians, 'Resuscitation from cardiopulmonary arrest: training and organisation', *Journal of the Royal College of Physicians* 21 (1987): 175–82.
10 C. E. Candy, ' "Not for resuscitation": the student nurses' viewpoint', *Journal of Advanced Nursing* 16 (1991): 138–46.
11 W. St C. Symmers, 'Not allowed to die', *British Medical Journal* 1 (1968): 442.
12 'Optimum care for hopelessly ill patients: a report of the Clinical Care Committee of the Massachusetts General Hospital', *New England*

Journal of Medicine 295 (1976): 362–4.
13 M. T. Rabkin, G. Gillerman and N. R. Rice, 'Orders not to resuscitate', *New England Journal of Medicine* 295 (1976): 364–6.
14 J. A. McClung and R. S. Kamer, 'Legislating ethics. Implications of New York's Do-Not-Resuscitate Law', *New England Journal of Medicine* 323 (1990): 270–2.
15 R. B. Schram, J. C. Kane and D. T. Roble, ' "No code" orders: clarification in the aftermath of Saikewicz', *New England Journal of Medicine* 299 (1978): 875–8.
16 R. I. S. Bayliss, 'Thou shalt not strive officiously', *British Medical Journal* 285 (1982): 1373–5.
17 ibid.
18 R. P. F. Scott, 'Cardiac arrests in general wards: three year follow-up', *Lancet* 1 (1983): 993; P. J. F. Baskett, 'The ethics of resuscitation', *British Medical Journal* 293 (1986): 189–90.
19 'Hospital resuscitation code call after "death sentence" ', *Guardian* (14 June 1991).
20 J. Rachels, *The End of Life. Euthanasia and Morality* (Oxford: Oxford University Press, 1986): 26.
21 National Conference of Catholic Bishops, *New World* 84 (1976): 17–18.
22 Pius XII, 'The prolongation of life', *The Pope Speaks* 4 (1958): 393–8 (reprinted in D. J. Horan and D. Mall (eds), *Death, Dying and Euthanasia* (Frederick, MD: University Publications of America, 1980)).
23 T. A. Brennan, 'Incompetent patients with limited care in the absence of family consent. A study of socioeconomic and clinical variables', *Annals of Internal Medicine* 109 (1988): 819–25.
24 P. Ramsey, 'The indignity of "death with dignity" ', *Hastings Center Studies* 2 (1974): 47–62.
25 P. Ramsey, 'Death's pedagogy', *Commonwealth* (20 September 1974): 497–502.
26 S. Braithwaite and D. C. Thomasma, 'New guidelines in forgoing life sustaining treatment in incompetent patients: an anticruelty policy', *Annals of Internal Medicine* 104 (1986): 711–15.
27 H. R. S. Harley, 'Reflections on cardiopulmonary resuscitation', *Lancet* 2 (1966): 1–4.
28 J. S. Yudkin, L. T. Doyal and B. S. Hurwitz, 'Interpreting survival rates for the treatment of decompensated diabetes: are we saving too many lives?', *Lancet* 2 (1987): 1192–5.
29 B. Lo and A. R. Jonsen, 'Clinical decisions to limit treatment', *Annals of Internal Medicine* 93 (1980): 764–8.
30 D. Brahams, 'Unwanted life sustaining treatment', *Lancet* 335 (1990): 1209–10.
31 Symmers, op. cit.; S. H. Miles, R. Cranford and A. L. Schultz, 'Do not resuscitate orders in a teaching hospital: considerations and a suggested policy', *Annals of Internal Medicine* 96 (1982): 660–4.
32 J. L. Puma, D. L. Schiedermayer, S. Toulmin, S. H. Miles and J. A. McAtee, 'The standard of care: a case report and ethical analysis', *Annals of Internal Medicine* 108 (1988): 121–4.

33 S. E. Bedell and T. L. Delbanco, 'Choices about cardiopulmonary resuscitation in hospital. When do physicians talk with patients?', *New England Journal of Medicine* 310 (1984): 1089–93; S. E. Bedell, D. Pelle, P. L. Maher and P. D. Cleary, 'Do-not-resuscitate orders for critically ill patients in the hospital: how are they used and what is their impact?', *Journal of the American Medical Association* 256 (1986): 233–7. See also S. J. Youngner, W. Lewandowski, D. K. McClish, B. W. Juknialis, C. Coulton and E. T. Bartlett, 'Do not resuscitate orders. Incidence and implications in a medical intensive care unit', *Journal of the American Medical Association* 253 (1985): 54–7; R. M. Veatch, 'Deciding against resuscitation: encouraging signs and practical dangers', *Journal of the American Medical Association* 253 (1985): 77–8.

34 P. S. Appelbaum and T. Grisso, 'Assessing patients' capacities to consent to treatment', *New England Journal of Medicine* 319 (1988): 1635–8.

35 K. V. Iserson, 'Forgoing prehospital care: should ambulance staff always resuscitate?', *Journal of Medical Ethics* 17 (1991): 19–24; G. A. Sachs, S. H. Miles and R. A. Levin, 'Limiting resuscitation: emerging policy in the emergency medical system', *Annals of Internal Medicine* 114 (1991): 151–4.

36 J. R. A. Mitchell, '"But will it help my patients with myocardial infarction?" The implications of recent trials for everyday country folk', *British Medical Journal* 285 (1982): 1140–8.

37 S.E. Bedell, T. L. Delbanco, E. F. Cook and F. H. Epstein, 'Survival after cardiopulmonary resuscitation in hospital', *New England Journal of Medicine* 309 (1983): 569–76.

38 D. J. Murphy, 'Do-not-resuscitate orders. Time for reappraisal in long term care institutions', *Journal of the American Medical Association* 260 (1988): 2098–101.

39 J. C. Hackler and F. C. Hiller, 'Family consent to orders not to resuscitate. Reconsidering hospital policy', *Journal of the American Medical Association* 264 (1990): 1281–3.

40 T. Tomlinson and H. Brody, 'Futility and the ethics of resuscitation', *Journal of the American Medical Association* 264 (1990): 1276–80.

41 K. Prager, 'Implications of New York's Do-Not Resuscitate Law', *New England Journal of Medicine* 323 (1990): 1838–9.

42 F. G. Ingelfinger, 'Arrogance', *New England Journal of Medicine* 304 (1980): 1507–11.

43 D. Hume, 'Of suicide', in T. H. Green and T. H. Goose (eds), *The Philosophical Works of David Hume* (London: 1874–5) (reprinted in P. Singer (ed.) *Applied Ethics* (Oxford: Oxford University Press, 1986)).

44 T. Tomlinson and H. Brody, 'Ethics and communication in do-not-resuscitate orders', *New England Journal of Medicine* 318 (1988): 43–6.

45 B. P. Gardner, F. Theocleous, J. W. H. Watt and K. R. Krishnan, 'Ventilation or dignified death for patients with high tetraplegia', *British Medical Journal* 291 (1985): 1620–2.

46 R. F. Uhlmann and R. A. Pearlman, 'Perceived quality of life and preferences for life-sustaining treatment in older adults', *Archives of Internal Medicine* 151 (1991): 495–7.

47 E. J. Emanuel, 'A review of the ethical and legal aspects of terminating medical care', *American Journal of Medicine* 84 (1988): 291–301.

48 NHS Management Executive, *A guide to consent for examination and treatment* (London: HMSO, 1990): 10 and 12.

49 President's Commission for the Study of Ethical Problems in Medicine and Biomedical and Behavioral Research, *Making Health Care Decisions* (Washington DC: US Government Printing Office, 1982).

50 B. Lo and L. Dornbrand, 'The case of Claire Conroy: Will administrative review safeguard incompetent patients?', *Annals of Internal Medicine* 104 (1986): 869–73.

51 *In re Claire Conroy.*

52 Brennan, op. cit.

53 J. Areen, 'The legal status of consent obtained from families of adult patients to withhold or withdraw treatment', *Journal of the American Medical Association* 258 (1987): 229–35.

54 A. S. Brett and L. B. McCullough, 'When patients request specific interventions. Defining the limit of the physician's obligation', *New England Journal of Medicine* 315 (1986): 1347–51.

55 Bedell, Delbanco, Cook and Epstein, op. cit.

56 D. L. Schiedermayer, 'The decision to forgo CPR in the elderly patient', *Journal of the American Medical Association* 260 (1988): 2096–7.

57 G. E. Taffett, T. A. Teasdale and R. J. Luchi, 'In-hospital cardiopulmonary resuscitation', *Journal of the American Medical Association* 260 (1988): 2069–72.

58 D. J. Murphy, A. M. Murray, B. E. Robinson and E. W. Campion, 'Outcomes of cardiopulmonary resuscitation in the elderly', *Annals of Internal Medicine* 111 (1989): 199–205.

59 Murphy, op. cit.

60 S. J. Youngner, 'Futility in context', *Journal of the American Medical Association* 264 (1990): 1295–6; S. J. Younger, 'Who defines futility?', *Journal of the American Medical Association* 260 (1988): 2094–5; S. H. Wanzer, S. J. Adelstein, R. E. Cranford, D. D. Federman, E. D. Hook, C. G. Moertel, P. Safar, A. Stone, H. B. Taussig and J. van Eys, 'The physician's responsibility towards hopelessly ill patients', *New England Journal of Medicine* 310 (1984): 955–9; P. J. Podrid, 'Resuscitation in the elderly: a blessing or a curse?', *Annals of Internal Medicine* 111 (1989): 193–5; B. Lo, 'Unanswered questions about DNR orders', *Journal of the American Medical Association* 265 (1991): 1874–5.

61 Tomlinson and Brody, 'Futility and the ethics of resuscitation', op. cit.

62 Council on Ethical and Judicial Affairs, American Medical Association, 'Guidelines for the appropriate use of do-not-resuscitate orders', *Journal of the American Medical Association* 265 (1991): 1868–71.

63 L. J. Blackhall, 'Must we always use CPR?', *New England Journal of Medicine* 317 (1987): 1281–5.

6

ICU Triage: the ethics of scarcity, the ideal of impartiality and the inadvertent endorsement of evil

Stuart F. Spicker

INTRODUCTION: SERIOUS RATIONING AND THE INTENSIVE-CARE UNIT

A number of ethical issues have recently emerged as a result of *informal rationing* of high-technology medicine including uneven patient access to intensive-care unit (ICU) services.

In 1989, Elisabeth Rosenthal of The *New York Times* noted that:

> Intensive care units across the country are overflowing, often crowded with hopeless patients who will derive no long-term benefit from their stays while short-changing the people they were intended to serve, critically ill patients who need temporary support to survive a medical crisis.[1]

Since hospital patients today are typically older and sicker, and since ICU technology enables many of them to be maintained on a variety of machines indefinitely, the burden on nurses, partly reflected in the nursing shortage, is severe. This additional pressure concerning human resources – the inadequate number of nurses – contributes to a high number of deaths of patients whose care is provided on the normal wards, but who would have benefited had they been admitted to or had they remained in the ICU, which in the average US hospital is running at 100 per cent capacity virtually all the time. However, the question remains whether or not *all* of these beds have been appropriately filled, i.e. whether the patients truly benefit from ICU care.

A hospital's ICU, of course, constitutes the principal locus where physicians, nurses, therapists and technologists typically work to save the lives of patients usually admitted *in extremis*. Indeed, in 1986 H. T. Engelhardt Jr and M. Rie[2] had already informed us that such care is a very costly, often very wasteful and medically futile, mode of medical intervention, though the US is notably a nation whose citizens continue to delude themselves into believing that economic burdens regarding the delivery of health care, including ICU care, do not really exist.[3] But the facts speak otherwise: it is not unusual for intensive care to account for 15–20 per cent of hospitals' operating budgets.

There is an argument for advocating a *patient-based* rather than a *societal-based* approach to shortage and *scarcity* – what I prefer to call *serious rationing*.

A patient-based approach is one that respects the choices of individual members of society, and enables them freely to choose among health care options for which they will pay, either directly out-of-pocket as the result of their labour or indirectly through other forms of social revenue acquisition to which they contribute in various ways. It is difficult to argue against this approach if one is committed, as I am, to the moral worth of citizens in a democratic polity.

Consider, as an illustrative example, an ethically problematic context – the ICU. Here I shall not merely assume that serious rationing under conditions of scarcity is already upon us, but I also believe it is important further to analyse the ICU ethical problematic in terms wherein the initial decision, for example, to *admit* a particular patient, does *not* typically permit communication and engagement with the patient in order adequately to determine his or her preferences beforehand. During admission to the ICU, such patient participation is frequently impractical. However, once admitted, patients could be queried on their values, for example:

> Do you wish to remain here at all, or for a short stay only, or for a longer stay, once I explain the prognostic probabilities and you fully understand them as well as your diagnosis? That is, do you prefer a short stay (life?) absent extensive and expensive life prolongation measures, or do you prefer a longer stay (life?) where the sky's the limit?

Of course, this conversation presumes virtually no shortage of ICU beds and the patient's awareness and decision-making capacity.

The reader may be familiar with (or have even used) a 'severity of illness' measure designed to determine objectively a patient's likelihood of survival, but such measures, in seeking so-called objectivity based on strictly clinical judgments of a patient's condition and prognosis, tend to ignore the patient's preferences and values, for example, how long to prolong or not to prolong the life of a particular individual in the ICU in terms of the values and preferences that patient holds and expresses.[4] As some have rightly stressed, *being alive*, mere survival, is not always the highest value or preference voiced by a patient, since chronic pain and suffering, extensive ICU followed by normal ward stay and quality of life considerations also must be weighed by the patient in making what is frequently a choice based on what it means to the patient to *have a life*, and not just remain alive.

In short, we can and must answer the question of how much ICU care should be provided to persons who not only could, but wish to benefit from such treatment. Moreover, we shall have to reconsider where properly to draw the line concerning who is and who is not to receive ICU treatment.

Since I believe that societies should avoid deceitfulness in responding to serious rationing (a serious worry if we decide to adopt social rationing schemes), and since patient preferences rarely coincide with physician preferences, it is quite difficult to determine or to rely on with confidence a patient's stated preferences in the highly emotionally charged ICU setting.[5] Thus we shall have to look more closely at ICU triage, especially *admission decisions* on the part of hospital physicians. This effort should enable us to see how, if at all, physicians and nurses may treat a particular set of patients *in extremis* fairly, justly, without deceit and especially without endorsing, being the instruments or 'gatekeepers' of, or being accomplices to a socially manifest evil. Indeed, the notion of *evil* has, perhaps, inadvertently been omitted from bioethical discussions for far too long. This is partly due, one might conjecture, to our preoccupation with good intentions, good fortune and the ends of fairness and justice.

SCARCITY, SORTING AND PATIENT ABANDONMENT

In order to develop my argument, I shall tentatively adopt a few premises at the outset: first, neither *health* nor *health care* are highly valued by most healthy members of society; second, any attempt to work to overcome the misfortune of others who might benefit from ICU services does *not* in itself logically entail the

STUART F. SPICKER

obligation to work to overcome *all* misfortune brought about by ill health; and third, that economic conditions of *scarcity* exist (regarding both material goods and human health care resources and services) is a reasonable working hypothesis, that is, a ubiquitous disproportionality obtains between medical judgment and patients' needs for imminent ICU services.[6]

Here I should not fail to point out that I shall be adopting the traditional triage model for sorting patients: first, those *in extremis* for whom treatment is medically futile, who are medically judged not to be expected to survive very long however much medical attention is provided, that is, those destined to die soon, but who, if treated, will require an enormous investment of dollars and other resources;[7] second, those not too seriously ill, but who have a potential for sudden deterioration and might benefit from ICU care, but who are quite likely to recover with 'normal ward' or 'step down' care, but without prolonged ICU attention; finally, the *morally most important priority group*, those who are clinically judged to require ICU care if they are to recover, but who, if they receive such care for a reasonable period of time, are (except in a few unavoidable cases where a triage error occurs) very likely to survive the traumatic episode and be discharged from hospital. What is most important for what follows is one additional assumption or hypothesis (what is for many hospitals already descriptive of their real world): that not all those in the *priority* group will be served, and therefore extensive suffering and abandonment (to let them die) is a certain outcome for them.

My thesis, then, is that the acceptance of abandonment (not treating many of those who would significantly benefit and recover) is not morally warranted or justified; that the withholding of ICU care for persons in the ICU priority group is not morally acceptable – that the acceptance of suffering, abandonment and the avoidable premature death of this proportion of ICU 'eligibles' entails at a minimum the tacit endorsement of suffering, premature death and *evil* – even if due to lack of adequate moral reflection and thus a truly inadvertent result, since most serious rationing is by default. Put another way, our society mistakenly but *truly believes* that being *impartial* by randomly selecting (by lottery) for treatment those patients in the priority group enables us all to remain morally blameless. (Here, of course, we should recall Bertrand Russell's distinction between having a true belief and *having knowledge*.)

94

THE IDEAL OF IMPARTIALITY: THE MORAL 'COP OUT'

The typically tri-fold sorting signalled by the term 'triage' (where tri-fold is in no way derived from 'triage', which is etymologically linked to the French *trier*, not *trois*) is actually practised today in a large number of US neonatal and other ICUs; indeed, it is not uncommon for US hospitals to 'code' patients admitted to the ICU by designating them with the numbers '1', '2' and '3' in order actually to apply the tri-fold distinction noted above. I hasten to add that these three classes are not always neatly circumscribed. That is, there are times when a patient's status (i.e., diagnosis and/or prognosis) is not easy to determine and the physician or nurse is not certain of the appropriate ICU classification. Sometimes the patient remains on the regular floor until he 'crashes'. Once the triage classification is determined, however, those in the priority group are supposed to be treated *impartially*, i.e., what is right for one person or group must be right for every similar person or group in similar circumstances; in our example the circumstances have been qualified by triage.

But this is problematic regarding ICU admission, for I know of no sound argument whose conclusion demands that we should be impartial – that deduces the moral injunction that we be impartial. Moreover, what would it mean to be impartial in the ICU context? As I have suggested, this will at least involve classifying and treating some but not others in the priority group, and not just simply not treating those who are hopelessly or terminally ill, having been given a poor prognosis for recovery. I should add that physicians are more and more likely to carry out what was not so long ago an unthinkable act: withdrawing or withholding critical care technology from certain patients by simply discharging them from the already overtaxed ICU. The upside of this is that the science of predicting who will survive and who will not survive ICU care has greatly improved, and physicians today can be more confident when they decide to withdraw or withhold intensive-care measures from patients who are unlikely to recover. Still, the decision to refuse to discharge a neocortically brain-dead (PVS, or deep coma) patient from the ICU is very problematic for physicians, part of the problem being due to the debate between the total brain dead versus the neocortically brain dead 'schools', i.e., whether one must wait either for confirmation of total brain death (including the entire

95

brainstem) or only confirm the diagnosis of neocortical necrosis in order to declare the patient dead. Here clinical objectivity and impartiality must take precedence, especially since laws in most countries require that *total* brain death be diagnosed, should brain criteria rather than traditional criteria for diagnosing death be relevant.

Returning from our digression, impartiality, i.e., *being* impartial, is frequently assumed to make for a just selection, where inclusion and exclusion from a class is judged prudentially necessary. When prospective ICU patients and their attending physicians are virtual strangers or at most casual acquaintances it is, of course, possible to treat them 'impartially'. But it may be a mistake to assume that such impartial treatment is appropriate in the ICU context; indeed, it may be important to acknowledge particular features of each patient that make psychological familiarity and equitable discretion essential to *each* patient's welfare. Hasn't the general public been critical of such impartiality in their search for the proper physician–patient relationship? Is it not ironic, with serious rationing facing us, to be asked to classify (triage) patients for admission to the ICU in a medically impartial manner by stressing their virtual *anonymity*? Such quandaries are formidable.

Here I might mention a very interesting proposal by Doctors H. T. Engelhardt Jr and M. Rie for determining the eligibility of prospective ICU patients for intensive care. It includes the suggestion that we undertake an intellectual exercise wherein we begin by thinking metaphorically, i.e., to cover ourselves against future unpredictable losses, we frequently elect to purchase various forms of *insurance*. To actually do so, of course, we must allocate our financial resources in as rational a way as possible, since insurance premiums all require an investment of the fruits of our labour, and we often wish to protect ourselves and our loved ones from the exigencies of an unpredictable and uncertain future. Applying this insurance metaphor to the allocation of material goods and human health care resources in, say, a hospital's ICU, we can ask our collective selves to think out just how important such ICU care is to us, given the likelihood of our future medical needs; we may then elect to purchase the appropriate level of health care insurance.

It is certainly just that we have a voice in the allocation of this and other health care resources, and I have no quarrel with this value as far as it goes. But we should note that Engelhardt and Rie's suggestion or thought experiment – the insurance metaphor – only enables us to determine, presuming we are successful, the *criteria* on the basis of which ICU admission (and expedited discharge) could be efficiently and *economically* determined. Their suggestion, which includes an *impartial* view of those directly affected, does *not* really help us to determine those *particular* patients who should and those who should not be assigned to the ICU *priority group*, but only to determine the *general profile* of those who should properly be assigned to (or are entitled to membership in) the priority group.[8]

At this point we have set the stage for a morally serious predicament: to what moral principle (or ethical theory) can we appeal to justify not treating everyone eligible for inclusion in the ICU priority group? In response to this question, I believe that Margolis's analysis[9] logically entails his important conclusion: the denial of treatment to those in the highest priority group cannot be justified on utilitarian, egalitarian or other traditional moral principles, including the impartiality principle, where a moral argument for patient selection must presume that the names of the patients are irrelevant since the names of those on the list are fungible or interchangeable. The paradox is, however, that while we quite easily treat our fellow man abstractly, having no difficulty accepting his or her anonymous misfortune, we also quickly acknowledge critical differences between our relations with our family members, intimate friends, immediate colleagues and sometimes our neighbours. How often does the nurse or physician demonstrate *partiality* towards patients whom they know personally? Isn't the physician and nurse expected to appreciate each patient's individuality? In doing so, don't they frequently make allowances in approaching them, or when classifying them as eligible for ICU services? Indeed, it seems that random patient selection (on to the priority group) by lottery for ICU treatment will not only not vindicate us ethically, it will not work practically or fairly either. Thus it may be inappropriate to rely on the principle of *impartiality* in ethics (a rather Kantian notion) since it is for many no longer viewed as a reasonable principle to apply in the hope of avoiding the apparent evil inherent in abandoning those persons in the priority group by the quick-claim deed of accepting their misfortune or their bad luck in the draw. Here we come to the core of my concern.

How may we avoid the unreasonable demand of those who would have us provide health care to all on the basis of a universal rights claim, irrespective of expenditure, and at the same time avoid ignoring those in the highest priority group who will be left untreated and condemned to premature death by the all too easy

STUART F. SPICKER

appeal to the psychological need to accept the misfortune of these 'abstract' others in the ICU? In short, I am dissatisfied with the line of argument that concludes that selecting patients under such conditions of scarcity, although surely unfortunate, is not also *unfair* and/or *unjust*. Indeed, upon further reflection such acceptance appears worse than unfair, since the issue before us is not identical to distributing limited goods not critical to human welfare, as we might distribute unhealthy foodstuffs, tobacco, cosmetics, etc. (I should add parenthetically that I cannot recall ever being accused of moral squeamishness in being ready, as I am, to acknowledge the personal sacrifices that necessarily follow from the unpleasantness of rationing; but *here* I believe we are compelled to reconsider a particular context that social policy can and perhaps must soon address.)

As you may have noticed, I have not said, nor have I even suggested, that the principal triage agents – physicians and nurses – are morally culpable here. Indeed, it is my belief that we are far better off not foisting on them the role of gatekeeper concerning those limited ICU beds designated for the priority group, an obligation that has fallen on them by default rather than by design. What we can, indeed must, do is confront at its source the *moral evil* we have identified (what for particular patients and families is personal tragedy), and set out to eliminate it from our future. This obligation falls to any society that deems itself a good society. Only by establishing innovative health policy (irrespective of all unsubstantiated claims to social entitlements or rights to health care) may we be in a position to intervene in the final outcome and appropriately provide ICU care to all patients medically belonging to the highest priority group. Once again, we must have surveyed and reassessed the economic landscape and in the process, we may, perhaps, skilfully apply the Engelhardt and Rie insurance metaphor.

The vexing issue with which I began, then, is one that requires nothing short of *social anticipation and innovative health policy*, not one that would benefit from further piecemeal tinkering by a few health care administrators or health professionals in a few hospitals' ICUs attending to a few patients.

OBJECTION AND CONCLUDING WORD

Objection: is it possible that the evil outcome of not treating the eligibly treatable can be avoided or dissolved before our eyes?

98

Surely we can discover a way morally to justify not treating those who would benefit from treatment in the ICU priority group other than the traditional appeal to the principle or ideal of impartiality, i.e., selecting patients for non-treatment on the basis of lottery, or, if that is unacceptable, on the basis of 'first come, first served'.

Suppose the citizens of a society, having fully understood this particular predicament, agree by social referendum or *contract* to accept, in each particular case, the luck of the draw under conditions of ICU priority bed scarcity. Suppose that we can all formally voice our assent *prior* to taking our respective chances should the time come to select persons for treatment and non-treatment in the ICU priority group. Surely we avoid blaming others for outcomes that are unavoidable when they are acceptable to us on the basis of our previous, but autonomous (contractual) decisions. Can we conclude, then, that the negative outcomes for the non-treated need only be unfortunate but not also unfair or evil by appealing to the autonomy of individuals expressed through specific referenda? Perhaps the contractarian will convince us that we can so conclude. Surely we have not had ample opportunity to voice our communal views on this and similar critical macro-allocational issues involving future social sacrifice. Furthermore, aren't such 'agreements' implicitly in force? Since we seem tacitly to agree that withholding an available but scarce life-saving resource from everyone would be morally reprehensible, isn't it quite fair to give what little we have to the few whom it will assist? What might one say to the following policy proposal already suggested in the extant literature: it is no longer permitted for surgeons to participate in transplantation of hearts to anyone in medical need, even if the patient has the financial means to pay out-of-pocket for such an intervention; that is, such expensive (two-tier) programmes shall be prohibited by legislation? On the other hand, what is morally wrong with maximising utility by giving our limited health care resources to a selected proportion of those in need, like those who need hearts, livers, lungs or admission to intensive-care units? Can we not be satisfied with utilitarian trade-offs here, and simply do the best we can for the greatest number of patients?

To raise these questions (and to suggest utilitarian criteria) is, in my view, to have inadvertently come full circle: that is, we have already tainted ourselves with evil, having tacitly, by default, accepted the status quo in failing to respect those patients whom we have elected to condemn to a premature death – patients whose names appear on proposed ICU admission rosters that may ironically (and perhaps unfairly and unfortunately) one day also include our own.[10]

ACKNOWLEDGEMENT

The author takes this opportunity to thank Richard J. Castriotta M.D. for his helpful suggestions following a careful and critical reading of the manuscript of this chapter.

NOTES

1 E. Rosenthal, 'Crowding causes agonizing crisis in intensive care', New York Times (22 August 1989): 17, 21.
2 H. T. Engelhardt Jr and M. A. Rie, 'Intensive care units, scarce resources and conflicting principles of justice', Journal of the American Medical Association 9 (1986): 1159–64. See also G. R. Winslow, Triage and Justice (Berkeley, Calif.: University California Press, 1982).
3 Rosenthal, op. cit.
4 M. Danis, et al., 'A comparison of patient, family and physician assessments of the value of medical intensive care', Critical Care Medicine 16 (1988): 594–600. And see D. Margolick, 'Patient's lawsuit says saving life ruined it', New York Times (18 March 1990): 1, 21.
5 J. F. Childress, 'Who shall live when not all can live?', in T. A. Shannon (ed.), Bioethics (Mahwah, NJ: Paulist Press, 1981): 501–15.
6 Rosenthal, op. cit.
7 Engelhardt and Rie, op. cit.
8 ibid.: 1162.
9 J. Margolis, 'Triage and critical care', in J. C. Moskop and L. Kopelman (eds), Ethics and Critical Care Medicine (Dordrecht: D. Reidel Publishing Co., 1985): 171–89.
10 Other important bibliographical references on which this essay has drawn include M. L. Bach, E. E. Bakkan and J. V. Toscano, 'Minnesota planners reject rationing', New England Journal of Medicine 321(16) (1989): 1130 (letter); N. K. Bell, 'Triage in medical practices: an acceptable model?', Social Science and Medicine 15-F (1981): 151–6; R. W. Chang, S. Jacobs and B. Lee, 'Use of APACHE II severity of disease classification to identify intensive-care-unit patients who would not benefit from total parenteral nutrition', Lancet 1 (28 June 1986): 1483–6. J. DeCecco, 'Is triage ethical?', Emergency 18(5) (1986): 60–3. H. T. Engelhardt Jr, 'Moral tensions in critical care medicine: "Absurdities" as indications of finitude', in Moskop and Kopelman, op. cit.: 23–33. J. D. Golenski and S. R. Blum, 'The Oregon Medicaid Priority-Setting Project [Report]: Conducted by Medical Research Foundation of Oregon' (Portland, Oregon: 1989), Bioethics Consultation Group, Berkeley, Calif., 1–18. T. Halper, The Misfortunes of Others: End-Stage Renal Disease in the United Kingdom (Cambridge: Cambridge

University Press, 1989). J. Kitzhaber (report), 'The Oregon Basic Health Services Act', (Salem, Oregon: Oregon State Senate State Capitol, 1989): 1–16. W. A. Knaus et al., 'APACHE II: a severity of disease classification system', Critical Care Medicine 13 (1985): 818–29. W. A. Kraus et al., 'Apache III prognostic system: risk perception of hospital mortality for critically ill hospitalised adults', Chest 100 (1991): 1619–35. J. M. Luce, 'Ethical principles in critical care', Journal of the American Medical Association 263(5) (1990): 696–700. J. E. Ruark et al., 'Initiating and withdrawing life support: principles and practice in adult medicine', New England Journal of Medicine 318(1) (1988): 25–30. R. B. Schiffer and B. Freedman, 'The last bed in the ICU: commentary', Hastings Center Report 7(6) (1977): 21–2. N. G. Smedira et al., 'Withholding and withdrawing of life support from the critically ill', New England Journal of Medicine 322(5) (1990): 309–15. S. F. Spicker, 'Rights, reasonable expectations, and rationing: a commentary on the essays of Ruth Mettheis and Baruch Brody', in H.-M. Sass and R. U. Massey (eds), Health Care Systems: Moral Conflicts in European and American Public Policy (Dordrecht: Kluwer Academic Publishers, 1988): 237–53. C. L. Sprung et al. (The Society of Critical Care Medicine Ethics Task Force), 'Society of Critical Care Medicine consensus statement on the ethics of forgoing life-sustaining treatments in the critically ill', Critical Care Medicine (1990). C. L. Sprung et al. (The Society of Critical Care Medicine Ethics Task Force), 'Attitudes of critical care medical professionals concerning forgoing life-sustaining treatments', Critical Care Medicine (1990). M. J. Strauss et al., 'Rationing of intensive care unit services', Journal of the American Medical Association 255(9) (1986): 1143–6. J. E. Zimmerman et al., 'The use and implications of do not resuscitate orders in intensive care units', Journal of the American Medical Association 255(3) (1986): 351–6. R. Zussman, Intensive Care: Medical Ethics and the Medical Profession (Chicago and London: University of Chicago Press, 1992).

7

From vision to system: the maturing of the hospice movement

Nicky James

INTRODUCTION

Idealism, enormous popular enthusiasm, vigorous growth and diversification are the hallmarks of the modern hospice. For a quarter of a century energetic community groups – schools, churches, women's groups, rotarians – have joined with major charities, NHS staff and eventually government to plan and finance a thirty–fold increase in hospice provision. The sense of local ownership, of 'our hospice', is crucial but intriguing. It suggests that in the late twentieth century British public imagination was and is sufficiently captured by a 'vision' to want to invest in a local death service. While life and death, mortality and morality are ancient enigmas they have contemporary manifestations.[1] Hospices are one such manifestation.

Questioning why modern hospices developed when they did and how they did is one way of examining death and the modern psyche. The canvas is enormous and the big philosophical and moral issues alluring. But as we face new solutions to the old chestnut of limited health resources universal concerns with dying and death become transposed to the mundane. Health policy is a means of transforming our management of death as the hospices move from the initial lively vision to systematic implementation. For despite the anguish and the comfort, the fear, pain and hope, the loneliness and spirituality, the loss and disbelief which accompany death, hospices and palliative care services have to take their place alongside all the other specialist health interests competing for priority, resources and skilled labour. A 'vision' may have given impetus to the growth of the hospices but it is their success which generates powerful economic, policy and social issues. The issues emerge in a variety of forms from testing ethical and cultural questions about the relation of hospice services to euthanasia, to government concerns about efficiency and organisational quandaries about how to give personal care from an institution. Underlying them all are our values about death and the changing principles by which we manage modern mortality.

To those whose faith and personal investment brought hospices into being, dispassionate reflection on policy can be felt as a betrayal of the humanity and personal nature of death, an example of the distancing of death from our society. However, using this chapter to explore changes in hospices offers an opportunity to examine the ways in which empathy and aspirations towards *euthanatos* – the good death – may become compromised.

This chapter is divided into three parts. The first section explains 'the vision' and suggests that in the early phase modern hospices offered a radical critique of the impersonal and medicalised management of death as well as being a counterbalance to the euthanasia movement. The second section explores how the 'hospice' has diversified and 'the vision' has become legitimised, and the final section looks at the tensions which the success of the hospice movement creates. In conclusion I speculate on what the hospices have offered us.

For the purpose of this essay it is convenient to divide developments in the hospice movement into three phases. The first, the pre-hospice phase is the postwar period until 1967 and the opening of St Christopher's Hospice. The second, the early hospice phase is from 1968–80; in 1980 three major evaluative events took place. The third phase, the current period, is from 1980 to the present.

THE VISION

'Visions' are intensely personal. If the circumstances are right a 'vision' can be shared by a committed group who become disciples and in turn share their 'vision' with others.[2] Though this 'hero' view of history is generally treated with scepticism, the story of one woman's vision and achievement has become a powerful, symbolic persuader for the hospice movement. The story which is part of hospice folklore is of Dr Cicely Saunders's shared experience with a patient. After an intense two-month friendship listening with David

103

Tamsa as he was mortally ill, the needs of the dying and their contribution to the living 'crystallised' for Saunders.[3] She in turn shared her aspirations for 'a home' with him, and on his death in 1948, he left her £500 in his will 'to be a window in your home'. It was the first donation to the home that opened as St Christopher's Hospice in 1967.

Like many of the case studies used by hospices to explain their work,[4] this oft-repeated story is intended to convey something of the depth of emotion, growth and hope that the dying can bring the living as well as explaining a source of Saunders's impetus to convert an ideal into a reality. The enlightenment of listening with the dying and hearing their manifold needs had a significance and power for early hospice planners that should not be underestimated. But part of the strength of 'the vision' derived from the positive, active caring which contrasted with fear and concern at the impersonal management of death. Understanding health care organisation and the public mood about death before hospices offered an alternative is a means of understanding the power of 'the vision' and also the enormity of the task.

Hospices as a radical critique of postwar terminal care

One interpretation of the development of the hospices is that the cumulation of a series of factors led to an active search and support for an 'alternative way of dying'.[5] The supportive rituals of the past identified by Aries had been eroded by the combined effect of industrialisation, 'civilisation' and 'soulless medicalisation' to the extent that Britain could be characterised as a 'death denying society'.[6]

While each of the factors considered below contributed to the development of the hospice movement, the opportunity for change arose from postwar circumstances that provided a framework and a willingness to challenge the status quo.

Rose and Rose[7] record that postwar developments in medical care enlarged areas of what was deemed to be relevant research. For the first time psychology was accepted as a legitimate part of medically organised study, together with biochemistry, biophysics, genetics and molecular biology. This has been interpreted as part of a massive medical expansionism which was a move to integrate 'support' with 'cure', 'compassion' with 'assessment' and saw 'the patient become a person', 'the feeling, thinking, subjective patient –

the whole person – becomes the new object of medical inquiry'.[8]

Arney and Bergen describe the effects of this change as leading to debates about the organisation of medicine and how it would consist of the health care team and support group networks 'deployed over a wide social space'.[9] The health care team aimed to 'individuate the whole person' and to be fully effective would give 'total care'.

These ideas are almost identically reflected in the organising principles of the hospices where the 'team' supports the 'individual' to achieve their own death with dignity by treating 'total pain' – that is social, spiritual, psychological and physical pain. It is notable that hospices too aimed to 'deploy over a wide social space' not through an expansion of medical professionalism, but by extending the services they offered by using volunteers and involving the clergy and social workers – all this as a means of meeting the requirements of 'total care'.

While the organisation of health care planning may have helped create an opportunity for change, it was personal experience, or rather impersonal experience, which generated the feeling that 'something must be done'. Postwar literature from a wide variety of sources suggested that death and dying raised fearful spectres. Such diverse literary artists as C. S. Lewis, Simone de Beauvoir, Vera Brittain and Noel Coward[10] wrote with feeling of the sorrowful death of someone they loved, while fiction writers brought these experiences to wider audiences.[11] Global accounts of the treatment of death from Ariès, Fulton and Elias,[12] disturbing research from academics such as Gorer, Sudnow, Glaser and Strauss and Cartwright, Hockey and Anderson[13] and the work of academic practitioners[14] serve as a reminder that it was individuals' grim experiences that gave impetus to the search for alternatives. The threat of unacknowledged pain, denial of opportunity to talk about dying, impersonal institutions and technologised death provided a focus for popular movements working to allow an individual to reclaim their own death.

Evidence from studies during this period show that there was good ground for fear. Sheldon,[15] writing in 1961, referred to 'human warehouses' and 'storage space for patients'. Work by Armstrong and Davies[16] in Britain and Quint Benoliel in the United States[17] suggests that nursing at that time was instrumental and routine – with the emphasis on hygiene rather than on the modern ideology of 'care'.[18] But Cartwright, Hockey and Anderson[19] showed that nine out of ten people spent at least part of the last year of their life living at home, so that it was domestic as well and institutional care that was problematic. In 1952 the joint National Survey on 'care of patients with cancer being nursed at home' highlighted problems in domiciliary care, referring to people living in 'appalling conditions', 'often short of the right sort of food, warm clothing and bedding'.[20] It was clear that death, and especially death from cancer, caused fear of pain, isolation and abandonment.

More encouraging were techno-medical developments. Doctors could offer new hope to some, but were also increasingly challenged to consider their responsibilities as intermediaries between life and death. As a matter of real concern delegates from the International Congress of Anaestheologists questioned Pope Pius XII: 'Does the anaesthesiologist have the right, or is he [sic] bound in all cases of deep unconsciousness, even those that are considered comparatively hopeless, to use modern artificial respiration equipment?'[21] The Pope's response was that 'life, health, all temporal activities are in fact subordinated to spiritual ends',[22] but he also asserted that 'the task of determining the exact instant of death is that of the physician'.[23] However erudite the professional debates, the ethical implications of the new technology were matters of widespread concern. Terse phrases about 'pulling the plug' and 'spare part surgery' conveyed something of the public ambivalence about the new techno-medical opportunities. In the 1970s, the reports of 'brain-dead' Karen Ann Quinlan and her family, subsequently published as *Karen Ann Quinlan; Dying in an Age of Eternal Life*,[24] exemplified this concern with newly-exposed dilemmas of life and death. The reports were disturbing on two counts. First, at an abstract level they raised legal and moral questions about what we mean by 'life' and 'death'. Second, and much more distressing, was the anguish of the family in their conflict with caring professionals – a conflict resolved only in court. *Re Quinlan* highlighted the direct connection between legal definitions and heart-rending decisions about life, and death. It is perhaps unsurprising that in the atmosphere of uncertainty about who had the power of decision in these matters, legal enforcement of 'the living will' was increasingly advocated in the United States. In Britain the Voluntary Euthanasia Society (VES) grew.

Though the VES was formed in Britain in 1935 it expanded enormously in the 1970s and early 1980s – a period in which hospice ideas began to take effect. When the second Euthanasia Bill was introduced to the British House of Commons in 1969 hospice and euthanasia groups were well used to joint debate, and the two groups have continued their discussion both formally in government proceedings[25] and informally in newsletters and other exchanges.[26]

The most frequently cited reason for joining the VES in 1980 was 'to be able to control myself in the circumstances of my own death'.[27] This appeared to arise from the observed powerlessness of the dying, so that advocates of euthanasia like hospice supporters had identified the inadequacy of services for the terminally ill. As Saunders said of their common purpose, 'both sides in the debate have a vendetta against pointless pain and impersonal indignity'.[28]

While both hospices and euthanasia supporters were concerned to make death personal and to give it meaning, their underlying philosophies differed. Instead of ensuring an individual's control of the timing of death as legalised euthanasia would do, the hospices aimed through good example and education to show that dying can be a positive part of living. From this perspective, death with dignity involves the relief of physical symptoms to encourage human potential for creativity despite the formidable nature of the occasion. Hospices emphasised humans as social beings able to make their lives meaningful through interaction with others, while also emphasising the potential and responsibility communities have for offering support.

While welcoming the hospices, the Voluntary Euthanasia Society was clear that they could not adequately fulfil every individual's physical and mental needs.[29] The contribution of the euthanasia movement to bringing 'death denied' into the open could thus be said to be a brutal, if hopeless realism. For every successful 'case study' offered by early hospices in support of their cause, the Voluntary Euthanasia Society could counter with one of distress and pain. The euthanasia movement's arguments have served as a reminder of the obstacles to reinterpreting dying and death in terms of growth and success, instead suggesting that, for some, living is so unbearable that death is preferable. Without the inclusion of euthanasia debates the enormity of hospice aims are diminished. For what hospices are aiming to achieve is care of the dying that is so effective that, to quote Saunders again, 'no-one should reach that desperate place where he could only ask for his life to be ended'.[30]

Connections between developments in medical technology, the influence of the euthanasia supporters and the hospices were noted by Saunders, who believed in the need for an alternative to euthanasia and to the impersonal medical interventions:

The spread of generally applicable knowledge was especially called for at a time when on the one hand many demanding active treatments were becoming technically possible and on the other the Voluntary Euthanasia Society was working to make legal the option of a quick death for any patient with an incurable illness considered likely to cause distress.[31]

Of relevance both to the euthanasia movement and to the hospices was the ageing population. As people live longer, so they are more likely to die of cancer and to need institutional care. Despite common misconceptions cancer was and is a disease predominantly of older people. Nevertheless, cancer was perceived as a terrifying disease striking randomly at the young, so when 'the vision' made care for cancer patients a particular focus it offered hope to young and old. It also directly confronted the taboo on talking about cancer.

In summary, although there is evidence that Saunders's and St Christopher's Hospice played a significant symbolic and practical role in making 'the vision' real, the 'hero' view of history is inadequate on its own. Demographic, medical, legal and attitudinal change set the context in which realising 'the vision' became possible.

Vision – the early phase

If the context was set, the debates in progress and the terminology available, it was the hospice ideals, that is 'the vision', their presentation and the alacrity with which they were accepted and developed that was the real mark of the early phase of the hospices. The essence of the early 'vision' was synthesised in Saunders's explanation of 'What is St Christopher's Hospice', of which the first three points were:

1 St Christopher's Hospice is a Christian Foundation, ecumenical and practical, searching for God's plan for its work and development.
2 It is a medical foundation, seeking to offer the best professional standards of care to patients with chronic and terminal pain, both in its wards, and in their own homes, especially, though not exclusively, to those with advanced malignant disease.

3   It is a community of people gathered together to welcome and help the whole family during such illness and after the patient's death.[32]

St Christopher's became not *a* model hospice, but *the* model hospice, 'the final step in the synthesis of the modern form of hospice' in Britain and throughout the world.[33] The joining of the medical and spiritual foundations to generate a particular sense of community with high standards of care directed towards cancer sufferers were key aspects which were replicated in many subsequent hospice services. The 'vision' offered was of 'an approach',[34] a 'concept of care',[35] a 'movement'[36] and, for Stoddard,[37] a 'caring community'. Corr and Corr[38] referred to it as a 'philosophy not a facility'. The strength of 'the vision' was that it offered not just an idea but the means of implementing it both at an individual and an organisational level.

'Total pain' was a key concept and listening to the dying was the only way to identify all the pains. While physical pain in particular has an immediacy which tended to mean that symptom control was accorded primacy, social, psychological and spiritual pain were given a legitimacy uncommon during the 1970s. 'Individual patient assessment', now commonplace, had a significant impact then in setting standards about dealing with each and every pain in fine detail. With the patient, as the 'leader of the team',[39] and the family, 'the unit of care' with the patient at the centre, a sense of the significance of each individual was conveyed as well as a refreshing explicitness about the interpersonal difficulties families faced in coming to terms with death in a period of 'death denied'.

The ideal was for the patient, with their family, to be given the opportunity to emphasise the 'living' that was left and to choose their own dying. Through the creation of an atmosphere of hope and support and a willingness to try out what patients were asking for – whether it was fish and chips, a night out at a party or the chance to die at home – it was life rather than death that was the essence of hospice care, though death was not denied. Once a family is truly integrated into decision-making and caring, the needs of the bereaved are more easily recognised, and so the hospice vision of the good death went beyond the moment of death through the first year of mourning.

It is easy to understand that the 'total pain' of patients and families demands a response such as 'total care'. This in turn meant that no single aspect of the 'total pain' was the duty of a particular specialist group, for everyone was recognised as having a contribution to make when they had a relationship with the patient. A prerequisite of dealing with 'total pain' was to be able to speak about the unspeakable, cancer and death. It also demanded a response to family fears and tensions, and being close enough to the patient to be their 'family' if they had no one else.[40] If a patient chose to open their heart to a hospice cleaner it necessarily meant that the cleaner was an important part of the caring team, and so everyone became involved in the responsibilities of 'total care'. These demands in turn required a rethinking of the traditional professional distance between patient and doctor or nurse and meant that the professionals themselves needed 'support'. To facilitate communication between professionals – poor communication often being described as being a cause of piecemeal rather than holistic patient care – team members had to recognise each others' skills in terms of patient needs rather than in terms of their established hierarchies.

All these factors meant creating a different kind of 'team'. Staff had to create the atmosphere, make 'the home' of the symbolic vision, so not only did traditional hierarchies and professional preciousness have to be overcome, but the team needed to be broadened to deal with the 'total pain'. Clergy, social workers, volunteers, the family dog, as well as health care specialists, were to be integral to the organisation, not just marginal extras to be brought in when necessary. Furthermore, the practice of medicine itself needed realignment, with a philosophy of 'care' rather than 'cure' meaning that staff had to relearn their prognostic skills in a way that accepted the consequences of chronic illness and death in young and old.

Finally, there was the recognition of the need for research and education. Perhaps it is these two elements which best suggest the early emphasis placed on 'spreading the message' and the planned intention to change practice on a wide scale. It is this element which is also said to distinguish the 'modern hospice' from those already in existence.

Presentation of 'the vision'

And so it was that 'the vision', like all visions, was an uplifting and inspiring message. The presentation of case studies with photographs illustrating dying patients transformed to active, pain-free participants in their social world were a way of highlighting hospice aims, keeping the message personal while serving to show the value of hospice services. At conferences, local groups, in journals and papers and on television, those speaking had the power of their personally-felt convictions. They offered a sense of a future to be strived for, and the active portrayal of dying as a time of growth for those involved overcame the negative taboo on talking about death. For many the faith was rooted in their Christianity as well as their aspiration to improve terminal care.

For the most part information given about hospice aims was highly prescriptive and derived from a handful of charity-status, purpose-built, renowned centres of excellence. Looking back at some of the literature from the early hospice phase,[41] the freshness, drive and uncritical naivity are in contrast to the more recent studies.[42] Unintentionally the early hospice literature created for some a new and equally illusory version of 'death denied'.[43] It was possible to get the impression that somehow hospices could make death acceptable and could take away the 'total pain' which includes sorrow and loss and the restrictions of illness and old age.

So the early hospice 'vision' emerged from individuals' personal convictions to become a descriptive ideal, dedicated, critical of former practice and with the intention of disrupting former patterns of care of the dying. Committed to listening to patients, to perceiving death as a time of growth, to offering an alternative to euthanasia by providing skilled, compassionate care for people dying of cancer, hospice aspirations were on a grand scale and the need for 'the vision' to be taken up was pressing. Nevertheless, the success of this proselytising could hardly have been anticipated.

THE SYSTEM

To those who have observed the proliferation of hospice services with disquiet, the idea that the current hospice phase is one of increasing systematisation may appear ludicrous.[44] Yet since 1980 the influence of national and publicly accountable groups has grown, creating a national hospice framework even while the 'vision' continues to carry the power to inspire new projects outwith the framework.

New schemes, new teams

Both individual and group 'vision' have been vital, for the collective power of personal commitment was the initial source of innovation and dynamism. It is a movement which has been taken forward by a handful of notable individuals and their immediate supporters, but more than that it has appealed to millions of people who have raised and continue to raise millions of pounds towards the building and upkeep of hospices, and the thousands of volunteers who make hospice work possible. It has generated national pressure groups with regional networks to put its point of view, and it has had government and health authority support. This prolific effort is a reflection of massive public support and of a demand-led service.

In 1967, when St Christopher's 'modern' hospice opened, there were a few Catholic hospices already in existence in Britain and Eire, together with the nineteen beds allocated in the Royal Cancer Hospital London (established 1909), the ten Marie Curie homes opened in 1952–3[45] and the education given by the National Society for Cancer Relief. By 1982, fifteen years later, there were 139 hospice services of various kinds. In 1991, only nine years later, the St Christopher's Hospice Information Service Directory of Hospice Services listed almost 430 existing hospice services with a further twenty-nine planned.[46]

A form of 'standard' classification became one means of monitoring services. Key divisions are now listed by beds available (almost 2,700 in 1991) and by hospice in-patient care (159 – of which 100 are independently registered charities), home-care services (321), hospital support teams (140), day hospices (151), overseas (forty countries) and education.[47]

This system, however, obscures almost as much as it reveals because the combinations of different services, with variations in remit, personnel and resourcing are enormous. Some hospices consist of a group of home-care nurses working in liaison with general practitioners, some started with medically-directed in-patient facilities and gradually developed home-care services, education and day support and others offer day care only. At some hospices bereavement services are offered by co-ordinated volunteers on a regular follow up, in others a 'bereavement visit' is made once or twice by a nurse and others have no bereavement service at all. In Wales, seven 'mini-units' were developed in cottage hospitals where two to three beds were designated for terminal care when necessary, whereas other in-patient units vary from five to sixty-two beds. Some services are nurse led, some are doctor led and at others decision-making is equally shared among nurse, doctor and social worker. Some home-care services offer 24-hour medical and nursing cover, whilst others are advice services with one nurse available during office hours. Most hospices require GP or hospital doctor approval to accept a referral, and some only accept referral from their own hospital. A few hospices are specific to AIDS patients, many hospices accept patients for respite care and some have patients with motor neurone disease or multiple sclerosis, though the vast majority of beds are for people with malignant disease. A network for paediatric advice is growing, and there are three hospices specially for children. Some services cover hundreds of square miles of sparsely populated rural land, and others a few square miles of urban conurbation. The vast majority are free, though welcoming donations, but a few charge.

As the services have proliferated, so have the titles and specialities associated with hospices. 'Terminal care' has become 'palliative medicine' which from 1988 became a sub-speciality recognised by the Royal College of Physicians as offering a medically acceptable career path. Hospices, too, have become known by other names such as 'continuing care units' and 'cancer care units' for a variety of reasons, one of which was to offer a more positive image of 'care' than the 'death house' image. 'Home-care services' are also known as 'domiciliary services', and 'hospital support teams' are known as 'symptom control/support teams', 'pain control teams' or 'Macmillan support teams'. Doctors are 'medical directors', 'associate specialists', 'medical supervisors' and 'physicians in palliative medicine'. Specialist advisers and counsellors are one of the more recent developments with nurses appointed specifically to support children with cancer and their families, radiotherapy patients or those with breast cancer.

Although not all variations are covered in these descriptions, they give an idea of the diversity of facilities which go under the name of 'hospice' – a diversity which in practice makes it difficult to specify hospice services available and still more difficult to specify outcomes.[48] So while from early on it was argued that hospices must be relevant to their locality, the patchwork of services obscure identification of what it is they are collectively achieving relative to the early hospice aims.

Diversification and legitimation

It is a peculiarity of the 1980s in the hospice movement that while the 'vision' with all its early innocence still has a compelling appeal which brings in new disciples, established services face the shift from striving aspiration to maintenance. They have to cope with regular staff turnover, their reputation as 'a place where people die', the problem of a succession of medical directors, and people becoming involved in hospices not because they see it as a great plan for the future, but because they want a career or need a job. This is an inevitable part of the ageing of any organisation and creates the impetus necessary to consolidate existing services.[49]

While consolidation is built on the assurance of experience, it poses different kinds of risk or challenge – those of maintenance of standards, routinisation and professionalisation. The two research reports on the hospice conference for 1980 help shed some light on this process for they were the first systematic reflections of hospice developments on any scale. The reports are discussed below, and the conference in the next section (p. 119).

Scepticism of the 'status quo' and its ability to tolerate innovation meant the early hospices were established outwith the mainstream system. As Taylor's relatively early analysis (1983) of hospices suggests:

For a number of reasons, hospices do value their independence outside the NHS. Not only has it given them the opportunity to develop their own models of care, which have subsequently been influential, but also it has enabled them to establish standards of excellence against which other forms of provision can be measured, and it has provided a useful base for training and research.[50]

The implication of this is that the NHS restricted development of care, training and education, and found it hard to establish standards of excellence. Hospices therefore have reason to be wary of how 'the vision' fares upon reintegration into mainstream health systems, yet the 1980 Wilkes Report shows that policy-makers were increasingly wary of over-enthusiastic visionaries.

The Wilkes Report was the result of a Working Group on Terminal Care.[51] Its most famous recommendation was that a large increase in hospice in-patient facilities was inappropriate. Instead greater dissemination of principles was preferred, so that the primary care sector (GP services), the hospital sector and the hospice movement might become better integrated. The report did not elicit the hoped-for response. Local initiatives for purpose-built in-patient units were carried forward by 'the vision', and an array of local groups established themselves as independent charities and built 'their hospice' anyway. Provided hospices fulfil the criteria of nursing homes' registration procedures and inspections, there is no restriction or accountability for what goes on in them. On a national scale, this became a matter of some concern. A government circular in 1987 instructed health authorities to draw up their plans for care of the terminally ill, and by the end of the decade, in 1990, the pressure group 'Help the Hospices' was urging health authorities only to give funding to those voluntary hospices which complied with the plan. Far from encouraging work 'outside' the system, the pressure group was urging greater conformity with it. To assist in the process they produced a set of hospice definitions and standards. So despite Taylor's observation on the need to develop standards outwith the NHS, by 1990 Help the Hospices noted: 'NHS support for the voluntary hospice sector can play a vital role ensuring that comprehensive services are available, and in raising and maintaining good and appropriate standards'.[52] This change of emphasis to dependence on an established system to ensure standards raises the question of actual standards relative to the initial hospice aims. In the rapid growth, some hospices have not delivered what they initially promised. As economic constraints on health authorities increase, the question of 'standards' and compromise will inevitably affect hospices as it affects other services. For instance, where cleaning services have been contracted out and staff turnover increased hospice cleaners are unlikely to be as integral a part of the team as early aspirations suggested.

The second report of significance in 1980 was by Lunt and was presented to the First National Conference on Hospice Finance and Administration in London in 1981.[53] It was the result of a survey of regional distribution of hospice provision, and indicated wide variations. Lunt also made calculations about the number of beds necessary for a given population, and the number of 'home nurses' necessary to support those at home. The same year Lunt carried out his fieldwork, Cancer Relief committed an extra 2.5 million pounds to expanding its domiciliary Macmillan nursing teams and by 1990 there were nearly 800 Macmillan nurses acting as a resource to hospital and community staff and helping to plug the main gaps in differential provision.[54] This development raised questions as some hospice advocates feared that it might be a 'dilution' of full hospice services, while some GPs and district nurses felt their role and their skills with the dying were being undermined. The need to monitor and support the growing number of 'palliative care' staff coincided with the 1987 government circular to health authorities demanding a plan for 'terminal care'. Cancer Relief, in negotiation with thirteen of the fourteen health authorities in England sought to establish posts, which are essentially co-ordinating and development posts, for a 'Regional Nurse in Continuing Care'. And so it is that as the hospices have spread their message and their influence, it has also become necessary for the hospices to adapt to changing demands for resources and the changing context of health resource allocation.

Accountable money

Had financial viability been a primary concern, the early hospices would not have opened, for innovative schemes are a financial risk. Yet while capital costs may be the initial headache, it is revenue costs that bring projects down. Now hospices have to jostle with other specialities when arguing that revenues must be maintained to ensure service quality. Help the Hospices notes: 'Hospice care is a high cost service and can only be delivered satisfactorily and effectively at high cost even with the help of volunteers.'[55] They go on to note that the future of 'good hospice care' depends on whether public services will want to buy the services and how much they will be prepared to pay. There must surely be tensions for health authorities as they are offered the choice of expensive hospice beds or the compromise of a cheaper though less specialised service in some spare hospital beds. The choice is not easy and the dilemmas for health planners allocating restricted resources are genuine. It requires hard reflection to justify five nurses on a shift with sixteen hospice patients when the local elderly care unit has three nurses for twenty patients.

In the new health world purchasers have great power over providers, and arguments over why high trained-staff:patient ratios must be sustained will require sophisticated arguments. The need for adequate quantities of drugs used on day and night shifts on in-patient units and covered by the Dangerous Drugs legislation is one argument for keeping up the staff:patient ratios. Another is the importance of continuity of care at such a vulnerable time in

116

people's lives. It means that experienced staff, skilled in psycho-social as well as physical care, fulfil each patient's needs themselves. The alternative is a task allocation system, probably hierarchial, where untrained staff carry out some elements of patient care but trained staff carry out other aspects, such as assessment of need, information giving or cleaning wounds. Yet high trained-staff: patient ratios lead to expensive salary bills and occasionally to an overprovision of staff since patient numbers and dependency levels are unpredictable. Yet if hospice nurses are treated merely as an expendable part of a general nursing workforce, moved here and there to fill in staff shortages on other wards, the sense of 'special-ness' and clarity of hospice purpose is diminished.

The initial hand-to-mouth financing of hospices has had to be-come more systematic. Early incomes derived from a combination of funding systems, including prayer, endowment, paid fund-raising and charitable donations, though during the 1980s public monies became increasingly important. With increasing public funding comes increasing accountability, and the need to explain what is being achieved.[56] And while many supporters agree it is vital to use research to verify hospice claims, it is a moot point whether research instruments and outcome measures are yet refined enough to be relevant gauges of the intangibles such as the feelings, the spirituality, the sense of community growth which hospices left the mainstream system to develop. With moves towards fifty:fifty voluntary:government contributions to hospices (the 'pound for pound' system) it is unsurprising that the government is 'support-ing' research into palliative care standards,[57] yet we also know that necessary research 'measures' are in their scientific infancy. While there is some hope that Britain will not go the same way as America,[58] it is worth bearing Kastenbaum's dictum in mind: 'The good death will be determined by its cost efficiency indicators running through a bureaucratic formula.'[59]

Hill and Oliver[60] point out that under new health evaluation systems such as QALYS (Quality Adjusted Life Years) the hospices have nothing to offer and emerge as an undeserving cause. So as hospices are poised at what is probably the peak of their growth, carrying with them a measure of our social investment in death, they are subject to the crude indicators by which we decide on the distribution of resources.

Prior's neat phrase that death is 'physically bounded but socially defined'[61] encapsulates social essence within physical determinants.

117

In practice it is the social parameters surrounding death which pose as much of a challenge as the physical effects. If the initial, disruptive aims of changing the system of terminal care were to be achieved, it was necessary that the hospices acquire legitimacy and systematic support both nationally and within the mainstream health care system that would make the knowledge and services available to everyone, not just the few living in the right areas. Only a system developed outwith the NHS generated the impetus to challenge the practice of the mainstream services, but as the movement has grown so the forms hospices take have diversified and expectations and standards vary. At the same time hospices are increasingly making claims on the national system for core funding, a claim which brings with it a greater standardisation than hospices founded on 'the vision' have been used to.

THE TENSIONS OF SUCCESS

The challenge issued by the early hospices was radical – to change the care of the dying. Now the hospice vision is familiar, hospices are having to confront the conundrums of their success. They face challenges of a new kind as they move from striving to establish themselves to becoming part of the establishment. The source of the challenge is twofold. First, the quest from within the movement is how optimally to manage the organisational transition from youthful enthusiasm to realistic maturity without losing the 'vision'. The second challenge is from outside and comes from the conservatism and conformity of the biomedical system which the early hospices had to escape in order to develop.

Challenge from within

Hospices like other charities and health interventions are part of fashion cycles. In time the lively public support the hospices have enjoyed over the last twenty years will wane and so they must respond and change to ensure their survival. The good will, long hours and strenuous money-raising efforts of the pioneer staff and volunteers as they strived to do something new and exciting cannot be sustained in the same way by the third-, fourth- and fifth-generation staff. For these staff, many of them young, will never have known a world without 'the vision' of the modern hospice, where doctors rarely spoke of cancer and death and where teamwork was not part of health care rhetoric. Regardless of their drive and commitment, hospices for them will not represent the scintillating breakthrough that offered so much hope and such a sense of urgency twenty-five years ago.

More than that, as hospices have come of age, staff are having to learn to compromise as they struggle to keep pace. The preparatory courses and in-house training of the early years, in which new staff learned of the hospices' philosophy and the skills that were expected of them, have disappeared in some units, though are more thoroughly established in others. *In extremis*, agency nurses are used by some hospices even while the medical cover is improving in others. An innovative medical Diploma in Palliative Medicine started in Cardiff in 1990 but at another hospice student nurse training status was withdrawn because the nursing care in the unit was deemed to be too 'task'-oriented. None of this is to decry the manifold achievements of the hospices, rather it is to draw attention to the different challenges of establishing a 'vision' and maintaining a system.

The 1980 'Bar Mitzvah' St Christopher's Conference completes the trio of evaluative events in that year.[62] The Parliamentary Under-Secretary of State for the DHSS helped celebrate hospice achievements as the conference participants considered the successes, weaknesses and future. Sir George Young welcomed the service the hospices had rendered the country in identifying the needs of the dying and promoting the understanding, knowledge and skills necessary to improve their lives. He noted the high quality care and the way in which hospices were expanding their community services, complementing existing health provision. But at that conference and since, other challenges were identified, challenges in which critical reflection on hospice principles has had to take place in conjunction with organisational issues.

Long recognised as a problem in the implementation of 'the vision' has been the sustained focus on cancer patients. Although a vast amount of the financial, educational, clinical and moral support for 'the vision' came from cancer charities, in particular the Cancer Relief Macmillan Fund (formerly the National Society for Cancer Relief) and to a lesser extent the Marie Curie Foundation, hospices and their policy-makers exercised their own self-censorship. Despite claims a decade ago from hospice advocates that the hospice concept should be applied to 'a much broader segment of medicine',[63] the specialist skills of hospice staff are still appropriated

119

mainly for people with malignancies. The lack of response seems to be a sign of growing comfort and domesticity, a settling of the hospice role and a measure of the slowing down of the momentum for innovation.

Associated with the hospice emphasis on terminal illness and cancer have been debates over the best types of service to provide. Should care of the dying be managed by specialists or by 'general' health-workers with a specialist interest in terminal care? The first option means the consolidation of yet another health care specialism in which experts refine their skills by serving only one, highly specific type of patient. In this option the potential for 'bands of people marching up the garden path' each offering their own particular speciality is not so far-fetched. The second option follows a generalist model in which staff take a 'special interest' in terminal illness, while retaining their availability to more people, some of whom will not be terminally ill. In this option it is unlikely that staff skills will ever be as well developed as those of the specialist for they do not have the same opportunity to concentrate their effort. Either option has implications for the future of the hospices and their service, education and research functions. Consideration of these options raises questions of whether hospices should seek to maintain their reputation as innovators, actively leading a medical field into new concerns and areas, or whether they should adjust their role to one of maintaining services for the known 10 per cent of terminally ill cancer patients who face problems of symptom control.

Also to be faced are apparently more mundane but equally testing issues of allocating resources. Questions concerning resource allocation are inextricably linked to the values and aspirations upon which the service is founded. With analyses of costs and skills come questions about how appropriate it is, when there are limited funds, for an expensive nurse to 'befriend' a person imprisoned in loneliness in their home. In terms of 'total care', humanity and death with dignity, it makes perfect sense. But in terms of allocating staff it raises the vexed question of whether a five-star service should be available to a few or a lesser service to greater numbers.

A fourth and final challenge is the problem of succession – should 'the vision' be sustained and if so how should it be done through successive generations and types of staff. As the staffing of units changes from the original 'devotees', one of the difficulties is how to raise staff consciousness about the 'differentness' of the hospice approach without appearing to be 'prissy moralists'.[64] While those who have become disciples of hospice ideals have long been urged not to follow the ideals slavishly, lack of clarity about the purposes of hospices and lack of knowledge of the criticisms which brought them into being will dilute the hospice message, and compromise the practice. Though initially hospices had to maintain a separateness of purpose and philosophy in order to clarify their aims and refine their practice, this separateness creates a problem of exclusiveness – of making services available only by the few 'specialist' staff to the relatively few, carefully selected patients. Integration with mainstream health services, therefore, appears to be vital, but it necessarily raises questions of compromising the initial hospice aspirations for managing 'total pain'.

Adapting to the status quo

Early hospices were to some extent exclusive and excluding. To join them staff had to become part of them and take on the 'vision'. If you didn't like it you left. But as the 'separateness' of the hospices diminishes, so does the protective barrier that it offers to the purity of the ideals. In its place comes a different protection, the protection of being part of the establishment, for as Miles, quoted by Punch, observes, 'No Utopia can afford its members the solid security provided by the established order.'[65]

As the hospices move back into the mainstream by becoming increasingly dependent on state funding, by setting up central controlling systems and by conforming to mainstream professional career paths, they do so for their own protection as well as fulfilling part of their stated aim to 'influence others'. Hence the old influences, some of which the hospices sought to escape, are reasserted. The early hospice amateurism has given way to a professionalism. But as reintegration into the mainstream health systems continues, professionalism is increasingly associated with professionalisation and all that is associated with 'professionals' – be they doctors, nurses, managers, social workers or other specialists in our predominantly biomedical health system.

Hospice proposals for change in the multidisciplinary team were genuinely radical, attempting to widen ideals about 'the caring team' and break down inter- and intra-professional hierarchies in order to achieve 'total care'. Yet each health care discipline has a long history of protecting its own interests and intra- and inter-professional

121

hierarchies are strong. An historical perspective suggests that the two most resilient manifestations of biomedical health services will be the professional territories and the emphasis on the physical rather than the psychosocial. If the old professional traditions assert their authority over hospice principles of teamwork and are coupled with new pressures of accountability and resource allocation, the effect is likely to be the medicalising of hospices and the remedicalising of care of the dying.[66]

In 1980 Eric Wilkes suggested that hospices should be 'planning for our own obsolescence', an obsolescence based on passing vital clinical and counselling skills on to professional colleagues. Further he advocated: 'a competent deprofessionalisation of care led by professionals exceptionally competent in their field, who will carry the hospice approach . . . throughout the health service'.[67] Instead, the quantity of specialist buildings, finance, doctors, nurses, social workers, administrators, fund-raisers, tutors and co-ordinators has burgeoned, even while staff have become more precise about what they can realistically achieve. So not only has the specialism grown apace, but the specialisations within the specialism have consolidated. Each now boasts its own interest group, and each clarifies its specific expertise, development needs, career path and, inevitably, its authority. Even the disturbing analogy of the family triumvirate[68] as it relates to health care, with father, mother, child becoming doctor, nurse, patient, is commandeered as administrators see themselves as head of the family: 'The father is the Administrator. He is the provider of resources and the organiser of support. He knows the patient and sees that they are welcomed and cared for.'[69] Naive though this may be, it is an illustration of how hospices, professionals and the health care system can patronise patients as the organisation takes over. There is already evidence of professional realignment in hospice organisation; in place of the current diversity of hospice teams a more standard 'core team' will emerge. The pressure group 'Help the Hospices' emphasises the need for in-patient services to have constant clinical supervision from doctors and so we may observe hospices' increasing conformity to mainstream patterns of staffing and responsibility. Some will consider this to be a realistic reassertion of appropriate standards; while others, conscious of the traditional power relations and professional self-interest, may see it as a loss of opportunity to experiment with new types of team for the patient's benefit.

Similarly, re-evaluation of the limits on staff time and skills may be part of a new realism or a way compromising hospice ideals. In the early years of the 'modern' hospice, the idea that staff would be 'friend' or 'family' if that was required, was strong. But with the greater understanding of the skills and knowledge necessary to offer effective psychosocial support it becomes clear that the appropriate training is extensive, and that expert staff are an expensive 'professional' commodity. Such a reassertion of professional skills tends to stretch the notion of being 'family' or 'friend' to their limit. Instead of being happy to spend time chatting about the progress of the local football team or the difficulty of buying good bread, paid staff become time-limited. Patients are astute at noticing 'time' allocations, and while they may be appreciative of the 'care-full' attention they receive, they may not feel a swift, skilful and supportive assessment as being of the same essence as 'friendship'. 'Befriending' may become an expensive, optional extra, delegated to volunteers or other agencies.

With growing professionalisation comes careerism and professional development. Inevitable though these may be, they bring about a change in emphasis. The early hospice pioneers who believed passionately in the importance of their mission took it up without any assurances for their futures. These pioneers are being, and will be replaced by those who, albeit committed to their specialist discipline, work in a now established specialism and look for peer credibility and recognition in pay, status, research and career prospects. Traditionally the biomedical system emphasises the physical. Hospice services which initially strived for a balance of 'total care' may observe the primacy of physical interventions re-emerge.

In a fascinating paper entitled 'What do hospices do?', Johnson et al. note that there is much variation in the ways in which hospice care is delivered. However, they also noted that where there is a full-time medical director the hospice is more likely to make use of 'invasive procedures and patients are more likely to be referred for palliative surgery and organ donation'.[70] Johnson et al. also revealed that such units were more likely to be described in 'technical' terms ('a pain relief centre', 'a specialist medical/nursing unit') than 'non-technical' ('a peaceful haven', 'just like the family'). Taken in conjunction with Help the Hospices' standards which require a doctor to be readily available for in-patient units, it seems likely that these trends towards intervention and a 'technical' approach will increase – some would argue in direct contravention of early hospice aims.

123

In placing the patients' needs first, 'the vision' held the potential for generating a radical change in the decision-making structure of the care of the dying. Yet how this placing the patient at the centre emerges in practice will surely depend on a much more difficult change – that of the biomedical hierarchies and priorities which shape our system of health care.[71] Hospice staff are trained within the mainstream health system and so hospices have set themselves a significant task in seeking to realign inter-professional balance.

THE ART OF THE POSSIBLE?

One of the great attractions about ideals is their glorious simplicity. Yet while they appear simple, the ways and circumstances in which they are applied are not. To be useful ideals and principles have to be translated into policies and practice, and as soon as that process begins, the simplicity is sullied. We need nonconformists to offer us alternative views, yet they are risky and threatening; we need 'visions' to strive for, yet we know they will be flawed in delivery. This does not mean that visionaries are not valuable, on the contrary, but it does mean that their aspirations are likely to be compromised by the art of the possible and what is deemed to be socially desirable.

With twenty-five years behind them now, much has changed both in the hospices and in the health services with whom they work. As in-patient hospices are likely to be nearing a peak in their numbers with the national network nearly complete, and as community services extend their reach, a fourth phase may soon emerge. If the first phase was the pre-hospice stage, the second phase, that of 'the vision' and the third phase the spread of hospice ideals through diversification and legitimation, the fourth phase is likely to be one of formal consolidation and standardisation, for hospices are an established and establishment part of British health care provision.

Where hospices once, implicitly, criticised others by highlighting deficiencies in terminal care, so now they too are in an uncomfortable position. Along with many other providers of health care, hospices have to explain and account for what they do. The broad, impersonal policy questions of 'does the hospice system work?' and, if so, 'for whom?' are difficult to answer when our auditing measures are blunt – especially when it comes to measuring social and psychological, let alone spiritual effects.

It is difficult to establish the precise nature of hospice influence.

I suggested at the beginning of the chapter that hospices expanded during a mood of concern about dying and already changing expectations of health services. Would the 1986 NAHA (National Association of Health Administrators) conference have come up with guidelines for hospital care of the dying if the hospice movement did not exist;[72] similarly, would there have been enough focused pressure to change the attendance allowance system to accommodate the care of the dying in 1990? It is unlikely that the Royal College of Physicians would have created a specialism of palliative medicine with all that implies in terms of training and research had it not been for a focus of attention on care of the dying. Yet none of these effects can be measured within conventional auditing systems.

Perhaps one of the main functions of hospices in all their diverse forms is to serve as a focus for our concerns about death. At a policy level we might want to use hospices as a litmus test of how well we manage the care of the dying in our society. Yet hospices are not appropriate for everyone. Furthermore, we must remain conscious of the less publicly-accountable services and less visible circumstances in which terminal care takes place. While the quality of care of the dying has been transformed for some by the presence of a hospice movement, in many nursing and residential homes 'good' policies for care for the dying are sparse. These types of facilities are likely to increase in the future with demographic change causing an increasingly ageing population and fewer people to care for them. As the system of purchasing hospice services extends under the National Health Service and Community Care Act 1990, with money becoming a more overt part of the process, we will need to know who chooses to buy access to which aspects of hospice services and those who do not use them at all.

However, there is another level at which hospice development has contributed, and that is as part of a broader debate on the value and meaning of life and death. While hospices have achieved much, the Voluntary Euthanasia Society has 11,000 members in Britain and the numbers are growing. It will be interesting to see how history interprets the morality of a society in which two contrasting groups, each with deeply committed views on human dignity, develop in parallel.

ACKNOWLEDGEMENTS
This essay owes much to the St Christopher's Hospice *Directory of Hospice Services* produced by staff of the Information Service. My thanks go to the staff for their unfailing help and cheerfulness over many years. Many thanks also to the staff of Help the Hospices for their assistance and to Cancer Relief for the regular mailings. David Field and Ruth Elkan have been of great assistance in discussing the chapter.

NOTES

1 Philippe Ariès, *The Hour of Our Death* (New York: Vintage Books, 1982); Joseph Campbell, *Masks of God* (Harmondworth: Penguin, 1986); Sally Humphreys, *The Family, Women and Death* (London: Routledge & Kegan Paul, 1982).
2 Max Weber, *Economy and Society* (Berkeley, Calif.: University of California Press, 1978): chs III and XIV.
3 Shirley Du Boulay, *Cicely Saunders: the Founder of the Modern Hospice Movement* (London: Hodder & Stoughton, 1987): 54–9.
4 For a 'feeling' of the varieties of ways case histories were used see, for example, Cicely Saunders, *Care of the Dying*, 2nd edn, *Nursing Times* 72(26), (1 July 1976); Robert Twycross, 'Relief of pain', in Cicely Saunders (ed.), *The Management of Terminal Disease* (London: Edward Arnold, 1978). Olga Craig, 'The role of the social worker', in Derek Doyle (ed.), *Terminal Care* (Edinburgh: Churchill Livingstone, 1979).
5 An elaboration of an 'alternative way of dying' is in ch. 2 of Veronica James, 'Care and work in nursing the dying', unpublished Ph.D. thesis, Aberdeen University (1986).
6 Ariès, op. cit. For a comment on the effects of industrialisation on death, Vanderlyn Pine and Derek Phillips, 'The cost of dying: a sociological analysis of funeral expenditure', *Social Problems* 17 (1970): 405–17; for the effects of 'civilisation' on death see Norbert Elias, *The Loneliness of Dying* (Oxford: Blackwell, 1985); and on medicalisation of death see Lindsay Prior, *The Social Organisation of Death* (London: Macmillan, 1989).
7 Hilary Rose and Stephen Rose, *Science and Society* (Harmondsworth: Pelican, 1969).
8 William Arney and Bernard Bergen, 'The anomaly, the chronic patient and the play of medical power', *Sociology of Health and Illness* 5 (1983): 12.
9 ibid.: 13.
10 C. S. Lewis, *A Grief Observed* (London: Faber & Faber, 1961); Simone de Beauvoir, *A Very Easy Death* (Harmondsworth: Penguin, 1978); Vera Brittain, *Testament of Youth* (London: Virago, 1984).
11 Evelyn Waugh, *The Loved One* (Harmondsworth: Penguin, 1958); Lisa Alther, *Kinflicks* (Harmondsworth: Penguin, 1977).

12 Ariès, op. cit.; Robert Fulton, *Death, Grief and Bereavement: a biblio-graphy*, (New York: Arno Press, 1977); Elias, op. cit.

13 Geoffrey Gorer, *Death, Grief and Mourning in Contemporary Britain* (London: Cresset Press, 1965); David Sudnow, *Passing On* (Englewood Cliffs, NJ: Prentice Hall, 1967); Barney Glaser and Anselm Strauss, *Awareness of Dying* (New York: Aldine Publishing Co., 1965); Ann Cartwright, Lisbeth Hockey and J. Anderson, *Life Before Death* (London: Routledge & Kegan Paul, 1973).

14 John Hinton, *Dying* (Harmondsworth: Pelican, 1972); Elisabeth Kubler-Ross, *On Death and Dying* (London: Tavistock, 1970); Colin Murrary-Parkes, *Bereavement: Studies of Grief in Adult Life*, 2nd edn (London: Tavistock, 1986).

15 J. H. Sheldon, *Report to the Birmingham Regional Hospital Board on its Geriatric Services* (Birmingham Regional Hospital Board, 1961), cited in Hinton, op. cit.

16 David Armstrong, 'The fabrication of nurse–patient relationships', *Social Science and Medicine* 17 (1983): 457–60; Celia Davies, 'Experience of dependency and control in work; the case of nursing', *Journal of Advanced Nursing Studies* 1 (1976): 273–82.

17 Jean Quint-Benoliel, 'Dying in an institution', in Hannelore Wass (ed.), *Dying: facing the facts* (Washington, DC: Hemisphere Publishing, 1979).

18 Nicky James, 'Care, work and carework', in Jane Robinson, Alistair Gray and Ruth Elkan (eds), *Policy Issues in Nursing* (Buckingham: Open University, 1991).

19 See Cartwright, Hockey and Anderson, op. cit.

20 This article was drawn upon in the Marie Curie Memorial Foundation's anniversary publication, *40 Years of Caring* (Marie Curie Foundation, 28 Belgrave Square, London SW1X 8QG: 1988).

21 Cicely Saunders, 'The problem of euthanasia', in *Care of the Dying*: 5.

22 Robert Veatch, *Death, Dying and the Biological Revolution* (New Haven, Conn.: Yale University Press, 1976): 106.

23 ibid.: 58.

24 B. D. Cohen, *Karen Ann Quinlan; Dying in an Age of Eternal Life* (New York: Nash Publications, 1976); and see *Re Quinlan*, 70 NJ 10, 355 A 2d 644 (1976) for the judgment of the Supreme Court of New Jersey.

25 Department of Health and Social Security, *Care of the Dying – Proceedings of a National Symposium on 29th November 1972* (London: HMSO, 1973).

26 For example, the hospice/euthanasia debate was in evidence in the Voluntary Euthanasia Society newsletter *Exit* (spring 1981); at the British Psychosocial Oncology Group conference in London in 1988 where Drs Sheila Cassidy and Pieter Admiral spoke; and in 1990 Marie Curie Cancer Education advertised a medical ethics seminar on 'Should euthanasia be legalised?'

27 Rosalind Lam, 'Who is concerned about the right to die with dignity? A postal survey of Exit members', occasional paper. (London: Institute for Social Studies in Medical Care, 1981).

28 Cicely Saunders, *St. Christopher's Hospice Annual Report* (1976–7): 7.
29 Voluntary Euthanasia Society information leaflet, 1990. See also Nicky Smith, 'Some conflicts and anomalies in terminal care movements', in Rex Taylor and Anne Gilmore (eds), *Current Trends in British Gerontology* (Aldershot: Gower, 1982).
30 Saunders, *Annual Report*.
31 Saunders, *Care of the Dying*.
32 ibid.
33 Robert Fulton and Greg Owen, 'Hospice in America', in Cicely Saunders, Dorothy Summers and Neville Teller (eds), *Hospice: the Living Idea* (London: Edward Arnold, 1981): 9.
34 Constance Holden, 'The hospice movement and its implications', *Annals of the American Academy of Political and Social Science* 447 (January 1980): 59–63.
35 Robert Buckingham, *The Complete Hospice Guide* (New York: Harper & Row, 1983).
36 Paul Dubois, *The Hospice Way of Death* (New York: Human Sciences Press, 1980).
37 Sandol Stoddard, *The Hospice Movement: a Better Way to Care for the Dying* (London: Jonathan Cape, 1979).
38 Charles Corr and Donna Corr, *Hospice Care: Principles and Practice* (London: Faber & Faber, 1983).
39 Richard Lamerton, *Care of the Dying* (Harmondsworth: Pelican, 1980).
40 Nicky James, 'A family and a team', in Anne Gilmore and Stan Gilmore (eds), *A Safer Death: Multidisciplinary Aspects of Terminal Care* (New York: Plenum, 1988).
41 Saunders, *Care of the Dying*; Lamerton, op. cit.; Doyle, op. cit.; Stoddard, op. cit.
42 For examples of recent research-based analyses of hospices see Vincent Mor and Susan Masterson-Allen, *Hospice Care Systems; Structure, Process, Costs and Outcome* (New York: Springer, 1987); Clive Seale, 'What happens in hospices; a review of research evidence', *Social Science and Medicine* 28(6) (1989): 551–9; idem., 'A comparison of hospice and conventional care', *Social Science and Medicine* 32(2) (1991): 147–52; Ian Johnson, Corrinne Rogers, Bronwen Biswas and Sam Ahmedzai, 'What do hospices do? a survey of hospices in the United Kingdom and Republic of Ireland', *British Medical Journal* 300 (24 March 1990): 791–3.
43 For examples of how this view is uncritically reported and perpetuated by some see Aries, op. cit.; and Denise Winn, *The Hospice Way* (London: Optima, 1987).
44 There is evidence of disquiet in the report of the Standing Medical Advisory Committee (Chair: Eric Wilkes), *Terminal Care: Report of a Working Group* (London: HMSO, 1980) and from the pressure group 'Help the Hospices' in the guidelines for hospices issued in 1990. See also Nicky James and David Field, 'The routinisation of hospice', *Social Science and Medicine* (1993): 1363.
45 From information on the Marie Curie Memorial Foundation, op. cit.
46 This information comes from the *1991 Directory of Hospice Services*.

47 ibid.
48 Audrey Ward, *Home Care Services for the Terminally Ill*, report for the Nuffield Foundation (Sheffield: Sheffield Medical School, 1985; Clive Seale, 'What happens in hospices', op. cit.
49 See Nicky James and David Field, op. cit., for a more detailed sociological analysis of the growth of bureaucracy in hospices.
50 Hedley Taylor, *The Hospice Movement in Britain: its Role and its Functions* (London: Centre for Policy on Ageing, 1983): 53.
51 Standing Medical Advisory Committee, op. cit. (the 'Wilkes Report').
52 Help the Hospices, *Hospice Care – Definitions and Qualifications* (including as appendix 1, 'A guide to good standards and practice') (London: Help the Hospices, April 1990).
53 Barry Lunt, *Terminal Cancer Care Services in Great Britain: the Current Picture and Future Developments* (1981) (available from St Christopher's Hospice, 51–53 Lawrie Park Road, London SE26 6DZ).
54 See *Cancer Relief Annual Report* (London: Cancer Relief, 1984) and *Cancer Relief News* (winter 1990–1).
55 Help the Hospices response to 'The National Health Service and Community Care Bill' prepared by Paul Rossi of Help the Hospices (March 1990).
56 See Frank Hill and Christine Oliver, 'Hospice – an update on the cost of patient care', *Health Trends* 20 (1988): 83–6.
57 Department of Health, November 1990.
58 A series of five articles comparing and contrasting American and British health care systems was written by Donald Light and published in *Health Services Journal* (October–November 1990) and sheds light on the differences of funding and organisation and the inappropriateness of Britain 'embracing competition American style'.
59 Robert Kastenbaum, 'New fantasies in the American death system', *Death Education* 6(2) (special issue) (summer 1982).
60 Frank Hill and Christine Oliver, op. cit.
61 Lindsay Prior, 'The rationalisation of death: the medico-legal system and the elimination of human agency', *Theory, Culture and Society* 2 (1984).
62 The proceedings of this conference were published in Cicely Saunders, Dorothy Summers and Neville Teller (eds), op. cit.
63 See Samuel Klagsbrun, in ibid.; and Paul Torrens, in ibid.
64 A reputation recognised by Eric Wilkes and referred to in Margaret Manning, *The Hospice Alternative* (London: Souvenir Press, 1984).
65 Miles, quoted in Morris Punch's highly pertinent article, 'The institutionalisation of anti-institutional ideas', *British Journal of Sociology* 25 (1974): 312–25.
66 Prior, *Social Organisation of Death*.
67 Eric Wilkes, in Saunders, Summers and Teller, op. cit.: 186.
68 Eva Gamrnikow was one of the first people to analyse this triumvirate and points out the inappropriateness of 'patient' being aligned with 'child', in 'Sexual division of labour: the case of nursing', in AnnMarie Wolpe and Annette Kuhn (eds), *Feminism and Materialism* (London: Routledge & Kegan Paul, 1978).

69 Desmond Graves, 'Models of hospice management' (p. 8), available from St Christopher's Hospice.
70 Ian Johnson *et al.*, op. cit.
71 Margaret Stacy gives a history of the 'biomedical' system in *Sociology of Health and Healing* (London: Routledge, 1989). The issue of hierarchies and inter-professional challenges was raised again in response to a questionnaire analysed by Andrew Heenan, 'Uneasy partnership', *Nursing Times* 87(10) (1991): 25–7.
72 Published as *Care of the Dying: a Guide for Health Authorities* (Birmingham: NAHA, 1987) (available from NAHA, 47 Edgbaston Park Road, Birmingham B15 2RS).

8

Animal rights and wrongs: medical ethics and the killing of non-human animals

Marie Fox

> Mankind's true moral test, its fundamental test (which lies
> deeply buried from view), consists of its attitude towards
> those who are at its mercy: animals. And in this respect
> mankind has suffered a fundamental debacle, a debacle so
> fundamental that all others stem from it.
>
> (Milan Kundera, *The Unbearable Lightness
> of Being* (London: Faber & Faber, 1984))

INTRODUCTION

Kundera's view is diametrically at odds with the views implicit in
most medico-legal literature in which the interests of animals are
generally not taken into account at all.[1] The purpose of this paper is
to challenge the implicit assumption that animals do not matter
morally, and that their interests may simply be overridden for
human ends. Such a view is symptomatic of how animals are treated
in wider philosophical writing. Treatises on rights and justice generally leave the issue of animal rights or interspecies justice out of
account as being 'too controversial'.[2] Hence what discussion there
is of such issues has been confined largely to specialist books and
articles, with the result that vivisectors and everyone else who
profits by such practices can easily avoid confronting the morality
of their treatment of animals. Such neglect is, of course, typical of
the lack of concern accorded to animals by our society as a whole.

However, any collection of papers on the ethics of death can
hardly afford to ignore the death of millions of animals in the name
of medical science, as well as commercial interest.[3] In 1990, 3.2

131

million animal experiments were carried out, many of them performed in the alleged interests of medical science.[4] In the context of this book it is important to consider the issue of our treatment of animals not only from the animal-welfarist viewpoint but also because all of the controversial issues surrounding the ethics of dying and killing are to some extent interrelated. The issue of what constitutes a 'person' is clearly central to debates on abortion and embryo experimentation, as well as experimentation upon animals,[5] whilst perhaps only in regard to euthanasia do we actually treat non-human animals more favourably than humans.[6] However, the issue is primarily important for the sake of the animals themselves – they are not mere scientific resources which we can use and abuse as we please.

Immediately we are faced with the question of *which* animals are important. Although for practical purposes many commentators limit their definition of animal to mammalian animals,[7] it seems preferable to define animals to include all vertebrates, given that considerable numbers of birds and fish are involved in research.[8] This position is now reflected in s. 1 of the Animals (Scientific Procedures) Act 1986 which defines a protected animal as 'any living vertebrate other than man'.[9] It is noteworthy that without any scientific justification the Act appears to accord certain species of animal *greater* value. Thus s. 5(6) provides that project licences should not be granted under the Act for experiments on cats, dogs, primates or equidae unless it is established that other species of animal are unsuitable or impracticable to obtain. There seem to be no clear reasons for such favouritism beyond the fact that the animals listed are either uncomfortably human-like, or are those which we have selected as companions or servants.[10] I believe that the debate on the morality of our treatment of animals has been cluttered with the drawing of such emotional and unjustifiably arbitrary lines, and that within the broad category of vertebrate animals it is impossible, without a considerable degree of arbitrariness, to construct a taxonomy which clearly delineates those animals which are objects of moral concern from those which are not. Similar problems plague attempts to divide human and non-human animals into two rigidly fixed dichotomous categories.

Another problem concerns not only *which* animals count morally, but which of their interests count. I assume here that the Cartesian view of animals as mere machines needs no further refutation. This is even accepted by vivisectors themselves – thus principle VI of the International Guiding Principles for Biomedical Research Involving Animals states: 'investigators should assume that procedures that would cause pain in human beings cause pain in other vertebrate species although more needs to be known about the perception of pain in other animals'.[11] Indeed, as Rose and Adams have posited, it may be the case that the experience of pain is worse for animals than for adult humans, as a major determinant of pain perception is the greater capacity for cognitive modulation possessed by adult humans, which means that they have a greater potential than animals or young children to attenuate or limit pain.[12] Yet despite this fact, animals are frequently subjected to pain without anaesthetics (in about 70 per cent of cases)[13] in worthless repetitive experiments. This makes it difficult to refute the charge of speciesism. It is simply assumed that animals are a lower form of life, or indeed mere tools[14] whose interests can automatically be overridden for human benefit or, more worryingly, simply for the sake of medical science/knowledge. Again this pursuit of knowledge is often simply self-evidently assumed, in philosophy[15] as well as science, to be a good without enquiring into the means used to obtain it. Moreover, it is not only the case that the infliction of *pain* is an unjustifiable means. As Rollin points out, it would be wrong to identify the needs and interests of animals solely with pleasure and pain, and thus to restrict the scope of moral concern to the scope of pleasure and pain. He argues that animals differ from machines and plants by virtue of having a *telos*, or intrinsic nature which is genetically imposed, and which causes them to strive to preserve life and actualise their potential. Thus, animals have interests because they possess some sort of conscious awareness of their needs,[16] an awareness which is ignored as their interests are routinely overridden in the alleged interests of medical science.

THE REALITY OF MEDICAL PRACTICE

Hitherto the main focus of debate in relation to the use of animals by medical science has been vivisection – a term which literally means the dissection of live animals but which has come to be more broadly used to include inducing disease in animals using them as vehicles to develop tumours, vaccines or for the extraction of medical products like insulin, and for educational purposes. The meaning of vivisection has thus changed through time to encompass new techniques of using animals as these become technically

133

possible. I would contend that since our focus is the killing of animals for medical purposes we must also widen the debate to encompass two other uses of animals – first, toxicity testing, much of which is carried out for the purpose of ascertaining the safety of new drugs for use by humans; and, second, the use of animals for xenografts, i.e., the transplantation of animal organs to humans, a procedure which poses additional ethical questions. Another way in which animals are used, allegedly in the interests of medicine, is in behavioural studies. Such experiments are outside the remit of this essay since they involve deprivation rather than physical torture and are less likely to entail the death of the animal. Moreover, since they are some of the least defensible experiments, morally or scientifically,[17] if experiments for which a stronger case can be made cannot be defended, the case for using animals in behavioural experiments necessarily crumbles as well. There is, I believe, a widespread reluctance to question all these uses of animals, dignified as they are by the name of medical science[18] and sanctioned by law. Too often it is treated as self-evidently the case that so-called 'lesser' animals should be 'sacrificed' for the sake of finding new drugs to alleviate human pain and disease, in the hope of finding out more about killer diseases such as AIDS or cancer, or in order to make up a shortfall in human organs which causes hundreds of human deaths each year. This perception betrays how far our reluctance to question medical science and the ends for which it is used has blunted our moral sensibilities, and made us willing to accept the use of dubious means for ends which are equally questionable. It seems to me that the reluctance to question the received morality of our treatment of animals stems from the fact that to do so will inevitably entail a radical change in our whole way of life. The use of animals in medical science is the pivotal case in the animal liberation debate because if the dubious basis of this practice is demonstrated, the case for other abuses of animals collapses. As Brophy has cogently argued, no other issue involves a moral dilemma at all.[19] In all other cases humans simply override the interests of non-humans without justification: choosing to hunt, wear fur or eat meat is not a choice *between* evils – it is simply a choice of evil. By contrast, the use of animals in medical science *appears* to involve a choice between the health, lives or suffering of animals, on the one hand, and those of humans, on the other. However, once the nature of animal experimentation is revealed, it becomes less clear that humans actually do benefit.

The use of animals to test the toxicity of drugs is regulated by the Medicines Act 1968. Of course not only drugs but also such trivial products as new or 'improved' household products or cosmetics are also tested on animals, such tests often being legally required by the Health and Safety at Work Act 1974 in the alleged interests of public confidence and consumer protection.[20] Frequently it is these experiments which are hardest to justify, *scientifically* as well as morally.[21] Such legislative requirements that substances must be routinely tested on animals, often in scientifically indefensible tests like LD50[22] and Draize,[23] reinforce the notion that animals are disposable scientific resources. In the United Kingdom, where animal testing provides clearance for the introduction of new products and compounds, industrial representatives are among the staunchest defenders of animal experimentation. Even where there is no mandatory legal requirement that new products be tested on animals, manufacturers will often test on animals as a safeguard against the risk of litigation due to any adverse reactions their products may cause. This raises the question whether the deaths of several thousands of animals per year can be justified on the grounds that it helps to protect corporations from financial losses incurred through compensation claims. Of course, aside from this factor, animal tests may be against the interests of manufacturers (on a cost–benefit analysis animal testing is expensive). Thus, whether industrialists support or oppose animal experiments depends solely upon the financial implications for them. By contrast to Britain, the comparatively strict regulatory regime of safety testing in the United States, which results in products being banned because of animal tests, leads to industrial pressure to abandon such testing. This illustrates Millstone's point that: 'arguments concerning the extrapolative validity of animal tests need to be understood in part by reference to their social contexts'.[24]

Apart from the testing of non-essential products like cosmetics, many new drugs which require animal tests are for trivial purposes. As Clark has pointed out, much of modern medicine is geared to allowing us to live a *pain-free* life rather than a genuinely healthy one. For example, it is clearly indefensible that many drugs are marketed, at the expense of great animal suffering, to remove conditions like expected hangovers or indigestion which could readily have been avoided.[25] Furthermore, many other 'new' drugs produce no tangible 'medical' benefit. As Ryder has shown, most animal experiments are performed to develop and test new drugs

MARIE FOX

and appliances which add more to the bank balances of multi-international drug companies than to the state of the nation's health.[26] A survey by the World Health Organisation in the 1980s showed that, of the 30,000–40,000 drugs available in Britain, a model list of 'essential' drugs numbered only 220.[27] Over one-third of all newly-marketed drugs are combinations or reformulations of existing drugs – which must be tested on animals – yet the World Health Organisation rarely deems such drugs essential. Indeed, a survey by the Medical Division of the DHSS revealed that in the decade between 1971–81 the new chemical entities marketed: 'have largely been introduced into therapeutic areas already heavily over-subscribed [and] for conditions which are common, largely chronic and occur principally in the affluent Western society. Innovation is therefore largely directed towards commercial returns rather than therapeutic needs'.[28] Hence many experiments, some of which will be performed in the name of medical science, are not justified even in the sense of advancing human interests. Undoubtedly great advances in animal welfare would be made simply by banning the testing of frivolous products – something the overwhelming majority of the population believes should happen.[29] Similarly, advances could be made through requiring *all* experiments to be published (particularly those which fail), imposing requirements that thorough literature surveys should be carried out before research is licensed in order to avoid unnecessary and painful duplication of research and prohibiting the use, particularly dissection, of animals in the education of scientists, medics and psychologists.[30] It has been contended that the real reason for dissection is to desensitise students,[31] and that simulated computer models, videos and the use of cadavers and animal corpses can obviate the need for such wasteful use of animals. However, working to achieve such practical gains in animal welfare, and reductions in the numbers of animals used, should not blind us to the more fundamental issue, which is whether we are ever justified in using animals for human ends even where tangible results *will* accrue or the anticipated benefits to humankind are great. Proponents claim that this is true of vivisection which has as one of its aims the saving of human life or the alleviation of human suffering.

Similarly, it is claimed that the use of xenografts, which has become a real possibility over the past decade, will also save countless human lives, as it is estimated that the knowledge and technology will be available within the next couple of years to make

136

routine successful transplants of animal organs to human beings who need them.[32] There exists a real probability of animals being bred solely to function as organ banks for humans. However, though the fundamental justification in both cases is the same, there are respects in which the issues of experimentation and toxicity testing differ from that of xenografts. Many people who profess no moral opposition to the carrying out of laboratory experiments or toxicity testing on animals are concerned about the practice of xenografts. The ethical issues raised have primarily been concerns about the use of genetic engineering, in particular suggestions that such techniques should be used to produce a 'transgenic' pig, with human genes inserted at the embryonic stage to make its organs match those of humans more closely and thus lessen the risk of rejection.[33] Lots of people clearly feel unhappy about the Orwellian idea of having a pig organ inside them.[34] Indeed, one of the central paradoxes of the whole animal liberation debate is the irony that the abuse of animals in the field of genetic engineering has actually succeeded in blurring still further the already hazy distinction between human and non-human animal.[35] I would suggest that this factor accounts for the 'particular horror' which Hursthouse contends most people feel about the idea of hybrid human–animals.[36] Yet even in the area of genetic engineering, with its merging of human and animal bodies, speciesism prevails. In April 1987 the United States Patents Office announced without prior public discussion that 'henceforth all forms of life *other than human* qualified as "patentable subject matter" ' (my emphasis). Thus animals' inferior status as human property was confirmed.[37] The second possible difference between xenografts and vivisection is that it could be contended that *once* (if) the techniques are perfected for transferring animal organs to humans the benefits from that practice are no longer speculative, as the protracted benefits of vivisection must inevitably be.

In the absence of serious debate on the ethics of xenografts, the prevailing view seems to be that the practice raises few ethical dilemmas and that these have little to do with the abuse of animals.[38] It is simply treated as self-evident that animals may be used as organ donors and the medical profession has come down strongly in support of the practice.[39] Opposing arguments have been portrayed by the media and medical establishment as originating from animal liberation extremists who care more about animals than people. Proponents of xenografts, if they bother to justify the practice at all, rely on the disingenuous argument that since we eat pigs it follows that it is justifiable to use their organs – which rather begs the question of whether killing animals for their flesh is morally justified.

Undoubtedly the shortage of human organs is a serious problem. It is estimated that in the UK there is a waiting list of about 4,000 patients awaiting organ transplants. Obviously the use of animal organs would be one way of solving this 'unmet need', but as the British Kidney Patients' Association point out, while they are not in principle opposed to such transplants, it is scandalous that huge resources should be devoted to expensive research programmes when so many human organs are buried or cremated daily.[40] Whilst Ian Kennedy's proposal that potential organ donors should have to opt out of having their organs used in the event of their untimely death may not solve the problem, it would go far towards meeting the need for organs, and it seems to me a more efficient and morally defensible strategy to adopt than breeding animals for use as donor banks.[41]

Clearly then there is a need for the medical profession to recognise that their use of animals does raise significant moral issues which require fuller debate. This lack of concern about the use of animals in medical science and for transplantation can be contrasted not only with concern about the use of adult humans in medical science,[42] but perhaps more pertinently with the ongoing debates in medical ethics about the moral and legal status of certain categories of 'marginal' human beings – the human embryo/foetus, anencephalic babies, the terminally ill and beating-heart cadavers. Indeed such humans may even lack the capacity to feel pain. Philosophers who approve of animal experimentation but do not then want to accept the logic of their argument that experimentation on such marginal humans must be permissible (particularly since it will almost certainly prove more fruitful) are forced back to the speciesist assertion that ultimately what is of moral significance is membership of the human race per se. Thus it is the case of such marginal humans which best demonstrates the problem of speciesism and begs the question of what really distinguishes human from non-human animals. It becomes apparent that all the criteria which supposedly demonstrate human superiority – intelligence, rationality, possession of language, self-consciousness – fail, because such borderlines cannot be drawn without including some animals within the compass of moral concern or excluding some humans.

What emerges is that such criteria are selected with the *aim* of differentiating us from animals. As Clark points out:

> it is not that we have *discovered* [animals] to lack a language, but rather that we define, and redefine, what language is by discovering what beasts do not have. If they should turn out to have the very thing that we have hitherto supposed language to be, we will simply conclude that language is something else again . . . we define our own being by opposition to theirs, and if they turn out to be rather different from our fantasy we will merely invent another and more subtle distinction.[43]

Ultimately, as Clark acknowledges, 'there are *no* such features that are entirely peculiar to man (except perhaps his *power*)'.[44] And power it seems is the crux of the issue – to reinforce our powerful position we have socially-constructed differences to make us feel superior, just as men have constructed sexual differences to preserve their power over women. Perhaps Midgley is right to suggest that we distance ourselves from the beast without for fear of the beast within,[45] and are reluctant to accept that we belong on the same biological/evolutionary continuum as them.[46]

The consequences of such essentialist thinking underpin many of the moral distinctions we make. For example, much attention has been devoted to the question of whether organs may be removed from 'beating-heart cadavers', yet it seems to me that the use of organs from 'brain-dead' humans poses many fewer ethical problems than those raised by breeding and killing healthy animals specifically for the purpose of organ donation. The justification that we kill animals for their meat anyway is clearly spurious; eating animal flesh is, it seems to me, much worse morally than taking an organ from a 'beating-heart cadaver', since the latter action can be defended, whereas I do not believe that the former can.[47] The fact that for many people it is the latter action which raises the greater moral dilemma is, I think, a good illustration of how pervasive speciesism is in our society. A more problematic category of human donor is the anencephalic baby, and much debate about infant organ supply has centred on whether such babies can be used as organ resources. Since such babies will die imminently, are incapable of pain (in so far as this can be ascertained)[48] and have not been purposely brought into existence for another's ends, the ethical objections to the use of such organs again appear to me to be less than in the case of using healthy animals which have an interest in living.[49] A possible difference between the cases of animals and anencephalic babies is the fact that the parents of an anencephalic child may suffer distress at their baby being used in this way (though in fact they often seem to derive comfort from the knowledge that their child's death has not been in vain).[50] However, it is problematic to allow moral status to hinge on the possession of caring relatives, and in any event in the usual speciest manner we ignore the distress which is routinely caused to animals by separation from their offspring.[51]

A similar lack of concern about animals as contrasted to humans is evident in other fields of medical ethics, most notably embryo experimentation. Discussion about according rights to foetuses/ embryos is paralleled by the lack of such discussion as far as animals are concerned, although they are sentient beings capable of suffering, whereas the early embryo is incapable of feeling pain. Indeed it is interesting that in the debates which preceded the Human Fertilisation and Embryology Act 1990 scientists who had for years been extolling the benefits of animal experimentation and the logic of extrapolating the results to humans were suddenly eager to point to the limitations of such experiments. Meanwhile, their opponents, who opposed experiments on embryos allegedly on humanitarian grounds, were all too willing to subject sentient creatures, which can undoubtedly feel pain, to torture and suffering. It is also worth noting how remarkably ill-informed the debate was. Those arguing for extensive legal regulation limiting what may be done to the human foetus pointed out that, unlike animals, the human foetus was currently accorded no protection, but they failed to examine how limited the legal protection given to animals is. Therefore, as with scientific practice, the legal reality must be examined.

THE LEGAL PROTECTION AFFORDED TO ANIMALS

Historically law has been, and remains, instrumental in constructing and reinforcing the subordinate position of animals. Even legislation portrayed as affording protection to animals is inevitably double-edged, as Brophy exposed in her condemnation of the Cruelty to Animals Act 1876. Her words remain true of its successor – the Animals (Scientific Procedures) Act 1986:

140

If it controls, it also licences. If it purports to protect the other animals, it also protects the vivisector from being prosecuted for cruelty. If it forbids him to perform his experiments as a public spectacle, it also prevents the public from seeing what happens in his laboratory.[52]

Despite this, the 1986 legislation has received a cautious welcome from animal welfarists who optimistically view the Act as providing a framework within which to effect real changes in the welfare of animals and phase out trivial research.[53] Hollands, in particular, stresses the potentially radical implications of s. 5(4) which states:

In determining whether and on what terms to grant a project licence, the Secretary of State shall weigh the likely adverse effects on the animal concerned against the benefit likely to accrue as a result of the programme to be specified in the licence.

Thus the Secretary of State (in practice her inspectors) is required to perform a cost–benefit equation before authorising any procedures on animals. One would expect, however, that in such a balancing process the odds will be heavily stacked against animals with human benefits continuing to be exaggerated whilst the extent of animal suffering is underplayed. Of course in such debates morally loaded language is virtually impossible to avoid, but Fox, for example, too easily concludes that '*tangible* (how is this measured?) *benefits* (are these proven? and what of failures?) of animal research far outweigh the animals' *discomfort*' (my emphasis).[54]

In practice therefore the 1986 Act does little to improve the position of laboratory animals. It was long overdue, and has effected little substantive change. A new licensing system was introduced which forms the cornerstone of the legislation and requires three licences. In the first place animal house facilities[55] must be licensed, and two persons designated[56] upon whom the statute imposes a duty to look after any animal whose well-being gives rise to concern. Second, a project licence must be granted in respect of each programme of research, and this will be granted only where a cost–benefit analysis under s. 5(4) has been carried out. Third, individual researchers must obtain a personal licence certifying their competence to carry out scientific procedures on animals.[57] The Act also established an 'Animal Procedures Committee' to advise the Secretary of State regarding the Act and to oversee the use of animals, and instituted a system of inspection of licensed establishments, but the practical effectiveness of such measures is debatable. The provision requiring that two-thirds of the committee must possess one of various stipulated qualifications has ensured that it is largely composed of those with a vested interest in the vivisection industry – who either perform experiments or are sympathetic to the practice of vivisection (for example, members of the Research Defence Society). As with most legislation, the real test of its efficacy will be how effectively it is implemented, and there is little room for optimism that it will be enforced any more effectively than its predecessor, under which prosecutions were virtually non-existent.[58] There is a miserly total of fifteen inspectors to inspect over 20,000 licences.[59] There had been hopes that the legislation would outlaw at least some of the most indefensible tests, such as the LD50 and Draize tests, and the controversial testing of cosmetic, tobacco and alcohol products or for psychological, behavioural and warfare purposes. However *no* tests were prohibited, nor were any targets set for reductions in the number of animals 'sacrificed' in experiments, despite the Home Office Minister responsible for the legislation – David Mellor – pledging in Parliament that: 'reduction in the number of animals used and the reduction of suffering is at the heart of the bill'.[60]

To fuel anti-vivisectionists' concern about the 1986 Act, Rodd has pointed out that it may actually have marked a lowering of moral standards in that, under the cost–benefit analysis to be carried out, the Animal Procedures Committee is now explicitly directed to take into account the interests of science *and industry*, whereas, theoretically at least, the 1876 Act permitted only experiments which were *medically* relevant and directed at relieving suffering.[61] The law thus recognises and sanctions the sacrifice of animals in the commercial interest. Moreover, for the first time, the 1986 Act permits the use of animals for the purpose of allowing scientists to gain manual dexterity, and allows experimenters to reuse animals which have recovered from anaesthetic, provided they will suffer only 'trivial' pain. Needless to say, it is up to the experimenter to make the judgment that the pain caused is trivial. All in all, one is forced to the conclusion that the British Union for the Abolition of Vivisection were justified in their conclusion that the 1986 legislation was simply a 'vivisectors' charter'.

It is true that Home Office guidance notes on the subject[62] expressly require the interests of animals to be taken into account. Thus paragraph 50 states: 'In assessing the basis of a project, the

Home Secretary is deciding whether or not it is in the public interest *(and for this purpose that includes the interests of animals)* that the project should be allowed' (emphasis in original). However, critically, this does not specify that the interests of a *particular* experimental animal should be taken into account, and is thus open to the interpretation that it applies to the interests of *all* animals. This allows the spurious argument to be advanced that if *any* animals may conceivably benefit from the procedure the licence should be granted. As Clark remarks, such arguments would never be countenanced were they advanced in relation to a group of humans – for example, the argument that experiments on Jews now may advance the interests of some other Jews in the future.[63] Moreover, as Morton notes, such a balancing of interests will not always be possible because: 'While good animal welfare, by and large, will lead to good science, there will be times when the animals' welfare will have to be compromised in some way in order for scientific objectives to be achieved.'[64] He seems to assume too easily that such scientific objectives can be equated with good science.

Certainly organisations like the Committee for the Reform of Animal Experiments (CRAE) and the Fund for the Replacement of Animals in Medical Experiments (FRAME) did press hard for the relatively minor concessions that were made during the passage of the legislation. And, as Hollands points out, the Act at least represents an improvement on the earlier legislation in so far as not only the pain and suffering of the animal but also other interference with welfare, such as facilities for housing, exercise and play, must be taken into account.[65] This should at least lead to minor improvements in the welfare of laboratory animals. However, at best such measures represent minor tinkering with the framework of the legislation protecting animals. Typical of the attitude to such amendments is the comment by Morton that certain species should not now be used if they 'cannot be kept without *undue* distress in a laboratory'.[66] Surely the fact that animals suffer such stress at all is indicative of the fact that animal experimentation cannot be meaningfully reformed. Furthermore, I fail to see how the Act really imposes public accountability. There seems no reason to believe that licences will not continue to be easily granted – there are nine 'permissible purposes' for which a licence may be granted, one of which is the hopelessly vague 'scientific research' which is nowhere defined in the Act. Such permissible purposes reinforce the prevalent idea that animals are lesser beings who may be sacrificed for

143

human convenience. Consequently I fail to share the optimism of some commentators – it seems probable that the law will continue to fail to adequately protect animals.

STRATEGIES FOR ENDING ANIMAL ABUSE

Given that law adopts this non-neutral stance of effectively condoning the practice of animal experimentation and testing, and has as yet shown no inclination to regulate or control xenografts, the question becomes whether and to what extent animal liberationists should engage with law and seek to control vivisection through the use of legislation. I would suggest that, hitherto, working for legal reform and legal rights for animals has been constructed as too central in the strategy of the animal liberation movement. This is also true of attempts to construct a defensible philosophical theory in which to ground legal rights/protection for animals. I would question the significance of both these strategies in fostering concern for and awareness of animal suffering. Of course, a variety of other arguments have been made against animal abuse. Some are methodological – hence animal experiments may be attacked on the grounds that they are scientifically invalid – i.e., that the results of animal experiments cannot safely be extrapolated to humans.[67] However, as Regan has pointed out, animal liberationists should be wary of placing too much weight on such methodological challenges because they invite continuation of research on animals in the hope of overcoming the defects.[68] Also in this regard I think much of the animal rights debate has been wrongly focused. A great deal of attention has been devoted to the issue of whether animal experiments have benefited humankind or not. Opponents of vivisection point to the fact that aspirin is fatal to cats; that drugs such as penicillin and digitalis may never have been used had there been the extensive testing on animals now legally required; and that though thalidomide was extensively tested on animals this failed to prevent the tragic deformities that resulted, though research on tissue cultures did give warnings that thalidomide was dangerous to humans.[69] Moreover, it is undoubtedly the case that many of the advances claimed by medical science can actually be attributed to improved social and economic circumstances.[70] Animal experiments have also consumed valuable resources which would otherwise have been available for epidemiology, clinical observation, the use of tissue and cell cultures and other forms of alternative research which, because of their focus on humans, are more scientifically accurate. Thus, though it is impossible to *prove* claims that the use of vivisection may have held back advances in medical science, as Brophy remarks, it is equally true that: 'no one is in a position to assert that all the discoveries achieved by vivisection could not have been achieved by other methods'.[71] Nonetheless, in my view it is better to concede that *some* useful advances have been made through vivisection in the past,[72] but argue that our society has now reached the point where it should recognise that we can no longer legally sanction the use of vivisection on the utilitarian ground that it produces medical benefits for humans.

The abuse of animals has also been castigated in consequentialist terms, because of the effect of cruelty to animals on human nature – the Kantian notion that it debases humans to treat animals badly.[73] The problem with this view is that animals themselves are not regarded as worthy of respect. Related to it is the notion of vivisection as a corrupting force – a version of the 'slippery slope' argument that so often rears its head in moral debate. Thus parallels have been drawn with the Nazi experience, and the argument advanced that the desensitisation induced by vivisection may lead to a loss of moral inhibition about experimenting on groups of humans. However, at best such arguments must be used with extreme caution[74] and at worst they represent a seriously flawed version of moral reasoning.[75]

The final strategy of the animal liberationist is to rely on the argument that it is simply morally wrong to experiment on animals, test drugs on them or use their organs. Undeniably this is the crux of the whole issue. Thus the task of the animal liberationist is to demonstrate why such practices are morally wrong. To do so calls into question the rarely challenged assumption that human life is self-evidently more important than animal life. In this vein Fox claims that critics of animal experiments do not acknowledge the 'simple truth' that humans are more important than animals. But whether this is simply true is open to question. Fox has argued that the differences he points to between humans and other animals are sufficiently substantial to amount to a difference in kind rather than degree, but he fails to satisfactorily explain how the differences on which he places so much weight do actually differ in degree – to me they more closely resemble differences in degree.[76] An example often chosen to 'prove' the vivisectionists' point that humans are more important is that persons faced with a situation where they were forced to choose between saving the life of a human and a non-human animal would almost invariably, and we would certainly think *rightly*, choose to rescue the human, and that this would remain true even if one human were weighed against the last surviving pair of a species. These however are fanciful examples as the choice in such situations and in those where animals are selected for use in medical science for human ends are simply not comparable – with animal experimentation, testing and xenografts we are concerned with the conscious decision to systematically oppress all species except our own. Emergency situations are by definition those in which tragic choices must be made, and this equally applies where the choice is between humans – for example, choosing which of two drowning humans to save. This may involve one in making a rapid calculation of the relative value of different human lives but even if one were in such a situation to determine that some humans lived lives which were in some sense less worthwhile or of lesser value than others, this would not justify a conscious decision to *routinely* treat such persons less favourably than other humans. Godlovitch has made the point that the greater value of human life:

> appears as a guideline for crisis situations rather than a principle in the ordinary sense. It presupposes two principles, 'Human life is valuable', and 'Animal life is valuable' and then offers a decision about priorities. It must be emphasised that the sense in which it does this is the same sense in which the welfare of a loved one would be valued more highly than a stranger.[77]

Since I would evidently not be morally justified in requiring a stranger to sacrifice her vital organs in order to benefit one of my loved ones – nor indeed to undergo an experiment which would save my entire family – it becomes clear that one can quite consistently acknowledge that human life is more valuable than that of animals, but still be morally obliged to condemn medical research on animals.

This is not to claim that in such situations morality is irrelevant, but rather that in such special situations (but not in everyday ones) it is appropriate to make a decision on the basis that a lesser value ought to be attributed to an animal than a human life. As Brophy has demonstrated, we should be wary about making selective extrapolations from such examples:

the obligation which [these] examples place on us is to avoid
such crises . . . every driver knows that, if he has to choose
between a single pedestrian and a mother, two toddlers and
baby in a pushchair, he must run down the single pedestrian.
Extrapolation from this maxim would allow us to vivisect ten
humans in order to save the lives of a thousand.[78]

Moreover, such arguments misconstrue the case of the animal liberationists. As Singer points out, the animal liberation movement does
not contend that all animals are of equal worth or that all interests of
humans and other animals are to be given equal weight, no matter
what those interests may be.[79] Rather, the claim is that where
animals and humans have similar interests, for example, in avoiding
suffering or continuing to live, their interests are to be counted
equally. In the exceptional situation presented by one of the 'tragic
choices' outlined above it may well be the case that human interest
weighs more heavily.

The argument about the relative values to be placed on human
and animal lives (and how law should reflect such estimates of
value) almost inevitably takes one into the philosophical territory of
rights argument, given the tendency of virtually all interest groups
to adopt the rhetoric of rights.[80] However, as far as the animal
liberation debate is concerned, it is the other main competing strand
of modern liberalism, utilitarianism, which has traditionally been
more concerned with animal welfare. From Bentham onwards utilitarian philosophy has contributed significantly to enlightened
thinking on animal rights. His widely-quoted declaration that:

The day *may* come when the rest of the animal creation may
acquire those rights which never could have been withholden
from them but by the hand of tyranny. . . . The question is
not, Can they reason? nor, Can they *talk*? but, Can they
suffer?[81]

has been hailed by many as the criterion to apply to our treatment
of animals. Hence in his classic formulation of how to calculate
society's welfare Bentham stipulated that each *person's* interests
were to count equally and that the interests of animals were to be
weighed in the calculus. It is on this theory that Peter Singer's
influential *Animal Liberation* is based. To counter the obvious flaw
that utilitarianism fails to attach sufficient importance to the
capacity of each person to decide for herself on a conception of the

good – to choose her own aspirations and ideals – Singer adopts a modified version of preference utilitarianism whereby one seeks to maximise the extent to which persons can attain their own preferences. Applying this to animals, Singer contends that since they have a preference to go on living and not to suffer or experience pain, this makes killing, or the infliction of pain, a wrong done to those individual animals, since the moral principle of equal consideration applies to animals as it does to humans. Hence Singer's case for improving our treatment of animals does not depend at all upon the notion of moral or legal rights, but is based instead on preference utilitarianism and the principle of equality of treatment, i.e., that *all* interests and preferences must be taken into account.[82] But, as with all teleological theories, it is the *end* that matters and not all of the consequences of Singer's arguments may be acceptable to animal liberationists. In a later article he allows that vegetarianism is not morally obligatory provided the animal to be eaten has been well-reared, humanely killed, is not self-conscious and is thus 'replaceable'.[83] Though this theory, applied to experimentation, would rule out the most immoral experiments, it would allow the continuation of the minority of experiments where the animals were kindly treated, anaesthetised and painlessly killed. Such an approach denies the animal any intrinsic value and leads to Singer's moderate reformist position on vivisection in *Animal Liberation*:

> All that we need to say is that experiments serving no direct and urgent purpose should stop immediately [these are notoriously difficult to define], and in the remaining areas of research methods involving animals should be replaced as soon as possible by alternative methods not involving animals.[84]

Consequently his theory fails to adequately protect the interests of animals.[85]

Hence the 'rights' view appears more radical in the protection it affords animals, and the case for animal rights has been convincingly made by Tom Regan.[86] He demonstrates that even Singer's modified version of utilitarianism is flawed in that it fails to provide a foundation for the claims of individuals (animal or human) over those of a collectivity. He therefore proposes that in order to safeguard animals from human oppression it is necessary to attribute rights to animals on the basis that these are moral claims which affirm that certain treatment is owed or due. For him the basic moral right which all persons (i.e., those who are the subject of a life and therefore possessors of inherent value – a category which he argues must extend beyond humans to mammalian animals) are owed is to be respectfully treated. Any harm done to them must be consistent with recognition of their equal inherent value and their equal prima facie right not to be harmed. He concludes that adherents of the rights view require the total abolition of the harmful use of animals in medical science because it violates *their* rights regardless of anyone else's utility. In this sense rights theory is stronger than utilitarianism – it gives animals a privileged moral status – no being is treated as if she were reducible to the best possible utility to others.

However, though I find this convincing in the sense that, *if* rights matter there seem to me no good grounds for distinguishing between humans and animals, it raises the issue of the *necessity* of attributing rights to animals or to any other entity. Having cogently criticised utilitarianism, Regan, in my view, makes the mistake of treating the rights-based approach as the only alternative to utilitarianism – apart from a cursory discussion of what he calls cruelty/ kindness views.[87] But though summarily dismissed by Regan, in my opinion this approach could provide a fruitful third avenue to according better treatment to animals. Of course, as Regan points out, kindness may be misplaced and therefore unjust, whilst the absence of cruelty does not of itself guarantee that a person's actions are right.[88] Clearly then kindness and cruelty are not synonymous with right and wrong, but it does not therefore follow that we need to make the quantum leap to a fully-fledged theory of moral/legal rights for animals. Indeed ultimately it can be questioned how different the rights-based and utilitarian approaches actually are. In practice these competing liberal theories often appear to collapse into one another. As Glover remarks, although utilitarians do not believe in absolute rights, the utilitarian approach produces a de facto recognition of frontiers which closely correspond to rights.[89] Moreover, if animals are deemed to possess a right to equal respect or not to be caused unnecessary suffering,[90] utilitarian calculations seem inevitably to enter, in deciding whether equal concern means equal *treatment* in practice, or what degree of suffering is *necessary*. Once such calculations are allowed to enter the equation it seems that any suffering animals may endure can be justified provided it is for our benefit.

In my view, having demonstrated the deficiencies with utilitarianism, Regan overlooks the inherently problematic character of appeals to rights. In my critique of the rights-based approach I wish to draw on feminist and critical legal theory to suggest that there are good reasons for animal liberationists to abandon rights arguments. Such analyses of rights suggest that they are problematic on three related levels – philosophically, it may be impossible to postulate convincing or conclusive arguments to the effect that animals or humans have rights; politically, it is questionable how effective rights discourse is; and, practically, even if moral/legal rights are conceded they may produce little. I would contend that animal liberationists have much to learn from feminist experience, given that throughout history there has been a certain commonality between the oppression of women and animals – both categories have been defined as the 'other' in contradistinction to man.[91] Similarly, Spiegel has convincingly and movingly demonstrated the parallels between the treatment of black slaves in the eighteenth and nineteenth centuries and contemporary treatment of animals, exposing such links as being rooted in power, domination and notions of supremacy.[92] Certainly the early proponents of animal rights, like Salt, explicitly located their work within an historical process of moral enfranchisement in the tradition of Paine and Wollstonecraft,[93] whilst Singer borrowed the idea of animal liberation from the political discourse of earlier liberation movements.[94] Thus the notion of animal liberation can be located within a genealogy of such political movements and lessons can be drawn from earlier struggles. Some commentators (generally male)[95] have contended that the drawing of such parallels is in some sense offensive to earlier liberation movements they deem more important, whether those of slaves, women or blacks, but again this seems to me an example of unreflective speciesism. As Spiegel points out:

> Comparing the suffering of animals to that of blacks (or any other oppressed group) is offensive only to the speciesist; one who has embraced false notions of what animals are like. . . . To deny our similarities to animals is to deny and undermine our own power. It is to continue actively struggling to prove to our oppressors, past or present, that we are *similar to our oppressors*, rather than those whom our oppressors have also victimised. . . . Let us remember that to the *oppressors*, there is often very little difference between one victim and the next.[96]

In terms of what rights strategies actually achieve, the lesson to be drawn from feminist theorising seems to be that animal liberationists should be wary of placing too much faith in rights arguments. As Carol Smart has demonstrated in the context of women's liberation, now that law no longer denies women formal rights which it accords to men, rights strategy may have outlived its usefulness and perhaps even become oppressive, although she acknowledges its worth at an earlier stage in the struggle.[97] However, though it may be the case that the women's liberation movement is 'entering a new era in which rights claims may be becoming less valuable',[98] this may not be true of the animal liberation movement. Few would now seriously contend that women or blacks lack the capacity for having certain basic human rights ascribed to them (if these can be said to exist at all) such as the right to life or to freedom from torture; but many would *argue* that animals do not possess such rights, whilst the vast majority of the population simply *act* as though they do not. Given then that the law is still a long way from recognising the formal equality of animals (and nor is it likely to do so in view of the problems it has with accommodating the formal equality of women) it could be contended that it is first necessary to convince law-makers that animals have philosophical rights. It is probably for this reason that just as the feminist movement has been reluctant to fully embrace the critique of rights,[99] the animal liberation movement has shown little sign of abandoning rights discourse. However, the fact that law does not accept any notion of formal equality between humans and animals may actually reinforce the view that there should be less reliance on animal rights tactics. Whilst there is a dialectical relationship between legal rights and public perceptions of certain groups,[100] as a society we are currently so far from conceding that animals should be accorded equality of treatment that, in a sense, it is too early to rely mainly on the tactic of pressing for legal rights. Without a gestalt shift in public perceptions, any legal rights that are granted are virtually certain to be very partial and limited and to reinforce the separation between human and animal.

Of course there are perceived to be disadvantages in abandoning the rights strategy. As Elizabeth Kingdom has argued in a feminist context:

The proposal to dispense with the discourse of rights does not usually meet with easy assent. Resistance is typically based on two positions, both pragmatic. The first is that feminists are understandably uneasy about walking down from the high ground of moral rights and on to the slopes of what they see as an *ad hoc* and unprincipled struggle. The second is that an alternative vocabulary has not been developed.[101]

Another problem with abandoning this discourse, as Smart has pointed out, is that rights have a strong rhetorical appeal aimed at protection of the weak against the strong, regardless of how effective this may prove in practice.[102] However, pragmatic arguments also count against the use of rights strategies; abandoning them would avoid some of the unfortunate associations in the public mind with the animal rights' movement's militancy, and also the ridicule which the animal rights' strategy can attract. It seems easier to defend the idea that rats should be compassionately treated than that they (and frogs or spiders?) should be accorded legal rights. There is some truth in Fox's argument that the appeal to rights when allied to sensationalist tactics of the sort favoured by animal rights 'extremists' is clearly calculated to polarise public opinion.[103] Therefore, on issues such as vivisection, where there is already a broad measure of consensus *against* such experiments, as evidenced by public opinion surveys and the decision of multinational firms like Avon and Revlon to halt animal experimentation in a blaze of publicity, it *is* counter-productive to alienate popular support by such tactics as the bombing of university campuses.[104] It would be much more productive to concentrate on educating the public in the very valid objections that 'respectable' scientists and philosophers have to such experiments.

Turning from pragmatic arguments to the critique of rights on a philosophical level, Rollin refutes an argument which suggests that animals cannot be the subject of rights because rights and duties are correlative concepts, and since animals owe us no duty they cannot be the subject of rights. As he points out, such arguments, like those designed to show that humans and animals are essentially different, overlook the fact that whilst animals may lack the capacity to be moral agents, they do nonetheless possess rights as objects of moral concern, which we are obliged to protect.[105] However, in itself this defence of animal rights seems to me to reinforce the inferior status of animals by perpetuating the subject/object dichotomy.

Other arguments against rights suggest that rights discourse has become totally debased and meaningless in recent years. An example is Minogue's argument that the concept of rights has become contaminated by entering the political rather than the moral arena. He contends that whereas rights used to be metaphysical entities in terms of which claims might be supported, i.e., they were *preconditions* of politics rather than part of politics, they have now simply become political demands.[106] In part this explains the currency of rights arguments, because any political movement can frame its demands in rights discourse.

In my view a more compelling argument against adopting the rights approach is Tushnet's point that legal rights, like all forms of legal reasoning, are inherently unstable and indeterminate, and make sense only when located within a full social and legal context.[107] This draws on Marxist theory, and, in similar vein to Salt, suggests that granting equal rights to *unequal* persons or beings will produce unequal effects.[108] Thus, whilst rights arguments may sound convincing in the abstract, as is the case when one looks at the writings of Regan and Rollin, once one considers how they would work in a real social context it becomes clear that granting animals formal legal rights is unlikely to effect any real change in their position, just as granting women, blacks, children and other oppressed groups rights has not led to real equality in their treatment.

Further, as Olsen contends, rights arguments are ultimately incapable of settling meaningful conflicts.[109] They simply set up a system of adversarial claims which polarise groups into opposing factions whose positions become irresolvable and more entrenched as new rights claims are generated. Moreover, they are particularly ill-equipped to settle the conflict between an asserted right of animals to a life free from human interference and the right which humans claim to the putative benefits of animal research. Once the argument is framed in these terms it seems to me inevitable that animals will lose out. Rather than settling the matter on any rational basis, it is decided so as to protect the interests of the most powerful group. Granting animals legal rights will not redress this power imbalance – on the contrary it will reinforce the power structure and entrench the dichotomies upon which it is based. As Livingston argues: 'The difficulties inherent in these discussions [of animal/environmental rights] arise in great measure from the failure to acknowledge that concepts of rights arise in human social environments which are built on dominance, hierarchies or *other forms of power relationships*' (his emphasis).[110] These formal and hierarchical qualities demonstrate that rights are ultimately an exercise of power. Hence, just as MacKinnon has argued that abstract rights will authorise the 'male' experience, so they will valorise *human*

153

experience and inevitably give priority to the interests of humans –
legal rights would be granted to animals only to the extent that they
don't really impact upon human interests. This is because law does
not provide a *rational* basis for choosing which right to protect in
any particular case. The point can be illustrated by a consideration
of the 'hard cases' where rights conflict. Those liberals who pay lip-
service to the importance of rights face problems with certain rights,
particularly where it is alleged that the right to do one thing causes
harm to others, but the nature of the 'harm' or the status of the
'others' is not clear.[111] Thus, for example, liberals who have come to
treat the right to free speech as a shibboleth, are reluctant to restrict
freedom of pornographers to express themselves, ignoring the harm
this causes women in the way that society perceives them, unless a
causal connection between pornography and sexual violence can be
demonstrated.[112] Similarly, the reluctance of many humans to give
up their 'freedom' to eat meat blinds them to the fact that animals
are 'others' who can thus be possessors of rights. Rights analysis,
rather than settling such conflicts, merely restates them in a new and
obscured form. As Frey contends:

> obfuscation is nearly always the result of the invocation of
> moral rights. What inevitably ensues is that we turn away
> from the immediate and important problems of whether, say,
> our present treatment of animals is right and can be justified
> and away from the necessary task of thrashing out the prin-
> ciples of rightness and justification of treatment. Instead we
> come to focus upon the much less immediate, important and
> easily resolvable because wholly speculative, questions of
> whether there really is this or that moral right which some
> people, but not others, allege that there is, and of what the
> criteria are, for the possession of that right.[113]

What rights arguments obscure is the different types of question
we could pose. In another context Simon Lee has contended that the
simple question whether there is an absolute right to freedom of
speech has obscured the fact that there are really two separate issues
involved in that debate; the more important of which is *not* whether
one has a right to speak freely, but whether it is right or wrong to
exercise that freedom in given circumstances.[114] Similarly, there
are two separate issues involved in considering the 'right' treatment of animals: first, the question whether animals have a *right* to
equal respect/life/freedom from suffering; and, second, the more

fundamental question of whether it is right or wrong to treat animals as we do – killing and torturing them for human purposes. It seems fairly self-evident that the second question is the more important as regards our treatment of animals.

However, rather than dealing with this fundamental question, rights arguments frequently lapse into sterile debates carried on at a high level of abstraction amongst philosophers, which are unlikely to improve the lot of animals through their impact on either scientists or society at large. The language is symbolic and reified, and these factors partly account for the fact that rights strategies have promised more than they have produced. As Hutchinson and Monaghan observe, in consequence the whole rights debate, of late at least, has been remarkably unproductive.[115] According to Frey, this is because rights strategies inevitably become an end in themselves which entails more important ends taking a back seat, and few practical gains for proponents of such rights.[116] That rights arguments do actually produce very little in substantive long-term gains is only now beginning to shake faith in liberal rights strategies.[117] As the North American experience demonstrates particularly well the protection of rights is vulnerable to changes in the political outlook of the legislature or judiciary. Thus, even where rights are granted, unless the power relations in society are addressed, they can easily be taken away again. Rights will be productive only if the basis of power in society is changed. As Salt proclaimed:

> It is of little use to claim 'rights' for animals in a vague, general way, if with the same breath we explicitly show our determination to subordinate those rights to anything and everything that can be construed into a human 'want'; nor will it ever be possible to obtain full justice for the lower races so long as we continue to regard them as beings of a wholly different order, and to ignore the significance of their numerous points of kinship with mankind.[118]

Indeed, perhaps the most pressing strategic problem with rights arguments is that, in part because of the obfuscation they create, they may actually exhaust the transformative potential of social movements. As Olsen points out, ultimately, rights strategies are fairly limited because they effect only a very partial change in power relations within society. Therefore the emphasis on rights can be politically stultifying – it may constrict visions of possible change and deflect attention from the need for the social reconstruction necessary to meet the needs of animals currently abused. The premise of rights arguments is inherently individualistic and thus may weaken social cohesiveness and foster antagonisms by magnifying disagreements within and conflicts between groups over rights. A focus on securing legal rights can result in the movement's inability to take account of the range of political strategies available and to determine appropriate reforms. Olsen has contended of feminist legal criticism that it:

> is at its most successful as it moves away from [rights] norms and into the risky territory of real concerns that are political rather than neutral or impartial. Abstract rights and neutral rules are devices used by feminists to deny what we really want while getting what we want indirectly.[119]

I would suggest that the same is true of the animal liberation movement – we too should 'stop trying to fit our goals into abstract rights arguments and instead call for what we really want'.[120] What is needed is a change in the conditions which make rights seem necessary. In the final analysis the struggle is not a legal one but a cultural and social conflict,[121] and consequently, as Tushnet suggests, demanding that *needs* be satisfied now is much more important than characterising such demands, or actions to support them, as being concerned with the enforcement of rights. Animal liberationists should demand change in how animals are perceived in society, rather than simply fighting for legal change which merely tinkers with the status quo, saps the power and energies of social movements, allows trade-off for the sake of trivial human pleasures and ultimately reinforces and concretises the inferior position of animals. By allowing the state to define the movement's goals legal strategies based upon rights discourse will enable the battleground to be contained – the debate will only be allowed to operate within defined parameters. Indeed, as Smart points out, the exercise of rights may not actually empower weaker individuals, but instead draw the state's attention to a situation and bring about consequences which are quite disastrous for the individuals involved – 'legal rights do not resolve problems . . . they transpose the problem into one that is identified as having a legal solution'.[122]

Moreover, as Olsen has demonstrated, one person's 'right' will almost certainly conflict with that of another.[123] Thus, it seems inevitable that the discourse of rights will generate arguments that cut in both directions.[124] As Smart has remarked, the trend towards counter-claims is unmistakable and poses a real problem for (feminist) rights strategy in the future.[125] Drawing on the work of Kingdom and Smart in the area of equal rights it seems reasonable to assume that the law would be structurally more likely to uphold the claims of humans as opposed to those of animals which are still viewed in law, as women historically have been, as man's property. Thus, if animal liberationists do couch their demands in terms of animal rights, opponents of those rights, such as vivisectors and drug companies, will be quick to post counter-claims in terms of rights which the law may be structurally more inclined to uphold. If the battle-lines are drawn up as pitting human rights versus those of animals (as opposed to viewing the two as self-supporting) it is easy to predict how the law would mediate, and how this would serve to symbolically reinforce animals' subordinate position in our society.

Aside from law's (perhaps unconscious) partiality to one side, another problem with a concentration upon securing legal rights is that law is inherently unpredictable in its effects, and will almost certainly work in unexpected ways and produce unintended side-effects.[126] Thus, legal rights, even where they are conceded, can operate in an unforeseen manner. What can be predicted with some confidence is that dominant groups are likely to benefit as much, as analyses of anti-discrimination legislation have demonstrated.[127] The conflicting approaches to rights which pervade the whole arena of birth, life and death[128] make it probable that the courts would be particularly free in this area to interpret any legal rights granted as they thought fit. Livingston makes the point that:

> The custom which dictates that ethics and law cannot recog-
> nize rights in sensate beings drawn into power relationships, is
> a manifestation of the *a priori* assumption that all non-human
> life is dedicated to human service. The law cannot deal with
> this obstacle because it is neither a moral nor a statutory issue.
> It is a cultural predisposition. . . . The assumption legitimating
> our discretionary power transcends all moral philosophy, all
> law. It is a *given*. (his emphasis)[129]

Consequently, as was demonstrated in relation to the animal protection legislation which purportedly regulates vivisection, such
legislation is inevitably double-edged, licensing and legitimating
certain forms of animal abuse whilst outlawing and controlling

others – and at the same time serving to deflect and allay public concern. The securing of animal rights would be a hollow victory without a change in the social context in which they operate. As Petchesky has pointed out: 'rights, to be meaningful, must carry the necessary enabling conditions that will make them *concretely realizable and universally available*'.[130]

Therefore, notwithstanding the difficulties, it seems to me that it would be wise to concentrate on other tactics than relying on rights. The most productive approach for anti-vivisectionists is to concentrate on the rightness/wrongness of our treatment of animals – an approach which takes account of both the intrinsic merits of our treatment of animals and the consequences of it – as any 'credible moral theory' must.[131] To this requirement could be added Rodd's stipulation that 'any satisfactory moral system has to give some account of the way we ought to treat non-human animals as well as a theory about the relationships between humans'.[132] Thus rather than concerning ourselves with the problematic concept of rights I believe that, primarily for strategic reasons, we should shift our focus to questioning whether our treatment of animals is morally right or wrong, and concentrate on restructuring society to ensure that animals are not exploited. It remains a matter of justice to treat animals properly, but this claim is not dependent on them being possessors of rights. It seems to me that adopting such an approach avoids both the dubious consequences of utilitarianism and the philosophically inconclusive and politically dangerous strategy of engaging in the rights debate.

As far as consequences are concerned, my position should be distinguished from those, such as Frey, who have argued that from the fact that animals do not possess rights it follows that we owe only limited moral duties to them. In the first place I do not wish to deny that animals may be the possessors of moral and, consequent upon them, legal rights; indeed I personally find many of Regan's arguments persuasive. I would only claim that this is not of central importance to the issue of how we should treat animals, and it may be a misplaced strategy. Rights may have a role to play, but it is a limited one and they should be seen as part of a total revolutionary programme rather than being viewed as static and abstracted from social conditions. Similarly the centrality of law and the aim of securing legal rights for animals must be questioned. Legal reforms, like philosophical arguments, may have their place – both have an educative and symbolic role to play in addition to the minor changes which they might effect in the welfare of laboratory animals. In any event securing legal rights must be recognised as only the beginning of the struggle, not the end.

THE FOSTERING OF MORAL CONCERN

Thus, what is more important than the construction of a meta-narrative is the fostering of concern and awareness of commonality of interests of human and non-human animals. A gestalt shift in thinking from cures based on animal research and suffering to prevention is required. Animal liberationists need a more broadly-based strategy, which views securing legal reform as only one step, and is concerned also with education, consciousness-raising and direct action to achieve animal liberation. Such strategies should be aimed at fostering the level of concern which in the late 1980s led to the rise in 'green consciousness'. Numerous philosophical trea-tises by Stone or Tribe[133] are unlikely to convince the general public that trees or the environment have rights but once con-sciousness of the issues is raised people's attitude to the environ-ment changes for the better.[134] The success of enterprises like the Body Shop and its host of imitators have helped fuel the type of public concern which has caused multinationals like Avon and Revlon to stop animal testing amidst much publicity. Such gains have not been made as a result of any general acceptance that animals have rights. Rather they are the product of increased public awareness of the cruelty inflicted on animals for minimal human benefit. Ultimately, I believe, the fostering of such concern about the reality and extent of animal abuse in society will be more productive than struggling to convince people that animals have moral and legal rights. From the conclusion that the issue of rights is not crucially important, I would argue that any moral code on how we treat animals would be *very* demanding – more so than has been suggested by some of those who have argued for limited rights to be extended to animals – and that it must seek to climin-ate the conditions that make possible the oppression of non-human animals. Hence I would agree with Regan[135] that the only acceptable position is the total abolition of the harmful use of animals in science, and for the reason that animals do matter in-trinsically – not because they possess rights, but for similar reasons which explain why some commentators do accord them rights, for example, their sentiency, capacity to feel pain, have other interests, etc., i.e., their similarity to humans in *relevant* respects. Moreover, a persuasive case can be made out that human liberation entails animal liberation as it is only through a rejection of oppression and institutionalised suffering that we will secure a long-term freedom and justice for all.

To adopt the moral position that the fostering of such concern should lead to the abolition of the use of animals in medical science is to expose oneself to the hackneyed charges of being anti-humanitarian and anti-scientific. However, this is to assume too easily that the interests of humans and animals are irreconcilable. Fox's very questionable assumption 'that much of the attention and energy committed to improving the lot of animals would be put to *better* use ameliorating human need and suffering and in fact constitutes a diversion from this more important and indeed critical task' (my emphasis)[136] seems to me wholly misplaced. Fox is entitled to believe that this is a *better* and more productive way to spend his time, but others are entitled to disagree. Valid moral reasons exist for others to legitimately devote *their* time to the cause of animals – either because they are the most oppressed group in society or because of a belief that human liberation entails animal liberation. Thus a convincing case can be made that the causes of humans and animals are ultimately reducible to the same ends – a healthier environment, diet, better use of preventive medicine, increased respect for the diversity of life,[137] but of course reduced profits for the drugs companies and scientists. To accuse anti-vivisectors of 'caring more about animals than people' ignores the fact that more human suffering can be ameliorated through distribution of existing medical and scientific knowledge to people who need it, and devoting greater resources to preventive medicine rather than inflicting needless suffering on animals for few or dubious medical advances.

As for the claim that anti-vivisectionists are also anti-science, as Singer points out, anti-vivisectionists seek to do 'no more than broaden the scope of the existing restrictions in scientific research' so as to include animals.[138] To be true to science means searching for alternatives which avoid inhumane treatment of animals. Sadly scientists are all too often blinkered by their training and by the fact that research funds tend to be channelled into existing methods of research (particularly those where the anticipated returns for commercial interests are great) to pursue the test for real alternatives.[139] But it should not be simply left up to scientists to pursue alternatives, it is up to everyone else to demand that they do so. As Brophy concedes:

It is not easy for the laity, the public, to charge science with superstition [but] science is an instrument of society and society has the right to insist that it stays within the limits of a morality which society can demonstrate to be reasonable.[140]

We must face this challenge and in questioning the methods of science, particularly medical science, we must not allow ourselves to be blinded by scientific expertise. The issues we face are social and moral in nature rather than purely scientific or medical.

CONCLUSION

Apart from those with a vested interest in maintaining the present system of animal oppression – the researchers and those who profit commercially plus those who have an often misplaced belief in the ability of vivisectors to find a cure for disease – there now appears to be a fairly broad consensus that animal exploitation, like meat-eating, cannot be *rationally* defended. Philosophers who care to address the issue seriously generally concede that it is the animal liberationists who occupy the moral high ground and put forward the more defensible philosophical justifications for their stance. The 'conversion' of Fox, perhaps the leading philosophical opponent of animal liberation,[141] further illustrates the difficulties in defending the use of animals, even on medical grounds, for human purposes. It is now up to researchers and those who 'benefit' from animal experimentation to ask if the suffering and death of millions of sentient animals per year can really be justified in the name of medical science. As Brown says:

those who see no problems in the use of animals in research are often researchers themselves. The perceptions of some are masked by career ambitions, the desire for personal reputation and reward, or by obsessive preoccupation with *scientific curiosity of a kind which tends to extinguish humanity*. (My emphasis.)[142]

Once it is accepted that animals are beings which have a moral status, the question of whether or not they are possessors of rights becomes purely secondary. As we become more aware of our moral obligations and duties of justice to an expanded circle of beings[143] it becomes incumbent on medics to question why under the Declaration of Geneva (as amended at Sydney, 1968) they are pledged only to 'maintain the utmost respect for *human* life from the time of conception' and whether they are not guilty (contrary to the Declaration of Tokyo, 1975) of 'countenancing, condoning or participating in the practice of torture or other forms of cruel, inhuman or degrading procedures' in failing to question the torture and sacrifice of animals for human ends. They should address the issue of why the duties imposed under the declaration drawn up by the Council for International Organisations of Medical Sciences are much less onerous than those involving human subjects.

However, complicity in such practices is by no means confined to medics or researchers.[144] In part the widespread apathy to animal abuse can be explained by the fact that there are many who have a vested interest in concealing the reality of animal experimentation. As Spiegel points out, secrecy is essential to the maintenance of the whole system, and certainly animal abusers go to great lengths and considerable cost to keep the public in ignorance of the full horrors of vivisection. However, this alone cannot explain the public's unwillingness to challenge animal abuse. Another explanation is Midgley's suggestion that we have a very divided attitude towards animals based partly on attraction – a sense of kinship with the animal kingdom – and partly on revulsion – a desire to deny our similarity to animals. As Midgley suggests, such confusion has the consequence that: 'We do not really put this issue [our treatment of animals] outside morality; we simply find it very confusing, and therefore handle it (as we do other doubtful cases) by avoiding thinking about it as much as possible.'[145]

This is a severe abdication of our moral responsibility, which can in no way be excused by apathy and an unwillingness to forgo the benefits of animal exploitation. At the moment our apathy, combined with their ambivalent feelings about animals, allows researchers to desensitise themselves in relation to their dealings with animals, and to treat them as replaceable scientific resources. Such a process is fostered, not only by training which encourages such desensitisation, but also by the fact that our language is insufficiently developed to describe our relationships with animals. As I have argued, the legally sanctioned use of animals by the medical profession in vivisection and potentially as organ banks is the pivotal issue in the animal liberation debate and an important ethical issue. If such use cannot be justified then the moral basis for any form of animal abuse is undermined. However, as Spiegel and Rollin contend, the realisation that the animals we turn into mere laboratory tools are in fact living creatures which cannot be distinguished from humans on a non-arbitrary basis would require of most of us immense changes in lifestyle. If animals must be brought under the umbrella of moral concern, the comfortable sense of right and wrong which governs our daily existence is no longer tenable and we can no longer carry on our lives in the same untroubled way.[146] For some this would mean giving up certain dietary or fashion choices, for others forgoing the chance of a wonder-cure. However, given that the chances of finding such a cure are slight, perhaps it is not after all such a major sacrifice as proponents of animal research have alleged. In this regard they are eager to point to the possibility of a cure for cancer or AIDS, but the chances of such a cure resulting from vivisection are remote. As Sharpe points out:

> Huge resources have been expended on animal-based cancer research yet artificially induced cancers in animals have often proved quite different to the spontaneous tumours which arise in patients . . . [and] since no animal tumour is closely related to a cancer in human beings, an agent which is active in the laboratory may well prove useless clinically.[147]

Indeed this is a field of medical research where vivisection may in fact have hindered advances since, as Sharpe suggests, the traditional emphasis in this area on animal-based research has diverted attention, and resources, from efforts to understand the underlying causes of the disease, in the so far fruitless search for a cure which has cost the lives and suffering of millions of animals and founded a multinational industry.[148] In fact research on animals has been used to supposedly *disprove* the linkage between radiation and the high incidence of cancers which seem to occur in the vicinity of nuclear power stations, which directs attention and resources to seeking a cure while quite possibly obscuring and wrongly discounting potential causes of the disease.[149] Similar problems would seem to beset animal research into AIDS. Chimpanzees are the only other species to maintain the HIV virus in their bodies when injected with it, but they do not go on to develop full-blown AIDS. Again the vested interest of the scientific and pharmaceutical industries in maintaining animal research and seeking profitable new drugs is likely to lead to an overemphasis on seeking to cure rather than prevent the disease. Certainly if the resources which are currently devoted to maintaining the institution of vivisection or ploughed into high-status and expensive transplant surgery were devoted instead to education, preventive medicine and the study of disease in humans, both in this country but more importantly in Third World countries, the overall consequences may well be a more significant reduction in killer diseases and a healthier population than can ever be realistically expected from the investment in animal experimentation.

However, even if this were not the case, at a more fundamental level it is my belief that we must be prepared to forgo some benefits that may accrue from the continuation of animal abuse. Whatever the historical achievements of vivisection, in a more enlightened society they no longer justify continued experimentation on animals, any more than it would be possible to justify experimentation on a class of human slaves. Undoubtedly it could be argued that in the past men have profited from denying women equal opportunities, and similarly whites in South Africa have profited at the expense of the black majority, but we no longer feel that this justifies male oppression of women or apartheid. Similarly, though one could expect with reasonable confidence that the use of animal organs would eventually save human lives (although they could be saved, and more efficiently, were such resources diverted instead to increasing the number of intensive-care wards or providing better screening facilities for various forms of cancer), it could equally be argued that such lives could be saved by using the organs of those human beings who are so mentally defective as not to appreciate that they are being sacrificed for someone else's benefit. I believe that this action would be so fundamentally immoral that no one would seriously countenance it,[150] and therefore since no one has succeeded in convincingly demonstrating relevant differences between non-human animals and such humans, except their membership of a different species, I believe that no resultant benefits could justify the immorality of such uses of animals. Hence, as a society we should refuse to countenance the use of animals as organ banks, and divert the resources such research consumes to the prevention of illness through education and preventive health care. As this example shows, we all have a responsibility to reconsider the use of animals in medical science, and in the process to re-evaluate our beliefs and assumptions on the value of life. My argument is that we should not confine our discussion of the ethics of killing to the human species alone, and nor should we limit our discussion to academic debates about the nature of rights. It is important that such conceptual issues be examined in their practical context, and what we are concerned with is of much more than purely academic interest – the lives of millions of animals are at stake in the name of a profession supposedly dedicated to the prolongation of life and alleviation of suffering.

NOTES

1 For example, I. Kennedy and A. Grubb, *Medical Law: Text and Materials* (London: Butterworth, 1989); J. Mason and A. McCall-Smith, *Law and Medical Ethics*, 3rd edn (London: Butterworth, 1991); M. Brazier, *Medicine, Patients and the Law*, 2nd edn (Harmondsworth: Penguin, 1992); P. Skegg, *Law, Ethics and Medicine* (Oxford: Clarendon, 1988). An exception is the American casebook T. Beauchamp and L. Waters, *Contemporary Issues in Bioethics*, 3rd edn (Belmont, Calif.: Wadsworth, 1989).

2 For example, J. Rawls, *A Theory of Justice*, (Oxford: Oxford University Press, 1973); T. Campbell, *The Left and Rights* (London: Routledge & Kegan Paul, 1983); and idem., *Justice* (London: Macmillan, 1988). R. Nozick is a notable exception – see *Anarchy, State and Utopia* (Oxford: Blackwell, 1974): 35–42.

3 See Manchester Anarchists, *Dirty Fingers in Dirty Pies* (Manchester: Raven, 1986) for an illustration of the extent of commercial investment in the (ab)use of animals.

4 Home Office, Statistics of Scientific Procedures on Living Animals, Great Britain, Cm. 2023 (1991).

5 See R. Hursthouse, *Beginning Lives* (Oxford: Blackwell, 1987): esp. 59–64.

6 See P. Singer (ed.), *In Defence of Animals* (Oxford: Blackwell, 1985): 8.

7 See Stephen R. L. Clark, *The Moral Status of Animals* (Oxford: Oxford University Press, 1977): 34; T. Regan, *The Case for Animal Rights* (London: Routledge & Kegan Paul, 1984): 28–30.

8 In 1990 109,295 procedures were carried out on birds. They may suffer particularly severely because of their sociable nature.

9 Such animals are also 'protected' in their foetal form from the midway point of gestation or incubation. Section 132 of the Medicines Act 1968 similarly defines 'animal' to include any bird, fish or reptile. Whilst I agree with B. Rollin, *Animal Rights and Human Morality* (Buffalo, NY: Prometheus, 1981): 38, that all animals with nervous systems have needs and hence the category of vertebrate animals is insufficiently broad; for the purposes of this essay, which is concerned solely with those animals used in medical research, it is unnecessary to consider invertebrates.

10 See also K. Tester, *Animals and Society: The Humanity of Animal Rights* (London: Routledge, 1991): esp. 42–4, for an interesting discussion of why the concept of animal rights 'is restricted to those animals that are most like us', i.e., mammals. He suggests that:

> [a]nimal rights may be understood as a taboo which helps to maintain the differential ordering of living objects. It establishes precisely how and why humans are different from the animals they most closely resemble; it makes humanity different by making humanity moral . . . [t]he human/animal distinction is most likely to blur with mammals, and so they are the ones we must take most pains to distinguish ourselves from. Animal rights makes mammals *a part* of the human social system and *apart* from it; because they are congruous and incongruous, and therefore taxonomically ambivalent, their treatment must be subject to inhibition.

See also Clark, op. cit.: 120, who suggests that we discriminate among animals not for realistic reasons but for symbolic needs, according to the meaning with which we invest particular animals.

11 Extracted in Beauchamp and Walters, op. cit.: 423–4.
12 M. Rose and D. Adams, 'Evidence of pain and suffering in other animals', in G. Langley (ed), *Animal Experimentation: The Consensus Changes* (London: Macmillan, 1989): 62. See also Rollin, op. cit., who notes, p. 33:

> the argument cuts both ways. If animals indeed cannot anticipate, or remember, then an animal in pain cannot anticipate an end to pain or remember a time without pain, as we can. The entire horizon of its universe is filled with pain, whereas we can see an end to suffering.

13 In 1990, out of a total of 3,207,094 procedures, 2,205,360 were performed without anaesthetic.
14 See note 31 *infra*.
15 See J. Finnis, *Natural Law and Natural Rights* (Oxford: Oxford University Press, 1980): 59–80.
16 Rollin, op. cit.: 38.
17 See C. Hollands, 'Trivial and questionable research on animals', in Langley (ed.), op. cit.: esp. 129–31; and M. Fox's attempted, and in my view rather weak, defence of such experiments: *The Case for Animal Experimentation: An Evolutionary and Ethical Perspective* (Berkeley, Calif.: University of California Press, 1986): 96–113.
18 As Brazier, op. cit.: 6 points out, few professions stand so high in general public esteem as that of medicine, although as Dressler has noted public perceptions of science and medicine are no longer so uniformly positive due to disillusionment with a variety of scientific ventures. R. Dressler, 'Research on animals: values, policies and regulatory reform', *Southern California Law Review* 58 (1985): 1147–201, 1150.
19 B. Brophy, 'In pursuit of a fantasy', in S. Godlovitch, R. Godlovitch

and J. Harris, *Animals, Men and Morals* (London: Victor Gollancz, 1971): 125–45. Brophy actually confines her discussion to vivisection, but I would suggest that it should be expanded to include toxicity tests and xenografts, as broadly the same alleged justifications are made to support each practice. As R. Rodd, *Biology, Ethics and Animals* (Oxford: Clarendon Press, 1990): 139–43, points out, to this dilemma perhaps one should add the problem of how to deal with animal pests.

20 1990 Home Office statistics indicate that toxicity testing of 'non-medical' products accounted for 266,843 procedures – 659 of these related to the toxicity of tobacco which is already well-established, 5,851 to cosmetic and household products and most of the remainder concerned substances used in industry or agriculture.

21 McCloskey however contends that even though such cosmetics are not necessary they should nonetheless be tested so long as they are available to be used by humans. J. McCloskey, 'Moral rights and animals', *Inquiry* 22 (1979): 23–54.

22 The Lethal Dose 50% test involves animals being force-fed a substance, often by stomach tube, to see how much of that substance is needed to kill half of the animals in the group. The LD50 commonly kills the animals through the sheer quantity of material being pumped into their bodies rather than by poisonous effect. It is widely used to test the toxicity of drugs, cosmetics, pesticides, household and industrial products. No pain relief is given.

23 In the Draize Eye Irritancy Test, rabbits have a test substance dripped or sprayed into one of their eyes (the other eye is the 'control') whilst they are immobilised in stocks. No pain relief is given. Rabbits are used because they are cheap, docile and have large eyes which lack tear ducts to wash away painful substances.

24 E. Millstone, 'Methods and practices of animal experimentation', in Langley (ed.), op. cit.: 72–8.

25 Clark, op. cit.: 67.

26 See R. Ryder, 'Me-too drugs', *Liberator: Campaigning Journal of the BUAV* (July/August 1987).

27 Cited in A. Walden, 'Pharmaceutical firms – danger to health' (BUAV leaflet, undated).

28 Cited in R. Sharp, *The Cruel Deception: The Use of Animals in Medical Research* (Wellingborough: Thorsons, 1988): 290.

29 In September 1989 an opinion poll conducted by MORI on behalf of the BUAV found that 85 per cent of respondents were opposed to the use of animals to test cosmetics. However, the results of such opinion polls depend very heavily upon how the questions are phrased, and as Dressler points out (op. cit.: 1150 n.14) although such surveys reveal a high level of concern for animal suffering they also reveal behaviour and habits inconsistent with such concern.

30 See Russell and Burchs's classic programme for the reduction, replacement and refinement of the use of laboratory animals – W. P. S. Russell and R. L. Burch, *Principles of Humane Experimental Technique* (London: Methuen, 1959).

31 For example, B. Rollin cites a conversation with one researcher who

MARIE FOX

confessed 'it makes my job as a researcher a hell of a lot easier if I just act as if animals have no awareness': *The Unheeded Cry: Animal Consciousness, Animal Pain and Science* (Oxford: Oxford University Press, 1989): 23. See also M. Midgley, 'Are you an animal?', in Langley (ed.), op. cit.: 1–18, who contends that such a desensitisation process crucially underpins the system of animal oppression.

32 Already, back in 1984, in the celebrated Baby Fae case a baby girl lived for twenty days after the heart of a baboon was transplanted to her by surgeons in California. In 1992 in Los Angeles a woman received a pig's liver in a transplant operation designed to save her life until a human liver becomes available (*Guardian* (13 October 1992)).

33 N. Hodgkinson, 'Pigs to be used for transplants', *Sunday Times* (31 July 1988); O. Bowcott, 'Heart "breakthrough" found by chance', *Guardian* (1 August 1988); J. Sandgrove, 'Will pig transplants save our bacon?', *Guardian* (2 August 1988).

34 G. Orwell, *Animal Farm* (Harmondsworth: Penguin, 1989): 95.

35 Much as the technical possibility of 'sex-change' operations has blurred the biological dividing line between the sexes.

36 R. Hursthouse, op. cit.: 62; see also S. Lee, *Law and Morals* (Oxford: Oxford University Press, 1986): 37–8.

37 Cf. the approach of the Warnock Committee to embryos of the human species. See Carol Grunewald, 'Monsters of the Brave New World', *New Internationalist* (January 1991).

38 So much so that much newspaper coverage of the issue has focused on the issue of whether one of the pioneers of such research should have disclosed details of the research without first discussing it with colleagues, rather than the more fundamental matters at stake. For example, N. Hodgkinson, 'Ostracised: the surgeon who talked too soon', *Sunday Times* (7 August 1988); A. Ballantyne, 'Surgeon quits after "pig transplants" row', *Guardian* (2 August 1988).

39 O. Bowcott, 'BMA sees no ethical bar to pig organ transplants', *Guardian* (1 August 1988).

40 *Guardian* (2 August 1988).

41 I. Kennedy, 'The donation and transplantation of kidneys', in his *Treat Me Right* (Oxford: Clarendon Press, 1988): 237–56.

42 For example, contrast the public outcry over the buying of human organs which led to the passage of the Human Organ Transplants Act 1989, with public apathy about the use of animal organs.

43 Clark, op. cit.: 96.

44 ibid.: 157.

45 M. Midgley, 'Concept of beastliness', *Philosophy* 48 (1973): 111–35.

46 See Tester, op. cit.: esp. 17–47.

47 See Regan, op. cit.: 333–7 on why our taste and culinary preferences cannot justify killing animals.

48 Though see A. Davis, 'The status of anencephalic babies: Should their bodies be used as donor banks?', *Journal of Medical Ethics* 14 (1988): 150–3.

49 However, I would suggest that on balance such organs should not be used, mainly due to the difficulty in drawing the line between those

168

beings whose organs it is permissible to use and those whose use is impermissible.

50 See 'Anencephalic newborns: can organs be transplanted before brain-death', *New England Journal of Medicine* (August 1989): 388–90.
51 Rodd, op. cit.: 131–2.
52 B. Brophy, op. cit.: 125–45, 134.
53 B. Rollin, *Unheeded Cry*, op. cit.: 181–5; Hollands, op. cit.; D. Morton, 'The scientist's responsibility for refinement: a guide to better animal welfare and better science', and J. Hampson, 'Legislation and the changing consensus', all in Langley (ed.), op. cit.
54 See his own descriptions of such 'discomfort', op. cit.: 117–37.
55 Those which carry out scientific procedures on animals, or breed or supply animals for such establishments.
56 One a veterinary surgeon and another who has daily care of the animals.
57 For more detail on these licensing provisions see D. B. Morton, 'The scientist's responsibility for refinement: a guide to better animal welfare and better science', in Langley (ed.), op. cit.: esp. 179–87.
58 See Hollands, op. cit.: 120–3.
59 ibid.
60 Admittedly the numbers of animals used has fallen from a peak of 5.6 million in 1977, but this reduction in numbers was already a trend prior to the passage of the legislation and was not significantly accelerated by it.
61 Rodd, op. cit.: 87.
62 Home Office (1986) Guide to the Operation of the Animals (Scientific Procedures) Act 1986.
63 Clark, op. cit.: 127–8.
64 Morton, op. cit.: 180.
65 Hollands, op. cit.: 138.
66 Morton, op. cit.: 174.
67 See Sharp, op. cit.; and idem., 'Animal experiments – a failed technology', and Millstone, op. cit., both in Langley (ed.), op. cit.
68 Regan, op. cit.: 384.
69 See Brophy, op. cit.: 138.
70 See I. Illich, *Limits to Medicine* (Harmondsworth: Penguin, 1976).
71 Brophy, op. cit.: 140; see also Clark, op. cit.: 68–71.
72 See Fox, op. cit.: 94–7.
73 See also Tester, op. cit., who contends that even Bentham (*supra* p. 147) was in fact advocating a similar approach.
74 See B. Williams, 'Which slopes are slippery?', in M. Lockwood (ed.), *Moral Dilemmas in Modern Medicine* (Oxford: Oxford University Press, 1985): 126–37.
75 See S. Lee, 'Crucial battle for the moral high ground', extracted in S. Lee and M. Fox, *Learning Legal Skills* (London: Blackstone Press, 1991): 143–4.
76 See Fox, op. cit.: 36–44.
77 R. Godlovitch, 'Animals and Morals', in Godlovitch, Godlovitch and Harris, op. cit.: 164.

78 Brophy, op. cit.: 137–8.
79 P. Singer, 'Ethics and the new Animal Liberation Movement', in Singer (ed.), *In Defence of Animals*: 3. We could add that it is clear that not all human lives would objectively be deemed to be of equal value.
80 R. G. Frey, *Rights, Killing and Suffering* (Oxford: Blackwell, 1983): 43.
81 J. Bentham, *The Principles of Morals and Legislation* (Oxford: Oxford University Press, 1980 edn), ch. xvii, s. 1. See also Rousseau cited in Tester, op. cit.: 131.
82 See P. Singer, *Animal Liberation*, 2nd edn (London: Jonathan Cape, 1990): 8–9:

> If a being suffers there can be no moral justification for refusing to take that suffering into consideration. No matter what the nature of the being, the principle of equality requires that its suffering be counted equally with the like suffering in so far as rough comparisons can be made with of any other being. If a being is not capable of suffering, or of experiencing enjoyment or happiness, there is nothing to be taken into account. So if the limit of sentience (using the term as a convenient if not strictly accurate shorthand for the capacity to suffer and/or experience enjoyment) is the only defensible boundary of concern for the interests of others. To mark this boundary by some other characteristic like intelligence or rationality would be to mark it in an arbitrary manner. Why not choose some other characteristic like skin color?

83 P. Singer, 'Killing humans and killing animals', *Inquiry* 22 (1979): 145–56, 153. Furthermore, his controversial conclusions on the circumstances in which it is morally permissible to kill handicapped human infants may be deemed unacceptable.
84 Singer, *Animal Liberation*: 34.
85 Though see Clark, op. cit.: 78–80 on a method for making 'proper' utilitarian calculations which arguably might afford them a fuller protection than Singer seems to allow.
86 Regan, op. cit.
87 ibid.: 195–200.
88 T. Regan, 'The case for animal rights', in Singer (ed.), *In Defence of Animals*, op. cit.: 18.
89 J. Glover, H. Dupuis, L. R. Karhausen, S. Novacs, P. Riss, B. Schone-Seifort and L. Velayanni Moutsopoulou, *Fertility and the Family: The Glover Report on Reproductive Technologies to the European Commission* (London: Fourth Estate, 1989): 26.
90 Which some philosophers have contended are more fundamental and certainly seem less controversial than a right to life, for example see R. Dworkin, *Taking Rights Seriously* (London: Duckworth, 1977): 150–83.
91 See L. Birke, *Women, Feminism and Biology – The Feminist Challenge* (Brighton: Harvester, 1986): 119–21; A. Collett, *Rape of the Wild* (London: Women's Press, 1987); G. Corea, 'Egg snatchers', in R.

ANIMAL RIGHTS AND WRONGS

Arditti, R. Duelli Klein and S. Minden (eds), *Test-Tube Women* (London: Pandora, 1985): 37–52.

92 F. Spiegel, *The Dreaded Comparison: Human and Animal Slavery* (London: Heretic Books, 1988).

93 See Tester, op. cit.: 166–9.

94 See Singer, *Animal Liberation*: x–xi:

A liberation movement is a demand for an end to prejudice and discrimination based on an arbitrary characteristic like race or sex. . . . Discrimination on the basis of sex, it was said, was the last form of discrimination to be universally accepted and practiced. . . . We should always be wary of talking of 'the last remaining form of discrimination'. If we have learned anything from the liberation movements we should have learned how difficult it is to be aware of latent prejudices in our attitudes to particular groups until these prejudices are forcefully pointed out to us. A liberation movement demands an expansion of our moral horizons. Practices that were previously regarded as natural and inevitable come to be seen as the result of an unjustifiable prejudice. . . . The aim of this book is to lead you to make this mental switch in your attitudes and practices toward a very large group of beings: members of species other than our own.

95 For example, Fox, op. cit.: 58.

96 Spiegel, op. cit.: 25.

97 Carol Smart, *Feminism and the Power of Law* (London: Routledge, 1989): 139–41. However, even in the field of women's liberation, Smart admits that, whilst it is now generally possible to go beyond rights claims, in the case of abortion and reproductive rights we have not yet reached a stage where those rights have become taken for granted.

98 ibid.: 148.

99 See F. Olsen, 'The family and the market', *Harvard Law Review* 96 (1983) 1497.

100 See E. Schneider, 'The dialectic of rights and politics', *New York Law Review* 61 (1988): 589.

101 E. Kingdom, 'Birthrights: equal or special', in R. Lee and D. Morgan (eds), *Birthrights: Law and Ethics at the Beginning of Life* (London: Routledge, 1989): 33.

102 Smart, op. cit.: 143.

103 Though I would not agree that all the actions of groups such as the Animal Liberation Front (ALF) are necessarily counter-productive, for it seems to me manifestly obvious that some forms of direct action are much more productive than argument. Politically, carefully targeted direct action can be very productive in terms of amassing public support, for example, the tactics of the Northern Animal Liberation League (NALL) which concentrated on exposing the reality of vivisection laboratories to the public with the minimum amount of damage, and succeeded in heightening public awareness of animal abuse to a much greater extent than working within the allegedly democratic political process could have done. (For details see *Against*

171

All Odds: Animal Liberation 1972–86 (London: Arc Printing, 1986).) Practically, 'sabotaging' hunts may save more animal lives than any amount of non-direct action. Most importantly, direct action is successful in terms of hitting animal abusers financially. The most spectacular 'success' of the animal liberation movement in this regard has undoubtedly been the decision of major stores like Debenhams and Harrods to stop stocking furs. Though the campaigns of groups like Lynx have undoubtedly contributed to the unacceptability of wearing fur it is hard to believe that such decisions were not dictated more through fears of the economic effects of fire-bombing campaigns by the ALF.

104 See *The Times*, 12 June 1990. Although again it is difficult to dispute ALF claims that the amount of money which the vivisection industry has been forced to spend on security as a result of various forms of ALF action has reduced the number of animal experiments.

105 Rollin, *Animal Rights and Human Morality*: 9–16.

106 K. Minogue, 'What's wrong with rights', in C. Harlow (ed.), *Public Law and Politics* (London: Sweet and Maxwell, 1986): 209–25. Thus freedom of speech was, he suggests, clearly a right because it was the *precondition* for making a political demand rather than being itself a political demand.

107 M. Tushnet, 'An essay on rights', *Texas Law Review* 62 (1984): 1363–403.

108 K. Marx, *Critique of the Gotha Programme* (Peking: Foreign Languages Press, 1976): 8–17.

109 F. Olsen, 'Unravelling compromise', *Harvard Law Review* 103 (1990): 105–35.

110 J. Livingston, 'Rightness or rights', *Osgoode Hall Law Journal* 22 (1987): 309–21.

111 See Lee, *Law and Morals*: 22–5.

112 Admittedly the free speech/pornography issue is a particularly intractable one, and in other areas there have been attempts to resolve rights problems by liberal academics (see, for example, J. Waldron (ed.), *Theories of Rights* (Oxford: Oxford University Press, 1984); Dworkin, op. cit.), but it seems to me that ultimately the test of a theory must be how far it deals with such problematic issues.

113 Frey, op. cit.: 46.

114 S. Lee, *The Cost of Free Speech* (London: Faber & Faber, 1990).

115 A. Hutchinson and P. Monaghan, 'The "Rights" Stuff: Roberto Unger and Beyond', *Texas Law Review* 62 (1984): 1477.

116 Frey, op. cit.: 43–6.

117 See in particular the recent decisions severely curtailing a woman's 'right' to an abortion, for example, *Webster v Missouri Reproductive Health Services* [1989] 492 US 490; *Rust v Sullivan* [1991] 111 S. Crt. 1759 US; and *Planned Parenthood v Casey* [1992] 120 L.Ed (2d) 683.

118 H. Salt, *Animal Rights Considered in Relation to Human Progress* (London: Centaur, 1980 (originally published 1892)).

119 F. Olsen, 'The family and the market': 429, n. 199.

120 ibid.: 430.

121 R. Petchesky, *Abortion and Woman's Choice* (London: Verso, 1986): viii.
122 Smart, op. cit.: 144.
123 Frances Olsen, 'Statutory rape: a feminist critique of rights analysis', *Texas Law Review* 63 (1984): 387–432.
124 Frey, op. cit.: 43–4; and see also E. Kingdom, 'Legal recognition', in C. Smart and J. Brophy, *Women in Law* (London: Routledge & Kegan Paul, 1985); and E. Kingdom, 'Consent, coercion and consortium', *Journal of Law and Society* 12 (1985): 19.
125 Smart, op. cit.: 152.
126 See J. Morison, 'How to change things with rules', in S. Livingstone and J. Morison (eds), *Law, Society and Change* (London: Dartmouth, 1990).
127 C. MacKinnon, 'Reflections on sex equality under law', *Yale Law Journal* 100 (1991): 1309; see also Tushnet's illustration of how the First Amendment's protection of freedom of speech has been so interpreted by the courts as to act as a guarantor of privilege and an obstacle to progressive legislative efforts (pp. 1386–92).
128 See R. Lee and D. Morgan, 'Is birth important?', in Lee and Morgan (eds), op. cit.: 8–11.
129 Livingston, 'Rightness or rights?', op. cit.: 314–15.
130 Petchesky, op. cit.: xv.
131 Hutchinson and Monaghan, op. cit.: 1418.
132 Rodd, op. cit.: 123–4.
133 C. Stone, 'Should trees have standing – toward legal rights for natural objects', *Southern California Law Review* 45 (1972): 450–501; L. Tribe, 'Ways not to think about plastic trees: new foundations for environmental law', *Yale Law Journal* 83 (1974): 1315–48.
134 Although the complexity of these issues on a moral and practical level may be demonstrated by the fact that the production of environment-friendly goods may lead to a rise in animal-testing.
135 Regan, *Case for Animal Rights*: 393.
136 Fox, op. cit.: 4.
137 See Clark, op. cit., and in particular his idea of commonwealth of humans and animals (pp. 132–3): 'A world picture which permits the recognition of other living creatures as affectionate, appetitive and the like and allows us to live together in friendship.'
138 Singer, *Animal Liberation*: 86.
139 See Dressler, op. cit.: 1148–54; and T. Kuhn, *The Structure of Scientific Revolutions*, 2nd edn (Chicago, I.: University of Chicago Press, 1970).
140 Brophy, 'In pursuit of a fantasy': 143.
141 See G. Langley, 'Plea for a sensitive science', in Langley (ed.), op. cit.: 193–218, 209; citing 'Author reverses views on animal rights' (letter), *Scientist* (18 December 1986); and M. Fox, 'Arguing against animal research', *Whig Standard* (Canada) (4 April 1987): 5–7.
142 L. Brown, *Cruelty to Animals* (London: Macmillan, 1988): 117. However, as Dressler acknowledges (op. cit.: 1151. n. 21) the past few years have seen the emergence of a burgeoning group of scientists willing to openly scrutinise their use of animals.

143 P. Singer, *The Expanding Circle: Ethics and Sociobiology* (Oxford: Clarendon Press, 1981).

144 See Singer, *Animal Liberation*: 9–10:

> Most human beings are speciesists . . . the overwhelming majority of humans take an active part in, acquiesce in, and allow their taxes to pay for practices that require the sacrifice of the most important interests of members of other species in order to promote the most trivial interests of our own species.

145 Midgley, 'Are you an animal?': 17.

146 Rollin, *Animal Rights and Human Morality*: 4.

147 Sharp, 'Animal experiments – a failed technology': 109–10.

148 See Clark, op. cit.: 79; and R. Ryder, *Victims of Science: The Use of Animals in Research* (London: Davis-Pointer, 1975): 58.

149 Sharp, *Victims of Science*: 86.

150 However, whilst I think we should be extremely wary about drawing the parallels with Nazism which plague popular moral debate, memories of Nazi experiments should not blind us to the remote possibility.

9

Tailoring multiparity: the dilemmas surrounding death by selective reduction of pregnancy

Frances Price

The difficulty of deciding exactly what selective reduction is, when the foetus is killed inside the womb makes the position different from that of ordinary abortion. Therefore, miscarriage is regarded as the legally correct description.
(Kenneth Clarke, *House of Commons Official Report* 21 (June 1990) col. 1198)

Several well-publicised 'grand multiple' births and deaths have promoted public awareness that the acceptance of certain forms of medical assistance in the quest for a pregnancy may have untoward consequences. Widespread publicity was given to the Frustacis and their septuplets born in California in 1985.[1] Following the birth of their first child, conceived after Patti Frustaci had taken a fertility drug, the couple sought medical assistance for the second time. Her septuplet pregnancy followed a course of Pergonal. One septuplet was stillborn, three died within nineteen days and the three survivors – one girl and two boys – were to suffer from impaired vision, hernias, chronic lung damage and developmental delay. The two boys also had heart damage. Soon after the birth of their seven babies, the parents instigated malpractice litigation on the grounds that the Pergonal dosage was too high and the obstetric monitoring by ultrasonography inadequate.

The lawsuit was settled out of court in July 1990, with the fertility clinic agreeing to pay the Frustacis 450,000 dollars and give the three surviving children monthly payments.

Two years later, in 1987, Susan Halton gave birth to septuplets in Liverpool. No child lived longer than sixteen days. A simple headstone in a cemetery in Merseyside records the date of death of each child. These deaths created intense public and professional consternation. An editorial in *New Society* entitled 'Septuplets: time to play God' suggested that 'the most disturbing feature of this tragedy is that it need not have happened': 'there remained the possibility, once the seven embryos had implanted themselves in the womb, of selectively removing some of them to enhance the chances of survival of the rest'.[2]

Few people know about the procedure for reducing the number of live foetuses carried by a woman pregnant with twins, triplets or more. In the United Kingdom the practice has become known as 'selective reduction' of pregnancy. Although not widespread, this irrevocable intervention has been employed in the United States and the United Kingdom for more than a decade.

Initially, the procedure was employed only in situations following prenatal diagnosis of severe abnormality, or genetic anomaly, in one of a pair of twins. The development of the abnormal twin is halted, usually some time after the fourth month of pregnancy, with the hope that the surviving twin will flourish. The case of a pregnant woman, one of whose twins had Hurler's disease, who underwent a reduction was reported in the *Lancet* in 1978.[3]

The demise at an earlier stage of gestation of some, but not all, of the foetuses in a multifoetal pregnancy also has been effected. The intention is that the pregnancy continues with enhanced prospects for the surviving foetus or foetuses during development, at birth and thereafter. This use was first announced in a letter to the *Lancet* in 1986: a quintuplet gestation in the Netherlands was reduced to twins in the first trimester of pregnancy which resulted in the birth of two healthy females at term.[4] Subsequently, the outcomes for forty-two women who underwent a reduction of their pregnancies in France have been described:

> The treatment used in our department [of obstetrics and gynaecology] for reducing multiple pregnancies after induction of ovulation with or without IVF began in 1983. Forty-two patients have been submitted to reductions of one or more embryos. . . . From two sextuplets were obtained one monozygotic pregnancy and one failure; from 10 quadruplets: three twins, four monozygotic pregnancies and three failures; from 18 triplets: 11 twins, six monozygotic pregnancies and one failure; from 12 twins we obtained 12 monozygotics.[5]

In 1990 the *Lancet* carried an article about the outcomes for forty-six women referred to Ronald Wapner and his co-workers 'for reduction of fetal numbers with the aim of improving the outcome of a multifetal pregnancy':

There were three indications for the procedure: to improve perinatal outcome and to increase the likelihood that a term infant would be born in a multifetal pregnancy (34 women); to allow the birth of a healthy infant without the birth of a congenitally abnormal coexisting fetus (8 women); and to preserve a singleton pregnancy when the woman would otherwise have the whole pregnancy terminated (4 women). Of the 80 fetuses left after reduction 75 (94%) have survived.[6]

The term 'selective reduction' masks the directness of the action that brings about death: usually a lethal injection of potassium chloride into the heart of one or more of the foetuses. Some of the ethical dilemmas involved are suggested by other names for the procedure found in the medical literature: selective embryocide,[7] selective foeticide,[8] selective termination,[9] selective abortion,[10] selective birth,[11] selective survival.[12] The suffix – *cide*, from the Latin *caedo* (to kill), in the terms 'selective embryocide', 'selective foeticide' directly conveys that death is involved. One woman who underwent a selective reduction of her quadruplet pregnancy to a twin pregnancy at thirteen weeks described the procedure as it had been explained to her:

The doctor explained that he would inject special salty water and that the needle would go through my tummy and . . . and puncture the babies' hearts – they were going to do it like that. And the babies stay inside you – they don't come out or go rotten, they just stay there as tissue.[13]

An alternative term 'selective birth' focuses on the intention of the practice: the birth of some but not all of the foetuses. This may be the intention behind the practice. But it is not always the reality. The woman may lose the entire pregnancy, as did five of the forty-two women in the French series referred to earlier: all five developed an infection.

As the indication for reduction is the undesired number of foetuses, not their abnormalities, some commentators have represented the situation as analogous 'to reducing the numbers in an overloaded lifeboat in the open sea to improve the survival chances of those who remain'.[14] The analogy does not work well. Women with multifoetal pregnancies are not comparable to overcrowded lifeboats. Significantly, the decision to lighten the load aboard must come from *within* the lifeboat. The comparison does however provoke questions which have some resonance with the questions raised in relation to selective reduction in this chapter. How many is too many? How did the adverse situation arise? On what grounds are some to be doomed and others to survive? What are the implications in law? What is known about the social and psychological consequences for those involved?

This chapter details not only the dilemmas to be confronted in relation to selective reduction, but also at the outset introduces some of the uncertainties surrounding the bearing, rearing and provision for triplets, quadruplets and higher order birth children.

HOW COMMON ARE MULTIPLE BIRTHS?

Three, four, five, six, seven and more babies may be born of the same pregnancy. Many multiple birth sets are extremely premature. Sextuplets have sometimes all survived, but septuplets never have. Octuplets were born in Mexico City in 1967; none of the four boys and four girls survived more than 14 hours. A case of nontuplets (nine) is probably the largest recorded multiple birth; an Australian woman gave birth to five boys and four girls in 1971. Two boys were stillborn; the remaining seven infants died within a week.

Pregnancies with more than three foetuses are rare, however. Around the turn of the century, the German statistician D. Hellin suggested a formula (known as Hellin's Law) by which the incidence of higher multiple births in a given population could be calculated: if n is the incidence of twins in a population, n^2 is that of triplets, n^3 is that of quadruplets and so on. On this basis, for populations such as those in Europe and North America, where one set of twins is born once in about 100 deliveries, the incidence of triplets should be one in 10,000 and that of quadruplets one in 1 million. Other studies in the first half of this century appeared to support this mathematical relationship.

Missing from Hellin's formulation, however, was any distinction between the incidence of different types of twins, triplets and quadruplets and more. These children may arise from two, three or more separate zygotes (each the product of the fertilisation of one

178

egg with one sperm), from a single zygote that divides, or from a combination of the two.

Very little is known about the reasons separation occurs within a single zygote, but separation into two (a monozygotic, or identical, pair) is remarkably constant in all human populations at about 3.5 deliveries per 1,000; this is in contrast to the marked variations around the world in twins, triplets and larger births that arise from the fertilisation of separate eggs (dizygotic, trizygotic or higher order zygosity or non-identical sets). Rates of non-identical twinning are particularly high in parts of Africa such as Nigeria and particularly low in Japan. There may well be a genetic predisposition to multiple ovulation, which perhaps is modified by environmental factors. Also, the likelihood of a woman having a non-identical multiple birth increases both with advancing age, peaking in the late thirties, and with the number of children she has previously borne (parity) – the more children, the higher her chances.

NEW HORIZONS IN HUMAN CONCEPTION

What is of far greater significance in considering the incidence of multiple births, however, is the unpredictable impact of developments in the medical management of infertility since the mid-1960s – in particular the rapid rise in the number of triplet and higher order births around the world. In England and Wales, 208 sets of triplets, ten sets of quadruplets and two sets of quintuplets were born in 1991, compared with seventy sets of triplets and six sets of quadruplets in 1982: 31.7 sets per 100,000 deliveries in 1991 compared with 12.2 per 100,000 in 1982.

Human reproduction is remarkably inefficient, but, despite this, most women who attempt to conceive do so within a year. Usually in a woman's monthly ovulatory cycle, a dominant single egg develops in one of her two ovaries. This egg grows in a fluid-filled cyst (a follicle) until it is mature. During ovulation it bursts from the follicle and passes into one of her fallopian tubes. The developing follicle, which is visible on ultrasound scan, goes on to produce hormones that are detectable in the woman's body.

Usually, if conception is to take place, sperm meet the egg in the woman's fallopian tube. If fertilisation results, an early embryo is formed, which travels down the fallopian tube to the uterus. If the embryo implants in the wall of the womb, a pregnancy is established. If two eggs are released and fertilised, or if a released, fertilised egg divides, a twin pregnancy results. And so on for three, four or more.

Advice about twins is available, derived from a considerable literature on the hazards of twin delivery and twin development. But by comparison with twins, the very unusualness and geographical scatter of triplets, quadruplets and children of larger multiple sets has precluded systematic study of the complications and cumulative consequences for those concerned with their care. Such higher order multiple births remain uncommon and unexpected, despite an increase in recent years. Accurate assessments of specific risks associated with such pregnancies and birth are few, although the perils of preterm birth are well documented. Most publications suggest an appreciable risk of impairment for multiple-birth infants which is usually linked to the increased frequency of prematurity.

The increase in the number of triplets and larger births is to a great extent a consequence of the use of so-called fertility drugs and assisted conception procedures in the medical management of infertility to enable a woman to conceive. As some infertility problems arise as a consequence of a failure to ovulate, a common first line strategy to achieve this objective has been to attempt to induce ovulation, although it does not by any means follow that conception will, or can, occur subsequently. Ovulation is the result of a finely co-ordinated interaction between hypothalamic, pituitary and ovarian hormones and the causes of anovulatory states can be far from straightforward – quite apart from the complexity of various other menstrual cycle disturbances.

There is now ample evidence however that certain ovarian stimulants are associated with an incidence of multiple gestation well above the spontaneous occurrence rate. The drugs that are in established clinical use are very likely to stimulate multiple ovulation: more than one ovarian follicle develops and ruptures, and a number of eggs are released. If two or more are fertilised a multiple pregnancy is then possible.

One ovarian stimulant that has been in use for well over a quarter of a century is the drug clomiphene citrate (Clomid, Serophene). A relatively inexpensive ovulatory induction agent which can be prescribed by general practitioners, this drug has been shown to be effective in a wide range of anovulatory states such as hypothalamic–pituitary dysfunction, polycystic ovary disorder, post-oral contraceptive amenorrhoea and post partum amenorrhoea. All the early reports of this drug noted a good response in terms of ovarian follicle numbers after stimulation but a relatively small risk of a multiple gestation. The manufacturer of Clomid states that the drug is associated with a 6 to 8 per cent risk of a multiple pregnancy.

The risk of a multiple pregnancy is greater however with another drug in frequent use in specialist practice: human menopausal gonadotropin (hmG, Pergonal). This drug is given by intra-muscular injections in conjunction with human chorionic gonadotropin (hCG Profasi). The prescribing information for Pergonal provided by the manufacturer asserts that 'the incidence of multiple births following Pergonal/Profasi therapy has been variously reported between 10% and 40%: the majority of multiple conceptions are twins'.[15] Refinements in gonadotropin administration – utilising improved hormone monitoring by rapid assays and high resolution ovarian ultrasound scanning to monitor the growth of the follicles – may have lowered the risk of a multiple pregnancy somewhat. But treatments remain difficult to monitor. The difficulty of controlling the number of follicles that develop in response to this and other ovulation-inducing drugs and the consequent risk of such a pregnancy remains.

In recent years, some clinics have reported that they have improved their pregnancy rate per treatment cycle by combining ovulation stimulation with intra-uterine insemination (IUI). The rationale for this approach is to bypass the cervical barrier by depositing large numbers of washed, mobile sperm directly into the woman's uterus. Overstimulation of the ovaries is an acknowledged drawback. Figures published in June 1991 by the Hallam Medical Centre in London indicate that between 6 and 7 per cent of women undergoing IUI produce more than four follicles. The clinic's multiple pregnancy rate for treatment cycles with ovarian stimulation with IUI was higher than for treatment cycles with ovarian stimulation alone: 'out of the first 100 pregnancies resulting from our IUI programme, nine were multiple pregnancies, seven twins and two triplets'.[16]

Multiple egg and embryo transfer

A more recent concern is the rate of multiple pregnancies after doctors have transferred several eggs or embryos in assisted conception techniques such as *in vitro* fertilisation (IVF) and gamete intrafallopian transfer (GIFT). Many clinics practising IVF and

181

GIFT have achieved both high rates of egg recovery and of fertilisation. But, although early development of such embryos is satisfactory, the rates of implantation of these embryos in the uterus remain low.

There is considerable dissent about what constitutes 'good practice' in the field of IVF and GIFT. This turns, in part, on different evaluations of acknowledged clinical risks, on what is to count as evidence, on the professional priority to be given in each clinical case to establishing and maintaining a pregnancy and on whether it is possible to predict which women are at greater risk of a multiple birth. Certain IVF clinics encourage the idea of a multiple birth by including photographs of twins and even triplets in their publicity material.

During the early 1980s, the idea gained currency that the IVF pregnancy rate would increase with the number of embryos transferred in each treatment cycle.[17] Edwards later put forward the idea, since retracted, that a synergism exists which he called embryo 'helping': an embryo capable of implantation somehow facilitates other transferred embryos to implant.[18] By the mid-1980s, pooled counts from IVF centres around the world seemed to confirm such predictions and encouraged the transfer of between three and six embryos. If at least three embryos are transferred, the late Patrick Steptoe estimated in 1986 that the risk of a multiple pregnancy would be about 25 per cent, and he questioned whether the risks of high multiparity were justified.[19] But, apparently, neither he nor his colleagues envisaged the marked increase in triplet and higher order multiple pregnancies from 1985 onwards.

Better access to ovarian follicles with ultrasound-guided retrieval, along with new combinations of ovulatory drugs, have enabled larger numbers of eggs to be collected. In 1988, six or more eggs were collected in almost half of all IVF treatment cycles in which a pregnancy was established in Australia and New Zealand.[20] Some 80 per cent of the resulting pregnancies occurred after the transfer of three or more embryos. Obviously, a triplet pregnancy is a possible, if unlikely, outcome.

The statistical analysis of the United Kingdom IVF and GIFT data by members of the Interim Licensing Authority for Human In Vitro Fertilisation and Embryology (ILA, formerly the Voluntary Licensing Authority, VLA) show a clear association between the rise of multiple births from 1985 onwards and the increased use of IVF, GIFT and associated procedures.[21] The Medical Research

Council (MRC) Working Party on Children Conceived by In Vitro Fertilisation found that 23 per cent of deliveries following assisted conception by IVF or GIFT resulted in a multiple birth of twins or more, compared with about 1 per cent for natural conceptions.[22] There is an additional risk factor: a higher than expected frequency of identical (monozygotic) twins, not only after the induction of ovulation with drugs,[23] but also after IVF and GIFT.[24] Thus there are reports of three eggs or embryos being transferred in a GIFT or IVF procedure and the outcome being a quadruplet pregnancy.

From 1987 the voluntary guidelines issued by the ILA stated that no more than three eggs or embryos should be transferred in any one cycle unless there were exceptional clinical reasons when up to four eggs or embryos could be transferred.[25] And, in 1991, three became the maximum in centres licensed by the newly-established Human Fertilisation and Embryology Authority (HFEA) set up under the terms of the Human Fertilisation and Embryology Act 1990.[26] However, unless the procedure involves the use of donated eggs or sperm, the GIFT procedure is not covered by the remit of the HFEA. The framing of the 1990 Act was explicitly to cover research and clinical practice involving work with embryos. The GIFT procedure is excluded because it involves clinical work with eggs and sperm.

HOW MANY IS TOO MANY?

Little data exists on what people attending infertility clinics expect from the clinical services they might receive. However, women and men confronting infertility may view a multiple pregnancy in a positive light. The idea of twins is widely welcomed, for instance. At the Universitaire Baudelocque in Paris 90 per cent of couples in the IVF programme were ready to take the risk of a triplet outcome to maximise their chances of a pregnancy.[27] Some 7 per cent of people attending the clinic expressed reservations about the possibility of multiple pregnancy and a few (3 per cent) declared themselves incapable of envisaging bringing up twins, quite apart from triplets. In an unpublished survey in New Jersey, Leiblum and her co-workers report that of four groups of women (designated 'IVF, ovulation stimulation with human gonadotropins (hMG), donor insemination and female medical student'), the 'IVF women' were 'the most receptive to having quadruplets or even quintuplets rather than having no biological children'.[28]

Few people have known children from a triplet, quadruplet or higher order set. Even fewer have provided care or support for these children, for their parents and for any siblings. For most people, the prospect of triplets or more is too remote to be imaginable. Ignorance seems understandable: the problems faced by those responsible for their delivery, care and welfare are not widely known. When, however, clinicians advocate procedures that increase the risk of plural births, this ignorance becomes disconcerting. From 1986 onwards, shortages of both staff and cots in hospital intensive-care units made the difficulties of neonatal provision for these children even more apparent and neonatal paediatricians voiced their concern.[29]

In the late 1980s, as the rise in the numbers of these births became more marked in the United Kingdom in national registration data, and as paediatricians became more vocal about the neonatal consequences, support came from the Department of Health for a national study which has provided the first comprehensive data from Britain. Called the United Kingdom Study of Triplets and Higher Order Births (the National Study), it is also the first study in the world to look at the problems to be faced caring for these children.[30]

Information was collected, in three complementary surveys, about the problems encountered by parents and by the doctors concerned with 313 sets of triplets and twenty-seven sets of quadruplets, quintuplets or sextuplets born in the early to mid-1980s. Surveys of obstetricians, paediatricians, other specialists and of family doctors were conducted jointly by the Office of Population Censuses and Surveys (OPCS) in London and the National Perinatal Epidemiology Unit (NPEU) in Oxford. I undertook the survey of parents (the Parents' Study) which was based at the Social and Political Sciences Faculty at the University of Cambridge.[31] This study involved the mothers, and many of the fathers, of triplets, quadruplets and quintuplets born in the years 1979–88.

Multiple pregnancy places a much greater physical strain on the mother than a pregnancy with a single baby. The risk of a miscarriage is greater.[32] Complications (such as bleeding or raised blood pressure) are more likely to arise than in a single pregnancy and can arise earlier in the pregnancy.[33]

In the National Study over half of the quadruplets and just over a quarter of triplets weighed under 1,500 grams at birth. About half the quadruplet or higher order births included in the obstetric survey occurred before thirty-two weeks of gestation compared with a quarter of triplets and less than a tenth of twins. In contrast only 1 per cent of singletons sampled in the British Maternity Hospital In-Patient Enquiry (HIPE) were born before thirty-two weeks' gestation.

More triplets, quadruplets and quintuplets now survive than was the case in the 1970s and earlier. During the five year period from 1986 to 1990, in England and Wales, triplets and higher order multiple-birth babies had five times the stillbirth rate, and twelve times the infant mortality rate of singleton babies.[34] But their mortality rates have not fallen as rapidly as those for single births. Compared with singletons, triplets and higher order birth children have a higher rate of serious congenital malformations visible at birth.[35] Notified malformations of the central nervous system and of the cardiovascular system are about twice as common among multiple-birth children as among singletons. Complications of prematurity and uteroplacental insufficiency are the main contributors to perinatal morbidity and mortality. These children are at an increased risk of cerebral palsy, particularly spastic diplegia, squint, pyloric stenosis and repeated hospital admissions.

SOCIAL CONSEQUENCES: QUALITY OF LIFE

When the children come home from hospital, their caretakers face a very demanding situation: it is not possible for one person to cope alone for any length of time. Where space is confined, it is likely to become an issue of great consequence and difficulties with transport can be an impediment to outings. Mothers of triplets and more risk becoming isolated and housebound, particularly in the first two years, if they have neither someone with whom to share the responsibility for the children nor a companion to accompany them on outings to parks and play areas.

Reported difficulties are emotional as well as practical. One mother of 2-year-old triplets described the difficulties of coping:

> The problems seem to arise from the fact that I get no respite from them at all. My husband freely admits that he cannot cope with them either emotionally or physically, and friends feel intimidated with the sheer number of them to cope. . . .

Familiar timetables are disrupted, and relationships also. Seldom are these consequences anticipated. The situation is not normal:

185

attempts to behave 'as normal' usually had untoward consequences, especially when the parents' exhaustion is exacerbated by insufficient sleep.

Mothers of triplets in the study described the feeling of being 'a freak':

> I am, I suppose, a private person and I have found the amount of attention they attract difficult to cope with. I can't walk down the main street without people approaching me. At times people do, probably unwittingly, make you feel a bit of a freak.

> I would not like the last three and a half years again. I have got very annoyed with people in the street who think we are so different and ask the same old questions. I have found myself becoming very withdrawn and rude to a point where I don't stop when people stop me.

Such is the novelty of the situation and scale of the demands that the help, support and advice available from the health and social services, and also from the voluntary sector, may not begin to meet the needs as perceived by the parents. One local authority social services department manager summed it up when he wrote: 'Such cases do not easily "fit" in terms of local authority provision – i.e. not elderly, not handicapped, no real question of reception into care. Requires some "imaginative" and liberal interpretation of guidelines and legislation.'

TAILORING MULTIPARITY

Until recently, a question mark hung over selective reduction in the United Kingdom. Was it permitted by the law relating to abortion? Unambiguously novel and dependent on advances in obstetric ultrasonography, prenatal diagnosis and fetoscopy, the procedure was not envisaged when legislation was passed in 1861, 1929 and 1967. Confusion about its legality is evident in the literature. Lawyers deliberated, for instance, whether or not the procedure was caught by section 58 of the Offences Against the Person Act 1861. This section prohibits the administration of a noxious substance or the use of an instrument with intent to procure the miscarriage of a woman whether pregnant or not. The debate turned on the term 'miscarriage'. Does it refer to the expulsion of the foetus from the uterus, to the emptying of the uterus or to the failure of gestation in itself? The decision not to prosecute an obstetrician who undertook the procedure in a case involving a twenty-seven-week twin foetus with Klinefelter's syndrome in 1989 was not settled until 1991.[36] Reference was made to this case in Parliament during the passage of the Human Fertilisation and Embryology Bill.[37]

The tailoring of multiparity by terminating apparently normal implanted embryos or foetuses first received adverse publicity in the UK early in 1987.[38] At that time no Voluntary Licensing Authority guideline made explicit reference to the procedure: it featured in the Second Report of the authority in 1987 as an additional issue in relation to the newly-introduced guideline 12:

It would be improper deliberately to introduce more than four pre-embryos to the uterus and then, should a large multiple pregnancy result, to reduce the number of live embryos other than for legitimate clinical reasons such as malformation or ectopic pregnancy.[39]

In that same year, the chairman of the Licensing Authority, Dame Mary Donaldson, made it clear in a letter to *New Scientist* that the authority regarded selective foeticide after a multiple egg transfer in a GIFT procedure and multiple embryo transfer in an IVF procedure as 'unacceptable and unethical'.[40] However, in 1988, annex 5 of the Third Report of the VLA provided a definition of 'selective reduction of pregnancy' (which, misleadingly, makes reference only to embryos):

Selective reduction of pregnancy is the term used to describe the procedure whereby one or more embryos in a multiple pregnancy are selectively killed to allow others to develop. In multiple pregnancies resulting from infertility treatment the procedure is used to avoid large multiple births though the technique has originated to stop the development of abnormal embryos in a multiple pregnancy where the remainder were normal.[41]

Published legal opinions were to the effect that the use of this procedure did not fall within the terms of the 1967 Abortion Act. John Keown's opinion, included as annex 4 of the VLA's Third Report, was entitled 'Why selective reduction could result in criminal proceedings'. Legal uncertainties were assuaged only when the Human Fertilisation and Embryology Act of 1990 brought selective reduction under the 1967 Abortion Act.[42] Section 37(5) of the 1990 Act rewrites section 5(2) of the 1967 Act.

There is no public record of the number of selective reductions undertaken. Obstetricians are undoubtedly wary of the procedure and it is difficult in some countries to find an obstetrician to undertake it. At least one clinician in the United Kingdom is prepared to offer the procedure to women who are not already under his care, and others have stated that they would be prepared to consider the procedure for women under their supervision.[43] In France, by contrast, several clinics make selective reduction routinely available to women with triplet or higher order pregnancies.[44]

There are those clinicians who regard these pregnancies as a disaster for all concerned, besides spelling trouble for paediatric units. These doctors urge strongly that all possible steps should be taken to ensure that the risk of such a pregnancy is avoided. But here lies the dilemma. The transfer of three embryos or eggs is generally regarded, internationally, as 'normal' practice in IVF and GIFT for the best chance of a pregnancy. And there is no regulation of ovulation induction practices. In the policy arena, certainly in the United Kingdom, ideas about the standing of medical decisions in clinical practice remain highly influential and pave the way for certain policy conclusions. Institutional pressure has protected the privileged status of clinical judgement which is used to control the discourse about risk.

THE EXPERIENCE OF SELECTIVE REDUCTION

There has been no systematic study of the experience of those women who have undergone selective reduction of their multiple pregnancies. Articles in the press and in support group newsletters have indicated some of the concerns and confusions.[45]

One woman wrote of her experience in the *Support After Termination for Abnormality News* (SATFA):

In February last year I was faced with deciding whether to have selective feticide. This is a new procedure for termination of one twin. My Twin I was perfect but Twin II had spina bifida and hydrocephalus. The procedure involved inserting a needle through my stomach into Twin II. I would then carry

188

both babies until I gave birth. I was told there was a high risk of miscarrying both babies. I felt that after the initial shock and pain of being told one of my twins was very ill, I could face the fear of miscarriage. I really had no choice – I had to give my perfect baby every chance of survival.

The procedure was carried out at 22 weeks. I remember feeling so afraid that the needle would be painful – not only the physical pain but the mental pain really frightened me. I was to discover that the mental pain far exceeded the slight discomfort the needle caused.

After the first 24 hours the fear of miscarrying decreased. Then my imagination took over. What was going on inside me? Did Twin I know what had happened to its twin? Would Twin I miss the movement of Twin II? Had the doctors terminated the correct Twin? And more important were the doctors sure that Twin I was OK?

On August 11th 1988 all my fears were taken away when I gave birth to a 9lb 12oz lovely boy. He was just perfect, and so big! After the normal stay in hospital I went on holiday with my husband, parents and my baby.

This is when I started to think about Twin II more and more. Until now all my thoughts had been for Twin I. Although I cried while I was having the procedure it was for Twin I. Even at the birth I was only concerned that Twin I was perfect and not that they had taken Twin II away. But now I had Twin I, my true grief over losing Twin II was hitting me. As I cared for my baby I wondered if Twin II, although they were not identical twins, would have looked like his/her brother.

Was Twin II a boy or girl? Yet this question had been one that I told the hospital I didn't want to know because then Twin II would become a person in my mind, which I knew I wouldn't be able to cope with.[46]

Bryan's study conducted in the mid-1980s focused on the experiences of eleven of the first thirteen women to undergo this procedure for twin–twin discordancy who had one surviving child.[47] All had discovered that the foetuses in their twin pregnancy were discordant for an anomaly likely to cause severe physical or mental disability. All had undergone the procedure at eighteen to thirty-one weeks of pregnancy at one centre in England. None had known about selective reduction before the diagnosis.

Bryan suggested that the medical profession was in general insufficiently informed about selective reduction, that it failed to give appropriate advice and that the sense of loss at the time of the birth was neither acknowledged nor supported. Only one woman was offered bereavement counselling. Some women had to explain the procedures to their general practitioner, health visitor and midwife. Of the eleven women, nine had told close relatives and friends, some of whom were disturbed by the idea. One woman who had undergone the procedure was distressed by the horrified reaction of her friends. Only one was not planning to tell her surviving child. The others were concerned about how best to explain what had occurred.

WHERE TO DRAW THE LINE?

Will selective reduction of multiple pregnancy become more generally available and, if so, under what circumstances and for what order of multiplicity? What are the criteria for deciding? What are the public policy implications? Are twins to be regarded as a normal pregnancy outcome, or not?[48] Most women understand motherhood to be a deep commitment. If a pregnant woman diagnosed as pregnant with twins states that she cannot countenance the prospect of bringing up twins, should selective reduction be an option for her? Can there be an ethical distinction between an overt congenital defect and one that could be said to lie in the realm of the politics of social welfare? There are political and social issues in relation to selective reduction that merit attention in their own right.

Selective reduction raises questions about the meaning of, and respect for human life. Is a distinction to be made if the multiple pregnancy has come about spontaneously? Reports to date suggest that reductions have been undertaken only where the multiple birth has arisen after medical assistance.

The public policy issues in this field go beyond declarations that there should be an increased consumer voice and consumer choice in medicine. The extent to which the communication of information about these matters is in disarray has been effectively masked. Long-standing notions not only about the hermetic nature of the doctor–patient relationship but also about clinical freedom have powerfully structured the agenda for debate, particularly in relation to establishing guidelines, to external regulation, to informed consent and to the nature and extent of counselling at the 'interface' between doctor and patient. In the clinics the promotional language is of remedy.

Issues of even greater complexity are presented by a case in Italy where GIFT, genetic diagnosis and selective reduction were undertaken to enable twins to be born in 1990 to a woman and her partner who risked passing on β-thalassaemia to their offspring. All eight eggs recovered from the woman in the GIFT procedure were transferred with the intention of increasing 'the likelihood of a multiple pregnancy'. At six weeks a quadruplet pregnancy was diagnosed and, after genetic diagnosis, the four embryos were reduced to two. The medical team reported that the woman subsequently delivered a healthy 2,300 gram boy and a 2,430 gram girl at thirty-seven weeks' gestation.[49]

At least two of the larger licensed assisted conception centres in the United Kingdom have data that demonstrate that pregnancy rates are just as high when the number of embryos transferred is limited to two (when more than two are available) as they are when three are transferred.[50] Alternatives to drug-stimulated IVF – in particular the close monitoring of the hormonal fluctuations within a woman's natural menstrual cycle – are available in some centres. This enables the time of ovulation to be predicted so that the retrieval of a single mature egg can be assured with a high degree of confidence. Called natural cycle IVF, this procedure is far less stressful and is undertaken entirely on an out-patient basis. But it requires expertise in endocrinology and, as yet, the pregnancy rate is appreciably lower than the rate obtained in IVF programmes using ovarian stimulation.[51]

Selective reduction is always likely to be a problematic option for a pregnant woman. She may accept the option with relief but later may experience guilt and grief. Her partner may accept the option more readily and bring pressure to bear. No one has yet explored the psychological and social complications for the parents and the survivors. One woman who gave birth to two children after a reduction of her quadruplet pregnancy spoke of the emotional turmoil she felt when she came home from hospital with her two children. She felt unable to explain her grief to sympathetic neighbours because she felt guilty. Her partner remarked, 'There's always that awful doubt. If you'd carried on, would four have survived?'[52] There is risk and an inherent ambivalence with selective reduction. One life or more may be 'destroyed', 'spared' or transformed. Reduction not only entails the curtailing of life but also the surrender of potential identity as, for instance, 'the mother of twins', 'the parents of quadruplets'. The woman who has undergone a selective reduction of her multiple pregnancy and her partner may become victims. Any distress is compounded by the fact that few people are aware of the technique, or of the reasons for which it might be offered.[53]

NOTES

1 'Surviving septuplets stable', *The Times* (23 May 1985).
2 See 'Septuplets: time to play God', *New Society* (28 August 1987): 3.
3 A. Aberg, F. Miterian, M. Cantz and J. Geliler, 'Cardiac puncture of fetus with Hurler's disease avoiding abortion of unaffected co-twin', *Lancet* ii (1978): 990–1.
4 H. H. H. Kanhai, E. J. C. Van Rijssel, R. J. Meerman and J. Bennenbroek Gracenhorst, 'Selective terminations in quintuplet pregnancy during first trimester', *Lancet* 1 (1986): 1447.
5 J. Salat-Baroux, J. Aknin and J. M. Antoine, 'The management of multiple pregnancies after IVF', abstract 153 presented at the third meeting of the European Society of Human Reproduction and Embryology, Cambridge (28 June–1 July 1987).
6 R. Wapner, G. Davis, A. Johnson, V. J. Weinblatt, R. L. Fischer, L. G. Jackson, F. A. Chervenak and L. B. McCullough, 'Selective reduction of multifetal pregnancies', *Lancet* 335 (1990): 90–3.
7 D. F. Farguharson, B. K. Wittmann, M. Hansman *et al.*, 'Management of quintuplet pregnancy by selective embryocide', *American Journal of Obstetrics and Gynecology* 158 (1988): 413–16.
8 C. H. Rodeck, R. S. Mibastion, J. Abramowicz and S. Campbell, 'Selective feticide of the affected twin by fetoscopic air embolism', *Prenatal Diagnosis* 2 (1982): 189.
9 M. I. Evans, J. C. Fletcher, I. E. Zador, B. W. Newton, M. H. Quigg and C. D. Struyk, 'Selective first-trimester termination in octuplet and quadruplet pregnancies: clinical and ethical issues', *Obstetrics and Gynecology* 71 (1988): 289–96. M. S. Golbus, N. Cunningham, J. Goldberg *et al.*, 'Selective termination of multiple gestations', *American Journal of Medical Genetics* 31 (1988): 339–48.
10 J. Iskovitz, R. Boldes, I. Thaler *et al.*, 'Transvaginal ultrasonography-guided aspiration of gestational sacs for selective abortion in multiple pregnancy', *American Journal of Obstetrics and Gynecology* 160 (1989): 215–17.
11 F. O. Redwine and R. E. Petres, 'Selective birth in a case of twins discordant for Tay Sachs disease', *Acta Genet Med Gemellol* (Roma) (1984): 33, 35. T. D. Kerenyi and U. Chitkara, 'Selective birth in twin pregnancy with discordancy for Down's syndrome', *New England Journal of Medicine* 304 (1981): 1525–7.
12 A. Antsaklis, J. Politis, C. Karagiannopoulous *et al.*, 'Selected survival of only the healthy fetus following prenatal diagnosis of thalassemia major in binovular twin gestation', *Prenatal Diagnosis* 4 (1984): 289.

13 W. Varley, 'A process of elimination', *Guardian* (28 November, 1989): 38.
14 See 'Doctors' aid for childless may be illegal', *Guardian* (12 January 1988): 4.
15 Serono Laboratories UK Ltd, 'If nature can't deliver . . . ', pamphlet 170/0886 (1986).
16 The Hallam Medical Centre's information sheet, 'Intra-uterine insemination with superovulation' (18 June 1991).
17 J. D. Biggers, 'In vitro fertilisation and embryo transfer in human beings', *New England Journal of Medicine* 34 (1981): 336–42.
18 R. G. Edwards, 'In-vitro fertilisation and embryo replacement: opening lecture', *Annuals of the New York Academy of Science* 442 (1985): 375–80.
19 P. Steptoe, 'The role of in vitro fertilization in the treatment of infertility: Ethical and legal problems', *Medicine, Science and Law* 26 (1986): 82.
20 National Perinatal Statistics Unit, *IVF and GIFT Pregnancies: Australia and New Zealand 1988* (Sydney: National Perinatal Statistics Unit, 1990).
21 W. Thompson and V. English, *Statistical Analysis of the United Kingdom IVF and GIFT Data 1985–1990* (1992, available from HFEA).
22 MRC Working Party on Children Conceived by In-Vitro Fertilisation, 'Births in Great Britain resulting from assisted conception, 1978–87', *British Medical Journal* 300 (1990): 1229–33.
23 C. Derom, R. Vlietinck, R. Derom, H. Van Den Berge and M. Thiery, 'Increased monozygotic twinning late after ovulation induction', *Lancet* 1 (1987): 1236–8.
24 R. G. Edwards, L. Mettler and D. E. Walters, 'Identical twins and in-vitro fertilisation', *Journal of In-Vitro Fertilisation and Embryo Transfer* 3 (1986): 114–17.
25 Voluntary Licensing Authority (Joint Medical Research Council/Royal College of Obstetrics and Gynaecologists), *The Second Report of the Voluntary Licensing Authority for Human 'In-Vitro' Fertilisation and Embryology*, (London: VLA, 1987).
26 Human Fertilisation and Embryology Authority, *Code of Practice* (London: HFEA, 1991).
27 C. Contrepas, 'Information before pregnancy', *Multiple Births Foundation Newsletter* 5(2) (1989).
28 S. R. Leiblum, E. Kemmann and L. Takse, 'Attitudes toward multiple births', paper presented at the Ninth International Congress of Psychosomatic Obstetrics and Gynaecology, Amsterdam (28–31 May 1989).
29 M. I. Levene, 'Grand multiple pregnancies and demand for neonatal intensive care', *Lancet* 2 (1986): 347–8. D. C. Anderson, 'Licensing work on IVF and related procedures', *Lancet* 1 (1987): 1373. M. I. Levene, 'Assisted reproduction and its implications for paediatrics', *Archives of Diseases in Childhood* 66 (1991): 1–3. R. Scott-Jupp, D. M. Field and U. Macfadyen, 'Multiple pregnancies resulting from assisted

conception: burden on neonatal units', *British Medical Journal* 302 (1991): 1079.

30 B. Botting, A. Macfarlane and F. Price (eds), *Three, Four and More: A Study of Triplets and Higher Order Births* (London: HMSO, 1990).

31 See F. Price, ' "Isn't she coping well?" Providing for mothers of triplets, quadruplets and quintuplets', in H. Roberts (ed.), *Women's Health Matters* (London: Routledge, 1992).

32 See B. Botting *et al.*, 'Obstetric problems during multiple pregnancy', in Botting, Macfarlane and Price (eds), op. cit.: 70–9.

33 Blood loss later in pregnancy, known as ante-partum haemorrage, is more likely to occur in multiple pregnancies than with single pregnancies. This is because raised blood pressure, often now referred to as pregnancy-induced hypertension, or pre-eclampsia, is more common and this may be accompanied by placental abruption, which means that the placenta becomes detached from the wall of the uterus.

34 B. Botting, I. Macdonald Davies and A. Macfarlane, 'Recent trends in the incidence of multiple births and associated mortality', *Archives of Diseases in Childhood* 62 (1987): 941–50.

35 A. J. Macfarlane, A. Johnson and P. Bower, 'Disabilities and health problems in childhood', in Botting, Macfarlane and Price (eds), op. cit.: 153–60.

36 C. Dyer, 'Selective reduction', *British Medical Journal* 302 (1991): 1043. Klinefelter's syndrome is a prenatally detectable chromosome abnormality (47XXY). One in 1,000 males has this syndrome. They are usually asymptomic during childhood with normal performance IQ scores. In adulthood, however, they are invariably infertile.

37 Ann Widdecombe, *House of Commons Official Report* (London: HMSO, 21 June 1990): col. 1192–3.

38 D. Brahams, 'Assisted reproduction and selective reduction of pregnancy', *Lancet* ii (1987): 1409–10.

39 See Voluntary Licensing Authority, *Second Report*.

40 *New Scientist* (9 July 1987): 64.

41 Voluntary Licensing Authority, *Third Report* (London: VLA, 1988): 42.

42 D. Morgan and R. C. Lee, *Blackstone's Guide to Human Fertilisation and Embryology Act 1990* (London: Blackstone Press, 1991).

43 E. Bryan, 'I don't want so many babies', *Multiple Births Foundation Newsletter* 6(3): (1990).

44 F. Nantermox, P. Boulet, F. Molenat, J. Ray and B. Hedon, 'Psychological implications of embryonary reduction', presented at the Twelfth European Congress of Perinatal Medicine (Lyons 1990).

45 C. Steven, 'An agonising choice – which of your babies should die?', *Sunday Times* (5 November 1989): F7.

46 Anonymous, 'Selective feticide', *SATFA News* 1 (1989): 3 (Support After Termination for Abnormality).

47 E. Bryan, 'The response of mothers to selective feticide', *Ethical Problems in Reproductive Medicine* 1 (1989): 28–30.

48 See Wapner *et al.*, op. cit.

49 B. Brambati, L. Formigli, L. Tului and G. Simoni, 'Selective reduction

of quadruplet pregnancy at risk of β-thalassaemia', *Lancet* 336 (1990): 1325–6.
50 J. Waterstone, J. Parsons and V. Bolton, 'Elective transfer of two embryos', *Lancet* 337 (1991): 975–6.
51 The pregnancy rate depends on the cause of the infertility. Patricia Kohn of the Sheffield Fertility Centre reports that in 'uncomplicated "tubal" patients under the age of 40, the clinical pregnancy rate (i.e. a gestation sac is visible on ultrasound) is 17% per embryo replaced. In "unexplained" female infertility, the equivalent rate is 13% and when male factors are present it is 8%. 11% of these pregnancies abort. Not all the cycles get as far as egg recovery (although 90% do), and not all the eggs fertilise, so the overall rate per cycle is much lower than the specific rates per embryo transfer given above' (personal communication, Patricia Kohn, Sheffield Fertility Centre (11 February 1991)).
52 See Varley, op. cit.
53 Editorial, 'Selective fetal reductions', *Lancet* 2 (1988): 773–5.

10

Disasters: the role of institutional responses in shaping public perceptions of death

Celia Wells

Zeebrugge, Hillsborough, Lockerbie – now familiar names because disasters occurred there, places where a large number of people died at the same time from a common cause. Two hundred and seventy people died at Lockerbie when a Pan-Am aeroplane was blown up; one hundred and eighty-nine died off Zeebrugge when a car ferry capsized; fifty-three died at Bradford when a football stand caught fire; ninety-five died at Hillsborough when they were crushed against the perimeter fence of a football field; thirty-one died at King's Cross when a fire engulfed an underground station; and thirty-five at Clapham when faulty signalling caused a rail collision. One hundred and sixty-seven died when the *Piper Alpha* oil platform exploded in the North Sea; forty-seven died when a brand new Boeing 737 crashed at Kegworth; and, most recently, fifty-one died when *The Marchioness* pleasure cruiser was overrun by a dredger on the Thames.[1]

There is nothing new about disasters. But responses to them have changed. It is only lately that corporate manslaughter has become part of our everyday language. There was little if any talk of collective criminal liability following disasters such as those at Aberfan in 1966 and the Bradford football stadium fire in 1985. The trend towards responding to disasters in terms of corporate manslaughter seems to have begun with the capsize of *The Herald of Free Enterprise* at Zeebrugge in 1987. The reasons for this change are varied and complex, but they are not a result of any obvious differences in terms of negligence or neglect. What has changed has been our perception of corporate organisations and their responsibilities for mass

196

death. We have less faith in their ability or willingness to take safety seriously.[2]

Inquests have proved an important factor in promoting this change. The Aberfan inquest was concluded in four minutes. There is now much more pressure on coroners to allow grief to be vented at inquests. The growth of support groups and the development of legal specialists in disaster law can be noted too. Disasters generally provoke a public inquiry of some sort and there have been some individual criminal prosecutions leading to suggestions of scape-goating.[3] It is clear that there is more willingness to attach criminal liability to an individual than to a corporate body. This has per-plexed some and angered others. Under the elaborate system of criminal justice in England and Wales various institutions (among them the police, the Director of Public Prosecutions (DPP), the Crown Prosecution Service (CPS) and diverse regulatory bodies) are involved in processing people who are suspected of having committed a criminal offence. In many cases it will be clear, both in fact and as a matter of social construction, that an unlawful homi-cide has been committed.[4] This is not so as far as disasters are concerned: they are rarely caused by the stereotypical homicidal individual. The decision whether to explain a disaster in criminal terms or to allocate blame by way of criminal liability will emerge from a kaleidoscope of conflicting considerations. The only public corporate manslaughter prosecution, that of P & O for the Zeebrugge deaths, was aborted by the trial judge before the pros-ecution had even finished presenting its case.[5] The DPP has been unwilling, citing insufficient evidence, to mount any other man-slaughter prosecutions against corporations. This has not deterred a private prosecution against the owners of *The Bowbelle*, the dredger which collided with *The Marchioness*; and relatives of the *Piper Alpha* victims also expressed an intention to mount a private crimi-nal case.[6]

A full analysis of the cultural, legal and institutional forces con-tributing to the public and state reactions to these disasters is not possible here. In identifying some of the formal processes which they attract I seek to locate some of the background factors which both generate and reinforce cultural perceptions. What I do here is to explore more closely the institutional influences which may contribute to perceptions of disaster deaths as criminally caused,[7] in particular the roles played by the inquest and other forms of inquiry. The essay is in five parts. I begin with a brief account of the jurisdiction of coroners, including the inquest procedure. In the second part the roles, both explicit and implicit, of the inquest jury and the tasks which it is asked to perform are more closely, and critically, analysed. In particular I discuss whether inquests can avoid, as seems to be expected of them, playing a part in determining criminal liability. The interplay between inquests and other institutions of state response to mass death (public inquiries and the processes of criminal prosecution) is considered in the third section. This is followed by an analysis of corporate manslaughter law and I conclude with 'Death rites and death dues', a discussion of some of the broader questions raised by mass deaths.

CORONERS AND INQUESTS

One thing disasters have in common is that each death will have been the subject of an inquest,[8] as are the 18,000 deaths from external causes, injuries or poisoning which occur every year.[9] The office of coroner dates back to medieval times.[10] Its form and function has altered considerably. Originally established as a means of raising Crown revenue,[11] the office 'was at its zenith in the second half of the thirteenth century'[12] after which a combination of factors led to its decline.[13] Nonetheless, the coroner's role in respect of 'sudden' or 'unnatural' death was well established by the nineteenth century.[14] Gradually, the inquest has been subordinated to the medical profession, and more recently to the police and to the Director of Public Prosecutions. Because many 'sudden' deaths turn out to be from 'natural' causes the Coroners Act 1926 allowed coroners to hold a post-mortem without an inquest, unless the death was violent or unnatural.[15] The coroner has a discretion to hold an inquest in other cases in order to allay suspicion.

Between one-third and one-quarter of all deaths are certified by a coroner,[16] but only a small proportion (one in eight) of these now involve an inquest. In 1990 there were 22,000 inquests from a total of 180,000 certificated deaths.[17] During this century, the role of the inquest in relation to homicide has been curtailed formally in a number of significant ways. First, the power to commit a suspect for trial has been removed and the coroner's duty in homicide cases to sit with a jury has been abolished.[18] Second, coroners are required to adjourn inquests where a person has been charged with the unlawful homicide[19] of the deceased, unless the DPP notifies otherwise.[20] The police can ask the coroner to adjourn for twenty-eight days or longer if there are grounds for believing a person may be charged with the homicide.[21] Third, any inquest held after a criminal trial cannot return a verdict inconsistent with that of the trial.[22] These provisions, although designed to protect an individual whose trial may be prejudiced by the prior finding of an inquest, also have the effect of enabling the police and the prosecuting authorities to prejudge many of the questions of liability.[23] The fact that, until 1926, inquests always preceded criminal trials emphasises the extent of the erosion of the inquest's importance in the construction of crime. The Warwick Inquest Group[24] suggested as an analogy Hall's 'primary definition' in the social production of news[25] in describing the significance of the initial decision to prosecute. 'A decision not to prosecute in any case involving the death of a member of the public [in police custody], is a decision to present the circumstances of the death before an inquest.'[26] And from this the death would be seen as accidental, a result of misadventure, rather than the fault of the police.

The primary official decision with regard to prosecution plays a rather different role where disasters are concerned. The decision about prosecution is still pivotal here, but the crucial distinction is less whether or not a prosecution will be brought than whether one will be *considered*. A decision to consider prosecution is enough to delay but also to subordinate the inquest. As I argue later (p. 207), an initial triggering of the prosecutorial mechanism means that some of the inquest's options can be foreclosed. Furthermore, the critical impact of the prosecutorial decision does not turn on the possible effect of charges and subsequent trial (the DPP has shown little enthusiasm for corporate homicide, see pp. 206–7), but on whether the DPP has ruled, in advance of the inquest, that there is insufficient evidence to proceed. This executive decision then fetters all but the most determined coroner and/or jury. There is an additional point of difference between the role of the disaster inquest and others, including those concerned with deaths in police custody.

Postponement pending a prosecutorial decision may inhibit the later inquest. But disasters almost invariably provoke a public inquiry,[27] which in turn will often prompt the coroner to adjourn the inquest. This may actually assist those who want to use the inquest to expose corporate or other negligence by providing the necessary evidence to open up the possibility of a finding of unlawful death.

Thus, the prosecution issue and the inquiry may provide conflicting gravitational forces. Suspension awaiting criminal proceedings may fetter the inquest, postponement pending a public inquiry may assist. The underlying point, however, that the official construction of events will affect the conduct and outcome of the nquest, applies to disasters as much as to other 'sudden and unnatural deaths'.[28]

JURIES AND INQUESTS

Juries are not mandatory for all inquests.[29] The increasingly subservient role given to the inquest appeared at one time to suggest that inquest juries would quietly fade away.[30] The Brodrick Report in 1971 was concerned that the jury be preserved but unashamedly saw its function as mainly symbolic and to legitimate the decision of the coroner.[31] Until 1926 all inquests were held with a jury; by 1969 it had reduced to 31 per cent and by 1990 had dwindled to 6 per cent.[32] The Coroners (Amendment) Act 1926,[33] allowed an inquest without a jury except where there is reason to suspect that the death:

1   occurred in a prison[34] or in police custody or as a result of a police officer acting in the execution of her duty;[35]
2   was caused by an accident, poisoning or disease which statute requires to be notified to a government department;[36]
3   in circumstances the possible recurrence of which is prejudicial to public health or safety.[37]

This last exception was broadly interpreted by the Court of Appeal in 1980 when it overturned the Divisional Court and the coroner in the inquest into the death of Blair Peach. It was alleged that Peach was hit by a policeman using an unauthorised weapon during a demonstration in Southall. The Court of Appeal held that 'prejudicial circumstances' could include hypothetical events such as those alleged.[38] This decision disposed of any threat to the survival of the compulsory coroner's jury and, not long after, selection procedures similar to those for Crown Court juries were introduced.[39]

Juries, whether trial or inquest, have always been something of a double-edged sword for the state. Whilst they are recognised as a relatively cheap fact-finding body which can lend authority and validation to an official determination, they can occasionally rebel. If inquest juries have in the past decade amplified a growing move towards the acknowledgement of corporate crime, particularly corporate homicide,[40] they are merely echoing those trial juries which in the past have 'nullified' murder charges against individuals, forcing their reduction to a less serious offence of manslaughter.[41]

The Coroners Act 1988 does not set down a list of possible verdicts for the jury. Section 11(3)(a) merely provides that they shall 'give their verdict and certify it by an inquisition'; and subsection (5)(b) provides that 'an inquisition . . . shall set out so far as such particulars have been proved –

(i) who the deceased was and
(ii) how, when and where the deceased came by his death'.

Section (5) (c) gives the Lord Chancellor power to prescribe its form by Statutory Instrument. The current rules make a number of 'suggestions' including accident/misadventure, unlawful killing or an open verdict.[42] In order to bring in a verdict of unlawful killing, a jury needs to be convinced on the criminal standard of proof that the deaths were caused unlawfully.[43] Before 1980 juries could add a 'rider' to their verdict, but this was abolished on the recommendation of the Brodrick Committee.[44] However, this was at first ignored and the Bradford fire inquest jury attached a list of twenty-four recommendations to their findings.[45] The Divisional Court has, however, recently held that there is no such power and indeed that to make recommendations would contradict rule 36(2) that 'Neither the coroner nor the jury shall express any opinion on any other matters' (than who the deceased was, how, when and where she came by her death).[46]

The juries at the Zeebrugge, Glanrhyd (the rail-bridge failure in west Wales) and Clapham inquests were undaunted and refused to follow the cautious approach of the respective coroners.[47] They effectively ignored the instruction that the purpose of the inquest was not to determine criminal or civil liability.[48] This is understandable for, however often this is said by coroners, it cannot hide a fundamental contradiction in the role of the inquest. Historically, determination of criminal liability was part of the formal remit. It was only in 1977 that coroners' juries lost the power to commit a named individual for trial. This meant that the inquest functioned as an alternative to the process of police charge followed by magistrates' committal which is the normal procedure for bringing a person to trial on indictment. Perhaps it was anticipated that the abolition of the committal power would result in some change in the underlying function of inquests, but it is difficult to see how that could have been achieved given that the rest of the procedure was left intact. Inquest juries are told *both* that they are not concerned with criminal liability *and* that they are to reach a conclusion about how the deceased came to die.

This simple division between allocation of blame and establishing cause is not a distinction which recent disaster inquest juries have found easy to maintain. If they asked themselves what caused the deaths when *The Herald of Free Enterprise* capsized off Zeebrugge the jurors could answer at cumulative levels of specificity.

i) The deaths were caused by drowning;

ii) the people drowned because the ferry capsized;

iii) the ferry capsized because the bow doors were left open;

iv) the bow doors were left open because the assistant bosun did not shut them;

v) the doors were not shut because the chief officer did not check whether the AB had closed them;

vi) the ferry sailed with the doors open because the captain did not check that the doors were shut;

vii) the ferry sailed with the bow doors open because P & O had failed to respond to earlier requests by captains that door indicator lights be installed on the bridge[49] (. . . And so on.)

These are all valid causal explanations. Is the inquest a forum for answering the causal question at the furthest level of generality or is the answer expected to be more specific?

As the explanations become more specific, the causal explanations become more judgmental. Unless the assistant bosun was falsely imprisoned in his cabin or had been rendered unconscious by a heart attack, statement (iv) begins to allocate blame. It could also be said that Celia Wells did not shut the bow doors, but this, while having some causal validity (if I had, the capsize would not have occurred), is of no help to us since I was not on the ferry. Suppose that I had been. We still would not be very interested in my failure to shut the doors. We are interested in the assistant bosun because it was his job to close the doors. And therefore the judgment, that he should have shut the doors becomes relevant to the causal explanation. We are interested in the directors of P & O because, although they were not on the ferry, it was operating under their management. What I have tried to show is that the question posed to an inquest jury, that it should account for a death, to explain what caused it, cannot always be answered without playing a part in allocating blame. It is sometimes going to be a very short step from that to a determination of responsibility and thence to criminal liability. This conclusion is reinforced by the availability to the inquest jury of the verdict of 'unlawful killing'.

INQUIRIES, PROSECUTIONS AND INQUESTS

Major disasters are almost inevitably followed by some form of inquiry. Some of these are appointed ad hoc, others are statutorily mandated. Whereas it is fairly easy to assert the relationship between the *inquest* and *criminal proceedings*, it is almost impossible to predict any pattern in the sequence of inquest and inquiry. The Warwick Inquest Group suggested that inquests were often used by the authorities as an official whitewash in cases of deaths in police custody. Compared with a criminal trial an inquest provides 'a convenient platform for the public presentation of rehearsed and selective evidence'.[50] Can the same be said of the use of inquests following disaster inquiries?

The answer seems to be both yes and no. Aberfan yields the best example of a disaster inquest being used as an official cover-up. One hundred and forty-four people, mostly children, suffocated when slag-heap slurry cascaded on to a village in south Wales in 1966. The Tribunal of Inquiry concluded that the National Coal Board (NCB), both nationally and regionally, and a number of individuals were guilty of neglect in failing to ensure that there was a safe tipping policy.[51] The inquiry report gave neither the NCB, nor its chairman, an easy ride. The board had originally attempted to blame the tragedy on 'a coincidence of a set of geological factors, each of which in itself is not exceptional but which collectively created a particularly critical geological environment'.[52] The inquiry commented that this

> was the starting point of an attempt persisted in for many weeks by the National Coal Board, to persuade acceptance of the view that the concatenation of geological factors on Merthyr mountain was such as could not reasonably have been expected to exist. The observation . . . might conceivably have had some bearing on our task had there ever been an attempt to ascertain what the geological features were; but, since there was no investigation and no thought devoted to the subject, the claim carried one nowhere.[53]

Following the inquiry report, the Attorney-General concluded that there should be no criminal proceedings and no official pressure was put on the chairman of the National Coal Board to resign. The Secretary of State for Wales defended these negative decisions on the ground that those who could be blamed had suffered enough by their own neglect.[54] The coroner, when it came to his turn, then announced that neither questions of civil nor criminal liability were for him and adopted the conclusions of the tribunal as 'tantamount to a finding of Accidental Death in each case'.[55] Far from being a full investigation, then, the coroner allowed the inquest to be pre-empted by the inquiry report. It is difficult to believe that the inquiry would be regarded as the close of the issue if the accident had occurred today. The bizarre and outdated political and legal responses to Aberfan would seem to provide some evidence of a cultural shift in attitudes to corporate safety failures.

The inquest can also be something of a whitewash where it precedes the publication of an inquiry report. Many inquiries are public in their proceedings and their reports are published as a matter of course. However, in the case of inquiries conducted by the Department of Transport's Air Accident and Marine Investigation Branches secrecy is more common. Relatives and survivors of *The Marchioness* tragedy on the River Thames were angered that the accident report was withheld and the inquest postponed until the master of the dredger had faced trial for failing to keep a proper lookout.[56] The report into the Manchester air fire was not published until three and a half years after the disaster, and long after the inquest.[57] The final report into the Kegworth air crash was published five months after the inquest. The report's unequivocal finding of pilot error was in marked contrast with the presentation of evidence at the inquest which played down suggestions of pilot fault in favour of the more usual portrayal of pilot as hero.

Coroners themselves have been heard to complain of their subservience to the public inquiry. Following the Moorgate tube crash in 1975, the coroner complained that setting up a public inquiry had become a 'conditioned reflex without regard to the role of the ancient and honourable coroner's court'.[58] The Zeebrugge and Clapham inquests do not fit into this pattern, however, and certainly the Fatal Accident Inquiry into the Pan-Am air disaster at Lockerbie was the first time that detailed evidence about the baggage checks on such flights was given in public.[59] The most that can be said is that a public inquiry or a well-publicised campaign by relatives, as seen after Zeebrugge and Lockerbie, may encourage, whilst an unpublished departmental inquiry may inhibit, a more searching inquest.

The significance of the considerable procedural discretion bestowed both on coroners and on those conducting inquiries should not be ignored. This can dramatically affect the extent to which these formal investigations are regarded as having served the interests of relatives, survivors or other interested parties. Coroners vary in the amount of detailed evidence they allow[60] and, with the unavailability of legal aid, much depends on whether relatives can afford legal representation.[61] In public inquiries the government usually meets the reasonable costs of interested parties. The impact that this can have on the course of an inquiry is illustrated by the government's withdrawal of its promise to meet the legal costs of the Association of London Authorities at the King's Cross Inquiry: a decision taken after the ALA raised the issue of the effect of cuts in subsidy on safety policy. The report endorsed this decision in its recommendations to the Treasury as to whose costs should be met.[62]

The terms of reference of an inquiry can obviously determine the range of conclusions drawn.[63] Yet although at the King's Cross Inquiry, Desmond Fennell QC emphasised that levels of funding were outside his terms of reference,[64] he then made a point in his report of stating that there was no evidence that the subsidy to London Regional Transport (LRT) was inadequate to finance necessary safety standards.[65] In any case, terms of reference of both the King's Cross and Clapham Inquiries were based on the Regulation of Railways Act 1871, section 7 of which provides that the investigation shall be in 'such manner and under such conditions as [the persons holding the formal investigation] may think most effectual for ascertaining the causes and circumstances of the accident'.[66] It is unlikely then that Fennell would have been procedurally constrained by such broad wording. Inquests and inquiries alike vary according to the interpretation of their role adopted by coroners and chairs, but the formal structure may hinder or enhance their discretion. Unlike those into shipping or air accidents, rail accident inquiries are not covered by the Tribunals and Inquiries Acts 1958 and 1971. They are neither governed by any statutory rules of procedure, nor give rights to legal representation or cross-examination.[67]

It is not easy to construct a predictive model in terms of the relationship between inquest, inquiry and criminal proceedings.

Apart from the procedural variations already mentioned, a major influence on the potential for criminal prosecution is the timing of the inquest and the inquiry. A complex three-way interrelationship may develop. It seems incontrovertible that a jury finding of unlawful killing will exert pressure on the DPP to prosecute.[68] It is more difficult, although not impossible, for such a verdict where the DPP has beforehand already announced a decision not to prosecute. Is it possible to isolate the factors which led to the unlawful killing verdicts at the Zeebrugge, Glanrhyd and Clapham inquests? In terms of timing, it is noticeable that the sequence for Glanrhyd was, first, inquest, second, DPP decision not to prosecute, third, the inquiry report.[69] The Zeebrugge jury was well-placed since, on the one hand, it had the benefit of the Sheen Inquiry which was outspoken in its criticism of P & O's safety policies, but, on the other, was not hindered by a prior decision by the DPP. It is the Clapham verdicts which stand out as clear beacons of resistance to all the institutional pressures.[70] The DPP (unlike his response to Zeebrugge) had already announced his conclusion that there was insufficient evidence to prosecute.[71] Ironically, it would have been precisely because the Zeebrugge inquest had forced into the open the question of criminal prosecution in these sorts of cases[72] that the DPP was able to attempt to pre-empt the inquest by using his s. 16 power to have it adjourned.[73] In other words, it was as a result of the DPP's intervention that the question of criminal prosecution could be officially disposed of before the inquest. The inquest jury's finding may, however, have been instrumental in the Railway Inspectorate's decision to prosecute British Rail for endangering passenger safety.[74] As with Clapham, the DPP had already announced, in advance of the Hillsborough inquest, that there were to be no criminal prosecutions.[75]

Unlawful killing verdicts were strongly mooted with respect to King's Cross. That inquest took place shortly after the Fennell Inquiry closed but before the report was published. Despite strong pressure from the relatives and survivors, the coroner (perhaps fortified by the intervention of the Lord Chief Justice)[76] restrained the jury with the instruction that they were not entitled to bring in unlawful killing verdicts.[77] The Fennell Report was severely critical of London Underground management in terms which were reminiscent of the Sheen Inquiry into Zeebrugge.[78] Would the inquest, which relatives described as a 'farce',[79] have resulted in verdicts of accidental death if it had taken place after the publication of

DISASTERS

Fennell's damning criticism?[80] Although the Clapham inquest was antedated by the DPP's decision not to prosecute, it at least had the benefit of the Hidden Inquiry Report.[81] *The Marchioness* also discloses an unhappy relationship between the various institutional forces. The DPP had decided not to prosecute before the report of the Marine Accident Investigation Branch of the Department of Transport was published, and no inquest has yet been held. Two juries failed to agree at the trial of the dredger captain for failing to keep a lookout.[82] A private prosecution against the company which owned the dredger was then brought. The report, when it was eventually published, blamed failures by the Department of Transport and the marine industry to concern themselves with operational safety and monitor vessel design, rather than the inadequate supervision of the respective captains on the night of the collision.[83]

It appears that the DPP and the inquest can each be significantly influenced by the timing, and the findings, of each other and of any public inquiry. Reference has already been made to the recognition in the Coroners Act 1988 that the DPP or police can ensure that criminal proceedings are concluded or discounted before any inquest.[84] This can have the effect of reducing inquests merely to a formality, unable to contradict previous findings, albeit those findings having emerged from an entirely different forum. The dangers to individuals of having their trial prejudiced by an inquest verdict have to be taken into account. Where there is only one possible suspect the dangers are far greater. But few cases are so clear-cut. There is often room for doubt as to whether the right person was prosecuted or as to whether the evidence disclosed a criminal offence at all. With regard to the latter, the DPP is vested with enormous power. The decision that there should be no prosecution may effectively foreclose the issue. As the Clapham inquest shows, inquest juries can, if they feel strongly enough (and if the coroner allows them),[85] defy that assessment. But inquest juries are largely at the mercy of coronial discretion and of outside institutional forces.[86] The recommendation of the Fennell Report into King's Cross that the requirement to hold an inquest should be abolished where there has been a formal investigation into an accident would confirm and exacerbate this.[87] It is difficult to imagine that either the Zeebrugge or Clapham inquest juries could have returned unlawful killing verdicts had they not been anticipated by the publication of the official inquiry reports.

207

LEGAL CONSTRUCTIONS

The inquiries into the Bradford and King's Cross fires and the Clapham and Zeebrugge transport accidents all disclosed remarkably similar accounts of management dereliction in respect of safety policy.[88] Yet there has been only one prosecution for corporate manslaughter. The significance of the fact that the DPP had not considered prosecution prior to the inquest finding of unlawful deaths in relation to Zeebrugge has already been examined. An additional factor, which could also contribute to our understanding of the Clapham inquest verdict, is that in each it was possible to identify (at least) one employee who had failed in his or her duty, which failure could be identified as the *immediate* cause of the disaster.[89]

A collision between conventional legal conceptions of crime and changing cultural expectations and demands is evident. The notion of collective responsibility is antithetical to much thinking about criminal responsibility. While it is accepted that corporations are legal persons, little thought has been given to the suitable adaptation of criminal responsibility, with its assumptions about the autonomous individual, to deal with corporate culpability.[90] That is not to say that corporations cannot be held criminally liable but that the development has been both historically contingent[91] and concentrated in the area of less serious, regulatory offences concerned with, for example, consumer protection rather than in traditional offences of violence.[92] In order for a corporation to be guilty of such an offence it has to be shown that a senior employee, someone who could be 'identified' with the directing mind of the company, satisfied the requirements for that crime, in this case manslaughter.[93] So for P & O to be convicted at trial, it would be necessary that at least one senior manager should have been regarded as guilty also.[94] This approach to corporate liability is more restrictive than that adopted in many other countries in two respects. First, the company will be liable only for the crimes of those in its very highest echelons and, second, the negligence of a number of directors or senior managers cannot be aggregated. This second aspect, on which the trial judge relied in the P & O prosecution, has never been properly tested in the appellate courts.[95] Thus one of the compromises assured with the collapse of the P & O trial at such an early stage is that the restrictive rather than the aggregate view of corporate liability has become accepted almost by default.[96]

Survivor and relative support groups have consistently maintained that they are not interested in pursuing individuals; they want corporations to be accountable. If a condition of corporate liability is that the finger of criminal blame must first be pointed at an individual defendant, albeit a senior representative of management, then trial juries may be reluctant to convict. This assumes that cases will ever get as far as a jury. If the Zeebrugge charges could not stick, then it might be difficult to imagine ones that would. But this conclusion should not be too hastily drawn, even though it may influence the DPP in decisions about future prosecutions. The restrictive ambit of the identification doctrine was not, in this case, the problem.

The real obstacle in the P & O case was the judge's interpretation of the crime of 'involuntary' manslaughter.[97] This interpretation could of course itself be explained as judicial reflection of the legal system's resistance to a *corporate* prosecution, a resistance which might be anticipated given the relatively recent cultural move in the direction of collective blame. There are two main types of involuntary manslaughter, 'reckless' and 'unlawful act' manslaughter. The P & O prosecution was based on the first. Of the seven defendants on trial, three were sufficiently senior to be 'identified' with the company for the purposes of criminal liability. The numerous defence lawyers convinced the trial judge, Mr Justice Turner, that the prosecution had failed to make out a case that any of their clients had been reckless as to the drownings. None of them had ignored an 'obvious and serious risk that the vessel would sail with her bow doors open, when trimmed by the head, and capsize'. There was apparently no evidence forthcoming that 'any one of the defendants . . . would themselves, or should themselves, have perceived the risk of an open-door sailing [as] either obvious and/or serious'.

The test of recklessness on which the judge relied requires two questions to be put:

1   did the defendant create an obvious (and serious) risk of causing physical injury; and
2   did the defendant either fail to realise that risk or ignore it.[98]

Here the prosecution was not alleging that the defendants had foreseen the risk themselves. The question then was whether they had failed to realise that there was an obvious (and serious) risk of physical injury.

Little thought is given in legal literature to the problematic nature of the concept of risk. All the emphasis is on the question 'obvious to whom'? The alternatives proffered are 'obvious to the defendant if she had thought about it' or 'obvious to a reasonable/prudent person'. The debate centres around answering the question whether the reasonable person against whom the defendant is judged is to be endowed with the defendant's own frailties such as age, mental deficiencies and so on. The judicial answer to this has been that no concession will be made to any deficit in the defendant's capacities to appreciate the risk, even if she had thought about it.[99] The problem with P & O was the converse; they could be expected to know more than most about ferry operations. The judge's approach to this aspect of the case is discussed further below (p. 211), but first an examination of the concept of risk itself will be helpful.

The nature of the legal debate with its preoccupation with the pros and cons of cognitive awareness has meant that the nature of risk itself has been sidestepped. It is not made clear which type of risk it is alleged that a defendant has foreseen or ought to have foreseen: is it probability risk alone or does it also entail a utility calculus?[100] Nor is there any legal discussion of what 'obvious (or serious)' might mean. We tolerate different degrees of risk according to the nature of the activity, its social utility, any future benefits it might bring, the type of harm threatened and the cost of its avoidance. The risks taken in open-heart surgery, for example, might be high but the pay-off is too, while the prospects if the operation is not done are limited. Transport systems also have social utility. In the case of both surgery and transport we neither expect that all risks can be eliminated nor that 'clear' (obvious?) risks will be ignored by those who have the specialised knowledge and skill with which to assess them. Social utility is not the only variable, it has to be measured against *the cost/practicality of eliminating or reducing that risk* and the interest threatened (property, life, etc). To apply this to the P & O case would mean a calculation of the relative probability that the ferry might leave port with the doors open against the cost of providing foolproof information to the captain that the doors had been shut. Since there was evidence of previous open-door sailings known to management and since indicator lights were fitted on P & O's ferries shortly after the tragedy,[101] the puzzle as to why the case was stopped is ever more difficult to explain.

Culture, in the sense of 'actively invoked conventional wisdom', is seen by Douglas as the coding principle by which hazards are recognised.[102] The assignment of responsibility takes place through the emergence of cultural standards of what is to constitute a proper risk.[103] So, rather than an objective probability being the means by which a decision as to culpability is reached, it is the other way round. Communities use their shared experiences to determine acceptable risk-taking,[104] with the result that 'the cultural coding of responsibility is also the coding for perceiving risks'.[105]

Legal accounts of recklessness assume that while some risks are justifiable, others are not, without any attempt being made to calibrate them. The lack of attention paid to this perhaps adds credence to the type of cultural analysis outlined above. The phrase 'obvious and serious risk' is left to carry the burden of determining the acceptable levels of risk in any particular activity.[106] Reaching agreement on what are 'fair risks' is never going to be easy. There is probably no such thing as an intrinsically 'fair or acceptable risk', only risks which are judged acceptable by specific groups of individuals in specific circumstances.[107]

To return now to the prudent person against whom P & O's lack of foresight was to be judged; since a company which owns a car ferry cannot claim a deficiency of knowledge compared with a ferry operator it was appropriate that Turner J. should ask whether the risk of sailing with the doors open would have occurred to a prudent *ferry operator*. However, the course he took in order to establish whether P & O had failed to realise that which a prudent ferry company should have realised was more problematic. To begin with, Turner J. appeared to base his doubts about the strength of the prosecution's case on the evidence of witnesses who were at the time or had been in the past employed by P & O itself. It is difficult to see how such witnesses could have represented the foresight of a prudent ferry company since the company for which they worked was on trial for this very failure of foresight. One of the clear lessons of risk-perception surveys is that people who benefit from a risky activity underestimate the risks, while those who are its potential victims overestimate.[108] Whilst it is less easy to categorise the passengers in terms of benefit or victim, it is clear that the company was a beneficiary which would suggest that the risk foresight of its employees would not be particularly helpful.

It is possible that the selection of witnesses was due to a failure on the part of the prosecution to trawl a wider net of marine witnesses. There was no hint from the judge, however, that he would have expected different evidence had there been such witnesses.

Furthermore, he did refer to some evidence which had yet to be heard from chief officers who would have described the problems of being required to supervise the bow doors and be on the bridge when the ferry sailed. The judge apparently did not regard this as sufficient to make a bare case to answer. The judge's insistence on witness evidence was itself unusual, but the sidelining of this evidence seems to be strange. It might have assisted the jury in deciding whether the company had failed to see that which a prudent operator would have seen: that one person cannot both ensure that doors have been shut and be out of sight of them on the bridge.

There is another point; according to the judge, it was necessary in order for a jury to consider whether a prudent ferry company would have realised the risk of open-door sailing, actual evidence be led that *a particular person* had indeed had such foresight prior to the accident. This involves some slippage from the way juries are usually asked to apply a recklessness test. Although this is rarely articulated, a test of this type generally operates *ex post facto* so that the question to be asked is whether a prudent person would, on thinking about it, have realised that the system which P & O operated could lead to this disaster. This is very different from requiring evidence that *a particular person* did so realise before the accident. If the prosecution had been able to find a witness who could assert prior foresight of this particular risk that would have strengthened the case considerably. But their failure to find such a witness should not have led to the case being regarded as fatally flawed or inadequate. Conversely, the defence might well have been helped by witnesses who testified that no one in the shipping industry had ever heard of such an occurrence.[109]

Throughout Turner J.'s direction there are dubious assumptions: not only that there must be evidence that someone realised the risk before it happened but that it could only come from witnesses, and by implication only from witnesses within the company itself. Juries are usually able to make inferences about recklessness from the evidence given of the incident which has given rise to the prosecution in the first place. The point is made more clearly when it is considered that the prosecution was only concerned to prove an objective recklessness. One of the criticisms made of the concept of subjective recklessness is that it is inappropriate to require that the defendant had actual (as opposed to latent) knowledge of the risk taken. 'It is absurd to suggest that knowledge can be actual only if it is made . . . explicit.'[110] Basing objective recklessness on the actual foresight of someone other than the defendant is a singular approach.

The failure of the P & O trial will undoubtedly discourage further public prosecutions for corporate manslaughter.[111] The rarity of the corporate manslaughter prosecution can be explained partly by doctrinal legal limitations (although the same factors which led to those restrictions also militate in favour of their survival).[112] If corporate liability were more widely drawn, the arguments for prosecutions would undoubtedly have been strengthened in many of the disasters discussed here. But both the DPP and the trial judge in the P & O case have shown a distaste for corporate homicide charges which goes beyond technical restrictions. Their resistance is a product as much of the social construction of crime as a quintessentially individual act as of legal possibilities. In this respect it may be that their views, as legal history has so often shown, are lagging behind some public perceptions of criminal responsibility for safety.

DEATH RITES OR DEATH DUES

Death features in the work of civil and criminal courts as well as often being the motivation for the establishment of a public inquiry. But the inquest is the only formal state tribunal whose exclusive concern is death.[113] In this essay I have been concerned with the interaction of these institutions in their responses to disasters or mass death. I argue that the need to establish a cause merges inevitably into questions of blame allocation. Although this has not been my focus here, it can be observed that even the suicide verdict is more than a statement about cause of death. Suicides in prison, psychiatric institutions and so on raise wider questions about the responsibility of the relevant authorities.[114] Deaths, wherever and whenever they occur, are not straightforwardly categorised as natural – pollution, social circumstances, medical care and poverty might all be implicated.[115]

All deaths have an economic and a political component as well as the more obvious emotional and perhaps religious connotations. Cultural selection determines which dangers are recognised; the institutions of public inquiry and punishment are ways in which this selection is translated into action.[116] So when there are disasters such as those at King's Cross, Hillsborough and Zeebrugge (or any other), there is no simple account which can be given. The inquest

213

shares its place as a forum of public response and as a means of determining cause and allocating blame with the media, public inquiries and sometimes the criminal trial. Such is the confusion surrounding its proper function that its significance can vary from the symbolic to the instrumental. In most disasters the inquest appears to perform a ritualistic function which is absent from the public inquiry despite their being concerned with seemingly similar questions of cause, blame and prevention. It was after the inquests, and not the public inquiries, into Zeebrugge, King's Cross and Clapham that relatives articulated their hope that 'justice should be done'. That aspiration was focused on the power vested in the inquest to conclude with a condemnatory verdict of unlawful killing.

The inquest occupies an important place in allowing, through the jury, a voice for public reproach of corporations for their neglect of safety. It is strange that the forms and functions of inquests and inquiries should be so varied, so underexplored and so rarely questioned. It is clear that the timing of the inquest and inquiry can both affect and be affected by the decision as to the potential for criminal prosecution(s) disclosed by the disaster. As events from Aberfan through to Zeebrugge have shown, ideas about criminal responsibility are themselves not static. Accounting for the apparent growth in awareness of the concept of corporate liability and increasing calls to apply it to disasters is beyond the scope of this essay. It is clear that changes in perceptions of collective and individual responsibility, as well as different moods about civil and criminal spheres, are exemplified in formal public responses to disasters. My aim here has been to demonstrate the variety and complexity of these reactions and to highlight the significance of the initial categorisation and interpretation of a death and the consequent implications for potential criminal liability.

APPENDIX

Chronological Table

Disaster	Inquiry	Inquest	Verdict	Crim. Procs.
Aberfan Oct. 66	Jul. 67	Sept. 67	A/D	DNP
Moorgate Tube Feb. 75	Jun. 76	Apr. 75	A/D	(DNP)
Bradford fire May 85	(Popplewell) Jul. 85+ Jan. 86	Jan. 86	A/D	(DNP)
Manchester air fire Aug. 85	Mar. 88+ Mar. 89	Sept. 86	A/D	(DNP)
Zeebrugge Mar. 87	(Sheen) Jul. 87	Oct. 87	Unlawful	DP Jun. 89
Glanrhyd rail Oct. 87	Apr. 90	Jul. 88	Unlawful	DNP Sep. 89
King's Cross Nov. 87	(Fennell) Nov. 88	Oct. 88	A/D	DNP May 89
Clapham Dec. 88	(Hidden) Feb. 89	Sep. 90	Unlawful	DNP May 90
Lockerbie Dec. 88	Sep. 90	Oct. 90		
Kegworth Jan. 89	Feb. 89+ Oct. 90	May. 90	A/D	(DNP)
Hillsborough Apr. 89	(Taylor) Aug. 89+ Jan. 90	Mar. 91	A/D	DNP Aug. 90
Marchioness Aug. 89	Aug. 91	Sep. 89	Adjourned	DNP Sep. 90

Key
+ interim.
A/D = accidental death or death by misadventure.
DP = decision to prosecute for manslaughter.
DNP = decision not to prosecute.
(DNP) = prosecution apparently not considered.

215

ACKNOWLEDGEMENTS

I am grateful to Phil Smith and Mike Edwards for research assistance funded by Cardiff Law School.

NOTES

1 The appendix gives full details of the disasters which are the subject of this essay.
2 Cultural attitudes to misfortune are discussed by Mary Douglas in *Risk Acceptability According to the Social Sciences* (London: Routledge & Kegan Paul, 1985). It has been argued that all cultures share the same basic repertoire of explanations for explaining misfortunes (blaming the victim in a 'moralistic style', blaming unpopular groups or forces in an 'adversarial style' or deflecting blame in a 'no fault' style), M. Douglas and A. Wildavsky, *Risk & Culture* (London: University of California Press, 1982).
3 In the prosecution of seven P & O employees for manslaughter following Zeebrugge and of the captain of the dredger which collided with *The Marchioness*, see below n. 56.
4 This is discussed at greater length in Nicola Lacey, Celia Wells and Dirk Meure, *Reconstructing Criminal Law* (London: Weidenfeld & Nicolson, 1990): ch. 5.
5 Discussed in more detail below, text accompanying ns 96–110.
6 The case against South Coast Shipping Co. Ltd, owners of *The Bowbelle*, failed at committal stage in 1992; the plans to prosecute in relation to *Piper Alpha* were abandoned in January 1992.
7 See V. Swigert and R. Farrell, *Murder, Inequality and the Law* (Lexington, Mass.: Lexington Books, 1976); and W. Felstiner, R. Abel and A. Sarat, 'The emergence and transformation of disputes: naming, blaming, claiming . . . ', *Law and Society Review* 15 (1980–1): 632.
8 Or, in the case of Lockerbie, the Scottish equivalent, a Fatal Accident Inquiry under the Fatal Accidents and Sudden Deaths Inquiry (Scotland) Act 1976; see Contributed, 'FAIs-after Lockerbie', *Scots Law Times* 23 (1991): 225.
9 Most of these deaths are accidental. British Medical Association, *Living with Risk* (London: John Wiley & Sons, 1987; reissued by Penguin, 1990): 47, based on information from the OPCS, *Mortality Statistics, Causes 1984* (London: HMSO, 1985).
10 The office was established in 1194, almost coinciding with the replacement of trial by ordeal by trial by jury in 1215; see T. A. Green, *Verdict According to Conscience* (Chicago, Ill.: University of Chicago Press, 1985): 51. See generally on the early years, R. F. Hunnisett, *The Medieval Coroner* (Cambridge: Cambridge University Press, 1961); and for a general history, J. McKeogh, 'Origins of the coronial jurisdiction', *University of New South Wales Law Journal* 6 (1983): 191.
11 Hunnisett, op. cit.: ch. 1. The coroner at this time could be called upon to perform almost any duties, including that of full-time official to present Crown pleas.

12 ibid.: 190.
13 ibid.; Hunnisett notes the decrease in the number of appeals, the abolition of the murdrum fine, the cessation of the general eyre (a periodical circuit of justices which could hear all manner of pleas) and the rise of the local justices of the peace.
14 Warwick Inquest Group, 'The inquest as a theatre for police tragedy: the Davey case', *Journal of Law and Society* 12 (1985): 35, at 38.
15 Now Coroners Act 1988, s. 19. Various other statutes provide for a mandatory inquest following deaths in particular circumstances.
16 About 32 per cent of deaths (from a total of 550,000) were reported to coroners in 1990 which was a slight increase attributed to more use of deputising services by GPs such that the doctor attending death could not legally give a certificate: *Home Office Statistical Bulletin* 5/91 (25 April 1991).
17 ibid. The proportion of 12 per cent has remained constant over the last five years.
18 Coroners (Amendment) Act 1926, ss. 20 and 13(2)(a) as amended by Criminal Law Act 1977, s. 56. The provisions for juries are now to be found in Coroners Act 1988, s. 8. See also n. 30 below.
19 The term is used here to include murder, manslaughter, infanticide, causing death by reckless driving or aiding and abetting suicide.
20 Coroners Act 1988, s. 16. The section also requires an adjournment where the DPP informs the coroner that a person has been charged on indictment with an offence committed in circumstances connected with the death of the deceased.
21 And the DPP can so request in relation to offences in 'circumstances connected' with the deceased's death. Coroners Rules 1984, rules 26 and 27.
22 Coroners Act 1988, s. 16(7)(a). Section 16(3) allows the coroner to resume an adjourned inquest 'if in his opinion there is sufficient cause to do so'. In 1990, 1,050 inquests were adjourned and not resumed under these provisions, *Home Office Statistical Bulletin*, op. cit.
23 As seemed to happen in relation to the Clapham rail accident. The DPP announced in May 1990 that there was insufficient evidence for criminal prosecution but the inquest jury returned verdicts of unlawful killing at the inquest in September.
24 Warwick Inquest Group, op. cit.: 37.
25 S. Hall *et al.*, *Policing the Crisis. Mugging, the State and Law and Order* (London: Macmillan, 1978): 58.
26 Warwick Inquest Group, op. cit.: 37.
27 Air and marine accidents are investigated by the Department of Transport's Air/Marine Accident Investigation Branches. The publication of their reports can be delayed. The report into *The Marchioness* tragedy was delayed for two years. *Report of the Chief Inspector of Marine Accidents into the Collision Between the Marchioness and MV Bowbelle* (London: HMSO, 1991).
28 See the further discussion, pp. 203–7.
29 Coroners Act 1988, s. 8.
30 They have already been abolished in Scotland: Fatal Accidents and

Sudden Deaths Inquiry (Scotland) Act 1976. The Brodrick Report, *Report of the Committee on Death Certification and Coroners*, Cmnd. 4810 (London: HMSO, 1971): para. 16.49, recommended that the coroner should in all cases have a discretion whether to order a jury or not.

31 ibid. The report recommended that the mandatory provisions be abolished and the decision whether to summon a jury should be entirely a matter for the coroner.

32 ibid.: table N, p. 202; and *Home Office Statistical Bulletin*, op. cit.

33 Now Coroners Act 1988, s. 8(1). The Criminal Law Act 1977 abolished the requirement for a jury in relation to homicide and road accidents which had been retained by Coroners (Amendment) Act 1926, s. 13(2)(a) and (d).

34 Or other place or circumstances as require an inquest under any Act, Coroners Act 1988, s. 8(3)(a).

35 Coroners Act 1988, s. 8(3)(b). This was originally added by s. 62 of the Administration of Justice Act 1982.

36 Coroners Act 1988, s. 8(3)(c).

37 Coroners Act 1988, s. 8(3)(d).

38 *R* v. *Hammersmith Coroner, ex parte Peach* [1980] QB 211 [1980] 2 All ER 7.

39 Coroners Juries Act, 1983, ss. 1–3, now 1988 Act, s. 9.

40 See Celia Wells, 'The decline and rise of English murder: corporate crime and individual responsibility', *Crim. Law Rev.* (1988): 788.

41 Green, op. cit.

42 Coroners Rules 1984, sched. 4, form 22, note 4, S.I. 1984 no. 552. Over half of verdicts record accident/misadventure, 10 per cent industrial diseases and 1.3 per cent unlawful killing: *Home Office Statistical Bulletin*, op. cit.

43 I.e., beyond reasonable doubt that the deaths were caused by another's gross negligence. *R* v. *West London Coroner, ex parte Gray* [1987] 2 WLR 1020.

44 Brodrick, op. cit. See now Coroners Rules 1984, r. 36(2). Coroners are entitled to make recommendations in writing to relevant authorities if thought necessary to prevent the recurrence of fatalities, r. 43.

45 *The Times* (30 July 1985). Some of these were more far-reaching than those of the Popplewell Inquiry, *Final Report of the Committee of Inquiry into Crowd Safety and Control at Sports Grounds*, Cmnd. 9710 (London: HMSO, 1986).

46 *R* v. *Shrewsbury Coroner's Court, ex parte British Parachute Association* (1988) 152 J. P. 123.

47 9 October 1987, 22 July 1988 and 13 September 1990 respectively. See the appendix for details of inquest verdicts.

48 In the King's Cross inquest the coroner backed up his direction that verdicts of unlawful killing were not open to the jury by invoking the advice of the Lord Chief Justice: *Guardian* (12 October 1988).

49 As revealed at the company's manslaughter trial these requests were greeted with derision by its directors: *Guardian* (15 September 1990).

50 Warwick Inquest Group: 37. The same could be said of criminal trials themselves.

51 Under the Tribunals of Inquiry (Evidence) Act 1921 which bestows High Court powers to summon witnesses, send for documents etc. *Report of the Tribunal into the Disaster at Aberfan*, HC Paper no. 553 (1967).

52 ibid.: para. 190.

53 ibid.

54 *Hansard* 751, 5th series (1966/7): cols 1916–17. The minister quoted the Tribunal of Inquiry, para. 207.

55 *The Times* (29 September 1967).

56 *Guardian* (17 August 1990). The Marchioness Action Group unsuccessfully sought leave to challenge the DPP's decision not to pursue manslaughter charges: *Guardian* (30 October 1990). After two trial juries failed to agree on this, the Crown offered no further evidence: *The Independent* (1 August 1991). See also text accompanying n. 82.

57 The fire was on 22 August 1985, the inquest returned verdicts of accidental death on 22 September 1986 and the Air Accident Investigation Board published an interim report in July 1987 and a final report on 12 March 1989.

58 *The Times* (15 April 1975).

59 The inquiry opened on 1 October 1990. See above, n. 8.

60 One complaint about the King's Cross inquest was that it lasted only one week, compared with a month for Zeebrugge and 4 minutes for Aberfan.

61 The Legal Aid and Advice Act 1949 provided for legal aid to inquests but this has never been implemented. See Justice, *Coroners Courts in England and Wales* (London: Justice, 1986): 15.

62 *The Times* (4 May 1988); and Department of Transport, *Investigation into the King's Cross Underground Fire*, Cm. 499 (London: HMSO, 1988): para. 21.6 (Fennell Report).

63 John Prescott, Shadow Transport Secretary, criticised both the Fennell Inquiry into King's Cross and the Hidden Inquiry into Clapham because wider questions of public subsidy were omitted; see, for example, *Hansard* 143, 6th series (12 December 1988): col. 647. See also Fennell Report.

64 *The Times* (23 April 1988).

65 *The Times* (18 June 1988) and Fennell Report para. 19.6.

66 In a parliamentary question about the terms of reference for the Fennell Inquiry, David Mitchell's reply for the government that reference should be made to section 7 was somewhat unhelpful: *Hansard* 124, 6th series (18 December 1988): 776w.

67 Although the investigation has the powers of a summary court. See generally, H. Wade, *Administrative Law*, 6th edn (Oxford: Oxford University Press, 1988): 999; and R. E. Wraith and G. R. Lamb, *Public Inquiries as an Instrument of Government* (London: Allen & Unwin, 1971): 146–54.

68 After the Zeebrugge inquest the DPP announced the prosecution of P & O and seven individuals for manslaughter: *The Times* (9 October 1987); and the Clapham inquest was followed by BR's conviction for failing to ensure passenger safety, for which it was fined £250,000:

CELIA WELLS

Guardian (15 June 1991).
69 Three people died on 19 October 1987. The inquest was held on 22 July 1988, the DPP decided in September 1989 not to prosecute, but the Department of Transport's inquiry did not report until 27 May 1990: Department of Transport, *Report on the Collapse of the Glanrhyd Bridge on 19 October 1987* (London: HMSO, 1990).
70 *Guardian* (12 October 1988).
71 *The Independent* (19 May 1990). The dossier of evidence was prepared for the DPP by the British Transport Police.
72 The coroner's original ruling that corporate manslaughter was not an offence which existed at law was successfully challenged in *R* v. *HM Coroners Court for East Kent, ex parte Spooner* (1989) 88 Cr. App. Rep. 10.
73 Coroners Act 1988.
74 The decision to prosecute was announced shortly after the inquest ended in October 1990: *Guardian* (21 November 1990); see also n. 67 above.
75 *Guardian* (31 August 1990). The inquest was adjourned *pending* this decision on 18 April 1990, and was finally resumed in November 1990. Verdicts of accidental death were returned in April 1991. Both *The Marchioness* and the Hillsborough Action Groups applied for leave to bring actions for judicial review of the DPP's decision: see n. 56 above; and David Bergman, 'Recklessness in the boardroom', *New Law Journal* 140 (1990): 1496.
76 See n. 47 above.
77 *Guardian*, (12 October 1988); cf. text at n. 47.
78 *M.V. Herald of Free Enterprise, Report of the Court, No 8074* (London: Department of Transport, 1987).
79 *Guardian* (13 September 1990).
80 Fennell Report.
81 *Investigation into the Clapham Junction Railway Accident*, Cm. 820 (London: HMSO, 1989).
82 See n. 56 above.
83 *The Independent* (15 August 1991); see n. 27 above.
84 See n. 20 above.
85 Cf. the King's Cross inquest, n. 48 above.
86 For example, the East Kent coroner who was so reluctant to allow corporate manslaughter on to the agenda of the Zeebrugge inquest has displayed the same aversion to unlawful killing verdicts in relation to inquests into Channel Tunnel workers' deaths over which he also presides.
87 Fennell Report: para. 19.40. The Lord Advocate already has an equivalent discretion in Scotland.
88 See generally Judith Cook, *An Accident Waiting To Happen* (London: Unwin, 1989); and see *Guardian* (16 November 1988).
89 Comparison here can be made with the official action taken against the driver in the Purley rail crash in March 1989. He confessed immediately to having caused the accident by his failure to stop at a red signal, and pleaded guilty to manslaughter.

90 See C. Wells, *Corporations and Criminal Responsibility* (Oxford: Clarendon Press, 1993); and B. Fisse and J. Braithwaite, 'The allocation of responsibility for corporate crime; individualism, collectivism and accountability', *Sydney Law Review* 11 (1988): 468.
91 There have been very few appellate decisions. Each one therefore acquires a significance which is disproportionate to the issues of the particular case.
92 See Wells, op. cit.
93 *Tesco Supermarkets* v. *Nattrass* [1972] AC 153.
94 Although not necessarily convicted.
95 It was discussed but was not fully argued in *R* v. *HM Coroner for E. Kent, ex p. Spooner* (1989) 88 Cr App. Rep. 10. The P & O trial confirmed that corporate manslaughter is an offence known in law: *R* v *P & O (European Ferries Ltd)* [1991] 93 G App. R. 73.
96 It is not possible here to give a full account of the arguments for a broader conception of corporate liability; see Wells, op. cit.; and S. Field and N. Jorg, 'Corporate liability and manslaughter: should we be going Dutch?', *Crim. Law Rev.* (1991): 156.
97 So-called to distinguish it from murders reduced to manslaughter because of provocation or diminished responsibility, Homicide Act 1957.
98 [1982] AC 341. The 'serious' was added in *Lawrence* [1982] AC 510. See also *R* v. *Reid* [1992] 3 All ER 673.
99 *Elliott* v. *C* (1983) 77 Cr. App. Rep. 103; *R.(S.M.)* (1984) 79 Cr. App. Rep. 334.
100 I.e., probability times harm. Douglas, op. cit.: 20; and A. Irwin, D. Smith and R. Griffiths, 'Risk analysis and public policy in major hazards', *Physical Technology* (1982): 13.
101 Sheen Inquiry: paras 18.4 and 18.8.
102 Douglas, op. cit.: 67–8.
103 ibid.
104 ibid.: 69.
105 ibid.: 72.
106 See, for example, Di Birch, 'The foresight saga: the biggest mistake of all', *Crim. Law Rev.* (1988): 4.
107 Irwin, Smith and Griffiths, op. cit.: 262.
108 Douglas, op. cit.: 21.
109 Since this was manifestly not the case, as the Sheen Report showed, the mystery becomes deeper. Even those with a deep aversion to conspiracy theories might begin to wonder if their lack of cynicism has hitherto been misplaced.
110 R. A. Duff, *Intention, Agency and Criminal Liability: Philosophy of Action and the Criminal Law* (Oxford: Blackwell, 1990): 160.
111 And private prosecutions may be forced to surmount expensive legal hurdles: see, for example, *R* v. *Bow Street Magistrates, exp. South Coast Shipping Co. Ltd* [1993] 1 All ER 219. See also ns 6, 56 and 75.
112 One limitation which I have not pursued in detail here is that emanating from the decision in *Andrews* v. *DPP* [1937] AC 576 which artificially restricts the use of unlawful act manslaughter.

CELIA WELLS

113 Coroners still, for historical reasons, deal with treasure trove.
114 See, for example, *R* v. *Birmingham and Solihull Coroner, ex parte Sec. of State for the Home Department*, QBD: *The Independent* (2 August 1990), where a verdict of lack of care following a suicide in prison was quashed. The second inquest returned the same verdict: *Guardian* (25 October 1990).
115 Douglas op. cit.: ch. 5. See also A. Sen, *Poverty and Famines: An Essay on Entitlement and Deprivation* (Oxford: Oxford University Press, 1981).
116 Douglas, op. cit.: 54.

11

Relatively late payments: damages beyond death and bereavement

Derek Morgan

DEATH CAN SERIOUSLY DAMAGE YOUR HEALTH

Shock is something which forms part of a recognisable train of events associated with the death of a close relative or loved one. Such reactions also encompass anxiety, rage, acceptance and mourning. But sudden and unexpected death, especially in very public circumstances, amplifies the response. What distinguishes grief from remorse and disappointment from shame is not simply a determinate inner feeling but responses, actions, appraisals and situations in the social world.[1] As Jane Littlewood has recently observed on the social and emotional sequelae of mass death: 'Bereavement by disaster seems to intensify the features of grief associated with unexpected violent deaths in general, and, under these circumstances, it would be expected that there would be an increased risk of poor outcome following such bereavements.'[2] For many centuries it was not recognised that the fear surrounding an accident or injury, and the subsequent emotional reaction, could cause a person to become ill.[3] Anger and resentment and their juridical counterparts of retribution and reparation have been recognised and sanctioned variously in the Code of Hammurabi, the Old Testament, the Roman law of retaliation – or *lex talionis* – and other systems, including that of trial by battle.[4] Whilst these have been largely superseded, it is only in the relatively recent past that English law has been prepared seriously to entertain claims in respect of the emotional losses suffered by those whose relatives have been killed by others.

The gradual legal responses to claims following death may have been shaped by the way in which family relationships, emotions and death have traditionally been described in historical terms. Writing of the perceived fluidity and distance in family relationships in early modern England, Lawrence Stone has suggested that 'belief in the immortality of the soul and the prospect of salvation was a powerful factor in damping down such grief as might be aroused by the loss of a child, spouse or parent'.[5] More recently, however, Anne Laurence has challenged Stone's assertion that evidence for close family links does not exist. She has suggested that only with the popularisation of Freudian ideas about relationships within the family and their supposed breakdown during the twentieth century has a more rounded understanding of family dynamics and the effects of death and bereavement been available.[6] Laurence charts various attitudes to grief from the seventeenth century onwards and recalls that contemporary attitudes to death are removed from the stereotypical dispositions often recorded in historical accounts. In addition to affecting people's emotional and spiritual lives, 'grief . . . in seventeenth-century England . . . was also regarded as a potentially fatal affliction'.[7] Thus she recounts descriptions of reactions and responses to death in which it was averred that in the City of Westminster eleven deaths from grief were recorded in the Bills of Mortality in 1632, and 279 for the whole of London.[8] Similarly, she records that physician Richard Napier often included grief in the lists of symptoms of his patients, and if this did not lead directly to death, it was often associated with mental disturbance or madness; 'nearly a third of the episodes of illness, despair, and madness in bereaved patients were attributable to the death of a spouse'.[9] This is echoed by Littlewood who writes in Aspects of Grief[10] that:

> bereavement is known to result in an increased risk of morbidity, both psychological and physical, and in an increased risk of mortality. Although the metaphor of dying of a broken heart is an old one, it is also a powerful one which has at least some basis in reality.

Death, then, it has long been recognised could seriously damage your health. Since then, however, death has become covert; an examination of the way we die is a necessary part of rescuing death from the invisibility in which it has subsequently become entombed.[11] This chapter sets out to examine the legal construction and parameters of the emotional response to individual and collective death; it is an essay on the phenomenology of death and bereavement. In particular it addresses the legal parameters of harm to the bereaved through claims for damages for what has variously been called 'nervous shock', 'post-traumatic stress disorder' or, more generally, psychiatric harm.

SURVIVORS AND SENTIMENTAL DAMAGES

Common law held from at least the beginning of the nineteenth century that death could not give rise to an action vested in other people, even though they might have been dependent upon the deceased. This is thought to derive from the ruling of Lord Ellenborough in *Baker* v. *Bolton* that 'in a civil court the death of a human being could not be complained of as an injury'.[12]

Similarly, at common law, a person's death extinguished any causes of action subsisting against them or which they may have had against another. Allied with the rule that death did not confer an action against the person causally responsible for the death on any other person, this gave rise to the aphorism that it was cheaper to kill than to maim. Dependants of someone killed by another's negligence had no action in respect of their financial loss flowing from the deceased's death and no right to seek redress for any physical or emotional harm which the death may have occasioned. The survivorship of action rule was abrogated in 1934 (in large part as a consequence of burgeoning motor vehicle fatalities) by the Law Reform (Miscellaneous Provisions) Act. This provides in section 1(1) that on the death of a person all causes of action (except defamation) subsisting against or vested in him or her survive to the burden or benefit of the estate. An action brought by the estate under these provisions will be dealt with on the same basis as for a living plaintiff, with the measure of damages generally being the same.

It is widely accepted that the development of railways in England led to calls for the re-routing of *Baker* v. *Bolton*, and this was eventually first provided for in the Fatal Accidents Act 1846.[13] However, it was established soon after the passage of that legislation that whatever other novel claims it had created, and however broad the statutory language ('damages . . . proportioned to the injury resulting') it did not envisage compensation for mental suffering following bereavement. In *Blake* v. *Midland Railway*,[14] the court announced in a claim by a woman brought after her husband's death that the 1846 Act actions were limited to pecuniary losses. Lord

225

Wright in *Davies* v. *Powell Duffryn Collieries*[15] more graphically declared that 'there is no question here of what may be called sentimental damages, bereavement or pain and suffering. It is a hard matter of pounds, shillings and pence'.

In cases where the death involved a young child there was seldom a financial loss – sometimes indeed a saving[16] – and the human loss, particularly, went without even symbolic legal recognition.[17] This position was ameliorated by the Administration of Justice Act 1982 which introduced a set of arbitrary rules for the benefit of close relatives in fatal accident cases. Section 3 provides that an action under the Fatal Accidents Acts may include a claim brought by a) the deceased's spouse, b) either parent of a legitimate minor who had never married or c) the mother of an illegitimate child who had never married. In that action they may seek recovery of what are known as 'bereavement damages' – presently set at £7,500 – under the Fatal Accidents Act 1976 s. 1A[18]

This exclusion of claims for 'sentimental damages' under the Fatal Accidents Act led, perhaps not surprisingly, in the intervening 130 years to the development of a common law jurisprudence on the recovery of damages for mental distress, more usually in the earlier cases referred to as nervous shock. A review of that development follows, but first I introduce the medical and social contexts within which it took place.

SYMBOLISM AND THE NATURAL ORDER OF DYING

In denying compensation to a woman who had suffered severe shock and personal injuries when trapped in a buggy on a railway line as a train approached, the Privy Council in *Victorian Railway Commissioners* v. *Coultas*[19] advised that:

> Not only in such a case as the present, but in every case where an accident caused by negligence had given a person a serious nervous shock, there might be a claim for damages on account of mental injury . . . the difficulty which now exists in case of alleged physical injuries of determining whether they were caused by the negligent act would be greatly increased, and a wide field opened for imaginary claims.

Of course, these judgments need to be understood within the

context of the medical system which framed them. Herbert Page, writing in 1891 commented that:

> most of the strange nervous symptoms so commonly seen after railway accidents were not due to physical injury sustained by the spinal cord, but were the more or less immediate concomitants of the profound emotion aroused by the unquestionably special features and incidents of every collision.[20]

In this, he sought to depart from the current orthodoxy, represented by commentators such as J. E. Erichsen[21] who held that the 'molecular derangement' of the nervous system observable in symptoms following railway accidents indicated that the trauma was properly viewed as a physical and not an emotional one. Page's views were not generally accepted – indeed they were regarded as sufficiently heretical for Barbour to write that his work 'was so evidently written to combat Erichsen's as to be untrustworthy'.[22] There was, however, change and reappraisal under way, foreshadowed in a paper read by Sigmund Freud in 1886 to the Viennese Medical Society in which he described a case he had witnessed in Paris in which a man involved in a work accident had developed hysterical paralysis. The interesting feature of this case for Freud's argument was that it tended to show that hysteria was not, as previously thought, due to a disease of the female genital organs, as it appeared also to occur in men.[23] The effect of these early developments in psychological medicine and analysis were marginal; recall that even as late as 1939 it was stated that 'to most medical men psychological medicine is a closed book'.[24] Indeed, there is evidence that even experienced psychiatrists can have major difficulties diagnosing some disorders unless they have a high index of suspicion.[25]

In the more recent past what has perhaps misleadingly come to be known as post-traumatic stress disorder (PTSD) has surfaced in a number of claims following the death of a person in an accident, another's liability for which has been admitted or established. PTSD claims, such as those following the Hillsborough football stadium deaths in 1989 and those in the capsize of *The Herald of Free Enterprise*,[26] may be seen as attempts to attract the symbolic recognition of loss which – the inquest apart – is otherwise absent from the British legal system. The physical and emotional responses of survivors and their more recent recourse to the legal system to compensate for these emotional and material losses is an important facet of survivors' part in the ritual response to death.

With high mortality rates in previous centuries, 'the prospect of an after-life offered the hope of compensation for the likely brevity of earthly existence and the disruption of human relationships by death'.[27] An increase in average life expectancy and changes in the patterns of mortality 'have made deaths outside the older age ranges relatively rare occurrences. Many people now reach middle age without having any direct experience of bereavement'.[28] The legal response to claims by and on behalf of the deceased and their relatives and dependants has to take account of what might be called this 'natural order of things'. This includes the decline of widespread belief in possible alternatives to earthly existence, heightened expectations of lengthened opportunities to enjoy the passage and a recognition of the nature of the harm that sudden and unexpected death caused to another can wreak. The legal recognition of post-traumatic stress disorder, in its originating site of the battlefield, has been characterised by Koraniya as a recognition that human beings are there expected to face modern dangers with stone-age psychological equipment.[29] The metaphor can be properly adapted to the effects of sudden and unexpected civilian death, especially where that occurs in unusual, dramatic or horrific circumstances. One example of this, provided clearly by the deaths at Hillsborough, is that they exposed to bereavement not only those who had not yet reached middle age, but that, more unusually, the deaths were not those of older parents but of adult children. Again, this disrupts the 'natural order' of dying. Littlewood's taxonomy of responses to death where it involves the death of adult children suggests that anger over the death would appear to be a particularly common reaction to bereavement. It seems likely that all parents view the deaths of their children as untimely events which have occurred outside the 'natural' order, and bereavement by disaster may be a double blow to parents in that disasters are also events which are outside their everyday expectations. Furthermore, following a man-made disaster, many people have a target to focus their anger upon.[30]

Littlewood's account of reactions to grief accords in a direct sense with two classic descriptions of post-traumatic stress syndrome, both of which emphasise unnaturalness and the amplification of experience:

228

Posttraumatic stress syndrome . . . is the popular name currently given to anxiety neuroses resulting from severe external stress that is beyond what is usual and tolerable for most people. Such neurotic reactions can occur after any unusually stressful event such as an explosion, hurricane, flood, major fire, or aeroplane accident.[31]

Posttraumatic stress disorder is a syndrome which develops following a psychologically traumatic experience; the event which precipitates such a psychological reaction is one 'generally outside the range of usual human experience'.[32]

What is post-traumatic stress disorder?

Mendelson describes the typical symptoms of post-traumatic stress disorder as involving the intrusive re-experiencing of the event, avoidance of reminders of that event, anxiety symptoms and a numbing emotional responsiveness together with some degree of withdrawal from contact with the external world. He suggests that the current concept is essentially that of what in the past had been termed 'traumatic neurosis'. This, he avers, has been of considerable utility to the law of tort, in that it has 'fitted in well with the legal concept of nervous shock, which is compensatable at common law when resulting from negligence'.[33]

PTSD may be divided into nine sub-syndromes: depression and suicidal, isolation and withdrawal, sensation seeking, paranoid, profound psychic numbing, alienation and cynicism, problems with intimacy, fusion of stress syndrome with pre-morbid disposition syndrome and pro-social humanitarian.[34] The American Psychiatric Association's Diagnostic and Statistical Manual (DSM–III) classifies post-traumatic neuroses as anxiety disorders and lists the symptoms and findings necessary for an operational diagnosis. These symptoms may begin soon after the traumatic event or they may not appear until after a period of several days, months or even years. PTSDs differ from other neuroses in that the external source of stress was real rather than symbolic; the trauma may also have had some special significance. Before I turn to an overview of the legal responses to such claims, two caveats need to be entered. First, as McFarlane concludes in his study of disaster victims, a clinical assessment of 'the interaction between the individual's experience of the disaster and a range of psychological, social, and biological

229

characteristics' has to be considered in identifying 'vulnerability factors'. However, one clear inference is that 'it is possible to define disaster victims as being particularly at risk' of developing psychological difficulties and that those who (in this case of a large fire) 'lost both their homes and first-degree relatives would appear to be most at risk of pathological bereavement'.[35] The important qualification which McFarlane enters into his study has particular importance for the present discussion:

> A significant proportion of any population exposed to major adversity will be distressed and will develop stress-related symptoms. . . . The clinical significance of much of the data collected from disaster victims . . . remains to be established. . . . This problem cannot satisfactorily be investigated among victims of a disaster who were seeking financial compensation, . . . as this factor may influence the reporting of symptoms.[36]

Second, in each of the public 'disasters' which have been the focus of continued and critical study and reflection, the assumption which underlies the litigation is that all deaths and the bereavement reactions to them are uniform and that the quality of grief experienced from the deaths witnessed very publicly through, for example, the medium of television (as in the Hillsborough case which is considered more extensively below (p. 234)) is also uniform. This assumption may be challenged. Littlewood has observed that it seems unlikely that 'any two people, whatever their relationship or gender, will react to the same traumatic event in exactly the same way at the same time'.[37] Grief arising from the deaths of older children, however, is more likely to have a similar impact on both parents.[38] This relationship between grief and bereavement and the nature of the emotional response is an important one for English law; it has been reasserted many times that 'the court has to draw a line between sorrow and grief for which damages are not recoverable and psychiatric illness for which damages are recoverable'.[39] Nonetheless, as Lord Wilberforce in *McLoughlin* v. *O'Brian* put it:

> English law and common understanding have moved some distance since recognition was given to this symptom as a basis for liability. Whatever is unknown about the mind–body

relationship . . . it is now accepted by medical science that recognisable and severe physical damage to the human body and system may be caused by the impact, through the senses, of external events on the mind. There may thus be produced what is as identifiable as an illness as any that may be caused by direct physical impact.[40]

AFTER SENTIMENT

Although it remains the case that damages cannot be awarded for an allegation by the plaintiff that as a result of the defendant's negligence he or she has suffered fear, mental distress or grief, Landes and Posner have pertinently observed that psychiatric illness

is a real social cost. Courts formerly were inhibited about granting recovery. . . . The growth of our knowledge of emotional illness . . . has, by lowering the costs of establishing these facts, increased the net social benefit of allowing damages to be awarded in such cases.[41]

Where the 'shock' produces a more tangible physical reaction, such as a heart attack or a spontaneous abortion, or a mental reaction, such as a neurosis, it is now settled that cognisance will be taken of this, and the assessment of damages for pain and suffering[42] may reflect this.

In respect of psychiatric harm (or nervous shock) on its own, English law has moved in three stages. Where first it denied recovery for harm of such a type at all,[43] recovery was later recognised where the harm was a direct result of fear for one's own personal safety,[44] subsequently extended to encompass fear for the safety of one's immediate family,[45] but not to a 'mere' bystander who came upon the aftermath of the accident.[46]

Thus, while *Bourhill* established that the test for recoverability was reasonable foreseeability of harm from shock, what might be called the 'inner' limits to liability ensured that those who in the second stage recovered damages were limited to parents, spouses, children and cases where the plaintiff was intimately involved in, albeit not responsible for, the accident. Into this category could be placed both the fellow worker,[47] and the rescuer.[48] These 'participant liability' cases are those in which the person who complains of psychiatric illness was him- or herself involved in the primary accident as a participant – either:

231

1 in being threatened himself or herself by the defendant's action;
2 in witnessing or as good as witnessing the incident by coming upon its 'immediate aftermath', where threat has been to a near relative;
3 in being induced to go to the rescue of those injured and suffering injury after so doing (the rescuer cases), even though the 'shock' there is cumulative and experienced over a lengthy period;
4 in believing, albeit wrongly, that through the negligence of the defendant they have been or are about to be the involuntary cause of death or injury to someone else.

The 'outer' limits to liability in this second, expanding stage involved the denial or restriction of recovery on a number of bases. First, in the category of 'uninvolved persons' are those in which the injury is attributable to the grief and distress of witnessing misfortune to others where the plaintiff is not himself or herself directly involved as an actor in any of the above ways. Second, it was established that there can be no liability for 'merely being informed of or reading about the accident';[49] there can only be liability for shock sustained through 'the medium of the eye or the ear without direct contact'. Third, as yet there is no liability placed on an injured person (or if she or he is killed, their estate) where they have caused psychiatric injury through their negligently self-inflicted death, injury or imperilment. Where the primary victim is him- or herself the negligent party (as in *Bourhill* v. *Young*) and the shock arises from witnessing this victim's 'self-inflicted' injury, then again there will be no recovery.[50] This exclusion is said, once again, to be based not on logic but policy. Fourth, it remains unclear whether the sight or fear of physical injury caused other than to a human being resulting in shock is actionable. The House of Lords in *Bourhill* v. *Young*[51] criticised *Owens* v. *Liverpool Corpn*[52] in which shock was occasioned to mourners at seeing harm or affront to a corpse being carried in a coffin. But in *Attia* v. *British Gas*[53] – in which Bingham LJ described this as a 'question of far-reaching legal principle'[54] – none of the three Appeal Court judges was prepared to rule on a preliminary issue that damage to property could not in an appropriate case constitute the relevant incident triggering a claim for consequential psychiatric damage. Although Bingham LJ remarked that that case involved 'a special feature', of a pre-existing relationship between the victim and the tortfeasor (contracted to install central heating in the plaintiff's house),[55] he concluded that 'a legal principle which forbade recovery in these circumstances' could not be supported.[56]

The third phase of recoverability for psychiatric loss was initiated by the House of Lords' decision in *McLoughlin* v. *O'Brian* and cases which have followed, particularly *Alcock*. This third stage of development forms the basis for the final section of this essay.

COMPENSATING HARM AFTER DEATH

Once a claim for nervous shock was established in which it was not fear for oneself but for the safety of someone else, the courts originally demanded both the sufferer's presence at the scene and sight of the accident. Those requirements were gradually relaxed to extend to presence near the scene without any actual sight of the accident. Further developments culminated in the House of Lords' admission of the claim of Mrs McLoughlin who was 2 miles and over an hour away from the scene of an accident which devastated her family. She was told of the accident and taken to the hospital by her neighbour. She arrived to find her husband and surviving children in various states of distress and disarray and before they had been cleaned up and given full medical attention, as though she had come upon the immediate aftermath of an accident to victims to whom she was closely related.[57]

Following *McLoughlin*, the courts were left with a number of difficult questions and the speeches were subject to powerful academic criticism.[58] What henceforth was the proper test for liability; was it an untrammelled application of the reasonable foreseeability test as appeared to be the decision of Lords Bridge, Scarman and Russell in *McLoughlin*, or was the ambit of liability narrower? Was recoverability limited by 'considerations of policy' identified by Lords Wilberforce and Edmund Davies, such that the courts should additionally consider whether there were grounds for circumscribing the applicability of the doctrine of reasonable foreseeability, which has itself been called an accommodating screen behind which the real social drama is played out?[59]

Before a duty of care will be held to exist three requirements will need to be satisfied: first, foreseeability; second, proximity or neighbourhood; third, the court's assessment of what it considers 'fair, just and reasonable' to impose on one party for the benefit of the other – which can be applied to both defendant and plaintiff of course – i.e., that there are no special reasons making it just and reasonable to deny a duty which would otherwise exist.

Unfortunately, it is widely confessed with judicial candour that it is impossible to state precisely the scope and application which any of these terms or concepts import. The concepts of proximity and fairness are not susceptible to such precise definition as to give them utility as practical tests. In *Alcock* Lord Oliver underlined this in saying that:

> 'Proximity' is, no doubt, a convenient expression so long as it is realised that it is no more than a label which embraces not a definable concept but merely a description of circumstances from which, pragmatically, the courts conclude that a duty of care exists. . . . In the end, it has to be accepted that the concept of 'proximity' is an artificial one which depends more upon the court's perception of what is the reasonable area for the imposition of liability than upon any logical process of analogical deduction.[60]

The primary question which then arose in *Alcock* was whether psychiatric harm is properly regarded as a form of personal injury and, if it is, whether it is a direct form of injury giving rise to liability based on reasonable foreseeability alone, or whether something more than this – this elusive notion of proximity – is also required. It was always unlikely that the encompassing liability contemplated at first instance by Hidden J in *Wright* v. *Chief Constable of the South Yorkshire Police* would survive the appellate process. In the House of Lords, Lord Ackner suggested that the questions to which the appeal gave rise involved the determination of whether *McLoughlin* liability should be extended, first, by removing restrictions on the categories of people who could sue beyond a spouse or child; second, by broadening the means by which the shock is caused so that it includes at least simultaneous television broadcast to supplement the sight or hearing of the event or its immediate aftermath; third, by modifying the requirement that the aftermath be immediate in order to satisfy the test of proximity.

The plaintiffs and defendants in *Alcock* differed over the stability of these three elements of the chemistry of a claim for nervous shock – the nature of the relationship between victim and plaintiff; the proximity of the plaintiff to the accident in determining the immediate aftermath of the accident; and how the plaintiff experienced the accident – whether directly, indirectly through television reception or tangentially through being informed of the accident and its consequences by a third party. For the plaintiffs, it was argued that these elements were merely part of the process of deciding whether as a matter of fact the reasonable foreseeability test had been satisfied, and they relied on the untrammelled application of the reasonable foreseeability test. For the defendant Chief Constable, they constituted an additional ingredient in the equation, operating as a control or limitation on the requirement and application of the test of reasonable foreseeability. It was argued for the defendant that foreseeability does not of and in itself dispose of the issue and there must be added to that 'the law's judgment' – the invisible hand of justice – as to those who should have been in the defendant's contemplation, based on 'its standards of value or justice'.

Lord Ackner accepted that the application simpliciter of the reasonable foreseeability test is 'far from being operative'. For Lord Ackner, the satisfaction of the test of reasonable foreseeability, while a 'vital step towards the establishment of liability', does not of itself satisfy Atkin's neighbour principle.[61] Lord Keith and Lord Jauncey's conclusions on this point were to similar effect; Lord Oliver alone recognises the artificiality of suggesting that distinctions in this area rest upon some definable notion of foreseeability – the traumatic effect on, for instance, a mother on the death of her child is as readily foreseeable in a case where the circumstances are described to her by an eyewitness at the inquest as it is in a case where she learns of it at a hospital immediately after the event.[62] Nonetheless, a relationship of proximity has to be imported in order to limit the exposure of defendants to potential action.

Once the nature of the liability in claims for psychiatric harm had been concluded, and the appropriate direction of enquiry indicated, the legacy of Lord Wilberforce's tripartite approach in *McLoughlin* became evident. The House of Lords proceeded to analyse the various claims by considering the class of persons to whom a duty might properly be owed, their physical proximity to the primary accident site and the way in which they became aware of or experienced the primary accident. It is therefore convenient to adopt this taxonomy in addressing the question of the extent of liability for nervous shock or psychiatric harm following *Alcock*.

235

THE JUDICIAL CONSTRUCTION OF
RELATIONSHIPS AND EMOTION

The class of persons

The Court of Appeal had held that the category of those entitled to
recover damages for nervous shock was limited to those who fall
within the nature of the spouse/parent relationship with the victim.
This relationship would give rise to a rebuttable presumption as to
closeness and proximity. In the House of Lords there was a less
precise approach; Lord Keith disavowed an attempt to limit the
class by reference to particular relationships, such as husband and
wife or parent and child. The closer the tie (not merely in relationship but in care), the greater the claim for consideration. The kinds
of relationship which may involve close ties of love and affection are
numerous, and it is the existence of such ties which leads to mental
disturbance when the loved one suffers a catastrophe. 'The closeness
of the tie would, however, need to be proved by a plaintiff, though
no doubt capable of being presumed in appropriate cases.'[63] But
such proof could cut both ways; in the case of one plaintiff whose
brother and another whose brother-in-law had been killed, and who
were both present at the scene and indeed one of whom identified
bodies at the mortuary, Lord Keith said that there was no evidence
of 'particularly close ties of love or affection' and

> the mere fact of the particular relationship was insufficient to
> place the plaintiff within the class of persons to whom a duty
> of care could be owed by the defendant as being foreseeably at
> risk of psychiatric illness by reason of injury or peril to the
> individuals concerned.[64]

Lord Jauncey agreed with Wilberforce in *McLoughlin* that ties of
parents and spouses are allowed because it is readily foreseeable
by the tortfeasor that if they see, hear or are involved in the immediate aftermath of a serious accident then they are likely to suffer
nervous shock 'because of their close relationship with the victim'.[65]
He added, however, that there may be others whose ties of relationship are as strong, and that the task for the court in considering
each case is to decide whether the claimant has established so
'close a relationship of love and affection to the victim as might
reasonably be expected in the case of spouses or parents and children'.[66] Similarly, Lord Ackner accepts that there is a presumption,

236

which is rebuttable, that the love and affection normally associated with marital and parental relationships is such that if they suffer psychiatric illness they should be entitled to sue. As a generalisation, he said, more remote relatives and friends can reasonably be expected not to suffer illness from shock, but that there might well be relatives and friends whose relationship is so close and intimate that they should for the purpose of this cause of action be treated in the same way.[67] According to Ackner, whether the nature of the relationship was such that, given the proximity to the accident in time and space and the nature of the accident, liability should arise was to be decided on a case by case basis. Lord Oliver saw no logic or virtue in seeking to lay down as a matter of 'policy' categories of relationship within which claims may succeed and without which they are doomed to failure *in limine*. He emphasised, especially in his discussion of the cases of two plaintiffs actually at the ground, that their perception of the consequences of the disaster to those to whom they were related was gradual rather than sudden and dramatic, and hence not compensatable.

There is in each of these speeches a reflection of the sentiment expressed by Marris that 'the intensity of grief is related to the intensity of involvement, rather than of love'.[68] But these essays on the social construction of emotions and relationships leave us little further forward than *McLoughlin* and the earlier Court of Appeal judgment; indeed, on this question the House of Lords may be criticised for having acted very much as a second appeal court rather than as a judicial body charged with overseeing and shaping the development of the common law. It enables precious little to be said about cases which involve long family separation or distances, little of liability against the background of family feud and – even more imponderable – the position of someone in a long-standing relationship who has, first, just broken that relationship through divorce, separation or abandonment; second, just lost their relationship through unwilling divorce, separation or abandonment at the behest of the other party; third, enjoyed a turbulent relationship constantly broken off by the injured or deceased party, or one over which they have themselves vacillated for a long time. However, it is now clear that liability may on the appropriate facts extend to a newcomer to the nervous shock party; the unrelated bystander who is not a rescuer.

Lord Justice Atkin in *Hambrook* v. *Stokes*[69] clearly contemplated the possibility of a successful action at the suit of a mere bystander, given sufficiently horrifying circumstances. Until *Alcock*, however, it was assumed on a number of grounds that such a person could not recover. Lord Wilberforce in *McLoughlin* suggested that existing law would exclude the claim of the 'ordinary bystander' – either on the basis that the defendant could not be expected to compensate the world at large or because they must be expected to be possessed of sufficient fortitude to withstand or at least absorb the calamities of modern life. However, it is apparent from the speeches of Lords Keith, Ackner and Oliver that limitations drawn to exclude the bystander are too taut.[70] Lord Ackner suggested as an example – which Lord Oliver endorsed – a passer-by at the scene of a petrol tanker careering out of control into a crowded school and there bursting into flames.[71] Similarly, this extension might be thought to be applicable to catastrophes such as the bombing of the Pan-Am flight over Lockerbie in 1988, when bodies rained from the sky; the coal slip at Aberfan in 1966, in which over 180 people, mostly children, a large part of one generation of a small, closed community were wiped out in a devastating and sudden event; or Zeebrugge – at the capsize of *The MV Herald of Free Enterprise* – where some of the survivors attempted to act as rescuers. In each of these examples, the occasion, fashion and aggregate of horrific death in unusual and distressing circumstances are such that 'ordinary fortitude' could not prepare the most hardened bystander, even one usually unconcerned for the suffering of fellow human beings, for the instant tragedies. Both these hypotheticals and Ackner's tanker illustration might properly be separated from, for example, a gradual, creeping epidemic, such as meningitis or AIDS, where the opportunity to accustom oneself to the deaths of others is more easily seized. Similarly, this approach could account for an appreciable distinction between 'solitary' deaths; thus the casual observer of the immediate aftermath of an 'ordinary' traffic accident (*Bourhill* v. *Young*) might not be within the orbit of recovery, but one which involved a particularly unusual or unpleasant method of death (say a school student on work-placement seeing a workman decapitated by a machine) might be.

Proximity and the aftermath doctrine

Even if a plaintiff can establish that the appropriate relationship nexus exists, Lord Wilberforce allowed that their proximity to the accident could be another reason for denying them recovery, although as he put it: 'under what may be called the aftermath doctrine, one who, from close proximity comes very soon upon the scene, should not be excluded'.[72] The immediate aftermath is to be judged according to the plaintiff's proximity to the accident in both space and time and experience. Thus liability might be denied because although closely related to an injured person, although suffering a recognisable psychiatric illness, a person comes upon the scene of the accident or its aftermath too late, for a reason which is beyond that which the law will compensate, or because their experience of the accident or the aftermath is not sufficiently direct or immediate. In *Alcock*, both types of proximity question fell to be determined: first, whether those plaintiffs who were not immediately present at the scene of the tragedy but who came upon it or the aftermath of it or the deaths which it had produced some varying length of time later could successfully sue; and, second, whether those who while not present at the ground had seen a live television broadcast of the whole events as they unfolded, even though they had been unable to see specific individuals during the course of the transmission, were sufficiently proximate. It is convenient here to treat these sub-issues separately.

In the Court of Appeal, Nolan LJ had described Copec, who had watched the events on television, believed his son to be in the affected part of the ground, made telephone calls throughout the night and later went to the Sheffield hospital looking for his son, and thence to the mortuary to identify him, such that the 'aftermath of the initial tragedy continued . . . until after the identification of the body'[73] as being closest to the 'aftermath' requirement elaborated in *McLoughlin*, but nonetheless too remote. In the House of Lords what Lord Ackner called the 'post-accident identification cases', identifying the corpse at the mortuary 8 hours after the accident, could not be regarded as part of the '*immediate* aftermath' of the accident itself.[74] Lord Jauncey went further and said that not only the time which had elapsed since the accident counted against the plaintiffs, but also the reason why they attended the 'aftermath'. Eschewing any comprehensive definitional essay on the question, he preferred instead to suggest that 'what constitutes the immediate aftermath of an accident must necessarily depend upon the surrounding circumstances'.[75] Lord Jauncey then drew attention to the fact that in *McLoughlin* the plaintiff had arrived at the hospital and found her family 'in very much the same condition as they would have been' had she found them at the scene of the accident; that is, before her family had been attended to and cleaned up. Additionally, she had gone to the hospital more to comfort or to rescue her family, whereas here the reasons for attending their relatives or friends was 'purely' for the purpose of identification at the mortuary. This seems to introduce both an unfortunate element of what may be called 'ambulance racing' into the aftermath doctrine, and also what might be thought of as a simple but literal lack of respect for the dead. Is it clear why imminent attendance at the ultimate consequences of the defendant's negligence – to identify the body of a close relative – should demand any more phlegm and fortitude than witnessing the immediate consequences, before the ambulance attendants, hospital staff or morticians have sanitised the victim?

Of course, the 'aftermath' of an incident and the 'circumstances of the incident' will clearly differ from, say, the motor car accident and its 'aftermath' (which may be bodies lying in the road or blood thereon (*Bourhill* v. *Young*)) or the immediate untreated consequences at A & E (*McLoughlin*) which make it close to the plaintiff being at the scene, and examples such as Aberfan, the Lewisham train crash and possibly Hillsborough, where the incident itself extends over a prolonged period of time and there may be doubt whether someone comes upon the aftermath or upon the still unfolding incident. As Hidden J at first instance put it in a way which does seem to have survived the appellate process: 'the aftermath for any particular incident will depend entirely on the circumstances of that incident'.[76] What may amount to aftermath for one person may not do so for another, because of the interrelationship of the relevant factors, the class of persons, their proximity to the accident and the means by which the shock is caused.

Proximity and the television

Finally, I turn to consider the second 'proximity' element addressed in *Alcock*, the means by which the shock is caused and the method of communication. In *McLoughlin*, both Lords Wilberforce and Bridge enigmatically addressed this point. Lord Wilberforce said that 'the shock must come through sight or hearing of the event or of its immediate aftermath. Whether some equivalent of sight or hearing, eg through simultaneous television, would suffice may have to be considered.'[77] Lord Bridge set out the conundrum of a woman who knows that her husband and children are staying in a certain hotel and who reads in her morning newspaper that it has been the scene of a disastrous fire. She sees in the paper a photograph of unidentifiable victims trapped on the top floor waving for help from the windows, and she learns shortly afterwards that all her family have perished. She suffers an acute psychiatric illness:

> That her illness in these circumstances was a reasonably foreseeable consequence of the events resulting from the fire is undeniable. Yet, is the law to deny her damages as against a defendant whose negligence was responsible for the fire simply on the ground that an important link in the chain of causation of her psychiatric illness was supplied by her imagination of the agonies of mind and body in which her family died, rather than by direct perception of the event?[78]

It is evident after *Alcock* that the answer to this question is 'yes'. In *Jones* v. *Wright*, at first instance Hidden J said, rejecting arguments of the defendants that a simultaneous television broadcast may enhance or augment what is being seen by those actually present at the scene or be accompanied by extraneous commentary which can colour the visual impression, that observation through simultaneous transmission is sufficient to satisfy the test of proximity of space and time: 'it is in my view the visual image which is all important. It is what is fed to the eyes which makes the instant effect upon the emotions, and the lasting effect upon the memory'.[79] It was irrelevant, he said, that reception of such a broadcast was outside the control of the tortfeasor, or indeed that a distinction might be drawn between live radio and television broadcasts. In holding that it was reasonably foreseeable that negligence on the part of those responsible for crowd safety resulting in death or injury to those present might lead to psychiatric illness in the close relatives who saw the events live on television, Hidden J remarked that it was not only reasonably foreseeable to the defendant that television crews would be there, he had knowledge of this fact; that it was reasonably foreseeable that those cameras would, or might be used to transmit live pictures and that those pictures would be seen by many close relatives of those involved in the disaster.

On appeal, the court held that liability was such that it did not extend to relatives – even spouses and parents – who watched events unfold on television. Whereas the person present at the scene sees only that which can be seen through her own eyes from her own position in the ground, the television viewer's sense of the horror is amplified and augmented; a spectator from the far end of the north stand would, for example, see and appreciate far less of what was happening than a television viewer many miles away. In the House of Lords the majority opinion went with the parameters established in the Court of Appeal. Lord Keith thought that viewing the scenes cannot be equiparated with the viewer being within 'sight or hearing of the event or its immediate aftermath'.[80] Whilst the Chief Constable would indeed have known that there would be live broadcast of the match, he would also know that the broadcasting code of ethics provides that pictures of suffering of recognisable individuals would not be shown. Had they been shown, Lord Keith said, this would have been a *novus actus* such as to break the chain of causation between the alleged breach of duty and the psychiatric illness. However, he agreed with Nolan LJ's suggestion that simultaneous television broadcasts could not be ruled out as providing the equivalent of the actual sight or hearing of the event or its immediate aftermath in all cases. Lord Justice Nolan had suggested as an example a publicity-seeking organisation which organised the televising of a balloon flight by a group of children that their parents could watch. 'It would be hard to deny' he ventured

that the organisers were under a duty to avoid mental injury to the parents as well as physical injury to the children, and that there would be a breach of that duty if through some careless act or omission the balloon crashed.[81]

This may be seen to fall within the 'participant liability' penumbra identified above. On this analysis Nolan LJ may be thought to suggest that there must be some direct relationship between the person who is responsible for arranging the simultaneous broadcast of the pictures and the person whose negligence causes the injuries or deaths which trigger the psychiatric injury. This would maintain the direct causal link between responsibility for televising what turns out to be the accident and responsibility for the accident itself. Lord Oliver agreed that there might be circumstances in which the simultaneous television transmission of the actual injury suffered by the primary victim was sufficient to satisfy the requirement of direct visual perception. But, he said, that was not the case in any of the instant appeals where the shock arose not from the original impact of the transmitted image, which did not depict the suffering of recognisable individuals. The sense of loss was not immediate and perceived directly, but was in the words of Oliver more part of an 'elongated and, to some extent, retrospective process'.[82] Similarly, Lord Jauncey thought that a defendant can normally anticipate that pictures of people suffering and dying would not be transmitted and that a television programme such as this which involves many camera angles shows scenes which no one individual would see such that such a programme is not 'equivalent to actual sight or hearing at the accident or its aftermath'.[83]

CONCLUDING COMMENT

The way in which courts shape, fashion and control ambits of civil liability is part of the process of establishing and recognising the symbolic and emotional importance of death and bereavement. Quite apart from the deterrence aspects of liability, their decisions may have a decisive impact on the lives and experiences of the bereaved and the way in which the dead are received and remembered. In so far as compensation is an aspect of grief, its study assists in the identification of values and beliefs in the law. What informs those decisions enables us to draw conclusions about justice, fairness and certainty. But not forgiveness, sorrow or value.

NOTES

1 J. Coulter, 'Affect and social context: emotion definition as a social task', in Rom Harré (ed.), *The Social Construction of Emotions* (Oxford: Basil Blackwell, 1986): 122.

2 Jane Littlewood, *Aspects of Grief: Bereavement in Adulthood* (London: Routledge, 1992): 143.

3 L. Keiser, *The Traumatic Neurosis* (Philadelphia, Pa.: J. B. Lippincott Co., 1968). Developments in psychiatric medicine enable accounts of reactions to dramatic accidents to be subsequently reinterpreted. Thus the report given by Charles Dickens of a railway accident in which he was involved at Staplehurst on 9 June 1865, when several coaches fell from a bridge occasioning loss of life, and his reactions to that, now read like classic psychiatric responses (recalled in L. T. C. Rolt, *Red For Danger; A History of Railway Accidents and Railway Safety Precautions* (London: The Bodley Head, 1955)). Similarly, Samuel Pepys's description of his experience during and following the Great Fire of London in 1666 has been described by R. J. Daly, 'Samuel Pepys and posttraumatic stress disorder', *British Journal of Psychiatry* 143 (1983): 90–3, as providing 'an excellent record of the development of posttraumatic stress disorder'.

4 See Geoffrey Macormack, 'Revenge and compensation in early law', *American Journal of Comparative Law* 21 (1973): 69, for an evaluation of some of these provisions.

DEREK MORGAN

5 *The Family, Sex and Marriage in England 1500–1800* (Harmondsworth: Penguin, 1979): 88. These sentiments are echoed by Michael Mitterauer and Reinhard Sieder in their treatise *The European Family*, trans. K. Oosterveen and M. Horzinger (Oxford: Basil Blackwell, 1982): 61.

6 'Godly grief: individual responses to death in seventeenth-century Britain', in Ralph Houlbrooke (ed.), *Death, Ritual and Bereavement* (London and New York: Routledge, 1989): 62–76.

7 ibid.: 75.

8 ibid., citing *Observations upon the London bills of mortality more probably by Captain John Graunt*, in C. H. Hull (ed.), *The economic writings of Sir William Petty*, vol. II (Cambridge: Cambridge University Press, 1899): at 342, 351.

9 Laurence, op. cit.: 75, citing M. Macdonald, *Mystical Bedlam* (Cambridge: Cambridge University Press, 1983): 103, 159.

10 op. cit.: xii, and ch. 3.

11 ibid.: ch. 1.

12 (1808) 1 Camp. 493 As Jolowicz points out, this 'was only a ruling at Nisi Prius, not a single authority was cited and the report is extremely brief'. W. H. V. Rodgers, *Winfield and Jolowicz on Tort*, 12th edn (London: Sweet & Maxwell, 1984): 661. Reference should also be made to *Higgins* v. *Butcher (1606) Yelv. 89*; and F. Holdsworth, *History of English Law*, vol. 3 (London: Methuen & Co., 1897): 331–6 and 676–7. The rule was confirmed by the House of Lords in *Admiralty Commissioners* v. *S S Amerika* [1917] AC 38.

13 The Fatal Accidents legislation confers upon the dependants of a deceased rights to seek financial compensation if the deceased would have been able to bring an action in negligence in respect of the injuries which caused his or her death. In so far as this action is derivative, it is subject to any defences which a defendant might have been able to raise against the deceased, such as contributory negligence and *volenti non fit injuria*. The class of dependants entitled to bring an action under section 1 of the Fatal Accidents Act 1976 include a spouse, former spouse or cohabitee of the deceased, his or her parent or other ascendant, any child or other descendant, any person treated by the deceased as a parent or child, any person who is or who is the issue of, a brother, sister, uncle or aunt of the deceased. The section further provides for cases of relationship by marriage – treated as if they were relationships by blood – and half blood treated as if they were of the whole blood. The stepchild of any person is treated as their child and an 'illegitimate' person is treated as the legitimate child of the mother and reputed father.

14 (1852) 18 QB 93.

15 [1942] AC 601; and see to the same effect Viscount Haldane LC in *Taff Vale Railway* v. *Jenkins* [1913] AC 1 at 4; 'The basis is not what has been called solatium, that is to say damages given for injured feelings or on the ground of any sentiment, but damages based on compensation for a pecuniary loss.'

16 On the opportunity costs of child-rearing see Heather Joshi, *Women's Participation in Paid Work* (London: Department of Employment Research Paper No. 45, 1984).

17 There is a particularly good example of this, and of the concomitant rule (based on *Clark* v. *London General Omnibus Co.* [1906] 2 KB 648 – burial expenses are not recoverable) in *Barnett* v. *Cohen* [1921] 2 KB 461 where McCardie J held that the plaintiff's claim upon the death of his 4-year-old son was 'pressed to extinction by the weight of multiplied contingencies' (at 472) and that he could not recover incurred costs 'in deference to his religious duties' in procuring a watcher for the body of the dead child or the losses incurred in suspending business during mourning.

18 Damages for Bereavement (Variation of Sum) (England and Wales) Order 1990 (SI 1990 no. 2575) which came into force 1 April 1991 increased from £3,500 to £7,500 the sum which may be awarded to the spouse of a deceased or the parents of a deceased unmarried minor – but not for a stillborn child. The award does not require proof of financial dependency and there is no enquiry as to the plaintiff's grief; the award is a conventional sum which does not survive for the benefit of the spouse's or parent's estate. Such damages are available only in relation to an unmarried person under the age of 18 at the date of death, and not, following *Doleman* v. *Deakin, The Times* (30 January 1990), at the date of the accident which causes death. In *Doleman* the Court of Appeal held that bereavement damages were not recoverable by the parents of the deceased who had been injured in a road accident a few weeks before his eighteenth birthday, maintained on a life support machine for six weeks and died after his eighteenth birthday.

19 (1888) 57 L.J.P.C. 69. Judicially, it has been suggested that psychiatric illness or psychosomatic illness is a more modern and accurate description and to be preferred to nervous illness, see *Brice* v. *Brown* [1984] 1 All ER 997, at 1005. In *Attia* v. *British Gas* [1988] QB 304, Bingham LJ criticised the continued legal use of the term 'nervous shock', saying:

> Judges in recent years have become increasingly restive at the use of this misleading and inaccurate expression and I shall use the general expression 'psychiatric damage' intending to comprehend within it all relevant forms of mental illness, neurosis and personality change.

20 Herbert Page, *Railway Injuries: With Special Reference to those of the Back and the Nervous System, in their Medico-Legal and Clinical Aspects* (London: Charles Griffin & Co, 1891). See also his *Injuries of the Spine and Spinal Cord without Apparent Mechanical Lesion, and Nervous Shock, in their Surgical and Medico-Legal Aspects* (London: J. and A. Churchill, 1883).

21 *On Railway and other Injuries of the Nervous System* (London: Maberly & Walton, 1866).

22 J. F. Barbour, 'Cerebro-spinal concussion', *Journal of Nervous and Mental Disease* 18 (1891): 137–48.

23 S. Freud, 'Memorandum on the electrical treatment of war neurotics', in *Collected Works of Sigmund Freud; Standard Edition*, vol. 17 (London: Hogarth Press, 1955): 211.

24 E. Miller, *The Neuroses in War* (New York: The Macmillan Company, 1940).

25 Alexander McFarlane, 'Posttraumatic morbidity of a disaster: a study of cases presenting for psychiatric treatment', *Journal of Nervous and Mental Disease* 174(1) (1986): 4–14, at 9; and see T. Van Putten and W. H. Emory, 'Traumatic neuroses in Vietnam returnees', *Archives of General Psychiatry* 29 (1973): 695–8. J. D. Lindey *et al.*, 'Survivors: an outreach to a reluctant population', *American Journal of Orthopsychiatry* 51 (1981): 468–78, have emphasised that one of the main problems in diagnosis and treatment is created by the tendency for patients to go to considerable lengths to remove their painful and intrusive thoughts from awareness. Citing two examples of this, McFarlane reveals that one person's hyperventilation was treated as asthma for thirteen months despite normal respiratory function tests and repeated failure to respond to a range of medications and another whose blepharospasm was treated with plastic surgery before a psychiatric diagnosis was considered.

26 Explored by Celia Wells here in Chapter 10.

27 Ralph Houlbrooke, 'Introduction', in Houlbrooke (ed.), op. cit.: at 3.

28 Littlewood, op. cit.: 1.

29 E. Koranyi, 'Psychobiological correlates of battlefield psychiatry', *Psychiatric Journal of the University of Ottawa* 2 (1977): 3; cited in Jack R. Ewalt and Donald Crawford, 'Posttraumatic stress syndrome', *Current Psychiatric Therapies* (1981): 148.

30 Littlewood, op. cit.: 143.

31 Ewalt and Crawford, op. cit.: 146. The description continues:

> It is important to distinguish patients with anxiety neuroses from those who are suffering from posttraumatic syndromes that are believed to be secondary to minor brain damage occurring from accidents, athletics, or other head trauma. . . . The posttraumatic stress syndrome must be differentiated from depressive disorders, generalized anxiety disorders, phobic disorders, adjustment disorders, organic mental disorders, and the major psychoses.
>
> (ibid.: 151)

32 George Mendelson, 'The concept of posttraumatic stress disorder: a review' (1988) 29 *Wm. & Mary L. Rev.* 41: 45–62, at 46–7 (citing American Bar Association, 1980).

33 ibid.

34 See J. Wilson and F. Ziegelbaum, 'The Vietnam veteran on trial: the relation of post-traumatic stress disorder to criminal behaviour', *Behavioral Science and Law* 1 (1983): 70 at 72–3.

35 McFarlane, op. cit.: at 10.

36 ibid.: at 4, citing M. Horowitz, 'Stress response syndromes: character style and dynamic psychotheraphy', *Archives of General Psychiatry* 31 (1974): 768–81. A similar methodological difficulty is exposed and discussed in N. Brill and G. Beebe's study of a representative sample of 1,400 discharged after the Second World War with some form of neurosis; *A Follow-Up Study of War Neuroses* (Washington DC:

National Research Council, 1955), in which the authors report that 16 per cent felt that compensation for the neurosis had had a positive effect, 69 per cent felt that it had had no effect and 16 per cent that compensation had actually hindered their post-conflict readjustment with trauma. Of course, this studies the effect of compensation on the victim not the relative, but the linkage between compensation and neurosis may need further thought.

37 *Aspects of Grief*, op. cit.: at 147.
38 ibid.: at 145.
39 Lord Denning MR in *Heinz* v. *Berry* [1970] 1 All ER 1074. It has sometimes been asked why the law does not compensate for 'mere' grief, but only for something going beyond that to psychological harm. Alexander McFarlane notes that 'in examining the psychological consequences of disasters, such disorders [as post-traumatic stress disorder] can and need to be distinguished from emotional distress, which is common after any calamity'. ('Posttraumatic morbidity of a disaster: a study of cases presenting for psychiatric treatment', *Journal of Nervous and Mental Disease* 174(1) (1986): 4 at 11). Judicially this has been translated by Lord Bridge who opined in *McLoughlin* v. *O'Brian* [1983] 1 AC 410 at 431 that 'The common law gives no damages for the emotional distress which any person experiences when someone he loves is killed or injured. Anxiety and depression are normal human emotions.' One reason seems to me to lie in something of an essentially Schopenhauerean characteristic:

> If the immediate and direct purpose of our life is not suffering then our existence is the most ill-adapted to its purpose in the world; for it is absurd to suppose that the endless affliction of which the world is everywhere full, and which arises out of the need and distress pertaining essentially to life, should be purposeless and purely accidental. Each individual misfortune, to be sure, seems an exceptional occurrence; but misfortune in general is the rule.
>
> ('The vanity and sufferings of life', in his *Essays and Aphorisms*, trans. R. J. Hollingdale (London: Penguin, 1970): 41–5)

Tony Weir puts it equally prosaically:

> There is no doubt that it is a *harm* to be rendered unfit to cope with the daily exegencies of life, to have one's merriment turned to misery, to feel one's peace of mind shattered by a shocking occurrence. So, too, it is harm to lose a limb and have to hobble about. But there is no doubt that the public – crass and ignorant as it may be – draws a distinction between the neurotic and the cripple, between the man who loses his concentration and the man who loses his leg. It is widely felt that being frightened is less than being struck, that trauma to the mind is less than lesion to the body. Many people would consequently say that the duty to avoid injuring strangers is greater than the duty not to upset them. The law has reflected this distinction as one would expect,

not only by refusing damages for grief altogether, but by granting recovery for other psychical harm only late and only grudgingly, and then only in very clear cases. In tort, clear means close – close to the victim, close to the accident, close to the defendant. . . .
(T. Weir, *Casebook on Tort*, 5th edn (London: Sweet & Maxwell, 1982): 77)

But such an assessment is forcefully challenged by consultant psychologist William Davies, in a letter to *The Independent* (1 September 1990) following the release of a man who had been held as a hostage for many years; PTSD

means that . . . victims not only suffer and endure intrusive and distressing memories of their experience both by day and night [such that] the smooth running of every day life may seem trivial to them. These symptoms can take a long time to develop and it is this aspect which may lead to a lack of sympathy from others who feel that the sufferer should have 'pulled himself together'.

40 [1983] 1 AC 410 at 418.
41 G. Landes and R. Posner, 'The positive economic theory of tort', *Georgia Law Review* 15 (1981): 851, at 917–18.
42 Or of any aggravated damages or general damages recoverable for torts actionable *per se*.
43 *Baker* v. *Bolton* [1808] 1 Camp. 493; *Victorian Railway Commissioners* v. *Coultas* (1888) 13 App. Cas. 222.
44 *Dulieu* v. *White* [1901] KB 669.
45 *Hambrook* v. *Stokes* [1925] 1 KB 141; liability to a mother whose shock resulted from what she realised from her own unaided senses (i.e., saw or heard, or perhaps in the case of a blind deaf mother, smelt in the case of a fire engulfing her home) happening to one of her children (or fiancé (*Currie* v. *Wardrop* 1927 S.C. 538)).
46 *Bourhill* v. *Young* [1943] A.C. 92. Lord Oliver in *Alcock* v. *Chief Constable of the South Yorkshire Police* [1991] 4 All ER 907 (HL) (at p. 927) describes *Bourhill* v. *Young* as a good illustration of the coalescence of the two elements of reasonable foreseeability and proximity, but that it is otherwise of little assistance in establishing any criterion for the degree of proximity which would establish the duty of care, 'save that it implies necessity for a closer degree of physical propinquity to the event than has been thought necessary in subsequent cases'. But note that the case was not dismissed *in limine* on the basis that the plaintiff there was 'a mere spectator'.
47 *Dooley* v. *Cammell Laird* [1951] 1 Lloyd's Rep. 271.
48 *Chadwick* v. *British Transport Commission* [1967] 2 All ER 945.
49 *Per* Macmillan in *Bourhill* v. *Young* [1942] AC 92 at 103.
50 Lord Oliver in *Alcock* (at p. 932) cites with approval from the judgment of Deane J in *Janesch* v. *Coffey* (1984) 54 ALR 417. Lord Ackner in *Alcock*, citing Lord Ordinary Robertson's example given in *Bourhill* of a window cleaner who negligently loses his grip and falls impaling himself on railings below, agreed that he does not owe a duty to a

woman who suffers shock-induced psychiatric injury when she sees the fall from her window from the other side of the road.

51 [1943] AC 92.
52 [1939] 1 KB 394.
53 [1987] 3 All ER 455.
54 At p. 462.
55 At p. 462; such that difficult features of the existence of a duty and proximity were already established. As Bingham LJ elaborated at p. 463:

> It is not, I think, contested that the defendants owed her a duty to take reasonable care to carry out the work so as to avoid damaging her home and property. But it is said that the defendants owed her no duty to take reasonable care to carry out the work so as to avoid causing her psychiatric damage. This analytical approach cannot, I think be said to be wrong, but it seems to me to be preferable, where a duty of care undeniably exists, to treat the question as one of remoteness and to ask whether the plaintiff's psychiatric damage is too remote to be recoverable because it was not reasonably foreseeable as a consequence of the defendants' careless conduct.

56 At p. 464.
57 And see also *Jaensch* v. *Coffey* (1984) 54 ALR 417, in which the plaintiff had her first sight of the effects of the accident upon her husband hours later at the hospital.
58 For example, Anthony Ogus, 'Recent developments in negligence: the theatrical and cinematic dimensions', in Elizabeth G. Baldwin (ed.), *The Cambridge Lectures 1983* (London: Butterworth, 1984): at 256–67, castigated the majority (Lords Bridge, Russell and Scarman) for being content to apply the general foreseeability test unconstrained by specific guidelines and without undue concern for such consequences as the increased burden on tortfeasors, the difficulties of establishing valid claims and the uncertainty arising from the problem of anticipating where judges will draw the line. Ogus (ibid.: 260) suggests that this approach is subject to two powerful objections: first, the law of tort should be seen primarily as a means to lay down rights which enable the parties to settle their disputes without litigation; reliance on the 'vague foreseeability principle involves a failure to appreciate this fundamental characteristic of tort law' (ibid.: 260). Second, this enables the judges to avoid attempting a coherent answer to the admittedly difficult question of when we should order the compensation of negligently inflicted losses:

> The proliferation of *litigation* is to be sharply distinguished from the proliferation of *claims*. If a claim can be expedited without significant administrative costs, we must address a different set of policy issues. The question now becomes, whether it is socially appropriate to leave the uncompensated loss with the plaintiff or rather to shift that loss to the defendant when, combined with

other claims for compensation, it might impose a heavy burden on him. This is the crux of the compensation problem, so simple to state and yet so intractable in practice.

(ibid.: 263)

59 John Fleming, *Law of Torts*, 5th edn (London: Butterworth, 1977): 154.

60 [1991] 3 All ER at 926; for similar approaches see *Davis* v. *Radcliffe* [1990] 2 All ER 536 at 540; and *Murphy* v. *Brentwood District Council* [1990] 2 All ER 908 at 932 *et seq*. Lord Oliver.

61 [1991] 4 All ER at 918.

62 [1991] 4 All ER at 926.

63 [1991] 4 All ER at 915. He placed in such a category one whose son was killed and one who lost her fiancé; of both he said, 'the closest of ties of love and affection fall to be presumed from the fact of the particular relationship, and there is no suggestion of anything which might tend to rebut that presumption'. However, both these claims failed because they had not been at the scene of the accident nor witnessed scenes depicting suffering of recognisable individuals.

64 *Alcock* at p. 915.

65 *Alcock* at pp. 933–5.

66 *Alcock* at p. 936.

67 *Alcock* at pp. 919–20, citing with approval Stocker and Nolan LJJ in the Court of Appeal, [1991] 3 All ER 88 at 113 and 120 respectively.

68 P. Marris, *Loss and Change* (London: Routledge & Kegan Paul, 1986).

69 [1925] 1 KB 141 at 158–9.

70 *Alcock* at p. 914; ('psychiatric injury . . . could not perhaps be entirely excluded . . . if the circumstances of a catastrophe occurring very close to him were particularly horrific') p. 919; ('I see no reason in principle why [a stranger] should not [be able to recover] if in the circumstances, a reasonably strong-nerved person would have been so shocked') p. 930 respectively. Lord Jauncey did not express a view on this and Lord Lowry's five-line speech merely recorded his agreement with the unanimous conclusion of his four brethren in dismissing the appeals at hand.

71 *Alcock* at p. 919.

72 [1983] 1 AC 410 at 422.

73 [1991] 3 All ER 88 at 122.

74 *Alcock* at p. 921.

75 *Alcock* at p. 936.

76 [1991] 1 All ER 353 at 381j.

77 [1983] 1 AC 410 at 423.

78 At [1983] 1 AC 442.

79 *Alcock* at pp. 380d–e.

80 *Alcock* at p. 915 citing Wilberforce in *McLoughlin* at [1983] 1 AC 410 at 423.

81 Nolan LJ [1991] 3 All ER at 122.

82 *Alcock* at p. 931.

83 *Alcock* at p. 936.

12

Risking death by dangerous sexual behaviour and the criminal law

K. J. M. Smith

How far does and should English criminal law seek to limit the sexual activity of a person infected with a sexually-transmittable disease which may expose a partner to the risk of death? This chapter examines the case of Acquired Immune Deficiency Syndrome (AIDS), which whilst not the only serious sexually-transmittable disease,[1] is the only one where consequential[2] death is probably inevitable, and for which (according to current understanding) there is unlikely to be an effective vaccine or cure in the foreseeable future.

AIDS poses the question of the appropriateness of using the 'rough engine' of the criminal law to promote the individual and social interest in controlling the incidence and spread of a disabling or ultimately fatal disease. Some American state legislatures have enacted, or are in the process of introducing, criminal sanctions as one possible means of checking the growth in the incidence of HIV.[3] Prosecutors have resorted to a plethora of general offences in attempts to punish and deter behaviour perceived as carrying the risk of HIV transmission. Charges range from variations of assault through to attempted murder. As one commentator has suggested: 'The politics of AIDS is moving steadily in the direction of the use of compulsory powers of the state.'[4]

In the United Kingdom, the current level of reported HIV infection is over 19,500 with those who have developed AIDS more than 7,500. However, the true prevalance of HIV infection is thought to be between 40,000 and 50,000.[5] Against such a background this chapter examines the potential and desirable role which English criminal law might play in controlling the sexual transmission of the AIDS virus.

The only other numerically significant means of transmission is through blood transfusion and use of contaminated hypodermic needles or syringes. The former danger has now been largely eliminated, at least in England, through effective preventive measures taken by agencies responsible for the processing and use of human blood. Transmission of HIV through the use of an infected needle in the course of drug abuse, whilst subject to many similar concerns, does not raise in such an acute form as sexual transmission the dangers of counter-productive and indefensible degrees of intrusiveness by criminalisation of such an area of human conduct. Criminalising 'sexual transmission' represents the most problematic case, both for the formulation of acceptable culpability conditions and fair enforcement practice.

Consideration of possible criminal liability for sexual transmission of HIV under existing law (pp. 252–7) is followed by a review of the practical and policy arguments favouring the specific criminalising of sexual behaviour which carries the risk of transmitting HIV (pp. 259–62). The third section of this chapter (pp. 263–70) analyses the principal problems and possible solutions involved in devising such offences.

EXISTING OFFENCES CRIMINALISING THE SEXUAL TRANSMISSION OF DISEASE

Existing forms of liability seeking to criminalise certain risky conduct in order to prevent the transmission of disease relate to contagious diseases and quarantine regulations set out in public health legislation.[6] Beyond these regulatory provisions is a diverse collection of crimes where, although preventing the transmission of disease is not a central objective, each offence arguably carries such a potential use. These offences include some forms of assault, endangering[7] life or injuring[8] another by administering a 'destructive or . . . noxious thing', obtaining sexual intercourse by deception[9] and the rather more remote possibilities of rape and attempted murder. For some of these offences the informed consent of the victim or endangered party to run the risk of infection *may* have a bearing on the liability of the infected person.

Where the victim is unaware of the defendant's infectious condition

Assaults[10]

Suppose the defendant is aware of his diseased condition, three varieties of aggravated assault merit review: assault occasioning actual bodily harm,[11] unlawfully wounding or inflicting grievous bodily harm and wounding or inflicting grievous bodily harm with 'intent'.[12] Possible liability for one or other of these assaults will turn on several factors: first, the defendant's frame of mind or mental culpability; second, the nature of the harm caused; third, whether such harm was caused in the way recognised by a particular offence's definition.

Mental culpability

The mental culpability for an assault occasioning actual bodily harm is satisfied where the actor intends an assault and it was reasonably foreseeable that there was a risk of causing such harm.[13] Unlawfully causing grievous bodily harm requires actual 'awareness that [an] act may have the consequence of causing some physical harm to some other person. . . . It is enough that . . . some physical harm [is foreseen] albeit of a minor character'.[14] Causing grievous bodily harm with intent for the purposes of section 18 of the Offences Against the Person Act 1861, requires the defendant either to have the purpose of causing serious harm or at least to know (or believe) that such harm was virtually certain.[15] For different reasons neither form of mental state is a realistic possibility in the assumed circumstances. A defendant acting (and proved to have acted) with the purpose of passing on his infection to another is, of course, conceivable, but likely to be somewhat of a rarity.[16] Furthermore, because of the impossibility of designating infection a virtually certain consequence of sexual contact, the alternative form of mental culpability will have severely limited relevance. If it could be proved, however, that the defendant *believed* infection to be a virtually certain consequence then conviction for at least *attempt* to commit the offence would be a possibility. Nonetheless, a far more realistic prosecution prospect, where demonstrating the appropriate mental state would be less problematic, is under either section 20 or section 47 of the 1861 Act.

Nature of the harm caused

Is infecting another with HIV (or other sexually-transmittable disease) 'harm' recognised by the Offences Against the Person Act? Neither 'actual bodily harm'[17] nor 'grievous bodily harm'[18] would seem to exclude HIV or major examples of venereal disease. However, a likely challenge to such a conclusion might relate to whether the delay occurring between initial viral infection and the physical manifestation of some bodily disorder could be such as to exclude the harm from the scope of these assault-based offences. The argument carries most obvious appeal in the case of AIDS, where progression from asymptomatic infection with HIV to, at least, the AIDS-related complex (ARC) stage may take months or even years.[19] Such an uncertain and contingent delay may be viewed as making the identifiable harm too remote to be recognised as plausibly connected (for assault purposes) to the defendant's initial actions. However, the high probability, if not complete certainty, of a pattern of physical degeneration and death is such as ought to prevail over any objections of this nature. Recognition of prospective harm of such a degree of likelihood[20] as being criminal harm under the 1861 Act would not constitute an obvious distortion of the interests which the Act apparently seeks to protect.

Methods of causing harm

Even assuming that the early stages of infection may be regarded as harm for the purposes of the 1861 Act, can such harm also be said to have been brought about by an assault within the sense and terminology of the Act? The leading authority until relatively recently was the late Victorian case of *Clarence*.[21] Clarence, knowing himself to be infected with gonorrhoea, had sexual intercourse with his wife (V) without revealing this information to her. Following V's contraction of the disease, Clarence was charged with inflicting grievous bodily harm and assault occasioning actual bodily harm. The Court for Crown Cases Reserved quashed his original conviction on the basis that the commission of an assault was a prerequisite of both offences charged. No such assault had occurred because V's consent to intercourse had not been vitiated by Clarence's nondisclosure of a fact which would if known to V have led to her refusal of intercourse.[22] The rules relating to the vitiating of apparent consent were the same for assault as for rape, only fraud as to the nature of the act or the actor's identity could render consent ineffective.[23]

The apparent rigidity of the position adopted by the majority in *Clarence* (nine out of fourteen judges) as to the meaning of 'inflict' in section 20 offences has been softened by subsequent modern developments. In *Wilson*[24] the House of Lords settled that although 'inflict' does not imply an assault, it is narrower than 'cause' in that it requires the direct application of force.[25] Whilst certainly brought about directly, the harm in *Clarence* could still not comfortably be said to have been brought about through force. Moreover, a charge under section 47 would still falter even post-*Wilson*, as that offence explicitly requires an assault.

As a matter of policy the defensibility of such distinctions must be open to considerable doubt. First, as conceded in *Clarence*,[26] the notion of assault has been recognised as incorporating indirect forms of applying force or causing harm.[27] Second, section 18 employs the term 'cause' instead of 'inflict' in relation to grievous bodily harm. The logic or utility of this drafting distinction between the sections has never been convincingly demonstrated.[28] Also, an arguable corollary of treating simple non-disclosure of a fact material to obtaining consent as constituting misrepresentation is that sexual partners always implicitly warrant themselves free of transmittable diseases.[29] This highlights that, as a matter of attitude and policy, the court in *Clarence* was by no means hostile to criminalising conduct seen as being of an 'abominable nature',[30] and 'atrocious barbarity'[31] which 'Every one would . . . desire [to be punished]'.[32] Rather, the case's particular outcome was more a formalistic or technical solution governed by concern to hold the bounds of 'assault' within what was seen as indicated by a 'true construction'[33] of the terminology employed by the 1861 Act. This point is of significance when considering proposals (p. 263) for either the creation of a new form of liability or at least for a change in prosecutorial policy in respect of life-endangering sexual practices.

Rape and procuring sexual intercourse by false pretences

Where the victim consents to sexual intercourse but is unaware of any particular risk of infection, is apparent consent vitiated? The court in *Clarence*, by denying the occurrence of an assault (because what the court saw as the defendant's fraudulent implied claim of freedom from transmittable disease did not negative consent), excluded, a fortiori, the offence of rape.[34] The judicially recognised categories of vitiating mistake have been tightly limited to the nature of the act and the man's identity.[35] Considerable reluctance has been shown by courts to depart from construing 'nature of the act' other than narrowly.[36] Though in the case of an HIV-infected partner it might be maintainable that an act of intercourse which carries a strong risk of consequential death is so vitally distinct from non-life-endangering intercourse as to render apparent consent to the whole act quite unreal.[37] However, permitting such an extrapolated result from the idea of vitiated consent runs counter to the underlying substance of rape: that the core of the personal interest protected by the offence of rape is not harm in any physical sense, but rather the violation of individual emotional integrity and 'identity', which would arguably not occur in the imagined circumstances. The essence of this offence is probably not therefore present or appropriately represented in the situations being considered.

Much more convincingly capturing the nature of the interest violated is the crime of procuring sexual intercourse with a woman[38] by 'false pretences' or 'false representations'. But quite whether 'false pretences or false representations' would be found to extend to implied claims of belief in freedom from transmittable disease is impossible to predict with confidence. Other than indicating that the notion of vitiation of consent is wider than in rape,[39] the limited case law is unhelpful. A plain literal application of the offence's definition might well cover the conduct under review. However, a court might feel that the original *purpose* of the offence disqualifies its proper use in such cases. For, as has been rightly suggested, 'the conduct primarily struck at by the section was the inducement of women to go abroad on a statement that they would have employment as actresses, dancers and so on, when in fact they were meant to become prostitutes'.[40]

Endangering life or injuring another by administering a destructive or noxious thing under sections 23 and 24 of the Offences Against the Person Act[41]

'Administering' or 'causing', whilst not the most apposite expressions for passing on infection through sexual contact, do not clearly exclude such constructions: strained, perhaps, but not to such a degree as would be likely to deter a moderately determined court. Furthermore, as has been judicially observed, one could view 'infection [as] a kind of poisoning. It is the application of an animal poison'.[42] The willingness of some courts to construe the breadth of these administering offences in a liberal and flexible fashion[43] suggests their possible theoretical relevance to HIV cases may not be entirely fanciful, assuming presence of the appropriate criminal mental state.[44] Moreover, the variety of reckless endangerment offence under section 23 is not vulnerable to the problem, already considered, that the defendant did not inflict or cause immediate serious harm, an argument which might defeat a charge under section 20 of the Offences Against the Person Act.[45] Infection, especially in the case of HIV, immediately carries indisputably life-endangering potential, thereby satisfying the harm requirements of section 23.

Attempted murder

Supposing that on discovering that he has become infected with HIV, D decides to avenge himself against providence's cruelty by setting out to infect as many others as possible. If V, a sexual contact of D's dies, could D be prosecuted for V's death? The most obvious legal ground preventing his prosecution for murder (or man-slaughter if D had less than 'intention'[46] to kill or cause serious harm) would be the almost certain occurrence of V's death more than a year and a day[47] after D's initial act of infection. These problems would not arise, however, if *attempted* murder were charged.

Some American courts have been confronted with such attempted murder charges where the victim has not consented to the defendant's actions. For example, in *Barlow* v. *Superior Court*[48] a participant in a 'Gay Pride' parade in San Diego, believed to have AIDS, bit two police officers during a scuffle. A prosecution move to charge attempted murder and intent to inflict serious bodily harm was thwarted by the court's refusal to permit testing of the defendant's blood. Furthermore, pursuit of such charges was disabled by a separate Californian state provision prohibiting the disclosure of any HIV test results.[49]

K. J. M. SMITH

Where the victim is aware of the defendant's infectious condition and consents to sexual contact with this knowledge

The nature and force of human sexuality is such as to make quite conceivable cases where a non-infected party agrees to sexual activity whilst fully aware of his partner's infected state. If, as a consequence, infection is transmitted, how relevant will the 'victim's' awareness of the risk (that he or she was running) be to the question of the defendant's potential criminal liability? The apparent view[50] of some members of the court in *Clarence* was that (the risk of) quite serious harm, including venereal disease, might be freely consented to thereby making serious 'assault' lawful. However, whilst current English law suggests such opinion to be outdated it provides no clear answer as to exactly what level of harm is legally permissible: 'the intentional infliction of any degree of bodily harm, however slight, is a battery unless P consents *and* the action can be positively justified by some public interest, such as that which validates "manly sports" '.[51] To state the obvious, it can hardly be in the public interest to increase the incidence of AIDS, or even lesser diseases. Although aimed at situations where harm is an intended or virtually certain consequence of the activity involved, socially unjustified risky behaviour where there is resulting harm is almost certainly covered by this broadly conceived prohibition policy. It is an interpretation supported by the express exclusion from liability by relevant authorities of 'manly sports', such as boxing, football and rugby. Judicial condonation of sexual contact where one partner is infected with HIV is difficult to imagine considering that the chances of infection are substantial and that the consequence of infection is likely to be the partner's eventual death, and possibly also an increase in the incidence of HIV in the population.

Returning to the offences previously considered, the victim's consent to, or knowledge of, the risk of infection will, arguably, have no legal effect in the case of aggravated assault if any degree of bodily harm, however slight, cannot be consented to without positive justification. The same will also be true of potential liability under sections 23 and 24 of the Offences Against the Person Act.[52] Those arguments considered in relation to the inappropriateness of rape apply even more strongly where there has been disclosure and consent. As maintained above, whilst it is imaginable that apparent consent to intercourse might be regarded as vitiated by

258

misrepresentation as to the defendant's freedom from transmittable disease, the imposition of liability through a deemed vitiation of actual and informed consent on the basis of consent being contrary to public policy is not credible.

PUBLIC INTEREST, PROSECUTORIAL POLICY AND CRIMINAL SANCTIONS

Looking back over the range of criminal liability which might attach to sexual contact where one partner puts at risk or infects the other with a sexually-transmittable disease, it is apparent that the English substantive law's attitude is at most ambivalent. Until the last decade the only likely basis of any prosecution would have been the contracting of venereal disease.[53] For reasons which are necessarily largely speculative, reported cases where such prosecutions have been pursued are almost non-existent. This state of affairs can probably be attributed to the running together of three factors: unclear substantive law, unenthusiastic prosecutorial policy and apparent public indifference.

As for the substantive law, the least unnatural route to criminalising transmitting disease has been some form of aggravated assault. However, the hurdle of *Clarence*'s restricted construction of section 20 of the 1861 Act has, no doubt, deterred possible prosecutions. And after the liberalising of the meaning of 'inflict' for assault under section 20 by the House of Lords in *Wilson*, doubt still remains as to whether infecting another, even where there is no knowledge of the risk by the victim, would be within section 20. Endangering life or injuring another by administering a destructive or noxious thing may well, as suggested, provide a prosecution vehicle, but the strained or awkward use entailed makes it an unrealistic proposition for any but the most desperate or zealous of prosecutors. To a lesser extent this is true of using procuring sexual intercourse by false pretences.

In the case of venereal disease, long-standing social attitudes have quite possibly affected the likelihood both of bringing any prosecution and of being able in practice to adduce supporting evidence. Clearly in England the absence of a specific offence of sexually transmitting venereal (or other) disease is, at the same time, both a reflection of and a reinforcing mechanism for social values which do not regard such behaviour as worthy of criminalising. Consequently, the chances of an infected complainant coming forward willing to initiate and participate in a prosecution are likely to be rather small, probably mainly limited to cuckolded husbands, betrayed wives (or other partners)[54] or outraged relations.[55] Additionally, such charges may supplement those brought for under-age sexual intercourse when medical examination is likely to reveal the presence of venereal infection. Beyond considerations of this nature other factors that are likely to have inhibited prosecutions would be proving the defendant's knowledge of his diseased state at the appropriate time, and that he was *the* source of infection – something which would be highly problematic if the complainant had had more than one sexual partner over the relevant period. However, against the cumulative effects of such factors likely to have reinforced prosecutorial reticence are the arguably implicit public policy ramifications contained in *Attorney General's Reference (No.6) 1980*. Although the Lord Chief Justice concluded by cautioning[56] 'we would not wish our judgment . . . to be the signal for unnecessary prosecutions', the general thrust and substance of the judgment remained an unequivocal judicial condemnation of causing personal harm without some demonstrable countervailing justification. A previously hesitant prosecuting authority might feel emboldened by Lord Lane's intolerance of unjustified harm to test the waters.

These brief observations provide the necessary legal and social backdrop to direct consideration of the modern and infinitely more threatening problem of AIDS and the role, if any, criminal law should play in its containment. In approaching an answer three related areas of concern present themselves: does the magnitude of the problem justify the criminal law's intervention? Can a proper balance be struck between the infringement of individual liberty involved in the highly intrusive quality of law regulating sexual behaviour and the broad demands of public welfare? And how could the criminal law make an effective or worthwhile contribution to the overall strategy aimed at checking progression of the AIDS 'epidemic'?

Introducing the criminal law into any area of social or personal activity first requires clear demonstration of public or individual harm; can it be said that this base condition is met? Resort to details of diagnosed cases of HIV-infected people and predictive statistics issued by official and other informed bodies leaves no room for doubt as to the chilling extent and nature of the actual and potential harm.[57] These figures represent unquantifiable levels of probably many years of emotional and physical suffering of those infected together with the long-term anguish of relatives and partners. In the case of infected women, there is the additional high risk and trauma of transmission of the virus to the foetus during pregnancy;[58] a risk which counsels strongly against pregnancy for infected women.

Accepting the enormous dimensions of the individual and social harm involved, coupled with projected far-reaching and severe economic consequences in terms of the costs of necessary medical care, what degree of erosion of individual liberty and invasion of privacy is justified in seeking to meet and contain these dangers? For those adopting a broadly consequentialist approach to determining the limits of the criminal law's legitimate reach, the answer will rest largely on the extent of the harm to be avoided and the likely effectiveness of the measures taken. Just how far one ventures down such a path of consequentialist thinking will turn on the degree to which notions of immutable or irreducible personal rights are allowed to modify the pursuit of such logic.[59] However, as will be suggested here, the measures which might be adopted in criminalising certain forms of sexual activity would not constitute any noticeable departure from liability already widely accepted in the same or adjacent areas of human activity.[60] Offering illustrations of the criminal law's regulatory presence in similar areas of conduct is clearly not a complete or unanswerable response to those holding reservations or those who are openly hostile to such existing examples of criminalisation. Rather, it is maintained here that possible introduction of criminal measures dealing with the transmission of HIV should not, in principle, falter on the grounds of being seen as marking a novel form of erosion of basic or desirable personal liberties or rights to privacy.

Aside from questions of abstract ethics relating to the proper limits of criminal law and sanctions, there is the (related but distinct) vital practical question of the likely effectiveness of criminalising certain sexual activity. How susceptible is sexual behaviour to regulation? It is trite but nevertheless true that, as with probably all criminal activity, social norms and modes of behaviour are reinforced or buttressed by the criminal law rather than created by it.[61] In the particular instance of sexual behaviour and transmission of HIV, conviction for an offence involving criminalised sexual conduct (specified *infra* pp. 263–9) is likely to be of considerably less significance in influencing behaviour than the fear of infection. Moreover, the operative circumstances of sexual offences where there is no actual assault or immediately manifest harm make the imaginable detection rate for the offence exceedingly low. However, bearing in mind the extreme gravity of the harm in issue, even an anticipated low detection/deterrence rate would arguably be a worthwhile and justified return. But the criminalisation of certain HIV-related sexual activities is as much or more persuasively justified by the role it might reasonably be expected to play in the wider function of promoting changes in sexual mores and behaviour by most emphatically underscoring the social rejection of highly dangerous practices. This is admittedly a tenet of social faith hardly given to proof, or rebuttal, but one of considerable intuitive appeal enjoying weighty endorsement both in the recent past and in modern times.[62]

The historical evidence of jurisdictions, including England, where certain forms of sexual activity have constituted crimes has often been taken to suggest the law's general ineffectiveness (if not positive nuisance value) in proscribing or regulating any sexual behaviour.[63] But this frequently offered conclusion requires at least two important qualifications. First, assessing the broad social effects of criminalising behaviour is notoriously problematic, especially where the incidence of such activity, as in 'victimless' crimes, is so much a case of the roughest of estimations. Relatively small shifts in behavioural patterns in these areas, whilst not readily measurable, may well take place as a consequence of the criminalisation of the conduct. However, behavioural changes or responses even on a modest scale would clearly be a worthwhile gain in the context of preventing HIV transmission. Second, the enforcement history of these 'victimless' crimes and venereal disease related offences is relevant only up to a point. The generally understood consequence of HIV infection not only makes self-regulation or self-denial a more realistic expectation, it also makes the formal reinforcement through the criminal law of such social expectations more likely to succeed in modifying even entrenched behavioural patterns. These arguable differences could reasonably be claimed to distinguish in key respects other former, less defensible, attempts at employing the criminal law to influence intimate forms of human behaviour.

OUTLINE PROPOSALS FOR NEW OFFENCES OF ENDANGERING ANOTHER'S HEALTH THROUGH THE TRANSMISSION OR ATTEMPTED TRANSMISSION OF HIV-INFECTED BODILY FLUIDS

With no great leap of judicial imagination and creativity, one or two existing offences in English law could be enlisted to prosecute those who knowingly risk infecting (or actually infect) others with HIV. For several reasons this would be unsatisfactory and inexpedient. First, the urgency of the threat of the steady rise in incidence of AIDS contagion hardly needs stressing. Waiting for the chance conjunction of an adequately prepared prosecution brought by a competent prosecuting authority and heard by a moderately innovative court is no way criminally to regulate this particular area of great social concern and sensitivity. Furthermore, the limits of creative judicial legislation are such that even a usually inventive court might feel too tested to manufacture a form of substantive liability capable of tackling in an acceptable fashion sexual activity. An inept refashioning or use of one or other existing offence would also be a legitimate political target for those social or sexual groups[64] most likely to be affected by such changes, all of which may serve to discredit a proper, defensible development of the criminal law. Unless criminal measures are conspicuously fair in balancing reasonable public expectations and personal autonomy their social, educative and symbolic function will fail to realise their worthwhile potential. Finally, the relatively open and initially consultative nature of the legislative process is far more likely than judicial activity to ensure a considered and measured response to this particular social problem. It is also a process exposed to greater public attention for a longer formative period, thereby increasing visibility of new liability and its ability to influence attitudes and behaviour.[65]

Formulating new, specifically tailored offences, presents the legislature with significant fundamental choices as to their scope, both in terms of the range of conduct and circumstances covered, and the necessary level of accompanying mental culpability. These possibilities are now considered.

Endangering behaviour

What *behaviour* should constitute an offence? HIV is transmittable through bodily fluids. Activities which entail, or risk, such transmission must therefore be the focus of any offence.

Criminal liability from engaging in risky or endangering behaviour, rather than the demonstrated causing of harm, is by no means novel, at least in its specifically targeted forms.[66] Moreover, general varieties of endangerment liability have existed in a number of jurisdictions, particularly American state codes, for more than a quarter of a century,[67] and have enjoyed a steadily widening appeal with reformers and legislators.[68] This type of criminality has a twofold relevance to possible liability from risking transmission of the AIDS virus. First, although hardly conceived of for such purposes,[69] general endangerment offences offer the clear potential to prosecutors to bring transmittable disease connected charges, and such potential has not escaped some American prosecuting authorities.[70] Second, long-standing endangerment provisions so far restricted to venereal disease offer easy adaptable legislative vehicles for the prosecution of errant HIV-carriers.[71] In contrast, English law, whilst familiar with particular examples of endangering offences, has neither a general catch-all provision, nor the legislative model of criminal liability for the exposure of others to the risk of infection with venereal disease.[72]

In defining an endangering offence the various forms of sexual activities liable to or normally resulting in the transfer of bodily fluids[73] will require definition. One awkward initial policy question to be confronted is whether saliva should be an identified bodily fluid, thereby bringing social kissing by virus carriers within proscribed behaviour. Although apparently small, the risk of transmission through saliva is thought to exist.[74] However, the extreme social deprivation imposed upon those infected with HIV by such a measure coupled with the low transmission risk ought to rule out its inclusion;[75] moreover, such extreme, almost quarantine-type measures would have potentially damaging effects on the chances of the offence's more general acceptance.[76]

Rather than ground liability on demonstrable tangible harm, such as the relatively early symptoms of infection, or simply the diagnosed infection itself, the offence would, then, centre around exposure to the risk of infection through the actual or attempted transmission of identified bodily fluids. Such an approach avoids two predictable problems: first, showing that the victim is in an infected state; second, the grave evidential difficulties of showing that the victim's diseased condition is causally related to a particular action of the defendant.[77] As already suggested, the offence's principal purpose is to encourage a shift in social attitudes and behavioural changes which will significantly decrease the risk of infecting others. The pure chance of whether or not the disease is actually transmitted on a particular occasion should not be relevant to liability.[78]

These outline proposals concern potential infection through sexual activity – both heterosexual and homosexual in nature – as this constitutes the most socially sensitive and numerically most significant means of transmission. The other single most important method of transmission, through contaminated hypodermic or 'scratch' needles, should also be the subject of similar suitably adapted provisions. Except in relation to social sensitivity, most of the observations made in respect of liability for sexual contact will have similar relevance to the use of needles.

Mental culpability

Under existing English law dealing with aggravated assaults the gravity of the offence is partly determined by the level of mental culpability and partly by the degree of harm sustained. Although this is subject to some obscurity and inconsistency, the rationalised and remodelled system proposed by the Criminal Law Revision Committee[79] for aggravated assaults provides a useful scheme of liability which a new offence of endangering behaviour might very broadly parallel. Distinguishing at least two levels of liability is justified, more particularly: *intentionally*[80] transmitting or attempting to transmit bodily fluids whilst the actor believes or knows he is infected with HIV; and *recklessly*[81] transmitting or attempting to transmit bodily fluids. Here the defendant must be at least reckless as to whether he is infected and as to whether his behaviour will involve the transfer of bodily fluids.

However, the nature and circumstances of the harm that these two offences aim to prevent should prompt careful consideration of a third, negligence, or objective fault, based form of liability.[82] This follows from the fact that HIV is most virulent during the initial seropositive state, and when the victim is frequently asymptomatic.[83] It is this unfortunate combination of highest infectivity levels coupled with likely unawareness of infection that makes such people the most important category for preventive measures. Establishing this third form of liability – whereby it would be criminal to transfer bodily fluids which, although not actually known to the defendant to be infected, were objectively likely to contain HIV – runs counter to the generally subjectivist grain of modern developments in criminal liability.[84] Moreover, the practical reality of employing this basis of culpability would be that members of particularly high-risk groups – sexually active homosexuals and intravenous drug users[85] – would be under something approaching an obligation to ensure, so far as reasonable, that they were free from infection.

Whilst at one level general structural logic within the criminal law system may indicate the criminalising of negligent risk-taking, strategic and social objections require appropriate responses, not the least because of the risk of discrediting the general tenability of the proposed subjective fault-based provisions as well. More specifically, first, without fairly clearly articulated risk criteria the pool of potential offenders could be extremely large. It would, for example, be theoretically conceivable that any member of the two major high-risk groups – sexually active homosexuals and drug abusers – could be convicted of a negligence-based offence even if they were not infected but had failed to take steps to confirm this by submitting to testing. Further, opportunities for the exercise of investigatory and prosecutorial prejudice against members of high-risk groups would be considerably boosted where the grounds of liability lacked clear delineation. Legitimate concerns[86] of this nature could largely be met by the conditions of negligence liability being specified – either negatively (what factors would prevent liability) or positively (what factors were necessary to incriminate). In identifying such conditions the present realities of the distribution of infection cannot be ignored. Members of high-risk groups are by definition those (currently at least) most in danger of infection and of infecting others. It would, therefore, be absurd to attempt to eliminate these factors[87] from the calculation whether or not an individual has negligently endangered another. However, the apparent harshness of these provisions could be considerably mitigated by expressly enacting that sexual behaviour would not be regarded as negligently endangering another if the individual could establish either that he had taken reasonable precautions[88] to prevent the transmission of bodily fluids *or* had within a specified appropriate period produced a negative HIV test result.[89]

Clearly this still casts on high-risk groups a far more demanding standard of care than that applicable to the sexually-active population generally. Without knowledge or belief of infection members of such groups are effectively obliged either to submit to regular HIV-antibody testing or to take reasonable precautions against transmission of possibly infected bodily fluids.[90] This is a regrettable but unavoidable discriminatory consequence of the present distribution pattern of infection. It should, however, be regarded as an exceptional case warranted by the deadly seriousness of the dangers involved. Moreover, the measures required are moderate, and arguably more an incentive than a disincentive[91] for members of high-risk groups to submit to periodic testing.

Beyond these substantive issues possible additional procedural safeguards relating to prosecutions for any of the proposed offences, whether requiring intention, recklessness or negligence, merit brief consideration. Most especially, the dangers of unacceptably intrusive or opportunistic investigation might be best countered by restricting prosecutions to cases initiated by victim-complainants. The risk of prosecution for a negligence-based endangerment offence would, consequently, be small, but still not insignificant. For example, one sexual partner later discovered by the other to have deliberately understated the number of his recent sexual partners or to have lied about having recently taken an HIV-antibodies test,[92] might well provoke a retaliatory complaint. Once again, legitimate unease over the highly intrusive nature of the prosecution envisaged needs to be set against, first, the enormous individual cost to victims in terms of the sustained trauma and probably fatal outcome and, second, the broader social ramifications of failure to contain and reduce the incidence of those infected with HIV.[93]

The relevance of consent and prophylactic action

Several arguments can be marshalled against consent by the victim to run the risk of infection being relevant to liability. On paternalistic grounds harm of the magnitude being risked ought not be subject to lawful consent;[94] on the basis of legitimate public interest the incidence of the disease should be controlled so that the extensive economic costs of long-term care and medication would not thereby be incurred; for evidential reasons establishing the offence would inevitably be more protracted and problematic with likely disputes over whether consent was fully informed. Nevertheless, despite these strong public interest and paternalistic arguments opposing an informed consent defence (or making non-consent a definitional ingredient) an arguably more powerful counter-case favouring such a defence can be deployed. First of all, if consent were no defence then an infected party has less of an incentive to disclose his condition, thereby raising the real possibility of the informed potential partner declining an invitation of sexual contact. Moreover, a party consensually running the risk of infection is, realistically, most unlikely to act later as a complainant or provide incriminating testimony for any prosecution. Finally, public interest arguments aside, the degree of culpability involved in life-endangering activities is less when the 'victim' has acted with awareness of and consented to the risk.

In addition to informed consent, a defence of proof of reasonable precautions having been taken to ensure the non-transmission of bodily fluids would be a proper and necessary concession to human nature. Any attempt to proscribe sexual activity completely is not only inhumane but an unrealistically extreme expectation, more likely to discredit the law than achieve observance. It is also implicit in the culpability requirements of the proposed offences, including one based on negligence, that acting on apparently reliable medical advice, either as to the actor's freedom from infection or as to the effectiveness of certain prophylactic measures, would free the defendant from liability.

Public health regulations and criminal penalties

Public health offences occupy, in some senses, the territory between full (or recognised) criminal status and civil proceedings. The use of these regulations to contain or eliminate contagious or infectious diseases has a long and, generally, highly respectable pedigree. It has been strenuously argued by some commentators[95] that regulation of sexual conduct to limit HIV transmission, if carried out, ought to be through the mechanism and under the guise of public health provisions rather than by enlisting the criminal law. The claimed advantages of such a strategy would include the elimination, or reduction, of intrusive or contentious implicit moral judgments and inappropriate criminal law notions of culpability and retribution. Further, the generally modest level of penalties attaching to infringements of public health requirements would be more in keeping with HIV transmission offences than the more severe range of punishments normally available for fully-fledged crimes. Lastly, the enforcement personnel associated with public health regulations are by training and inclination more likely to exercise appropriate discretion in the process of investigation and prosecution of offences.

Whilst such claims undoubtedly carry some force, they can be met. Many might reasonably suggest that conduct which, at least, knowingly or recklessly puts at real risk the life of another for sexual gratification more than justifies strong moral condemnation; and, consequently, is most appropriately regarded as a *criminal* infringement of general social norms. The intimate nature of the act of such deadly endangerment hardly diminishes the legitimacy of such social condemnation. Comparisons with the range of criminal sanctions available for existing life-endangering offences, or even those involving the infliction of non-life-endangering harm, make a public health level of sanction appear wholly inadequate.[96] Most importantly, the potential for fostering and shaping of new attitudes through the criminalising of endangering behaviour would be lost or greatly diminished if public health regulations rather than the criminal law were employed[97] because criminal law is the most visible and unequivocal statement of the social rejection of certain forms of behaviour.[98]

CONCLUSIONS

Opposition to recent American legislative activity criminalising HIV-related endangering practices illustrates the predictable and fair concern not only among high-risk group organisations, but from less sectional quarters. There are dangers of criminal measures being misinterpreted as evidence of intention to isolate socially or alienate either those already infected or individuals most at risk. It is also accepted that there is continuing weight in the measured observations of Wills J in *Clarence* that:

> a wide door will be opened to inquiries not of a wholesome kind, in which the difficulties in the way of arriving at truth are often enormous, and in which the danger of going wrong is as great . . . and very possibly a fresh illustration afforded of the futility of trying to teach morals by the application of the

criminal law to cases occupying the doubtful ground between immorality and crime, and of the dangers which always beset such attempts.[99]

The case favouring liability arguably outweighs such understandable reservations. The criminal law is capable of playing a subordinate but not insignificant role in altering behavioural patterns at the very least through its power to act as a measured, unequivocal public statement of what is broadly felt to be unacceptable life-threatening conduct.

Current English law could with minimal or no modifications be employed to prosecute some practices dealt with by the proposed offences. Rather than marking a major substantive extension of criminal liability, or a disguised retreat from the laudable ethos of Wolfenden,[100] these new measures are more appropriately seen as approaching criminalisation of potentially fatal conduct directly instead of obliquely through use of the clutch of existing offences reviewed earlier. In coping with what they have identified as an 'AIDS epidemic', the declared strategy of governmental and official agencies is overwhelmingly voluntarist;[101] 'coercive' measures or 'legal sanctions' being regarded as ineffective or even counter-productive[102] in curbing the incidence of infection. Quite properly public education is the government's 'key weapon'; the 'message of the dangers of AIDS has to be told again and again and it must be unambiguous'.[103] However, it is suggested here that the generally acknowledged threat[104] of a steady and inexorable growth in the incidence of HIV infection is such as to require all reasonable measures of containment to be seriously examined, including use of the criminal law.[105] Specific criminal provisions could complement rather than subvert the existing principally educative and supportive measures by underscoring in the most 'unambiguous' fashion the nature of the moral and social issues at stake. When set alongside other varieties of existing criminalised harming and endangering conduct both the logical and moral symmetry of the proposed new offences become readily apparent.

NOTES

1 See for example generally, D. Llewellyn-Jones, *Herpes, Aids and Sexually Transmitted Diseases* (London: Faber, 1985).
2 Whilst opinion is not unanimous, the progression from infection to the complete AIDS state is believed virtually inevitable, although the rates of progression vary considerably.

3 See references cited by L. Gostin, 'A decade of a maturing epidemic: an assessment and directions for future public policy', *American Journal of Law and Medicine* 16 (1990): 1–7; K. M. Sullivan and M. A. Field, 'Aids and the coercive power of the state', *Harvard Civil Rights – Civil Liberties Law Review* 23 (1988): 135 at 157–8; S. Burris *et al.*, *Aids Law Today* (New Haven, Conn.: Yale University Press, 1993): 242. Outside American jurisdictions, see, for example, the New South Wales Public Health (Proclaimed Diseases) Amendment Act 1985, s. 50 N(3).

4 L. Gostin, 'The politics of AIDS: compulsory state powers, public health,and civil liberties', *Ohio State Law Journal* 49 (1989): 1017.

5 Department of Health Press release, Aids figures, May 1993; HIV figures, March 1993. See also the Health Education Authority, *HIV and AIDS: An Assessment of Current and Future Spread in the UK* (London: HEA, 1990): annex 1.

6 See *infra*, pp. 268–9.

7 Section 23, Offences Against the Person Act 1861.

8 Section 24, Offences Against the Person Act 1861.

9 Section 31 of the Sexual Offences Act 1956: 'it is an offence for a person to procure a woman by false pretences or false representations, to have unlawful sexual intercourse in any part of the world'. See B. Hogan, 'Modernising the law of sexual offences', in P. Glazebrook (ed.), *Reshaping the Criminal Law* (London: Stevens, 1978): 174, 183.

10 Used in the sense to cover batteries, as does s. 47 of the Offences Against the Person Act.

11 Section 47, Offences Against the Person Act 1861.

12 ibid.: sections 20, and 18, respectively.

13 Or even recognising that the victim may apprehend the application of force. *Roberts* (1972) 56 Cr. App. Rep. 95, confirmed in *Savage and DPP* v. *Parmenter* [1992] 94 Cr. App. Rep. 193.

14 *Mowatt* [1968] 1 QB 421, confirmed in *Savage and DPP* v. *Parmenter*, ibid.

15 See *Bryson* [1985] *Crim. Law Rev.* 669; *Burke* [1988] *Crim. Law Rev.* 839; J. C. Smith and B. Hogan, *Criminal Law* (London: Butterworth, 1992): 428.

16 But still a distinct level of culpability which ought to figure in any reformulated scheme of liability. See *infra*. Cf. *US* v. *Moore* 846 F 2d 1163 (8th Cir. 1988).

17 'Actual bodily harm includes any hurt or injury calculated to interfere with the health or comfort' of the victim, including injury to the state of the victim's mind; *Miller* [1954] 2 QB 282, at 292. In its Consultation Paper No. 122, *Offences Against the Person and General Principles* (1992), the Law Commission proposes that in relation to assaults 'injury' means '(a) physical injury including pain, unconsciousness, or any other impairment of a person's physical condition' (draft bill, section 1 (6)).

18 'Grievous bodily harm' means no less than the expression's natural meaning; *Smith* [1961] AC 290.

19 The development of AIDS entails three clinically identifiable stages: (i) in the asymptomatic seropositive condition, where an individual has HIV antibodies in his blood system; (ii) AIDS-related complex (ARC);

(iii) complete immune deficiency syndrome (AIDS). See generally, A. Mueller, 'The epidemiology of the human immunodeficiency virus infection', *Law, Medicine and Health Care* 14 (1986): 250.

20 In the consent case of *Donovan* [1934] 2 KB 498 the Court of Criminal Appeal spoke of harm as a 'probable consequence' (at p. 507). Contrastingly, in *Clarence* (1888) 22 QBD 23 it was suggested by Stephen J that not only did 'inflict' in the context of a s. 20 assault 'imply an assault' but also 'a wound or grievous bodily harm [which] is the manifest immediate and obvious result'. Cf. the year and a day rule for homicide responsibility considered by the Criminal Law Revision Committee, *14th Report Offences Against the Person*, Cmnd. 7844 (London: HMSO, 1980), paras 39–40.

21 (1888) 22 QBD 23. Contra the earlier decisions in *Bennett* (1866) 4 F and F 1105 and *Sinclair* (1867) 13 Cox 28. Cf. *State* v. *Lankford* 102 A 63 (1917): consent to sexual intercourse is not consent to risk infection (with syphilis) which may constitute an assault. See also similarly the American civil cases of *Long* v. *Adams* 333 SE 2d 852 (1985) and *Kathleen K* v. *Robert B* 198 Cal. Rptr. 273 (1984), both relating to the contraction of genital herpes.

22 Non-disclosure was equated by the court with a positive fraudulent misrepresentation (see, for example, (1888) 22 QBD 23, 55 and 59). Cf. the position of D capitalising on V's mistake as to his identity or the nature of the act; here consent has been held to be ineffective and intercourse non-consensual. See *Papadimitropoulos* (1957) 98 *Crim. Law Rev.* 249: 'it is not the fraud producing the mistake which is material so much as the mistake itself' (p. 260).

23 (1888) 22 QBD 23, 43 *per* Stephen J. A few years earlier in his *Digest of the Criminal Law*, 3rd edn (London: Macmillan, 1883): 177, Stephen had indicated that simply 'fraud' without qualification, could vitiate consent.

24 [1984] AC 242.

25 For the difficulties created by the requirement of direct force and how it differs from the wider notion of 'cause' see Smith and Hogan, op. cit.: 425. In its Consultation Paper No. 122, *Offences Against the Person and General Principles* (1992), the Law Commission proposes that assaults be reformulated so that 'A person is guilty of an offence if he . . . causes injury . . .' (draft bill, section 6); and see paras 8.16–8.19.

26 (1888) 22 QBD 23, 36 *per* Wills J, and 45 *per* Stephen J.

27 See D. W. Elliott, 'Frightening a person into injuring himself' [1974] *Crim. Law Rev.* 15.

28 In its *14th Report, Offences Against the Person*, Cmnd. 7844 (London: HMSO, 1980): para 153, the Criminal Law Revision Committee proposed a standardised use of 'causing' for remodelled offences replacing sections 18, 20 and 47.

29 At least that they have such a belief. Cf. A. Lynch, 'Criminal liability for transmitting disease' [1978] *Crim. Law Rev.* 612.

30 (1888) 22 QBD 23, 46 *per* Stephen J.

31 (1888) 22 QBD 23, 55 *per* Hawkins J, in a dissenting peroration of some indignation:

I cannot . . . be a party to a judgment which in effect would proclaim to the world that by the law of England in this year of 1888 a man may deliberately, knowingly and maliciously perpetrate upon the body of his wife the abominable outrage charged against the prisoner, and yet not be punishable criminally for such atrocious barbarity.

Hawkins J eyed extra-marital sexual relations more coolly: prostitutes 'tacitly' consented to 'take all risks'; for other women 'the circumstances of each particular case would have to be considered' (at pp. 54–5).

32 (1888) 22 QBD 23, 65 per Lord Coleridge CJ.

33 ibid.

34 Expressly recognised at ibid.: 33 and 43.

35 Olugboja (1981) 73 Cr. App. Rep. 344. Cf. the wider view of the nature and quality of the Act in Maurontonio [1968] 1 OR 145; and Makray (1982) 70 C.C.C. (2d) 479.

36 Williams [1923] 1 KB 340 displays an arguably less restrictive approach. See G. Williams, Textbook of Criminal Law (London: Stevens, 1983): 562.

37 On the question of the level of risk of transmission see below n. 46. As to consent, cf. the Criminal Law Revision Committee, 15th Report, conclusions (para. 2.29); with, for example, the more radical views of N. Lacey, C. Wells and D. Meure, Reconstructing Criminal Law (London: Weidenfeld & Nicolson, 1990): 338; and Hogan, op. cit.: 182–4.

38 Section 3(1) of the Sexual Offences Act 1956, initially created under the Criminal Law Amendment Act 1885, the offence existed at the time of Clarence. Like rape, this offence is limited to criminalising men for sexual intercourse with women per vaginam thereby excluding (O'Sullivan [1981] Crim. Law Rev. 406) transmission of disease through other sexual acts and between homosexuals.

39 Williams [1923] 1 KB 340. But cf. Christian (1914) 78 JP 112 and Landow (1913) 77 JP 364. And is the notion of implied claim of freedom from transmittable disease applicable where sexual contact is initiated by the healthy partner?

40 Williams, op. cit.: 563.

41 Section 23 of the Offences Against the Person Act: an offence punishable with up to ten years' imprisonment to 'unlawfully and maliciously administer to or cause to be administered to or taken . . . any person any poison or other destructive or noxious thing, so as to thereby endanger the life of such person, or . . . inflict . . . grievous bodily harm'. Section 24 creates a lesser offence subject to up to five years' imprisonment where the defendant acts in a similar manner (to s. 23) 'with intent to injure, aggrieve, or annoy'.

42 In Clarence (1888) 22 QBD 23, 42 per Stephen J. See also Williams, op. cit.: 216.

43 Cf. Gillard (1988) 87 Cr. App. Rep. 189, with the more restrictive approach in Dones [1987] Crim. Law Rev. 682 in relation to s. 24.

44 On the general obscurity of this see Smith and Hogan, op. cit.: 430–1.

45 Even harm sufficient for s. 47 may not have occurred simply through infection and during the asymptomatic seropositive stage.

46 *Hancock and Shankland* [1986] AC 455 and subsequent authorities. If death or serious harm of another were regarded as a virtually certain consequence of sexual contact with a person infected with HIV, then less than purposive action by D would suffice. However, it is generally believed that a single sexual contact does not carry such a high degree of risk of infection even though serious harm or death is generally believed to be an eventual virtual certainty after infection. On the levels of risk, see, for example, M. Friedland and K. Klein, 'Transmission of the human immunodeficiency virus', *New England Journal Medicine* 317 (1987): 1125.

47 See above n. 19. The rule is a common yet not a universal requirement in all American states, for example. See Annot, 'Homicide as affected by Lapse of Time between Inquiry and Death', 60 ALR 3d 1323 (1974).

48 236 Cal. Rptr. 134 (1987).

49 The general willingness of some American appellate courts to recognise the potential use of the AIDS virus in criminal proceedings is well illustrated by *US* v. *Moore* 846 F 2d 1163 (8th Cir. 1988). For a review of the extensive implications of this decision see L. Stansbury, 'Deadly and dangerous weapons and Aids: the Moore analysis is likely to be danger-ous', *Iowa Law Review* 74 (1989): 951.

50 See, for example, (1888) 22 QBD 23, 54 *per* Hawkins J, and 58 *per* Field J. But cf. *Coney* (1882) 8 QBD 534.

51 Smith and Hogan, op. cit.: 410 on the basis of the combined effect of *Donovan and Attorney General's Reference* (no. 6 of) (1980) [1981] QB 715. Similarly, Williams, op. cit.: 587. See also on *Donovan*, Lynch [1978] *Crim. Law Rev.* 612, 614.

52 Cf. *Cato* [1976] 1 All ER 260. It is, though, rather hard to see how there might be an offence under s. 24 through acting with 'intent to . . . aggrieve or annoy' where the victim consented to the actions.

53 And possibly genital herpes.

54 *Clarence*, *supra* n. 20. Where the offence does not involve violence there would be problems of compellability in respect of some witness/partners: section 80, Police and Criminal Evidence Act 1984.

55 *Bennett*, *supra*, n. 21.

56 [1981] 2 All ER 1057, at 1059. Followed by the House of Lords in *Brown* [1993] 2 All ER 75.

57 See, for example, Health Education Authority, op. cit.: generally.

58 Or during perinatal events. See, for example, the Health Education Authority, ibid.: 21–3; and the US National Institute of Justice, *Aids in Correctional Facilities XI*, 3rd edn (Washington DC: US Government Printing Office, 1988): 8–15.

59 The issue arises most acutely in respect of fully consensual sexual activity, where the victim is aware of the other's diseased state. Cf. generally, for example, J. Feinberg, *The Moral Limits of the Criminal Law vol. 3: Harm to Self* (New York: Oxford University Press, 1986): ch. 22; D. Lyons, 'Human rights and the general welfare', *Philosophy and Public Affairs* (1977): 6. And see 'consent' below.

60 See offences, pp. 252–9, above and 'endangering' liability considered below.

61 Cf., for example, H. Gross, *A Theory of Criminal Law* (New York: Oxford University Press, 1979): 400–1; E. Durkheim, *The Division of Labour in Society* (1893 trans. G. Simpson, New York: Macmillan, 1933): 108; W. Moberly, *The Ethics of Punishment* (London: Faber & Faber, 1968): 212–20; and J. Feinberg 'The expressive function of punishment', in his *Doing and Deserving* (Princeton, NJ: Princeton University Press, 1970).

62 Gross, op. cit.; and cf. N. Walker, 'Punishing, denouncing or reducing crime', in Glazebrook (ed.). op. cit.; and N. Walker, 'The ultimate justification', C. Tapper (ed.), *Crime, Proof and Punishment* (London: Butterworth, 1981).

63 Particularly sodomy and the transmission of venereal disease in jurisdictions outside England. See, for example, F. Brandt, 'Aids in historical perspective: four lessons from the history of sexually transmitted diseases', *American Journal Public Health* 72 (1988): 367; and R. Porter, 'History says no to the policeman's response to AIDS', *British Medical Journal* 293 (1986): 1589.

64 It has been suggested more than once that in the broad area of AIDS-related problems, prosecutions and new legislation, the 'courage of [American] political officials, public health officers and the judiciary has been less than remarkable' in responding to sectional pressure groups. Note, 'Fear itself: Aids, herpes and public health decisions', *Yale Law and Policy Review* 3 (1985): 479, 509–16.

65 For a more sceptical view see, for example, L. J. Moran, 'Illness: a more onerous citizenship', *Modern Law Review* 51 (1988): 343.

66 See K. J. M. Smith, 'Liability for endangerment: English ad hoc pragmatism and American innovation', [1983] *Crim. Law Rev.* 127; A. Ashworth, 'Defining criminal offences without harm', in P. F. Smith (ed.), *Criminal Law Essays in Honour of J. C. Smith* (London: Butterworth, 1987): 18; and A. Ashworth, 'Belief, intent and criminal liability', in J. Eekelaar and J. S. Bell (eds), *Oxford Essays in Jurisprudence* (Oxford: Oxford University Press, 1987): 16–17. And cf. *Khaliq* v. *H.M. Advocate* 1984 SLT 137 discussed by L. Farmer, P. Brown and J. Lloyd, *Scots Law Review* (18 December 1987): 389.

67 Smith (ed.), op. cit.

68 See, for example, the Law Reform Commission of Canada, Recodifying Criminal Law, Report 31 (1987) cl. 10(1): 'Everyone commits a crime who causes a risk of death or serious harm to another person: (a) purposively; (b) recklessly; or (c) through negligence', and cf. broadly similar provisions in the New Zealand Crimes Bill 1989, cls 130 and 132 considered by C. E. F. Rickett, *Victoria University of Wellington Law Review* 20 (1990): 183, 210.

69 See the revised *Model Penal Code Commentaries* (1980) on the rationale of endangerment liability in section 211.2 of the code: 198–203.

70 Cf. Sullivan and Field, op. cit.: 139, 157; the Health Education Authority, op. cit.: 36.

71 This process of legislative adaption of venereal disease offence provisions is already well under way in American states. See Gostin, 'The Politics of AIDS', op. cit.: 1017, 1041; and A. R. Spiegelman, 'Selective prosecution: A viable defense against a charge of transmitting Aids?', *Washington*

K. J. M. SMITH

University Journal of Urban and Contemporary Law 37 (1990): 337, 341.

72 Even the demonstrated transmission of venereal disease is not subject to any specific form of liability in England. Of indirect significance to notions of the criminal law's proper limits is the more restricted range of sodomy offences under English law (see Smith and Hogan, op. cit.: 476–7) compared with 50 per cent of American states. Cf. Spiegelman, op. cit.: 337, 341.

73 Also requiring comprehensive definition.

74 Cf. K. Roth, 'AIDS: medical aspects and policy considerations', *Law Society's Gazette* (1988): 25–6.: 74–5; and H. Hoe *et al.*, 'Infrequency of isolation of HTLV – III virus from saliva in Aids', *New England Journal of Medicine* 313 (1985): 1606.

75 Contra, for example, L. K. Burdt and R. S. Caldwell, 'The real fatal attraction: civil and criminal liability for the sexual transmission of Aids', *Drake Law Review* 37 (1987–8): 657, 695–6; and D. Robinson, 'Aids and the criminal law: traditional approaches and a new statutory proposal', *Hofstra Law Review* 14 (1985): 91, 103.

76 Cases where, for example, an infected prisoner bites or attempts to bite or even spits at a prison officer may require a specific offence.

77 Cf. Stephen J in *Clarence* (1888) 22 QBD 23, at 41.

78 It will, of course, in so far as 'victims' who do not contract the virus are less likely to furnish evidence leading to the prosecution of a partner.

79 *14th Report*, op. cit.; with differences in culpability reflected in the maximum punishment available for each offence.

80 In the sense proposed in the Draft Criminal Code Bill, Law Commission Report 177, *A Criminal Code for England and Wales* (London: HMSO, 1989): cl. 18.

81 ibid.; i.e. actual foresight of the risk.

82 For this offence there would need to be negligence both in the sense that the defendant ought to have realised both that he was possibly infected with the virus and that his behaviour carried the risk of transmitting infected bodily fluids.

83 *Supra*, n. 19.

84 Cf. Law Commission Report 177, op. cit.: para. 8.20, vol. 2.

85 Cf. Roth, op. cit.: 13–14, 72–9 and D. Levine and P. Bayer, 'Screening blood: public health and medical uncertainty in Aids, the emerging ethical dilemmas', *Hastings Center Report* (1985).

86 For example, Gostin, 'The politics of AIDS', op. cit.: 1052. On the broader question of the relationship between 'official' perceptions of AIDS and the framework of legal response note J. Montgomery, 'Victims or threats? – the framing of HIV', *Liverpool Law Review* 12 (1990): 25.

87 Individuals who are both sexually-active homosexuals and intravenous drug users are by a considerable margin most at risk. It is arguable that liability based on subjective recklessness would cover most of the situations and individuals likely to be brought within a negligence offence. The welter of propaganda surrounding the transmission of HIV would probably lead most courts to infer that the defendant, as a member of a high-risk group, knew he was particularly in danger of being a carrier of the virus.

88 It is accepted that prophylatic methods are not 100 per cent safe, but the alternative of a complete prohibition on sexual relations is unrealistic and likely to discredit the whole basis of any liability in this area.

89 Bearing in mind the circumstances, it would be unrealistic to cast a duty on the prosecution to prove that no reasonable preventive precautions were taken or that the defendant had not recently produced a negative HIV-antibodies test result.

90 After initial HIV infection many weeks or months may elapse before HIV antibodies develop in the blood system thereby making the individual capable of infecting others (seropositive state) and producing a positive test result. Mueller, op. cit.: 250; and Health Education Authority, op. cit.: 14–17.

91 Providing the individual confidentiality of testing and possible alleviative treatment is maintained. If this were not so the process of testing and any consequential treatment might reasonably be viewed by those affected as likely to increase their chances of being a possible source of attention or investigation by prosecution agencies. But cf. Sullivan and Field, op. cit.: 184; L. Gostin, W. Curran and M. Clark, 'The case against compulsory case finding in controlling Aids – testing, screening and reporting', *American Journal of Law and Medicine* 12 (1987): 7; C. Millman, 'Sodomy statutes and the Eighth Amendment', *Columbia Journal of Law and Social Problems* 21 (1988): 267; and A. Grubb and D. Pearl, *Blood Testing, AIDS and DNA Profiling: Law and Policy* (Bristol: Jordans, 1990): chs 1–2.

92 And claiming it to have been negative.

93 Cf., for example, the comments of the Californian appellate court on the ultimate primacy of public harm concerns in the genital herpes civil action of *Kathleen K* v. *Robert B* (1984) 198 Cal. Rptr. 273.

94 Clearly a judgment based on individual social and ethical inclinations.

95 Most cogently by Gostin, 'The politics of AIDS': 1054–5.

96 For example, under s. 15 of the Public Health (Control of Disease) Act 1984 deliberate infringement of regulations concerning the treatment of victims or preventing the spread of 'any epidemic endemic or infectious disease' is subject to a low scale of fines.

97 Cf. s. 17(1)(a) of the Public Health (Control of Disease) Act 1984 which makes it a summary offence for a person who 'knowing that he is suffering from a notifiable disease, exposes other persons to the risk of infection by his presence or conduct in any street, public place, place of entertainment or assembly, club, hotel, inn or shop'. This endangerment-based offence is aimed at the containment of highly contagious 'notifiable' diseases which do not presently include HIV infection or AIDS.

98 How widely known are the relevant provisions of the Public Health (Infectious Diseases) Regulations 1988 and Public Health (Control of Disease) Act 1984? They provide that on the application of the relevant local health authority a magistrate may: (i) order a person believed to be infected (among other diseases) with AIDS to be medically examined where expedient to do so in the interests of that person, his family or the public where the doctor treating him consents (s. 35); (ii) order, with the relevant health authority's consent the removal to a hospital persons

infected with HIV (see below regulation 5) if it is believed that proper precautions to prevent the spread of infection cannot, or are not being taken and that serious risk of infection is thereby caused (s. 37); (iii) order the detention of such a person already in hospital if similar risks as in (ii) exist. See J. Keown, *Professional Negligence* 5 (1989): 121; and Montgomery, op. cit.: 25, 41–4. Regulation 5 refers to Acquired Immune Deficiency Syndrome. It is unclear whether this includes HIV. If it does not the potential reach of the provisions is considerably reduced. See report in *The Times* (24 June 1992) of South Birmingham Health Authority's refusal to take any measures in relation to an HIV carrier believed to have infected four partners after confirmation of his HIV positive status.

99 (1888) 22 QBD 23, at 32–3. For a lucid modern version of such reservations (but aimed at victimless offences) see S. H. Kadish, 'The crisis of overcriminalisation', *Annals* 374 (1967): 157, 159.

100 *Report of the Committee on Homosexual Offences and Prostitution*, Cmnd. 247 (London: HMSO, 1957).

101 For example, Department of Health, *Aids* Cmnd 925 (London: HMSO, November 1989): para. 3. Cf. the contrary American view of the Report of the *Presidential Commission on the Human Immunodeficiency Virus Epidemic* (Washington DC: US Government Printing Office, 1988): 130–1: extending 'criminal liability to those who knowingly engage in behavior which is likely to transmit HIV is consistent with society's obligation to prevent harm to others and the criminal law's concern with punishing those whose behaviour results in harmful acts'.

102 See, for example, the DHSS evidence to the HC Social Services Committee, 3rd Report, *Problems Associated with AIDS* (1986–7), HCP 182, ii, 72; and Health Education Authority, *HIV and AIDS*, op. cit.: ch. 5. Even the making of HIV infection and AIDS notifiable diseases has so far been considered too 'coercive' in perception, if not reality. See Keown, op. cit.: 121–3. And on the legal aspects of testing see I. Kennedy and A. Grubb, 'Testing for HIV infection: the legal framework', *Law Society Gazette* 86 (15 February and 1 March 1989).

103 DHSS memorandum to the HC Social Services Committee, 7th Report, *AIDS: Minutes of Evidence* (1988–9), HCP 202, i, paras. 1.7 and 38.

104 See, for example, the latest Department of Health statistics (August 1991) and Health Education Authority, op. cit.: ch. 3. Cf. comments of Professor Ian Kennedy (in his oral evidence to the House of Commons Social Services Committee, *Problems Associated with AIDS: Third Report* (1986–7) HCP 182, ii) who was apparently not hostile to use of 'police power' against someone setting about to 'revenge' themself on others (p. 301) or who was 'clearly hell-bent on putting others at risk' (p. 305).

105 Cf. D. Brahams, 'The Aids letter', Royal Society of Medicine (5 February 1988): 1, and response of the Terrence Higgins Trust 1988, ibid. (7 May 1988): 3. See also brief Bow Group proposals in *AIDS* (1989): 4 and 34; and B. Amiel, *Sunday Times* (9 June 1991). Unformulated support is to be found in a trickle of parliamentary interventions; for example, 144 HC Debs, *Hansard* 144 (13 January 1989): col. 1158.

13

Deathly silence: doctors' duty to disclose dangers of death

Robert Lee

There is a series of jokes which commonly begin with the words 'Doctor, Doctor'. (There is little point in reciting these now, although some might argue that they would be a good deal more interesting than the essay which follows.) They have as a central theme some form of flippant rejection, by the doctor, of the complaint reported by the patient. As with much in humour, these jokes may hint at an area of concern or vulnerability which many of us share. In the nature of things, doctors may be strangers to us, and yet we must confide in them information which we would share perhaps with no one else, or certainly only with those with whom we are most intimate. The dismissive reaction of the doctor in all of these jokes is the realisation of our worst fears – that rather than take us seriously, the doctor might laugh at our petty or mistaken concerns, or hold us up to wider ridicule.

Conscious of such feelings, doctors have learnt to respect confidences. This may prove necessary if only to retain the repeat business of the patients. For their part, the patients, perhaps unable to determine at a technical level the quality of the service provided, may simply choose the services of the provider showing most apparent care and concern for the demands (if not the needs) of the patient.[1] The physicians themselves, aware of both the unsophisticated choices of the patient, and wishing to protect their own place within the market of potential providers, have long self-regulated their professional practice. One significant form of this self-regulation is that of respecting patient confidences. Thus the Hippocratic oath states that:

> whatever in connection with my professional practice, or not
> in connection with it, I see or hear, in the life of men, which

279

ought not to be spoken of abroad, I will not divulge as reckoning that all should be kept secret.

Similarly the Declaration of Geneva states that: 'I will respect the secrets which are confided in me even after the patient has died.' Finally the International Code of Medical Ethics words the duty as follows: 'A doctor owes to his patient complete loyalty . . . the doctor shall preserve absolute secrecy on all he knows about his patient because of the confidence entrusted in him.'[2] Although this final pronouncement sets it most clearly, all of these obligations would seem to be of an absolute nature. On the face of it, they permit no exceptions, and indeed this reflects the tradition in many continental countries.[3]

In Britain such an absolute duty is not recognised. Both the British Medical Association (BMA) and the General Medical Council (GMC) would allow exceptions.[4] The most obvious is patient consent, although the use of information for accredited medical research purposes or disclosure under statutory requirements or in consequence of a court order, may be permitted. In this essay, however, I intend to deal with a notion that there may be an overriding duty to society upon a doctor to make disclosure of information given in confidence. In particular, the area of concern is where the doctor is convinced, as a result of the confidence made, that a wider disclosure of this information could save a life or lives.

LEGAL CONTEXTS OF CONFIDENTIALITY

Before embarking on such a review, it is important to consider the context in which these questions may arise, since it will vary. One obvious arena for debate is that of the General Medical Council. Under section 35 of the Medical Act 1983, the GMC produce ethical guidelines to doctors, and in effect enforce such guidelines. First, they impose the strict duty on doctors to refrain from disclosure of patient-related information where this is learnt directly or indirectly in a professional capacity. Failure to abide by such a rule can lead to disciplinary action and, in an extreme case, to the removal of the doctor's name from the medical register. Equally, however, it may be possible for issues relating to confidentiality to arise at common law. This could take the form of an action based in breach of confidence.[5] As such, this will involve some form of injunction to restrain the breach of the confidence by the person in whom it was placed. So long as the information is not already in the public arena, then, irrespective of any contractual or proprietary interest in the information, the court may be willing to imply a duty of confidence such that recipients of the information may be restrained from disclosure.[6]

This whole concept of a duty of confidence arises out of particular relationships which the law has chosen to recognise. Typically, however, *dicta* in many of the cases has pointed to the doctor/patient relationship as a classic example of this legal recognition. Whilst injunctive relief is clearly possible, there is less certainty as to whether or not damages would lie for such a breach of medical confidence. The case of *Kitson* v. *Playfair*[7] is often mistakenly cited as a case in which damages were so awarded. In fact, however, this claim was based in defamation and not breach of confidence as such. Moreover, the absence of any contractual relationship between doctor and patient, within the NHS framework, will typically leave no damages claim for breach of any implied term, and, in the law of tort, no direct remedy would be available, even assuming that damages could be quantified. Nonetheless, there is an intriguing possibility that a third party might bring a claim for non-receipt of information confided in a doctor. This might arise where the doctor chooses to honour a confidence, rather than disclose to a third party information which shows imminent danger to that third party. When that very danger leads to death or personal injury to that third party, one might imagine that a claim could be brought against a doctor – a possibility considered below (p. 292).

Finally, it may be that the legal process may demand that the person in receipt of information, given in confidence, discloses that information in order to further the court process. Here the doctor has less protection than others working within the legal process. First, there is no parallel to legal privilege, and a doctor compelled to provide information to a court may risk punishment for contempt in refusing to break a confidence and make disclosure. Thus in *Hunter* v. *Mann*,[8] a doctor treating emergency patients involved in a car accident refused to disclose their identity, on the basis of confidences placed in him, when later approached by the police. This did not prevent his prosecution in the Magistrates Court under a section of the Road Traffic Act 1972 demanding that 'any . . . person . . . shall be required . . . to give any information which it is in his power to give and may lead to the identification of the driver'.[9] He appealed against this decision on the basis that, as the information was given in confidence, it was never 'in his power' to make disclosure. The appeal failed. It is something of a pity that Doctor Hunter's strong recognition of his ethical duty was not shared by the court. However, the case serves as a useful reminder of two issues. The first is that it is by no means uncommon in case law to find the courts taking their lead from the medical professional bodies, so that, in this case, the Blue Book[10] did recognise a permitted exception to the general rule of confidence in order to assist the police in the detection of crime. This is a point to which we shall return (p. 289). Second, that whatever the law or, for that matter, a professional rule says, doctors may be prepared to follow the dictates of their conscience in establishing the boundaries of their ethical duties.

There are a number of instances of the courts considering the disclosure of medical information in the absence of immediate threats to identifiable third parties, but where potential risks can be identified. Although outside the strict remit of this paper, such cases are illustrative of the manner in which the courts face such problems. Generally those whose disclosure might be restrained are ready to assert some reason why the information might enter the public, or a more public arena. Thus in X Health Authority v. Y,[11] freedom of the press was pleaded as a reason why a newspaper might print the revelation that two practising doctors with the authority were receiving treatment for AIDS. It was against this claim of press freedom that the court weighed the public interest in retaining the confidentiality of AIDS-related information. The public interest in confidentiality was said to substantially outweigh the other interest asserted – not least because the doctors, as patients themselves, ought to have their confidentiality respected in the hope of securing the wider public health, and encouraging patients with the virus to come forward in the future for treatment.

This seems unproblematic. If there was a likelihood of cross-infection from doctor to patient, and obvious irresponsibility on the part of the authority in refusing to guard against such a possibility, then the case might have posed greater problems. However, such cross-infection from patient to doctor is extremely rare[12] and, one supposes, from doctor to patient rarer still – though not impossible. Nonetheless, as Lord Wilberforce once wryly remarked, 'there is a wide difference between what is interesting to the public and what is in the public interest'.[13] Here the assertion of press freedom seems more to do with the former species of information than the latter.

BALANCING INTERESTS

In the formal balancing of the interest in *X Health Authority* v. *Y*, Rose J follows what had become a stereotypical formulation of dealing with confidentiality issues. Thus in a part of the *Spycatcher* litigation, *Attorney-General* v. *Guardian Newspapers* (no. 2), Lord Goff suggested that:

> although the basis of the law's protection of confidence is that there is a public interest that confidences should be preserved and protected by the law, nevertheless that public interest may be outweighed by some other counterveiling public interest which favours disclosure. This limitation may apply . . . to all types of confidential information. It is this limiting principle which may require a court to carry out a balancing operation, weighing the public interest in maintaining confidence against a counterveiling public interest favouring disclosure.[14]

One significant area in which this process has long been apparent is that of public interest immunity. In its earlier guise of Crown immunity it allowed the Crown on grounds of national security to refuse to disclose documents without which a legal remedy could not practically be pursued.[15] By denying such redress in the name of confidentiality it confers significant status on the confidences in the wider public interest. Nonetheless it is possible to point to examples of cases in which it seems legitimate to do so. Thus in *D* v. *NSPCC*,[16] D was justifiably aggrieved by allegations of child abuse which appeared to be untrue upon investigation by the NSPCC. The society refused, however, to disclose the identity of an informant, thereby depriving D of the possibility of an action against the society in negligence arising out of the manner of the investigation and confrontation. The House of Lords refused to order disclosure, finding a wider public interest in preserving the confidentiality of those stepping forward to identify the possibility of abuse, lest the 'sources of information . . . dry up'.[17] The narrow rule of this case is simply to confer upon the NSPCC the public interest ground open to the Crown, or to the police, not to disclose sources of information. However, Lord Edmund-Davies in this case offers wider guidelines. In his view, since there is considerable public interest in matters coming before the court, it is necessary to produce a clearly demonstrable case that the public interest is served by the exclusion of evidence. Where, on balance, there remains doubt, disclosure should be ordered.

Because of state involvement in the provision of health services in the United Kingdom, public interest issues in medical law may involve the Crown. Thus in *AB* v. *Scottish National Blood Transfusion Service*[18] an action of reparation was brought against the Scottish National Blood Transfusion Service by a patient alleging infection with HIV as a result of blood transfusions administered to him. In order to pursue an action in negligence against the donor also, the petitioner sought disclosure of the donor's identity. The decision in fact turned upon the success of the Secretary of State's claim that the documents fell within a class which would be afforded protection on ground of public policy, and that, having considered the matter, the Secretary of State was not prepared to infringe donor anonymity lest the supply of blood to the transfusion service was put at risk. The court found that it was not entitled to investigate the validity of the Secretary of State's claim unless it was patently unreasonable, or had been expressed on an erroneous basis. In the view of the Court of Session on the facts before it, although the arguments for and against disclosure might be finely balanced, the decision of the Secretary of State could not be so described.

The court did seem to show some sympathy for the plaintiff, and clearly indicated that, but for the state involvement, it would be 'legitimate for the court to consider the merits of the respondents' objection in the light of the nature of the work which they perform so as to determine whether or not the petitioner's interest shall prevail over that objection'. Thus they would have been prepared to make the sort of consideration made in *D* v. *NSPCC* but for the intervention of the Secretary of State asserting what in effect was a Crown immunity issue. Lord Morison considered the way in which the competing interests might have been decided had such a determination proved necessary, but we find oscillating arguments with no clear ranking. For example, the court laid considerable stress upon the fact that an action against the donor was not necessarily a disclosure to the public as a whole. Thus, in the view of the court, the donor's interest lay in an apprehension of legal action, rather than the publicity which might be attracted. Moreover, it was said to be 'offensive to any notion of justice that persons should be deprived of the ability to claim damages from those by whose negligence they have been injured'. Indeed Lord Morison went on to express the opinion that where there was a public policy requirement of non-disclosure 'it will be reasonable for public policy to provide also some alternative means of compensation'. Equally the court recognised that there may need to be some deterrent from persons abdicating all responsibilities when giving blood. Here the court was prepared to accept that the public interest might plainly be served if irresponsible donors were discouraged. At the same time the court said that given 'the very highest motives of altruism and commitment to the public welfare' shown by donors, it was not clear that the possibility of a threat of later legal action would deter donations.

Clearly, therefore, there are a number of arguments which weigh heavily down on the side of disclosure. Against these the court aired a series of objections. One of these was that it was 'impossible to hold that such a pecuniary interest [in damages for negligence] should prevail over a material risk to the sufficiency of the national supply of blood for purposes of transfusion'. The consequences of the loss of supply of blood were described as 'appalling'. Consequently:

> if there is any major risk of such an occurrence resulting from disclosure of the donor's name in the present case – and this is what I have to assume – it seems to be clear that the objection to that disclosure must prevail over the interest advanced on the petitioner's behalf.

Reading all of this one is left somewhat perplexed as to the view of the court, but the general drift seems to be that the court was not persuaded entirely that disclosure by the blood transfusion service would have resulted in a loss of blood supply, and that they would have needed convincing evidence that this was so. If so convinced, they may well have not permitted disclosure, but in the actual case itself the convincing obstacle to disclosure was simply the technical legal constraint, within the law of Crown Immunity, of accepting the Secretary of State's view.

The above cases illuminate the claim of the courts to be able to 'balance' factors and examine the tilting of the scales. However, as the analysis in the *Scottish Blood Transfusion* case demonstrates, there is no obvious weight to be given to any particular factor. Indeed the emphasis placed upon relevant considerations is vague throughout and identified by wording which is itself ambiguous: 'material', 'adequate', 'relevant' and the like. Moreover, it assumes that the interests are inevitably pitted against each other. Lord Morison in the passage on denial of compensation being 'offensive

285

to any notion of justice' indicates a preferred solution to awarding compensation and preserving anonymity. This would serve both interests and satisfy considerations of justice, yet it is not an option open to the law.

DANGEROUS PATIENTS

By far the most detailed analysis, in the medical context, of the balancing of interests is to be found in the case of *W* v. *Egdell*[19] which raised 'in an usually stark form the question of the nature and quality of the duty of confidence owed to a patient'. In that case a patient had been detained in a secure hospital without limit of time having killed five people and wounded another two. Ten years later he applied to a mental health tribunal for discharge, or transfer to a less secure unit. This application received some support from the authorities in the hospital in question in that they were prepared to sanction transfer to a regional secure unit. However, following opposition by the Secretary of State, W's solicitors, in an attempt to obtain a report in support of the application, instructed Egdell, a consultant psychiatrist. During his work with W, Egdell formed the opinion that W was suffering from a paranoid psychosis and pointed to the possibility that, underlying the mental illness, W might have a psychopathic deviant personality. Since this finding made it unlikely that W was or would be fit for release Egdell strongly opposed the application, and expressed concern, also, at the patient's possible transfer.

This report was sent to the solicitors acting for W, on the assumption that it would be placed before a tribunal. On receiving it, however, the solicitors withdrew the application. Egdell nonetheless sought to persuade the solicitors to forward a copy of the report to the hospital authorities. The solicitors took instructions from W who refused permission to disclose. At this point Egdell forwarded a copy of the report to the assistant medical director of the secure hospital, who, at Egdell's insistence,[20] forwarded a copy to the Home Secretary. The Home Secretary then referred W's case back to the tribunal, providing a copy of Egdell's report. W sought an injunction restraining the use of the report in the tribunal proceedings, and seeking damages for breach of confidence from Egdell.

At first instance, the application and claim were refused.[21] Scott J held that the duty of confidence owed to the patient was subordinate to the public interest in ensuring that there was a proper assessment of W's mental condition: 'I readily admit that W had a strong private interest in barring disclosure of the Egdell report to the Home Office . . . ', yet:

> the interest to be served by the duty of confidence . . . is the private interest of W and not any broader public interest. If I set the private interest of W in the balance against the public interest served by disclosure of the report . . . I find the weight of the public interest prevails.

Although the Court of Appeal dismissed the appeal by W, they rejected crucial aspects of the decision at first instance: 'in so far as the Judge referred to the "private interest" of W, I do not consider that the passage in his judgment accurately states the position'. In particular the Court of Appeal offered an analysis of competing public interests: 'there are two competing public interests . . . of course W has a private interest, but the duty of confidence owed to him is based on the broader ground of public interest'.

These competing interests, on analysing the Court of Appeal's judgment, break down as follows. The law should recognise professional duties of confidence and, in the particular situation, restricted patients under the Mental Health Act 1983 should have the right, as with patients generally, to independent private advice and the public interest requires that patients should speak freely, openly and without reservation to their medical advisers. Against this, to quote Bingham LJ:

> A consultant psychiatrist who becomes aware, even in the course of a confidential relationship, of information which leads him, in the exercise of what the court considers a sound professional judgment, to fear that . . . decisions may be made on the basis of inadequate information and *with a real risk of consequent danger to the public* is entitled to take such steps as are reasonable in all the circumstances to communicate the grounds of his concern to the responsible authorities. (My emphasis)

Thus the competing public interests are identified as the preservation of the confidentiality of the doctor/patient relationship pitched against the wider public safety. Put as baldly as that, the decision of the court seems unsurprising, but the question is whether the issues should or can be put as baldly as that. Before exploring this question, however, it is useful to reflect a little longer on the *Egdell* case.

The court allowed that in order to make disclosure there must be 'a real risk' of danger. Immediate concerns in this case were identifiable in view of W's medical history. Nonetheless W had on a previous occasion been recommended for transfer by medical advisers, which the Secretary of State had blocked. W received further support from doctors responsible for his everyday care on this, his second application, prior to Egdell's examination which pointed to a possibility of danger. Thus the 'real risk' in this case which the doctor feared had not been highlighted in previous medical assessments by other psychiatrists. Even so, the past medical history of W, leading to his detention at Broadmoor, is difficult to put aside. But it would be unfortunate if great inroads into medical confidentiality were allowed to rest upon the quite exceptional facts of this case. This is not to support the *Egdell* formulation as such, but merely to say that it does not represent the most difficult case which may have come before the courts.

Take, for example, the situation in which a patient with no documented history of mental illness seeks medical advice from a psychiatrist, who forms the view that this patient represents a genuine risk to public safety. Providing that this assessment is based upon professional judgment then the doctor would no longer be bound by any duties of confidence and could take steps immediately to ensure that the patient is securely detained. It could be that the assessment is inaccurate, but while the Court of Appeal speak of 'sound' judgment, in practice, if the doctor makes the assessment in good faith, it seems unlikely that a court, post-*Egdell*, would find a breach of confidence simply because other doctors later disagree, or because the anticipated incident never occurs.

If *Egdell* is not confined by W's particular medical history, might it be restricted to the formal processes under way in the case? Egdell's disclosure was made in the context of W's application for discharge or transfer. In the first instance decision, Scott J comes close to suggesting that because the report is prepared for use in a tribunal hearing, notwithstanding the fact that it was prepared at W's instruction, it ought to be disclosed to that tribunal. This seems unfortunate. The Mental Health Act 1983 gave the authorities no particular right to know the substance of the interview between the doctor and the patient. This may explain the reluctance of the hospital to disclose the Egdell report to the Secretary of State.

Moreover, in many parallel situations, the disclosure of this kind of report might have been resisted by invoking professional legal privilege. Indeed the Court of Appeal were adamant that the case was not one of legal privilege, but of confidentiality. In fact, the formal process may be seen to have loosened the constraints of professional confidence. At first instance, Scott J seems to allow that the duty of confidence owed in the circumstances of the application is less than the duty which might be owed ordinarily by psychiatrists to patients not governed by Mental Health Act procedures. However, it is not immediately apparent why this ought to be so, on the analysis of the preceding paragraph. Indeed this is a somewhat dangerous view as it might suggest that the right to confidence of a detained patient is less than that of a patient not so detained, and from there it may be a small step to say that rights of psychiatric patients in relation to confidentiality ought to be less well protected than those of patients generally.

It is clear from *Egdell* that the context is significant in another sense. The Court of Appeal are clear that Egdell's disclosure to a national newspaper would have amounted to a breach of confidence. Here legal and professional confines of confidentiality coincide. It is notable that, at both first instance and on appeal, the courts follow closely the rules of the *Blue Book*. In particular they relied upon rule 81(g) which stated that:

> rarely disclosure may be justified on the ground that it is in the public interest which, in certain circumstances such as, for example, investigation by the police of a grave or serious crime, might override the doctor's duty to maintain his patient's confidence.[22]

Of course this provides no immediate solution since, as Scott J accepted:

> These rules do not provide a definitive answer to the question raised in the present case as to the breadth of the duty of confidence owed . . . they seem to me valuable, however, in showing the approach of the General Medical Council to the breadth of the doctor/patient duty of confidence.

Here arises a problem apparent in other cases of medical law[23] – that standards are set in accordance with professional guidelines, notwithstanding that the 'rules do not themselves have statutory authority'.[24] Thus criteria which have never undergone the test of wider public debate effectively become the legally-enforced standard.

There is one final aspect of *Egdell* which requires consideration prior to returning to a consideration of the problem of balancing interests, and this is a problem which bedevils the law of confidentiality generally. It is impossible to reinstate the confidence once breached – a secret divulged is no longer a secret. This is a significant consideration in that it suggests that clear and unequivocal rules are necessary and that they should err, if at all, on the side of protecting confidences. Certainly, as the law stands, where a doctor breaches confidence there may be no remedy open to the courts, and indeed courts may be left with little option but to sanction the conduct. Thus *R* v. *Crozier*[25] represents a case in which, in the court's own words, the conduct of the doctor 'at first blush . . . seem[ed] entirely wrong' but which led to a finding that the doctor had acted 'responsibly and reasonably'.

In *Crozier*, the appellant, who had attacked his sister with an axe, was assessed while on remand by a psychiatrist, Dr Wright. Wright concluded that he was sane, though a continuing danger to his sister. This report was made available to the court, which, acting upon it, sentenced Crozier to nine years' imprisonment. The appellant had obtained an independent examination by another psychiatrist, Dr McDonald, which for some reason never reached the appellant's counsel. This suggested that the appellant was suffering from a psychopathic disorder within the Mental Health Act 1983 such that, representing a continuing danger to his sister, he ought to be detained in a maximum security hospital. Not having reached the appellant's counsel, the report was not disclosed before the court. Dr McDonald, arriving late at court, expecting to give evidence as to the appellant's condition, heard him being sentenced to imprisonment. Dr McDonald immediately approached counsel for the Crown and fully disclosed the contents of the report. It was this act of disclosure, to which the appellant objected most strongly, but which the Court of Appeal sanctioned:

> We would put Dr McDonald in very much the same position as Dr Egdell found himself. True it is that the appellant was not even charged with murder, but . . . he might very well have . . . murder[ed] his sister. We believe this too is a case where there was a strong public interest in disclosure of

Dr McDonald's views than in the confidence he owed to the
appellant.

Note that this is not the correct formulation, post-*Egdell*, since the
issue is not the duty of confidence owed to Crozier, but the wider
public interest in respecting medical confidences generally – but it is
clear the court intended to follow *Egdell*. Had the appellant
received the copy of Dr McDonald's report, he would have been in
a position to instruct his legal advisers. In the view of the Court of
Appeal, even if the appellant had asked that the report be kept fully
confidential, it would have supported Dr McDonald had he nonetheless felt it his duty to disclose the report. Similarly it was said
that once disclosed – even if wrongly disclosed – the judge, in
sentencing, 'could do no other than act on it in the public interest'.

Crozier represents small but significant extensions of *Egdell*.
These include the *dicta* immediately above concerning disclosure in
the face of adamant refusal and use of material wrongfully disclosed.
Like *Egdell* there was, at least initially, a conflict of medical opinion, but in *Crozier* the potential danger was not to the world at
large but to Crozier's immediate family. *Crozier* is also important
coming soon after *Egdell* on which it strongly relied, and seems to
have cemented the *Egdell* line on public interest issues for the
foreseeable future. It is the interpretation of the competing public
interests with which I now wish to take issue.

In the Court of Appeal judgments in both *Egdell* and *Crozier*, the
court considers competing public interests. Yet the patient may
have a powerful interest in restricting disclosure. Again, in the two
cases, the individual interest was significant, and concerned the
future liberty of the patient. Not to recognise this is short-sighted
and perhaps in error. The Law Commission have typified the action
for breach of confidence as 'a civil remedy affording protection
against disclosure or use of information which is not publicly
known and which has been entrusted to a person in circumstances
imposing an obligation not to disclose'.[26] This definition emphasises the obligation to the individual and allows for a strong personal interest in non-disclosure. It is the imparting of information in
confidence that establishes a prima facie rule of non-disclosure so
that the first consideration deserves to be the interest which the
individual possesses in the secrecy of the information. Thus coun-
terbalancing public interests are placed on scales which are already
firmly weighted down by the considerable burden of confidence

imposed on the holder of it. Thus it is suggested that the *Egdell* view of balancing of public interests pays insufficient regard to genuine and weighty private interests. In rejecting the analysis of Scott J, at first instance in *Egdell*, of private interest competing against the public interest, the Court of Appeal lost sight of the private interest altogether and found only two competing public interests. A preferred formula might be to weigh the strong private interest together with the general public interest in preserving doctor/patient confidentiality against any other public interest asserted.

DUTIES TO OTHERS

I wish to develop this argument further by reviewing situations in which disclosure is not to be made necessarily to the authorities but to third parties who might be at risk as a result of the patient's actions. It might be easier to make out a case for disclosure here since it might be possible, for example, to warn Crozier's sister of a danger so that she might take precautions without necessarily influencing decisions about Crozier's liberty in the future. Also, we do not inform the world at large, but a single person only. Moreover, the doctor dealing with a person thought to be mentally ill may doubt the capacity of the patient to make realistic assessments concerning the disclosure of medical opinions as to prognosis. By making such incremental changes to the facts of the *Crozier* case, it is possible that the case for disclosure made by the Court of Appeal becomes even stronger. Indeed some might be prepared to argue that not only would it be permissible for the doctor to disclose, but that the doctor has a positive duty to warn a third party of a known or suspected danger.

Precisely this issue has been faced in the Californian case of *Tarasoff* v. *Regents of the University of California*.[27] In this case the patient informed his therapist of an intention to kill a third party who, although not named, was clearly a girl with whom the patient had become infatuated. The patient did indeed murder the young woman two months later, in spite of attempts by the therapist to thwart such an act of violence. The parents of the murdered girl sued on the basis of the therapist's breach of a duty to warn her of the likely danger. It was held that 'a psychotherapist treating a mentally ill patient . . . bears a duty to use reasonable care to give threatened parties such warning as are essential to their foreseeable danger arising from [the] patient's condition or treatment'. The decision was largely upheld on rehearing by the Californian Supreme Court which would have additionally found the duty fulfilled by informing the appropriate authorities, or otherwise preventing the threatened act of violence. This is an obvious extension of the rule where there is a general danger to the community, although it has been argued that the *Tarasoff* duty only applies where there is an identifiable individual.[28] Issues concerning the extent of danger may affect forseeability, and there are other questions concerning the duty of care. Not least among these is the idea that there can be certainty of diagnosis with psychiatric illness. The American Psychiatric Association, in its *amicus* brief in *Tarasoff*, has argued that it is simply not possible accurately to predict potentially dangerous behaviour. If this is so, then, whatever the formal recognition of duty, it might be that the expected standard of care is so low as to render breaches virtually impossible. Nonetheless *Tarasoff* is regarded as a landmark case, and significantly it was cited in *Egdell*.

Tarasoff recognises not merely a permission to disclose, but an actual duty to do so. This duty has been admitted in the USA in other situations. In the words of *Doe* v. *Roe*:

despite the duty of confidentiality courts have recognised the duty of a psychiatrist to give warning where a patient clearly represents a danger to others . . . to disclose the existence of a contagious disease . . . to report the use of controlled substances in certain situations . . . and to report gunshot and other wounds. . . .[29]

Moreover, having asserted that there may be a duty to disclose, it is considerably easier to admit simple permissions to disclose. In an older established case, *Simonsen* v. *Swenson*, it was said that:

no patient can expect that if his malady is found to be of a dangerously contagious nature he can still require it to be kept secret from those to whom, if there was no disclosure, such disease would be transmitted. The information given to a physician by his patient, though confidential, must, it seems to us, be given and received subject to the qualifications that if the patient's disease is found to be of a dangerous and so highly contagious or infectious nature that it will naturally be transmitted to others, unless the danger of contagion is disclosed to them, then the physician should, in that event, if no other means of protection is possible, be privileged to make so much of a disclosure to such persons as is necessary to prevent the spread of the disease.[30]

Although this case dates back to 1920, in relation to AIDS, in more recent times, Californian and Texan legislation has permitted unauthorised disclosure by a doctor to a spouse of an HIV-positive patient.[31] In New York, even in the face of patient objection, known sexual partners and needle-sharers may be warned by the doctor.[32]

These matters remain open in the UK, although it is understood that the Blue Book is to be amended to allow an exception to the general duty of confidentiality in order to safeguard the well-being of third parties.[33] In view of the tendency of the courts to take their lead from medical ethical guidelines (highlighted above) it is by no means unlikely that, in the future, the courts may recognise at least a permission to warn partners of HIV-positive patients.[34] Rather than leave this matter to the developing common law, however, it might be possible that this area could be clarified by statute. There have long been regulations governing disclosure of information relating to communicable diseases.[35] In general, these impose additional duties of confidence and, in so doing, presumably reflect potential stigma which certain communicable diseases may attract. In the case of sexually-transmitted diseases, this doubtless reflects in part the methods of contraction of the particular disease. Similarly, in relation to AIDS, possible routes of infection include homosexual sex and intravenous drug usage. Thus, HIV-positive individuals may be members, or assumed to be members, of social groups whose activities we have long criminalised, and whose lifestyles are widely rejected in society as a whole. This may account in part for the widespread discrimination evident against persons who are HIV-positive in schools, at work or in hospitals, even though the particular virus is unlikely to be spread by casual or everyday contact.[36]

In view of this discriminatory experience, programmes of testing, counselling or treatment of the virus are already at risk. Such medical procedures are not assisted by activities of those, such as insurers, who might regard even the administration of a blood test as indicative of the likelihood that the person is in an at-risk group.[37] Yet given the rate at which the disease has already spread, and its capacity to continue to do so, public health programmes are vital. Chapter 12 in this volume has suggested that the criminal law may have a part to play in restricting the spread of the virus.[38] In that paper the suggestion that neglect may be a sufficient *mens rea* for the commission of the suggested offence takes us close to compulsory testing. Even if I was inclined towards criminalisation in this way, which I am not, I should reject the proposals on purely pragmatic grounds. I remain entirely unconvinced that a programme of health education can be advanced in any way whatsoever by the imposition of punitive sanctions for failure to comply with the public health requirements. Rather, it seems likely that in the face of possible criminal prosecution arising out of the sexual conduct of the infected person, that person would be reluctant in the extreme to step forward for the necessary counselling and medical assistance.

For similar reasons, too, it might be argued that the wider utility is served in protecting public health programmes by ensuring the absolute confidentiality of AIDS-related information. If we believe this, then this might outweigh the admitted public interest of informing a third party of the danger which they face. But whether or not this is so (and one would not be surprised to see a court take the contrary view) it does not represent a complete resolution of the argument, because, as was argued above, such formulation takes no regard at all of the private interest of the HIV-positive patient.

The interest of such a patient in non-disclosure is not encompassed fully by the fear that breach of confidence will lead to identification as a member of a discriminated group. This is because the patient must have some interest in ensuring that the doctor, as confidant, will not violate the doctor/patient relationship by divulging information against the patient's will. The patient has approached the doctor and has volunteered confidences only on the basis that these are necessary for the purposes of treatment, and will be subject to respect. Of course, if the doctor were to explain to the patient in advance, in line with the *Simonsen* formulation,[39] that if he were to diagnose the patient as dangerous, then there would be further disclosure on to third parties likely to be subject to that danger, then disclosure might be permissible where such events occurred. But this is not what is done, and it is not what is done because it is known that such contingent dealings would not illicit the full confidence of the patient. Consequently the interpretation of what happens is that the doctor teases the information from the patient with the promise of confidentiality, only immediately to breach that promise on finding what is actually divulged.

In the case of third-party warnings, to use a promise of

confidentiality to secure otherwise inaccessible information when it is known that such a promise may never be kept, is manifestly contrary to notions of fairness. The assurance of fair dealing which provided the basis of the doctor/patient relationship is known in advance by one party only (the doctor) to be contingent upon the possible disclosures of the patient. The patient assumes a mutuality of promises, but the doctor is prepared to act unilaterally. In the face of all of this, we should never place doctors under a duty to disclose, and if we are to permit doctors to breach that trust, then our reasons for doing so should be powerful indeed. This is not to say that they will never exist. For example, a difficult case might be that in which a male patient, having become resentful at having contracted the HIV virus by a single homosexual encounter, confides in his physician that he deliberately tends to spread his infection as a vengeful act. Faced with such evil intent, I may be prepared to argue that the doctor should be released from requirements of confidentiality assuming that it is possible to prevent the potentially fatal actions of the patient. However, this failure to recognise confidentiality as an absolute requirement does not greatly diminish the strength of the principle as a whole. Nor is there any great likelihood that HIV-positive individuals will purposely seek to infect others.

It follows that this example does not assist greatly with the more typical situation that the HIV-positive patient has a single sexual partner who is at risk of infection. It makes sense that in such a situation a doctor seeking disclosure to the third party should attempt to encourage the patient to disclose, or offer to make disclosure on that patient's behalf. Problems arise only when the patient steadfastly refuses either course of action. Here, it must be said that, unlike the psychiatric disclosure cases, there is no immediate reason to dispute the competence of the patient. Moreover, doctrines of consent must allow that patients can act against (what doctors view as) the best interests of themselves or others, without being considered incompetent or irrational. Although not always forceful in so doing, the law broadly supports this view.[40] In view of the discrimination suffered by HIV-positive patients, it is difficult to state that they act irrationally in insisting on absolute secrecy concerning their health state. Thus, in addition to the strong moral authority for respecting confidences, we place a considerable private interest against non-disclosure upon the scales before weighing a competing public interest in relation to warning third parties.

In relation to the wider interest in public safety, it is not always obvious that disclosure will offer widespread protection. Unless a specific third-party contact is known, it is difficult to see how disclosure might be effective, unless we are prepared to sanction open disclosure to the world at large. Other suggestions, such as tracing of sexual contacts, may constitute an unwarranted intrusion on the privacy not only of the patient, but also of those contacts, and is in any case an inappropriate task for the doctor. Even where there is risk to a known third party, it assumes that the third party when warned will act upon the information and will reduce the risk by, for example, not sharing a needle in the future. However wise such advice, there is no guarantee that it will be followed. As Gillon has stated: 'in most cases the probability of preventing death or severe injury by breaking medical confidentiality about HIV state will be low'.[41]

At the same time, on each occasion that a confidence is broken in this manner it becomes less likely that at-risk groups will deal with doctors on a sincere basis in the future. As trust is reduced, so too is the capacity of health care professionals to contain the spread of the virus. The promise of professional confidence becomes conditional, with the physician reserving the right to waive guarantees previously given. Patients may choose to refuse to deal with health care professionals who engage in such confidence tricks. Those wishing to combat the disease may have to ask whether it is better to treat an HIV-positive patient, but have no contact with his/her sexual partner, than never see the first patient at all. In *AB* v. *Scottish Blood Transfusion Service*,[42] the argument of the Secretary of State was that public health would be retarded by disclosure of blood donor identity, as potential donors were deterred. Protection of the donor's secrecy was necessary 'on the grounds of public policy to ensure that there is and continues to be a sufficient supply of donor blood to the health service nationally'.

If such arguments are accepted, then it would follow that not only does the doctor have no duty to warn, but that, in most situations, the doctor would breach confidence by third-party disclosure in the absence of patient consent. This does not mean that a doctor should not use best endeavours to persuade the patient to offer consent, but that a doctor may generally be considered bound by the refusal. This is not the line taken by the GMC,[43] nor that proposed by Grubb and Pearl in their work on confidentiality and HIV testing.[44] Broadly such views would permit disclosure to a

297

carer or contact where there is a serious or significant risk[45] of infection and where, in spite of counselling, it is thought that the patient will continue to refuse to disclose.[46] Grubb and Pearl would wish to see the court 'content itself by accepting . . . that a doctor had a discretion to inform those who are immediately and directly at risk, taking account of the HIV patient's attitude (and responsibility) to warning or protecting the sexual partner . . . themselves'.[47] Thus they express the hope that the court 'would reflect the need to impose a duty to warn upon the doctor'.[48] This may be a forlorn hope, for once a permission to disclose is allowed, a duty to disclose may not be far behind. For example, it may be that the sexual partner of an HIV-positive patient will be a patient of the same general practitioner. From the point of view of the law of negligence, that would mean that a doctor has a patient towards whom s/he owes a clear duty of care. That doctor knows that information which s/he holds could prevent readily foreseeable injury befalling the patient.[49] If disclosure of such information is permissible, then it may be difficult to escape the imposition of a duty to disclose and allow the prospect of damages to the third party in the event of non-disclosure. The safer course is to maintain a general rule forbidding the disclosure, and thus avoid the prospect of actions based on a positive duty to warn.

One final point which needs to be made is that medical practitioners are not neutral on questions of disclosure of AIDS-related information. In relation to the passage of information on HIV-positive patients between practitioners, GPs have argued that consultants are 'over-protective of confidentiality'. Yet it is not clear why a doctor should have the right to know information where the patient refuses to sanction disclosure. The general practitioner is not at risk ordinarily. Indeed the DHSS Advisory Group Report on AIDS found only nine reported cases worldwide in which HIV was transmitted from patients to health care workers.[50] It is apparent that in the course of treatment of any patient with a disease which is capable of being transmitted, a medical practitioner undertakes some degree of risk. It is not clear that disclosure outside the realms of patient consent should be allowed for this particular infection in advance of any other. It is true that restrictions on information may make it difficult to offer adequate treatment to the patient, but the patient must retain the right to decide this even in the face of therapeutic disadvantage.

Thus in the face of this disease, doctors have been willing to advocate departures from principles which might be considered ordinarily accepted. For example, the Royal College of Surgeons has advised that members suffering injuries from needles or scalpels may wish to test high-risk patients for the HIV virus even where a patient has not consented to such testing.[51] This questionable proposal of dubious legality illustrates the fragile nature of ethical standards when faced with cases of HIV-positive patients. Rather than being over-protective of confidentiality it may cause us to question the wisdom of allowing to the doctor a discretion to disclose in the majority of cases.

CONCLUSION

It is inescapable that from time to time doctors will be privy to information divulged to them in confidence which will indicate a danger of activity on the part of the patient which could be potentially fatal to third parties. It is not surprising that a profession dedicated to preserving life and health should recoil from such a prospect. Nonetheless a reaction which would lead to a breach of confidence would be ill-advised. Doctors must remain conscious of the processes by which confidences are illicited if, in the discharge of their work, they wish to retain such confidences generally.

The law, which should be better placed than the doctor to guard and preserve individual interests in confidentiality, should show a stronger respect for such interests than in the immediate past. Recent case law tends to have lost sight of the need to support individual privacy, focusing rather on public interest considerations, in which the dangers to third parties weigh most heavily. The law runs the risk of partiality in which these 'innocent' third parties are challenged by those for whom society has little regard or respect – groups such as mentally ill or HIV-positive patients. It is only by asserting strongly the rights of such groups to have their interest in confidentiality noted and taken into account that we can guard against the dangerous instincts not of patient, but of doctor.

NOTES

1 For a consideration of the problems of consumers of health care in judging their own best welfare see A. McGuire, P. Fenn and K. Mayhew, 'The economics of health care', in A. McGuire, P. Fenn and K. Mayhew (eds), *Providing Health Care* (Oxford: Oxford University Press, 1991).

2 For the texts of these declarations see the appendices of J. K. Mason and R. A. McCall Smith, *Law and Medical Ethics*, 3rd edn (London: Butterworth, 1991).

3 R. Lee, 'Disclosure of medical records: a confidence trick?', in L. Clarke (ed.), *Confidentiality and the Law* (London: Lloyds of London, 1990).

4 British Medical Association, *Handbook of Medical Ethics* (London: BMA, 1986); General Medical Council, *Professional Conduct and Discipline: Fitness to Practise* (hereafter the *Blue Book*) (London: GMC, 1991); and see L. Gordis and E. Gold, 'Privacy, confidentiality, and use of medical records in research', *Science* 207 (11 January 1980): 153.

5 See M. Thompson, 'Breach of confidence and secrecy', in Clarke (ed.), op. cit.

6 *Duchess of Argyll* v. *Duke of Argyll* [1965] 1 All ER 611; *Stephens* v. *Avery* [1988] 2 All ER 477.

7 *The Times* (28 March 1986); see the comment on this case by J. Jacob, *Speller's Law Relating to Hospitals and Kindred Institutions*, 6th edn (London: Lewis, 1978).

8 [1974] 1 QB 767.

9 See s. 168(b) Road Traffic Act 1972; see now s. 172(2)(b) Road Traffic Act 1988.

10 *Supra*, n. 4.

11 [1988] 2 All ER 648.

12 Department of Health and Social Security, *Report of the Advisory Group on Aids* (London: HMSO, 1988).

13 *British Steel Corporation* v. *Granada Television* [1981] 1 All ER 417, 455.

14 [1988] 3 All ER 545, at 659.

15 See, for example, *Duncan* v. *Cammell, Laird & Co* [1942] AC 624; and J. Jacob, 'Discovery and public interest', [1976] *Public Law* 134.

16 [1978] AC 171.

17 ibid., *per* Lord Diplock, at p. 218.

18 (1990) SCLR 263. For a discussion of the policy issues at stake in this type of case see R. C. Bollow and D. J. Lapp, 'Protecting the confidentiality of blood donors' identity in Aids litigation', *Drake Law Review* 37 (1986–7): 343.

19 [1990] 1 All ER 835.

20 Dr Egdell threatened to send a copy directly to the Home Office if the hospital did not themselves supply it.

21 [1989] 1 All ER 1089.

22 GMC, op. cit.

23 This is true for both consent to treatment where the law has moved from trespass to negligence where the standard in relation to disclosure of risk is set by reference to that accepted as proper by a responsible body of medical opinion: *Sidway* v. *Bethlem Royal Hospital* [1985] 1 All ER 643. On a wider front this is true of medical negligence and the standard of care generally: *Bolam* v. *Friern* HMC [1957] 2 All ER 118.

24 *Egdell* [1990] 1 All ER 835, at 843 *per* Sir Stephen Brown P.

25 (1991) *Crim. Law Rev.* 138.

26 Law Commission, *Breach of Confidence*, paper no. 110 (London: Law

Commission, 1981).

27 (1976) 17 Cal. 3d 425; 551 P. 2d 334; 131 Cal. Rptr. 14.

28 *Thompson* v. *County of Alameda* 27 Cal. 3d 741 (1980). For further discussion of this issue, see M. Jones, 'Medical confidentiality and the public interest', *Professional Negligence* (16 March 1990).

29 (1977) 400 NYS 2d 668.

30 (1920) 9 ALR 1250, at 1253.

31 For an analysis of such laws see L. Gostin, 'Public health strategies for confronting Aids – legislative and regulatory policy in the United States', *Journal of Americal Medical Association* 261 (1989): 1621; and D. H. J. Hermann and R. D. Gagliano, 'Aids, therapeutic confidentiality and third party warnings', *Maryland Law Review* 48 (1989): 55.

32 New York Health Code, section 2782 quoted (in part) in A. Grubb and D. Pearl, *Blood Testing, AIDS and DNA Profiling* (Bristol: Jordan, 1990).

33 Information provided by Clare Dyer in the course of the preparation of a centenary publication for the Medical Protection Society. See R. Lee 'Confidentiality and medical records', in C. Dyer (ed.), *Doctors, Patients and the Law* (London: MPS, 1992). The relevant passage of the 1992 *Blue Book* will read:

> Rarely cases may arise in which disclosure in the public interest may be justified, for example a situation in which the failure to disclose appropriate information would expose the patent or someone else to a risk of death or serious harm.

For an eloquent statement in favour of absolute confidence see M. H. Kottow, 'Medical confidentiality: an intransigent and absolute obligation', *Journal of Medical Ethics* 12 (1986): 117; cf. H. Emson, 'Confidentiality: a modified value', *Journal of Medical Ethics* 14 (1988): 87.

34 See the discussion in Grubb and Pearl, op. cit.: ch. 2.

35 See, for example, The National Health (Venereal Diseases) Regulations 1974 (SI 1974, n. 29) as amended by the Health Services Act 1980 (Consequential Amendments) Order 1982 (SI 1982 n. 288).

36 Presidential Commission of the HIV Epidemic, *Report of the Presidential Commission on the HIV Epidemic* (Washington DC: US Government Printing Office, June 1988): para. 119 *et seq.*

37 See M. Scherzer, 'Insurance', in H. Dalton and S. Burris (eds), *Aids and the Law* (New Haven, Conn.: Yale University Press, 1987); and R. P. Luculano, 'Life insurance', in W. H. L. Dornette (ed.), *Aids and the Law* (New York: Wiley, 1987).

38 See K. J. M. Smith, Chapter 12 of this volume.

39 *Simonsen* v. *Swenson* (*supra* n. 30).

40 See essay by J. Montgomery, Chapter 3 of this volume and also that by P. Aldridge, Chapter 2; and see also *Malette* v. *Shulman* (1988) 63 OR (2d) 243.

41 R. Gillon, 'Aids and medical confidentiality', *British Medical Journal* 294 (1987): 1675, 1676; and see also R. Gillon 'Confidentiality', *British Medical Journal* 291 (1985): 1634; and D. Pheby 'Changing practice on

confidentiality: a cause for concern', *Journal of Medical Ethics* 8(12) (1982).
42 *Supra* n. 18.
43 GMC statement of 25 May 1988 paras 17 *et seq.*
44 Grubb and Pearl, op. cit.: ch. 2.
45 Grubb and Pearl, ibid., would follow the formulation of the New York Health Code (*supra* n. 32).
46 Given that I have not proposed an absolute duty of confidence it may be that the difference between these views and my own may simply surround what is viewed as a 'serious or significant risk'. But I think not. In my example of the vengeful HIV-positive patient, it is the evil nature of the intention that dissuades me against respecting a confidence. Nonetheless I should assert as a norm that the policy should be that of non-disclosure in spite of the presence of a sexual contact.
47 Grubb and Pearl, op. cit.: at 55.
48 ibid. Other tortious issues arise here which might be more appropriately considered on another occasion. But a number of issues arise in relation to causation and quite possibly contributory negligence. For a consideration of this area see Hermann and Gagliano, op. cit.: 55.
49 R. Lee, 'Hospital admissions – duty of care', *New Law Journal* (1979): 567.
50 DHSS, op. cit.
51 Royal College of Surgeons, *Patient Consent to Treatment* (London: Royal College of Surgeons, 1990).

Index